Practical JavaScript for

Paul Wilton

Stephen Williams

Sing Li

Published by glasshaus Ltd,
Arden House,
1102 Warwick Road,
Acocks Green,
Birmingham,
B27 6BH, UK

Printed in the United States
ISBN 1-904151-05-1

Practical JavaScript for the Usable Web

web professional to web professional

Trademark Acknowledgements

glasshaus has endeavored to provide trademark information about all the companies and products mentioned in this book by the appropriate use of capitals. However, glasshaus cannot guarantee the accuracy of this information.

Credits

Authors
Paul Wilton
Stephen Williams
Sing Li

Technical Reviewers
Tom Farrell
Martin Honnen
Mark Horner
Christian Kenyeres
Ginnie O'Neal
David Schultz
Jon Stephens
Michael Walston
Stephen Williams

Proof Readers
Dan Walker
Agnes Wiggers

Commissioning Editor
Eleanor Baylis

Technical Editors
Amanda Kay
Simon Mackie

Managing Editor
Liz Toy

Project Manager
Sophie Edwards

Production Coordinator
Pip Wonson

Cover
Dawn Chellingworth

Indexers
Adrian Axinte

About the Authors

Paul Wilton

After an initial stint as a Visual Basic applications programmer at the Ministry of Defence in the UK, Paul Wilton found himself pulled into the Net. He is currently working freelance and is busy trying to piece together the Microsoft .Net jigsaw. Paul's main skills are in developing web front ends using DHTML, JavaScript, VBScript, and Visual Basic, and back-end solutions with ASP, Visual Basic, and SQL Server. He would like to thank his fiancée, Catherine, for all her patience and caring.

Stephen Williams

Steve recently co-founded Chimera Digital Ltd, a company that brings together expertise in the fields of education, video production and web technologies, and produces content packages suitable for business in training, promotion, marketing, and more. Prior to this he worked for Edison Interactive, where he was the lead Vignette developer for their Switch2 entertainment portal web site.

His interests in artificial life lead him from his PhD in Molecular Microbiology at the University of Birmingham, into object-oriented programming and the Internet.

Sing Li

Sing Li is an active author, consultant, and entrepreneur. He has written for popular technical journals and is the creator of the "Internet Global Phone", one of the very first Internet phones available. His wide-ranging consulting expertise spans Internet and Intranet systems design, distributed architectures, web services, embedded systems, real-time technologies, and cross-platform software design. He also participates in the Jini and Jxta communities.

Table of Contents

Introduction

If you want to learn client-side JavaScript fast, but effectively, then you're reading the right book. We'll move swiftly through the technology over the next ten chapters, dealing only with the aspects of JavaScript that you will need to use in your day-to-day web development tasks.

JavaScript can be tricky to implement: browser compatibility and usability issues are part of the web professional's working world. This book is written around exactly those issues. It's about 'intelligent' JavaScript, the JavaScript that improves the functionality of your web site without throwing error messages in the older browsers, or making the user jump through unnecessary hoops to accomplish what they came to your site to do.

We don't cover every angle of JavaScript here. For example, we won't be working with PDFs, or server–side JavaScript in this book. We'll be covering many other things though, including:

- Dealing with different browsers
- Implementing scripts that improve the look, feel, and functionality of your web site
- Advanced data validation techniques
- Writing JavaScript, from small pieces of add–in functionality to a full application with shopping cart functionality.

Who's this Book for?

This book will suit you if you've already been building HTML pages for some time and need to learn JavaScript fast.

It'll also suit you if you've dabbled with some scripts already. Maybe you've implemented some of those freely available on the web, but you want a thorough understanding of how the technology works in order to build your own.

You don't need any previous programming experience to understand the concepts and code that are presented here.

Whoever you are, and whatever your previous knowledge, we hope this book lives up to your expectations.

What do I Need to Begin?

All you need is a text editor (Notepad, Dreamweaver, or whatever you usually use) and a browser. Chapter 6 deals with DHTML for IE4 and NN4, so you'll need the relevant browsers to test this code with if you want to check out the differences between them. Other than that, all you need is access to the code download at *http://www.glasshaus.com* and somewhere to run your code. We've used Personal Web Manager, but any other server will do just as well.

Style Conventions

We've used a number of styles in the book to help you understand what's going on.

We've used the **important words** style to flag up new or important subjects.

Screen Text is used to indicate anything you'd see on the screen, including URLs.

New blocks of code are in this code foreground style:

```
<html>
<body>
<script language="JavaScript">

  var myCalc = 1 + 2;
  document.write("The calculated number is " + myCalc);

</script>
</body>
</html>
```

If we're amending a script, perhaps adding in a new line or making changes to an existing one, then we use the code background style for the code that you've already seen together with the foreground style to highlight the new code:

```
<html>
<body>
<script language="JavaScript">

  var userEnteredNumber = prompt("Please enter a number","");
  var myCalc = 1 + userEnteredNumber;
  var myResponse = "The number you entered + 1 = " + myCalc;
  document.write( myResponse);

</script>
</body>
</html>
```

To talk about code within text we use this `code in text` style, which is also used for filenames like `myFirstJavaScript.htm`

> Essential not–to–be–missed information is in boxes like this.

Asides to the current discussion are presented like this.

A Note About Code Formatting

We've tried to make the code as easy to read as possible. This does mean that there is sometimes whitespace in the scripts that would break the code if you used it exactly as it is printed. For example, this JavaScript code:

```
        output+="<a href=\""+getPageName(pages[i][j])+".html\" class=\"page\"
    title=\""+pages[i][j]+"\">";
```

will look like this in the book:

```
        output+="<a href=\""+getPageName(pages[i][j])+".html\" class=\"page\"
                title=\""+pages[i][j]+"\">";
```

The code in the download is without the whitespace.

Support/Feedback

Although we aim for perfection, the sad fact of book publication is that a few errors will slip through. We would like to apologize for any errors that have reached this book despite our efforts. If you spot such an error, please let us know about it using the e-mail address `support@glasshaus.com`. If it's something that will help other readers then we'll put it up on the errata page at *http://www.glasshaus.com*.

This address can also be used to access our support network. If you have trouble running any of the code in this book, or have a related question that you feel that the book didn't answer, please mail your problem to the above address quoting the title of the book, the last 4 digits of its ISBN, and the chapter and page number of your query.

Web Support

Feel free to go and visit our web site, at *http://www.glasshaus.com*. It features:

- **Code Downloads**: The example code for this, and every other glasshaus book, can be downloaded from our site.

- **On-line Resource Center**: We will be building up a definitive reference on the Web, containing all the up-to-date reference material that you'll need. We've decided to put this reference material on the Web rather than weighing down our books with hefty appendices. It will be added to over time, so if there is anything you feel isn't up there but should be, please let us know.

1

- What is JavaScript?
- Discussion of programming and concepts
- How to add JavaScript to a web page

Author: Paul Wilton

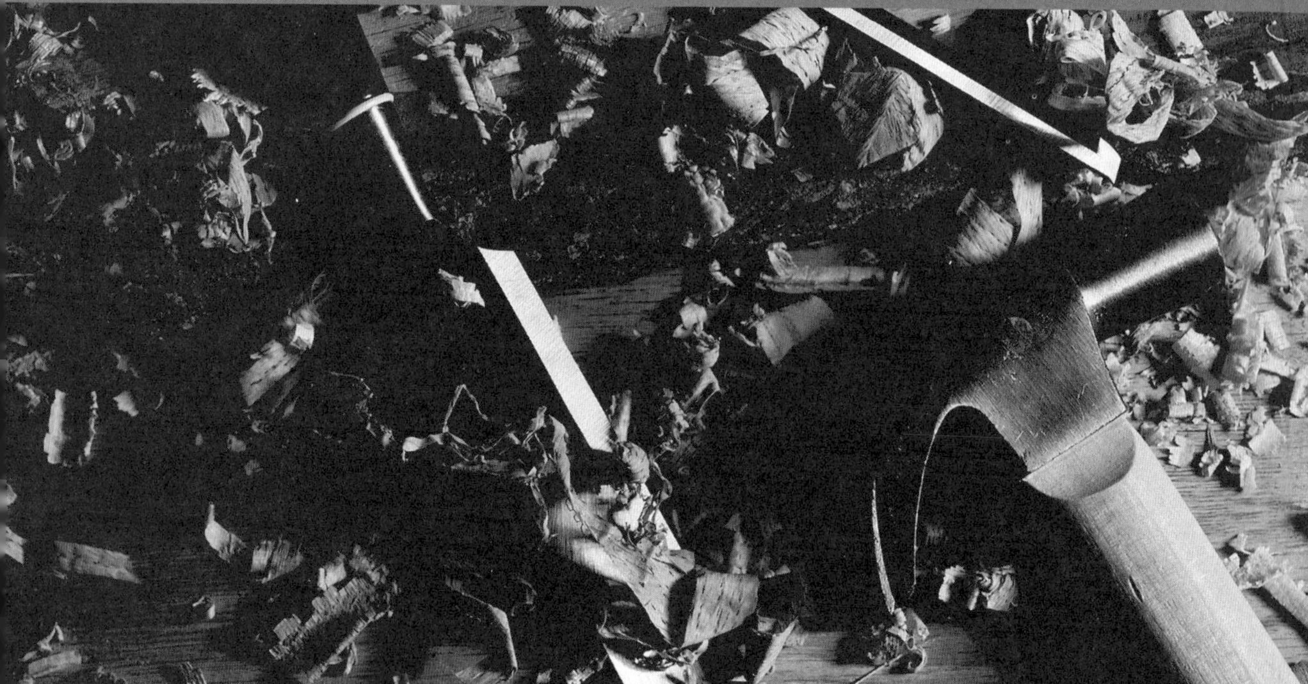

Getting Started with JavaScript

JavaScript has grown steadily in both popularity and capability since its inception and is now the number one browser scripting language. The technology has two key strengths: cross–browser support, and the ease with which it can be programmed. So successful has the JavaScript technology become that it's no longer used for browser–based programming alone, but also for programming PDF files and web server programming.

While the JavaScript language has been growing in capability, browsers themselves have also become much more programmable, enabling developers to access more of the page and its HTML elements. So JavaScript browser programming can now be extremely sophisticated and functional.

Consequently, a book about JavaScript might cover all sorts of things, so we've narrowed down the field of exploration to concentrate on using JavaScript to develop user interfaces for web pages and applications that are both usable and functional. In the first few chapters we will look at the essentials of the JavaScript language, and then move on to implementing it: using DHTML to dynamically change pages after they have loaded, validating data entered by the user, and building more interaction into applications than is possible with HTML alone.

We'll be creating a lot of short scripts in the chapters that follow, and we'll tie everything together into a large application that builds up through the book: an image viewer with shopping cart functionality. We'll start by constructing a web page that enables visitors to view large libraries of images, which would work well for sites with large numbers of images on them like a fanzine site. This part of the application will show you how to create effective user interfaces with JavaScript, and demonstrate how the usability of the web site can be improved with such an interface.

As we progress through the book we'll add e-commerce functionality to the site so that visitors can buy the images as well as view them. We'll look at how JavaScript can be used to create shopping baskets, to obtain the information needed to place an order, and to validate that information. We'll be concentrating our efforts on the front–end development process, leaving the server-side for another book.

Of course, it all begins here with this chapter, and this is where we'll set up the rest of the book by looking at:

1. What JavaScript is and what it can do for us
2. The advantages and disadvantages of JavaScript; the problems you are likely to encounter during JavaScript development, and the solutions to those problems.
3. JavaScript in a web page and essential syntax
4. Object Oriented Programming (OOP) – sometimes also termed Object Oriented Development (OOD) – in relation to JavaScript the web browser.
5. Writing and running a simple JavaScript program

Many of you will already have come across JavaScript, and already have an idea of what it is and what it can do, so we'll move quite swiftly through the language and its capabilities first.

What is JavaScript?

JavaScript started life as *LiveScript*, but Netscape changed the name, possibly because of the excitement being generated by Java, to JavaScript. The name does confuse people, though, who expect there to be a closer relationship between Java and JavaScript than actually exists. In fact there's little in common between the languages, although some of the syntax looks similar.

The JavaScript language was created by Netscape in 1996 and included in their Netscape Navigator (NN) 2.0 browser via an interpreter that reads and executes the JavaScript included in `.html` pages. The language has steadily grown in popularity since then, and is now supported by the most popular browsers: those produced by Netscape and Microsoft as well as less widely used browsers like Opera. The good news is that this means JavaScript can be used in web pages for all major modern browsers. The not quite so good news is that there are differences in the way the different browsers implement JavaScript, although the core JavaScript language is much the same.

The great thing about JavaScript is that once you've learned how to use it for browser programming, you can move on to use it in other areas. Microsoft's IIS uses JavaScript to program server-side web pages, PDF files now use JavaScript, and even Windows admin tasks can be automated with JavaScript code.

What Can JavaScript Do for Us?

The rollovers and DHTML tricks associated with JavaScript came along relatively recently in the history of the technology. In the early days JavaScript was primarily used for manipulating data before posting it to the server, saving the contents of a form as the user moved from one page of an application to another, and client–side form validation – in fact, much of the functionality that it's widely used to implement now.

Validating the user's data simply means checking that the data entered is appropriate before proceeding with the form. For example, if you want the user to enter a date in the format dd/mm/yy, then you can check that numbers and not letters have been entered, and that the numbers make sense: that the number representing the day isn't higher than 31, and that the number representing the month isn't higher than 12.

There are two very good reasons for validating data on the client's machine:

- User experience: the user doesn't have to wait for the form to be sent to the server, checked for validity, and then possibly sent back with error messages. Validating data on the client makes for a much smoother user experience.
- Server processing power: you're generating far less work for the computer hosting the web site by checking forms before they are sent to the server. The hosting machine won't have to handle the workload of validating the data and resending pages with errors in them to the user. Data checking on the server, although sometimes necessary, uses up bandwidth and will ultimately reduce the maximum number of visitors you can accommodate on your web site at any one time.

Since Netscape Navigator 2 and the first implementation of JavaScript, things have moved on quite a bit. As browsers have become more programmable, developers have been able to create more functional and interactive pages. A simple example of browser programmability in action is the image rollover, where one image is swapped for another when the user rolls her mouse pointer over it. A more sophisticated example is a JavaScript powered shopping cart, something we'll be creating later in the book.

As JavaScript has developed in its own right, developers and designers have been able to create much more impressive visual effects and interaction with the user. For example, JavaScript can be used to create a tree menu for web site navigation, like that one shown below which was on Microsoft's web site (*http://msdn.microsoft.com*):

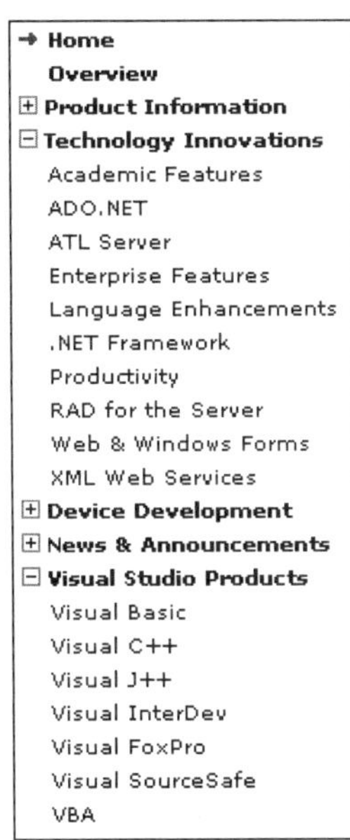

This particular example only works in Internet Explorer 4 and above, but it's perfectly possible to create a tree navigation structure that works for Netscape 6+, and we'll be doing that later on in the book.

> Special effects and inventive interaction can really enhance the user's experience, but they can also really get in the user's way if they are overused or inappropriately placed. It's the usability enhancements that you can make to your web site using JavaScript that will encourage users to come back again and again.

The Advantages and Disadvantages of JavaScript

We've already seen some of the advantages of JavaScript, like cross–browser support, validating data on the client, and being able to create more sophisticated user interfaces.

JavaScript effects are also much faster to download than some other front–end technologies like Flash and Java applets. In fact, unless you're writing a massive JavaScript application, it's quite likely that no significant extra download time will be added to a page by using JavaScript on it. Nor do users need to download a plugin before they can view your JavaScript, as they would with Flash for example, they simply need a browser that supports it – and, of course, most modern browsers do.

Other advantages include the fact that you don't need any extra tools to write JavaScript, any plain text or HTML editor will do, so there's no expensive development software to buy. It's also an easy language to learn, and there's a thriving and supportive online community of JavaScript developers and information resources.

The disadvantages of JavaScript, as with most web development, are almost entirely related to browser compatibility.

While the advances in browser programmability we've seen over recent years are, generally speaking, a good thing, if you don't implement them with care you can create a lot of inconsistencies and broken pages quite unintentionally using JavaScript. Code that works just great on IE4 might not work at all on Netscape 4, what works in NN6 doesn't always work in NN 4, and so on.

In essence, there are two main problems with JavaScript and browsers:

- The different JavaScript versions in different browsers.
- Browser programmability: the HTML elements and features of the browser that can be accessed through any scripting language. (IE4 , for example, makes most of the page and HTML accessible to scripts, but Navigator 4 limits what can be accessed and manipulated.)

JavaScript Version Differences between Browsers

The JavaScript language has gone through a number of versions, right from the first release, JavaScript 1.0, to the latest version, JavaScript 1.5 (supported by Netscape browsers, currently Netscape 6.2). Microsoft calls its own version of JavaScript **JScript**, which began with JScript 1.0, and is currently at JScript 5.6, (supported by IE 6).

While the names and numbers of the versions of JavaScript supported by Netscape and Microsoft may differ, the languages themselves are broadly, but not entirely, the same. And therein lies the problem: there are a significant number of small and sometimes subtle differences that can catch you out.

This table lists the different versions and indicates where IE and Navigator versions of JavaScript are roughly compatible:

Browser	NN3.0	NN4.0 - 4.05	NN4.06 - 4.76	NN6.0+
IE3.0	JavaScript 1.1			
	JScript 1.0			
IE4.0		JavaScript 1.2	JavaScript 1.3	
		JScript 3.0	JScript 3.0	
IE5.0				JavaScript 1.5
				JScript 5.0
IE5.5				JavaScript 1.5
				JScript 5.5
IE6.0				JavaScript 1.5
				JScript 5.6

The table only gives a very rough approximation, and in those terms JavaScript IE3 = NN3, IE4 = NN4 and IE5+ = NN6. An example of the small differences is the `try..catch` clause, which is supported in JavaScript by IE5+ and NN6+, but not in IE4 or NN4.

Although there are plenty of references you can use to look up such differences, the only way of being absolutely sure that a page will work on different browsers is to test it as widely as possible. Programs such as VirtualPC from *www.connectix.com* allows you to install and run multiple operating systems with different browsers from one host operating system.

Browser Programmability

While the language syntax and features of different versions of JavaScript are important, even more so is the browser being used to view your web pages. Let's go back to the basics to explain what this means in terms of JavaScript development.

JavaScript isn't able to do much without an environment, and in this book we're working with JavaScript in the browser. In this sense we could say that the browser is essentially the **host**. JavaScript's usefulness lies in its ability to manipulate the host environment, whether that's a web page, a `PDF` file, a web server, or Windows itself.

Each of these host environments makes itself available for programming. It does this by providing **objects** that allow JavaScript to learn about, and manipulate, the host environment. For example, the browser makes the document object that represents a web page available to JavaScript. This enables us to use JavaScript to add new HTML into a web page even as the user is viewing it. If we were using JavaScript in a Windows server then we'd find that the server exposes a very different set of objects with functionality related to the server.

So browsers themselves also have different levels of **programmability**: the collection of browser elements and features that can be accessed through a programming language. Just as the HTML supported by different browser versions varies, so too do the things we can access in the browser. A simple example would be the ability to change the image loaded in an `IMG` tag; this was supported by Netscape 3 but not by Internet Explorer 3, so attempting to access an `IMG` tag and change its source image will work great in one browser but fail completely in the other.

Not only do different browsers enable us to do different things in JavaScript, the way certain pieces of functionality are implemented can vary between browsers as well. For example, if we're creating pages accessible to IE4+ and NN4+ browsers, then we need to cope with three different ways of accessing HTML tags through JavaScript:

- The IE4+ way that works exclusively with IE4+
- The NN4 way that works exclusively with NN4
- The DOM Interface that works with IE5+ and NN6 browsers

We'll be covering each of these ways in depth in this book.

Coping with Different Browsers

You might be wondering how you can deal effectively with the panoply of JavaScript versions and web browsers' programmability. Well there's no denying that it can be frustrating, but there are strategies that you can adopt for dealing with browser issues that will make life that bit easier.

One option, and the one I prefer if possible, is to do two versions of a web site. The first version features maximum functionality and works on IE4+ and NN6. (As you'll see in later chapters, pages can be made to work with both IE4+ and NN6 with a little modification. Making IE4+ pages work with NN4 is much more of a challenge because of the limited programmability of NN4 compared with IE4, and the different ways that these browsers allow programmatic access.)

The second version is a more basic site, one that uses only simple HTML and limited JavaScript, if any at all, but which still allows access to most of the site's content. As long as I pay careful attention to the design of this second version of the site then I can expect it to work with 99% of browsers currently in use out there. Then when a visitor arrives at one of the pages in the web site I can use browser detection scripts, (which we'll be using later on), to redirect them to the version of our web site that works with their browser.

> If you use this approach to web development then you should ensure that the information for both versions comes from the same source; for example, a server-side database could be used to generate the HTML for both versions.

There will be times when this approach isn't going to work though. Sometimes the only way to make a web site function as well in NN4 as it does with IE4+ is to dumb down the original site specification. You'll also have to decide, on a site-by-site, audience-by-audience basis, whether you want to support older or less common modern browsers like Opera.

Three questions should help clarify which browsers your site needs to work with:

1. Who will visit the web site? If you're creating a web site dedicated to programming the Opera browser then it's going to have to work with Opera. Similarly, if you're developing for an Intranet where the browser and version is controlled then the question is answered for you.
2. What does the client want? If they demand it works with IE2.0 and remain oblivious to your raised eyebrows and sotto voce "you have got to be kidding", then that's what you're going to have to do.

3. Which browsers are most commonly used? This changes as new browsers are released and old ones go out of use. You also need to take into account the importance of making your web site accessible – while this is obviously a good idea, there are also legal obligations to make certain web sites accessible.

There are a number of web sites that offer general statistics about the browser versions in common use, and these can help you decide which browser you need to support in order for the majority of people to view the site. Try these for web browser stats:

http://www.upsdell.com/BrowserNews/stat.htm

http://browserwatch.internet.com/stats/stats.html

http://www.w3schools.com/browsers/browsers_stats.asp

This last site covers information such as operating system, screen size and the version of JavaScript being used – including the fact that as many as 1 in 10 people have JavaScript switched off. (If you were building for such an audience then you might opt to have a non-JavaScript version of the web site, or create individual non-JavaScript pages, or notify users that they need JavaScript to use the web site. We'll be looking at ways of dealing with this as well as dealing with different screen sizes.)

Remember, though, that many browser statistic web sites base their numbers on the people who visit their web site, and the people who visit such sites are unlikely to be representative of the average visitor to *your* site. In fact, if you're creating web pages for an existing web site, then that web site is probably the best source of browser statistics.

> However you find your statistics, always be aware that you should only alienate users for a good reason. Although you might be only losing 5% of your potential visitors statistically, if those 5% are an extremely vocal minority they can have a detrimental impact on your brand and good name. A shop that turned away 5% of people because they were wearing the wrong shoes wouldn't be able to expect much long–term success...

JavaScript in a Web Page

First things first: a web browser 'interprets' code by converting it to something the computer can understand, and then executing it. It won't, however, interpret and execute JavaScript code unless we tell it what is JavaScript and what is HTML.

We use the HTML tags `<script>` and `</script>` to tell the interpreter that the lines between the tags should be interpreted as JavaScript code and not HTML or text. Everything between the tags is considered JavaScript program code.

We can put the JavaScript code block anywhere in the page, and in more than one place, as well as have more than one script block:

```
<head>
<script language="JavaScript">
  // The forward slashes denote commented text that won't be executed
```

```
</script>
</head>
<body>

<H1>Test Page</H1>
<script language="JavaScript">
  // more commented text or code
</script>
</body>
</html>
```

This code won't actually do anything, it's just here to demonstrate the `language` attribute inside the `script` tag, and that you can add JavaScript in more than one place on a page.

Although IE supports VBScript as well as JavaScript, both IE and NN will assume that you're using JavaScript if you don't specify the language, so you can get away with leaving the attribute off altogether. However, the attribute can also be used to specify different versions of JavaScript:

Attribute Value	Example	Effect
JavaScript1.2	`<SCRIPT language="JavaScript1.2">`	Code will be executed only by IE4+ and NN4+. Browsers incompatible with this version will ignore it.
JavaScript1.3	`<SCRIPT language="JavaScript1.3">`	Only Netscape 4.06+ and IE5+ will execute the code. Incompatible browsers will ignore it.
JavaScript1.5	`<SCRIPT language="JavaScript1.5">`	Only NN6+ will execute the code. Incompatible browsers will ignore it.
JScript	`<SCRIPT language="JScript">`	Only IE4+ will execute the code. Incompatible browsers will ignore it.

Although we'll be specifying the language in the examples in this book, we won't specify a specific version of JavaScript, but use browser-checking code in the examples where the Internet Explorer and Netscape code is the same but for a few subtle differences. You'll find that most examples in the book work the same on IE4 and Netscape browsers.

JavaScript Syntax

Before we go any further we should discuss some JavaScript syntax essentials:

- `'//'` Indicates that what follows is a comment and not code to be executed, so the interpreter doesn't try to convert it to machine code and run it. Comments are a handy way of putting notes in the code to remind us what the code is intended to do, or to help anyone else reading the code see what's going on.

- '/*' Indicates the beginning of a comment that covers more than one line.

- '*/' Indicates the end of a comment that covers more than one line. Multi–line comments are also useful if you want to stop a certain section of code from being executed but don't want to delete it permanently. If you were having problems with a chunk of code, for example, and you weren't sure which lines were causing the problem, you could comment a chunk at a time in order to isolate the problem.

- Curly braces ('{' and '}') are used to indicate a block of code. They ensure that all the lines inside the braces are treated as one block.

- A semicolon defines the end of a statement, and a statement is a single command. Semicolons are in fact optional, but it's still a good idea to use them to make clear where statements end, because doing so makes your code easier to read and debug. (Although you can put many statements on one line, it's best to put them on separate lines in order to make the code easier to read.) You don't need to use semicolons after curly braces.

Let's put this syntax into a working block of code:

```
<html>
<body>
<script Language="JavaScript">
  //one-line comments are useful for reminding us what the code is doing

  /* this is a multi-line comment. It's useful for both longer comments but
     also blocking out segments of code when you're testing
  */

  /*script starts here. We're declaring a variable myName, and assigning its
    value to whatever the user puts in the prompt box (more on that in Chapter
    2), finishing the instruction with a semicolon because it is a statement
  */

  var myName = prompt ("Enter your name","");

  //If the name the user enters is Paul Wilton
  if (myName == "Paul Wilton")
    {
     //then a new window pops up saying hello
     alert("Hello Me");
    }

  //If the name entered isn't Paul Wilton
  else
    {
     //say hello to someone else
     alert("hello someone else");
    }
</script>
</body>
</html>
```

Some of the code may not make sense yet, depending on your previous JavaScript experience. All that matters for now is that it's clear how comments are used, what a code block is, and why there are semicolons at the end of some of the statements. You can run this script if you like – just copy it into an HTML page and run it through your browser.

Although statements like `if` and `else` span more than one line and contain other statements, they are considered single statements and don't need a semicolon after them. The JavaScript interpreter knows that the lines linked with an `if` statement should be treated as one block because of the curly braces. We'll be looking at variables and conditional statements (`if` and `else`) in the next chapter.

Code Execution

The browser reads the page from top to bottom, so the order in which code executes depends on the order of the script blocks. (Also note that it's not just the browser that can read our code, the user of our web sites can view our code too so it's not a good idea to put anything secret or sensitive in there.) There are three script blocks in this next example:

```
<head>
<script language="JavaScript">
     alert("First script Block");
     alert("First script Block - Second Line");
</script>
</head>
<body>
<H1>Test Page</H1>
<script language="JavaScript">
     alert("Second script Block");
</script>
<P>Some more HTML</P>
<script language="JavaScript">

     alert("Third script Block");

     function doSomething()
     {
           alert("Function in Third script Block");
     }

</script>
</body>
</html>
```

If you try it out, you'll see that the `alert` in the first script block appears first displaying the message *First script Block*, followed by the next `alert` command in the second line displaying the message *First script Block - Second Line*.

The interpreter continues down the page and comes to the second script block, where the `alert` function displays *Second script Block*, and the third script block following it with the `alert` statement that displays *Third script Block*. Although there's another `alert` command inside the function a few lines down, it doesn't execute and display the message. This is because it's inside a function (`function doSomething`) and code inside functions will only execute when they're called.

An Aside about Functions

We'll be talking about functions in much more depth in Chapter 3, but we should introduce them here because you can't get very far in JavaScript without an understanding of functions. Functions are blocks of code, surrounded by curly braces, which you create to perform a helpful task. JavaScript contains functions that are available for us to use and perform tasks like displaying a message to the user.

We can also create our own functions, which is what we did in the previous code block. Let's say we create some code that works out what browser the user has. We'd probably want to use it again and again in different situations. While we could cut and paste code blocks wherever we wanted to use them, this approach can make the code excessively long; if you want the same piece of code three or four times within one page it'll also get pretty hard to decipher and debug. So instead we can wrap the browser–checking functionality into a function and then pass in any information that the function needs in order to work using **parameters**. A function can also return a value to the code that called the function into action originally.

To call the function you simply write its name, but you can't do that, as you might expect, until the script has created it. We can call it in this script by adding it to the third script block like this:

```
<script language="JavaScript">

      alert("Third script Block");

      function doSomething()
      {
            alert("Function in Third script Block");
      }

    //call the function doSomething
    doSomething();

</script>
</body>
</html>
```

So far in this chapter we've looked at the pros and cons of the JavaScript language, some of the syntax rules, learned about some of the main components of the language, albeit briefly, and run a few JavaScript scripts. We've covered quite a lot of distance. Before we move on to a more detailed examination of the JavaScript language in the next chapter, however, we should talk about something key to successful JavaScript development: **objects**.

Objects

Objects are central to the way we use JavaScript in a web page. Objects in JavaScript are in many ways like objects in the world outside programming (it does exist, I just had a look). In the real world, an object is just a 'thing': a car, a table, a chair, and the keyboard I'm typing on. Objects have:

1. **Properties**: the red car
2. **Methods**: the method for starting the car might be *turn ignition key*
3. **Events**: turning the ignition key results in the *car starting* event

Object-Oriented Programming (OOP) tries to make programming easier by modeling real–world objects. Let's say we were creating a car simulator. First, we would create a car object, giving it properties like *color* and *current speed.* Then we'd need to create methods: perhaps a *turn ignition key* method to start the car, and a *press brakes* method to slow the car, into which we'd need to pass information about how hard the brakes should be pressed so that we can determine the slowing effect. Finally we would want some events, for example *gasoline low* event to remind us to fill up the car.

Object-Oriented Programming works with these concepts. This way of designing software is now very commonplace and influences many areas of programming – but most importantly to us, it's central to JavaScript and web browser programming.

Some of the objects we'll be using are part of the language specification: the String object, the Date object, and the Math object for example. The same objects would be available to JavaScript in a PDF file and on a web server. These objects provide lots of useful functionality. The Date object, for example, allows you to obtain the current date and time from the PC. It stores the date and provides lots of useful date related functions, for example converting the date/time from one time zone to another.

As we've already seen, the browser makes itself available for programming through objects. These objects allow us to find out information about the browser and to change the look and feel of the application. For example, the browser makes the document object that represents a web page available to JavaScript. We can use this from JavaScript to add new HTML into the web page being viewed by the user of the web browser. If you were to use JavaScript with a different host, with a Windows server for example, then you'd find that the server hosting JavaScript exposes a very different set of objects, their functionality being related to things you want to do on a web server.

We'll also see in Chapter 3 that JavaScript allows us to create our own objects. This is a powerful feature that allows us to model real–world problems using JavaScript. To create a new object we need to specify the properties and methods it should have using a template called a **class**. A class is a bit like an architect's drawing in that it specifies what should go where and do what, but it doesn't actually create the object.

> *There is some debate as to whether JavaScript is an object–based language or an object–oriented language. The difference is that an object–based language uses objects for doing programming but doesn't allow the coder to use object–oriented programming in their code design. An object–oriented programming language not only uses objects but also makes it easy to develop and design code in line with object–oriented design methodology. JavaScript allows us to create our own objects but its syntax is not as OO friendly as languages such as Java or C#, which have language commands and features specifically to enable OOP. However, we'll be concentrating not on debates about what is or isn't object oriented here, but on how objects are useful in practical terms in this book, and we'll look at some basic object–oriented coding where it helps make life easier for us.*

As we progress through the book we'll look in more depth at objects: the objects central to the JavaScript language, the objects that the browser makes available for access and manipulation using JavaScript, and creating our own custom objects. For now, though, all we need to know is that objects in JavaScript are 'entities' we can use to add functionality to web pages, and that they can have properties, methods, and events – although not all of them do: the Math object, for example, has only properties (like the value of PI) and methods (one such method generates a random number).

Simple JavaScript Example

We'll finish the chapter with a simple script that determines first the size of the user's screen and then loads up an image that fits. We'll do this using the `screen` object (in fact both a property of the `window` object as well as a property in its own right – but that's a distinction best left to Chapter 5, *Windows and Frames*). The `screen` object is a representation of the user's screen, and has an `availWidth` property that we'll retrieve and use to decide which image to load.

Here's the code:

```
<html>
<body>
<script language="JavaScript">
      //if width of the screen object is less than 650 pixels
      if (screen.availWidth < 650)
      {
            //load the small image
            document.write("<IMG src=SmallImage.jpg>")
      }

      //or if the width of the screen object is less than 1000 pixels
      else if (screen.availWidth > 1000)
      {
            //load the big image
            document.write("<IMG src=BigImage.jpg>")
      }
      //otherwise
      else
      {
             //load the medium sized
             document.write("<IMG src=MedImage.jpg>")
      }

</script>
</body>
</html>
```

You can download the images from *www.glasshaus.com* or use your own. The images in the download are sized to fit screens 640 * 480 (`SmallImage.jpg`), 800 * 600 (`MedImage.jpg`) and 1024 * 768 or larger (`BigImage.jpg`).

Although we'll be looking at the details of `if` statements and loops in the next chapter, you can probably see how this is working already. The `if` statement on the first line asks if the `screen.availWidth` is less than 650 pixels:

```
if (screen.availWidth < 650)
```

If the user's screen is 640 * 480 then it is less than 650 pixels, so the code within the curly braces is executed and the small image is loaded. (Assuming the user doesn't have any task bars on the left or right of the screen, the image will fit.)

```
if (screen.availWidth < 650)
{
      document.write("<IMG src=SmallImage.jpg>")
}
```

We're using another object, the `document` object, to write to the page (HTML document). The document object's `write()` method allows us to insert HTML into the page. Note that `document.write()` doesn't actually change the source HTML page, just the page the user sees on their computer.

In fact we'll find `document.write()` very useful as we work through the book. It's good for small examples that show how a script is working, for communicating with the user, and even for debugging an area of a program that you're not sure is doing what you think it should be doing. It also works on all version 4 and later Microsoft and Netscape browsers.

The code carries on checking the size of the screen images using the `else` statement. The final `else` only occurs if neither of the other evaluations have resulted in code being executed, so we are assuming that the screen is 800 * 600, and load the medium sized image accordingly:

```
else
{
      document.write("<IMG src=MedImage.jpg>")
}
```

It's also worth noting that we're measuring the screen size here, and the user may have a 800 * 600 screen but that doesn't mean their browser window is maximized. We may be making the user download a bigger image than they actually need by doing things this way.

Later on we'll be working with more complex examples that use JavaScript to ensure that the interface fits the user's screen. For now though, I hope this simple example gives you an inkling of the kind of flexibility you can add to your web pages using JavaScript.

Summary

In this chapter we've taken a look at what JavaScript is, how it works, and what its advantages and disadvantages are. We noted that one disadvantage, or at least something we have to be aware of, is the differences between browser versions. We looked briefly at how we might cope with browser differences and will look at them in more detail later in the book.

We've also run some JavaScript code, seen how to add comments to the code, and how to separate JavaScript statements using semicolons. We also saw that we can tell JavaScript to treat a group of lines of code as a single block belonging to a statement using curly braces, with the `if` statement, for example. We saw that we can add JavaScript to various places within a web page, and that JavaScript generally runs from top to bottom, and from the first `script` block to the last, with the exception of functions that only execute when we tell them to.

We also looked at objects, which are central to writing JavaScript. Not only is JavaScript itself very much dependent on objects, but the browser also uses objects to make itself available for programming through JavaScript. Finally, we looked at a simple example that selects an image of a size that would fit on the user's screen, using the `screen` object to find out information about the users screen and then the `document` object to write HTML to the version of the web page the user sees.

In the next chapter we'll cover the language fundamentals of JavaScript. We'll see how JavaScript stores and manipulates data, and uses it in calculations. We'll also look at creating 'intelligent' JavaScript programs using decision–making statements that allow us to evaluate data, do calculations with it, and decide on a course of action. With that chapter under our belt we'll have most of the foundation knowledge needed to go on to more exciting and useful web programming.

2

- Dealing with information
- Calculations and information manipulation
- Decision making

Author: Paul Wilton

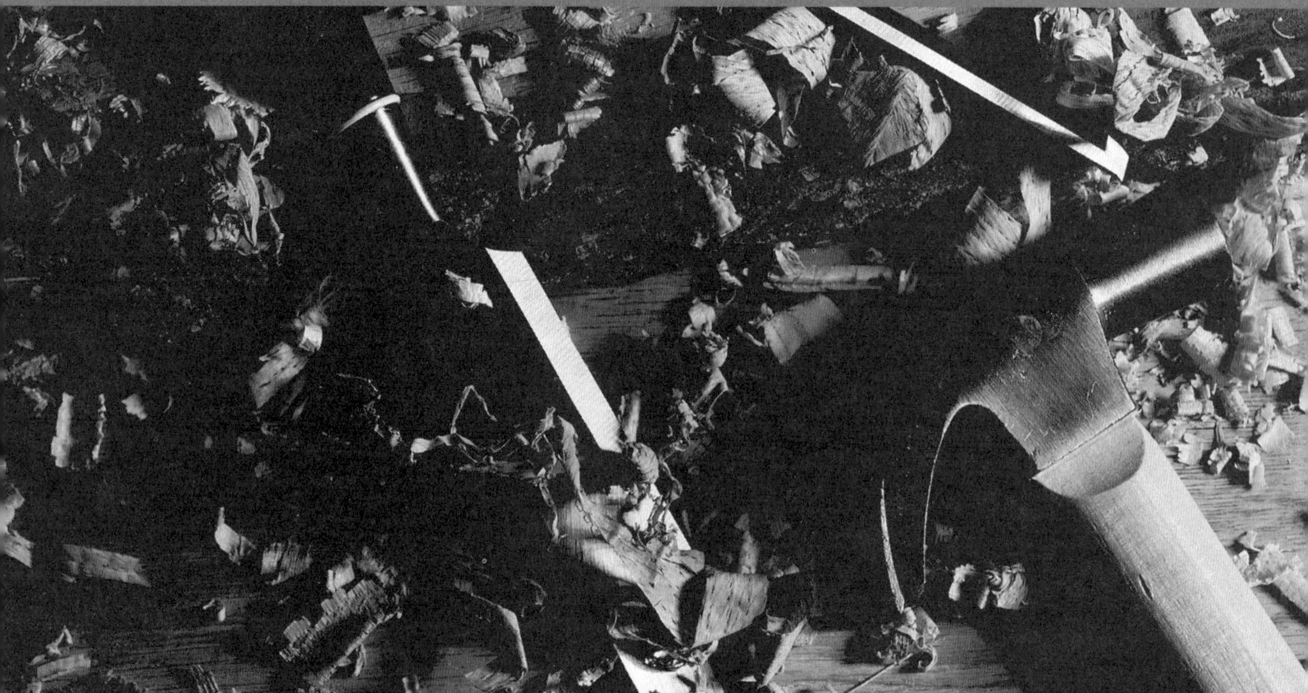

Data and Decisions

Data and decision-making are fundamental to every 'intelligent' program. We'll begin this chapter by looking at how JavaScript understands, or represents, data. This is important because JavaScript works with a number of **data types**, and manipulates data according to its data type. You can generate unexpected results by running manipulations on data of a different type to the one you were intending to work with, so we'll look at some of the more common data type problems, and see how to convert one type of data to another.

We'll also be working with conditional statements and loops: two of the most valuable tools for decision-making. In order to make decisions in a computer language we need to let the program know what should happen in response to certain conditions, which is where conditional statements come in. Loops, on the other hand, simply allow you to repeat an action until a specified circumstance is met. For example, you might want to loop through each input box in a form and check the information it contains is valid.

We'll be covering a lot:

- Classifying and manipulating information in JavaScript: data types and data operators
- Variables
- Converting data types
- Introducing data objects: String, Date and Math objects
- Arrays: storing ordered sets of data like the items in a shopping basket
- Decision–making with conditional statements, loops, and data evaluation

Data, Data Types, and Data Operators

Data is used to store information, and in order to do that more effectively, JavaScript gives each piece of data a **type**. This type stipulates what can or cannot be done with the data. For example, one of the JavaScript data types is **Number**, which allows you to perform certain calculations on the data that it holds. The simplest data types in JavaScript are primitive data types. Primitive in this sense just means that the data is stored directly. There are three primitive data types that store data in JavaScript:

- String: a series of characters: "some characters", for example
- Number: a floating point number, like 42 or 3.1415
- Boolean: can contain a true or false value

There are two slightly different primitive data types as well. These don't store information, but instead warn us about a particular situation:

- Null: indicates that there is no valid data
- Undefined: indicates that something has not been defined and given a value. This is important when you're working with variables.

We'll be working extensively with these data types throughout the chapter.

The String Data Type

The JavaScript interpreter expects string data types to be enclosed within single or double quotation marks (known as delimiters). This script, for example, will write *some characters* onto the page:

```
<html>
<body>
<script language="JavaScript">
  document.write("some characters");
</script>
</body>
</html>
```

The quotation marks won't be written out to the page because they are not part of the string, they simply tell JavaScript where the string starts and ends. We could just as easily have used single quotation marks:

```
<html>
<body>
<script language="JavaScript">
  document.write('some characters');
</script>
</body>
</html>
```

Both methods are fine, just as long as you close the string the same way you opened it and don't try to delimit it like this:

```
document.write('some characters");
document.write("some characters');
```

Of course, you might want to use a single or double quotation mark inside the string itself, in which case you need to use a distinct delimiter. If you used double quotation marks then the instructions will be interpreted as you intended:

```
document.write("Paul's characters ");
```

But if you used single quotations marks, they won't be:

```
document.write('Paul's characters');
```

This will give you a syntax error because the JavaScript interpreter can't tell whether the string ends before or after the final `s`.

> JavaScript syntax, like English syntax, is a set of rules that make the language 'intelligible'. Just as a syntax error in English can render a sentence meaningless, so a syntax error in JavaScript can render the instruction meaningless.

You can avoid creating JavaScript syntax errors like this one by using single quotation marks to delimit any string containing double quotes and vice versa:

```
document.write("Paul's numbers are 123");
document.write('some "characters"');
```

If, on the other hand, you wanted to use both single and double quotation marks in your string then you need to use something called an escape sequence. In fact, it's better coding practice to use escape sequences instead of the quotation marks we've been using so far, because they make your code easier to read.

Escape Sequences

Escape sequences are also useful for situations where you want to use characters that can't be typed using a keyboard (like the symbol for the Japanese Yen ¥ on a Western keyboard). These are some of the most commonly used escape sequences:

Escape Sequences	Character Represented
`\b`	Backspace
`\f`	Form feed
`\n`	New line
`\r`	Carriage return

Table continued on following page

Escape Sequences	Character Represented
`\t`	Tab
`\'`	Single quote
`\"`	Double quote
`\\`	Backslash
`\xNN`	NN is a hexadecimal number which identifies a character in the Latin-1 character set (the Latin-1 character is the norm for English speaking countries)
`\uDDDD`	DDDD is a hexadecimal number identifying a Unicode character

Let's amend this string, which causes a syntax error:

```
document.write('Paul's characters');
```

so that it uses the escape sequence (`\'`) and is correctly interpreted:

```
document.write('Paul\'s characters');
```

The escape sequence tells the JavaScript interpreter that the single quotation mark belongs to the string itself and isn't a delimiter.

ASCII is a character encoding method that uses values from 0 to 254. We specify characters using the ASCII value in hexadecimal with the `\xNN` escape sequence. The letter C is 67 in decimal and 43 in hex, so we could write that to the page using the escape sequence like this:

```
document.write("\x43");
```

The `\uDDDD` escape sequence works in much the same way but uses the Unicode character encoding method, which has 65,535 characters. As the first few hundred ASCII and Unicode character sets are similar, you can write out the letter C using this escape sequence like this:

```
document.write('\u0043');
```

ASCII and UNICODE information can get quite detailed so the best place to look for information is on the web. For Unicode try *http://www.unicode.org*.

Data Operators

JavaScript has a number of data operators that you can use to manipulate the data in your programs; you'll probably recognize them from math. Here are some of the most commonly used operators:

Operator	What it does
+	Adds two numbers together or concatenates two strings
-	Subtracts the second number from the first
*	Multiplies two numbers
/	Divides the first number by the second
%	Finds the modulus – the reminder of a division. For example, 98 % 10 = 8
--	Decreases the number by 1: only useful with variables, which we'll see at work later
++	Increases the number by 1: only useful with variables, which we'll see at work later

Here they are in use:

```
<html>
<body>
<script language="JavaScript">
  document.write(1 - 1);
  document.write("<br>");
  document.write(1 + 1);
  document.write("<br>");
  document.write(2 * 2);
  document.write("<br>");
  document.write(12 / 2);
  document.write("<br>");
  document.write(1 + 2 * 3);
  document.write("<br>");
  document.write(98 % 10);
</script>
</body>
</html>
```

You should get this output:

0
2
4
6
7
8

JavaScript, just like math, gives some operators precedence. Multiplication takes a higher precedence than addition, so the sum 1 + 2 * 3 is carried out like this:

2 * 3 = 6
6 + 1 = 7

All operators have an order of precedence. Multiplication, division, and modulus have equal precedence, so where they all appear in an equation the sum will be calculated from left to right. Try this sum:

2 * 10 / 5%3

The result is 1, because the calculation simply reads from left to right:

2 * 10 = 20
20 / 5 = 4
4%3 = 1

Addition and subtraction also have equal precedence.

You can use parentheses to give part of a calculation higher precedence. For example, you could add 1 to 1 and then multiply by 5 like this:

(1 + 1) * 5

The result will then be 10, but without the parentheses it would have been 6. In fact it's a good idea to use parentheses even when they're not essential because they help make the order of the execution clear.

If you use more than one set of parentheses JavaScript will simply work from left to right:

```
document.write( (1 + 1) * 5 * ( 2 + 3) );
```

This is how the sum is calculated:

(1 + 1) = 2

(2 + 3) = 5

2 * 5 = 10

10 * 5 = 50

As we've seen, JavaScript's addition operator adds the value on the left-hand side of the operator to the value on the right-hand side. What it actually does with the two values depends on the data type that you're using. For example, if you're working with two numbers that have been stored as the number data type, then the + operator will add them together. However, if one of the data types you're working with is a string (as indicated by the delimiters), then the two values will be concatenated. Try this:

```
<html>
<body>
<script language="JavaScript">
  document.write('Java' + 'Script');
  document.write( 1 + 1);
  document.write( 1 + '1');
</script>
</body>
</html>
```

Being able to use the addition operator with strings can be handy, but it can also generate unexpected results if one of the values you're working with happens to be of a different data type to the one you were expecting. We'll be looking at some example like this, and resolving them, later on.

It's less of a problem if you're working with **literal** values as we have been doing so far. However, much of the data you'll be working with in your programs will be entered by the user, or generated by the script, so you won't know in advance exactly what data you're going to be working with. This is where **Variables** come in. Variables are placeholders for data in your script, and they're central to JavaScript programming.

JavaScript Variables

You have to declare a variable before you can do anything with it, and JavaScript will throw a syntax error if you try to use a variable without first declaring it.

We declare a variable by giving it a unique name and using the `var` keyword. Variable names have to start with a letter of the alphabet or with an underscore, while the rest of the name can be made up of numbers, letters, and underscore characters, but can't include punctuation marks.

> Like most things in JavaScript, variable names are case-sensitive: `thisVariable` and `ThisVariable` are different variables. Be very careful about naming your variables; you can run into all sorts of trouble if you don't name them consistently.

Always give your variables meaningful names. In the next example we'll build, for example, we're going to write an exchange rate conversion program, so we'll use variable names like `euroToDollarRate` and `dollarToPound`. There are two advantages to naming variables descriptively: it's easier to remember what the code is doing if you come back to it at a later date, and it's easier for someone new to the code to see what's going on. As we'll see in the next chapter, code readability and layout are very important to the development of web pages. It makes it quicker and easier to spot errors and debug them, and to amend the code as you want to.

So, with all that said, let's start declaring variables. We can declare a variable without initializing it, (giving it a value):

```
var myVariable;
```

Then it's ready and waiting for when we have a value. This is useful for variables that will hold user input.

We can also declare and initialize the variable at the same time:

```
var myVariable = "A String"
var anotherVariable = 123;
```

Or we can declare and initialize a variable by assigning it the return value of the `prompt()` function, or the sum of a calculation:

```
var eurosToConvert = prompt("How many Euros do you wish to convert","");
var dollars = eurosToConvert * euroToDollarRate;
```

The `prompt()` function is a JavaScript function that asks the user to enter a value and then returns it to the code. Here we're assigning the value entered to the variable `eurosToConvert`.

Initializing your variables is a very good idea, especially if you can give them a default value that's useful to the application. Even initializing a variable to an empty string can be a good idea, because you can check back on it without bringing up the error messages that would have popped up if it didn't have a value.

Let's look at how variables can improve both the readability of your code and its functionality. Here's a block of code without any variables:

```
<html>
<body>
<script language="JavaScript">
     document.write(0.872 * prompt("How many Euros do you wish to convert",""));
</script>
</body>
</html>
```

It's not immediately obvious that this code is converting Euros to Dollars, because there's nothing to tell us that 0.872 is the exchange rate. The code works fine though; if you try it out with the number 10 you should get:

8.72

Supposing that we wanted to make the result a little more informative, like this:

10 Euros is 8.72 Dollars

Without variables, the only way to do it would be to ask the user to enter the Euros they want to convert twice, and that really wouldn't be user friendly. Using variables, though, we can store the data temporarily, and then call it up as many times as we need to:

```
<html>
<body>
<script language="JavaScript">
  //declare a variable holding the conversion rate
  var euroToDollarRate = 0.872;
  // declare a new variable and use it to store the number of Euros
  var eurosToConvert = prompt("How many Euros do you wish to convert","");

  //declare a variable to hold the result of the Euros multiplied by the
conversion
  var dollars = eurosToConvert * euroToDollarRate;

  //write the result to the page
  document.write(eurosToConvert + " euros is " + Dollars + " dollars");
</script>
</body>
</html>
```

We've used three variables: one to store the exchange rate from Euros to Dollars, another to store the number of Euros that will be converted, and the final one to hold the result of the conversion into Dollars. Then all we need to do is write out the result using both variables. Not only is this script more functional, it's also much easier to read.

Converting Different Types of Data

For the most part, the JavaScript interpreter can work out what data types we want to be used. In the following code, for example, the interpreter understands the numbers 1 and 2 to be of number data type and treats them accordingly:

```
<html>
<body>
<script language="JavaScript">

  var myCalc = 1 + 2;
  document.write("The calculated number is " + myCalc);

</script>
</body>
</html>
```

This will be written to your page:

The calculated number is 3

However, if we rewrite the code to allow the user to enter their own number using the `prompt()` function, then we'll get a different calculation altogether:

```
<html>
<body>
<script language="JavaScript">

  var userEnteredNumber = prompt("Please enter a number","");
  var myCalc = 1 + userEnteredNumber;
  var myResponse = "The number you entered + 1 = " + myCalc;
  document.write( myResponse);

</script>
</body>
</html>
```

If you enter `2` at the prompt, then you'll be told that:

The number you entered + 1 = 12

Rather than add the two numbers together, the JavaScript interpreter has concatenated them. This is because the `prompt()` function actually returns the value entered by the user as a string data type, even though the string contains number characters. The concatenation happens in this line:

```
var myCalc = 1 + userEnteredNumber;
```

In effect, it's the same as if we'd written:

```
var myCalc = 1 + "2";
```

If, however, we use the subtraction operator instead:

```
var myCalc = 1 - userEnteredNumber;
```

Then `userEnteredNumber` is subtracted from 1. The subtraction operator isn't applicable to string data so JavaScript works out that we wanted the data to be treated as a number, converts the string to a number, and does the calculation. The same applies to the `*` and `/` operators.

The `typeof()` operator returns the type of data that has been passed to it, so we can use that to see which data types the JavaScript interpreter is working with:

```
<html>
<body>
<script language="JavaScript">
  var userEnteredNumber = prompt("Please enter a number","");
  document.write(typeof(userEnteredNumber));
</script>
</body>
</html>
```

This will write *string* into the page.

The way to ensure that the interpreter is using a number data type is to **explicitly** declare that the data is a number. There are three functions you can to do this:

- `Number()`: tries to convert the value of the variable inside the parentheses into a number
- `parseFloat()`: tries to convert the value to a floating point. Anything non–numerical passed to the function will be discarded
- `parseInt()`: converts the value to an integer by removing any fractional part without rounding the number up or down. Anything non–numerical passed to the function will be discarded

Let's see how these functions work in practice:

```
<html>
<body>
<script language="JavaScript">
  var userEnteredNumber = prompt("Please enter a number","");
  document.write(typeof(userEnteredNumber));
  document.write("<br>");
  document.write(parseFloat(userEnteredNumber));
  document.write("<br>");
  document.write(parseInt(userEnteredNumber));
  userEnteredNumber = Number(userEnteredNumber)
  document.write("<br>");
  document.write(userEnteredNumber);
  document.write("<br>");
  document.write(typeof(userEnteredNumber));
</script>
</body>
</html>
```

Try entering the value 23.50. You should get this output:

string
23.5
23
23.5
number

The data entered is read as a string in the first line. Then `parseFloat()` converts 23.50 from a string to a floating point number, and in the next line `parseInt()` sends back only the fractional part, (without rounding up or down). The variable is then converted to a number using the `Number()` function, stored in the `userEnteredNumber` variable itself (overwriting the string held there) and on the final line we see that `userEnteredNumber`'s data type is indeed Number.

Try entering *23.50abc* at the user prompt:

string
23.5
23
NaN
number

The results are similar, but this time `Number()` has returned *NaN*. (*NaN* stands for 'Not a Number'.) The `parseFloat()` and `parseInt()` functions still return a number because they work from left to right converting as much of the string to a number as they can and then stop when they hit a non-numeric value. The `Number()` function will reject any string that contains non-numerical characters (anything other than digits, a valid decimal place, and + and - signs are allowed but nothing else).

If you try entering *abc* you'll just get:

string
NaN
NaN
NaN
number

None of the functions can find a valid number and so they all return *NaN*, which we can see is a number data type, but not a valid number. This is a good way of checking user input for validity, and we'll be using it to do exactly that later on.

So let's get back to the problem we started with: using `prompt()` to retrieve a number. All we need to do is tell the interpreter the data entered by the user should be converted to a number data type, using the `Number()` function with the `prompt()` function:

```
<html>
<body>
<script language="JavaScript">

  var userEnteredNumber = Number(prompt("Please enter a number",""));
  var myCalc = 1 + userEnteredNumber;
  var myResponse = "The number you entered + 1 = " + myCalc;
  document.write( myResponse);
```

```
</script>
</body>
</html>
```

And that's all we need to say about primitive data types and variables for now. Primitive data types, as we have seen, simply hold a value. However, JavaScript can also deal with complex data, and it does this using **composite** data types.

The Composite Data Types: Array and Object

There are two composite data types:

- Object: contains a reference to any object, including the objects that the browser makes available
- Array: contains one or more of any other data types

We'll look at the Object data type first. As you might recall from the discussion in Chapter 1, objects model real-world entities. These objects can hold data, and provide us with properties and methods.

The String, Date, and Math Objects

These three objects do three different things:

- String object: stores a string, and provides properties and methods for working with strings
- Date object: stores a date, and provides methods (but no properties) for working with it
- Math object: doesn't store data, but provides properties and methods for manipulating mathematical data

Let's start with the String object.

The String Object

Earlier we created string primitives by giving them some characters to hold, like this:

```
var myPrimitiveString = "ABC123";
```

A String **object** does things slightly differently, not only allowing us to store characters but also providing a way to manipulate and change those characters. You can create String objects explicitly or implicitly.

Creating a String Object

Let's work with the implicit method first: we'll begin declaring a new variable, and assign it a new String primitive to initialize it. Try that now using `typeof()` to make sure that the data in the variable `myStringPrimitive` is a string primitive:

```
<html>
<body>
<script language="JavaScript">
  var myStringPrimitive= "abc";
  document.write(typeof(myStringPrimitive));
</script>
</body>
</html>
```

We can use still use the String object's methods on it though. JavaScript will simply convert the string primitive to a temporary String object, use the method on it, and then change the data type back to string. We can try that out using the `length` property of the String object:

```
<html>
<body>
<script language="JavaScript">
  var myStringPrimitive= "abc";
  document.write(typeof(myStringPrimitive));
  document.write("<br>");
  document.write(myStringPrimitive.length);
  document.write("<br>");
  document.write(typeof(myStringPrimitive));
</script>
</body>
</html>
```

This is what you should see in the browser window:

string
3
string

So `myStringPrimitive` is still holding a string primitive after the temporary conversion. We can also create String objects explicitly, using the `new` keyword together with the `String()` **constructor**:

```
<html>
<body>
<script language="JavaScript">
  var myStringObject = new String("abc");
  document.write(typeof(myStringObject));
  document.write("<br>");
  document.write(myStringObject.length);
  document.write("<br>");
  document.write(typeof(myStringObject));
</script>
</body>
</html>
```

Loading this page displays this:

object
3
object

The only difference between this script and the previous one is in the first line where we created the new object and supply some characters for the String object to store:

```
var myStringObject = new String("abc");
```

The result of checking the `length` property is the same whether we created the String object implicitly or explicitly. The only real difference between creating String objects explicitly or implicitly is that creating them explicitly is marginally more efficient if you're going to be using the same String object again and again. Explicitly creating String objects also helps prevent the JavaScript interpreter getting confused between numbers and strings, as it can do.

Using the String Object's Methods

The String object has a lot of methods, so we'll limit our discussion of them to two of them here, the `indexOf()` and `substring()` methods.

JavaScript strings, as we've seen, are made up of characters. Each of these characters is given an index. The index is zero-based, so the first character's position in the index is 0, the second is 1, and so on. The method `indexOf()` finds and returns the position in the index at which a substring begins (and the `lastIndexOf()` method returns the position at which the substring ends). For example, if we wanted our user to enter an e-mail address, then we could check that they'd included the '@' symbol in their entry. (While this wouldn't ensure that the address was valid, it would at least go some way in that direction. We'll be working with much more complex data checking later on in the book.)

Let's do that next, using the `prompt()` method to obtain the user's e-mail address and then check the input for the '@' symbol, returning the index of the symbol using `indexOf()`:

```
<html>
<body>
<script language="JavaScript">
  var userEmail= prompt("Please enter your email address ","");
  document.write(userEmail.indexOf("@"));
</script>
</body>
</html>
```

If the '@' is not found then *-1* is written to the page. As long as the character is there in the string somewhere, its position in the index, in other words something other than *–1*, will be returned.

The `substring()` method carves one string from another string, taking the indexes of the start and end position of the substring as parameters. We can return everything from the first index to the end of the string by leaving off the second parameter.

So to extract all the characters from the 3rd character (at index 2) to the 6th character (index 5), we'd write:

```
<html>
<body>
<script language="JavaScript">
  var myOldString = "Hello World";
  var myNewString = myOldString.substring(2,5);
```

```
  document.write(myNewString);
</script>
</body>
</html>
```

You should see *llo* written out to the browser. Note that the `substring()` method copies the substring that it returns, and it doesn't alter the string we are creating the new string from.

The `substring()` method really comes into its own when you're working with unknown values. Here's another example that uses both the `indexOf()` and `substring()` methods:

```
<html>
<body>
<script language="JavaScript">
  var characterName = "my name is Simpson, Homer";
  var firstNameIndex = characterName.indexOf("Simpson, ") + 9;
  var firstName = characterName.substring(firstNameIndex);
  document.write(firstName);
</script>
</body>
</html>
```

We're extracting *Homer* from the string in the variable `characterName`, using `indexOf()` to find the start of the last name, and adding 9 to it to get the index of the start of the first name, and storing it in `firstNameIndex`. This is used by the `substring()` method to extract everything from the start of the first name – we haven't specified the final index so the rest of the characters in the string will be returned.

Now let's look at the Date object. This allows us to store dates and provides some useful date/time related functionality.

The Date Object

JavaScript doesn't have a primitive date data type, so we can only create Date objects explicitly. We create new Date objects the same way as we create String objects, using the `new` keyword together with the `Date()` constructor. This line creates a Date object containing today's date and time:

```
var todaysDate = new Date();
```

To create a Date object that stores a specific date or time we simply put the date, or date and time, inside the parentheses:

```
var newMillennium = new Date("1 Jan 2000 10:24:00");
```

Different countries describe dates in a different order. For example, in the USA dates are specified in MM/DD/YY, while in Europe they are DD/MM/YY, and in China they are YY/MM/DD. If you specify the month using the abbreviated name then you use any order:

```
var someDate = new Date("10 Jan 2002");
var someDate = new Date("Jan 10 2002");
var someDate = new Date("2002 10 Jan");
```

In fact, the Date object can take a number of parameters:

```
var someDate = new Date(aYear, aMonth, aDate, anHour, aMinute, aSecond,
aMillisecond)
```

To use these parameters you first need to specify year and month, then use the parameters you want – although you do have to run through them in order and can't select amongst them. For example, you can specify year, month, date, and hour:

```
var someDate = new Date(2003, 9, 22, 17);
```

You can't specify year, month, and then hours though:

```
var someDate = new Date(2003, 9, , 17);
```

NB: Although we usually think of month 9 as September, JavaScript starts counting months from 0 (January), and so October is represented as month 9.

Using the Date Object

The Date object has a lot of methods that you can use to get or set a date or time. You can use local time (the time on your computer in your time zone) or UTC time (Universal Time, once called Greenwich Mean Time). While this can be very useful, you need to be aware when you're working with Date that many people don't set their time zone correctly.

Let's look at an example that demonstrates some of the methods:

```
<html>
<body>
<script language="JavaScript">
  //create a new date object
  var someDate = new Date("31 Jan 2003 11:59");
  //retrieve the first four values using the appropriate get methods
  document.write("Minutes = " + someDate.getMinutes() + "<br>");
  document.write("Year = " + someDate.getFullYear() + "<br>");
  document.write("Month = " + someDate.getMonth() + "<br>");
  document.write("Date = " + someDate.getDate() + "<br>");

  //set the minutes to 34
  someDate.setMinutes(34);

  document.write("Minutes = " + someDate.getMinutes() + "<br>");

  //reset the date
  someDate.setDate(32);

  document.write("Date = " + someDate.getDate() + "<br>");
  document.write("Month = " + someDate.getMonth() + "<br>");
</script>
</body>
</html>
```

Here's what you should get:

Minutes = 59
Year = 2003
Month = 0
Date = 31
Minutes = 34
Date = 1
Month = 1

This line of code might look a bit counter-intuitive at first:

```
someDate.setDate(32);
```

JavaScript knows that there aren't 32 days in January, so instead of trying to set the date to the 32nd of January, the interpreter *adds* 32 days to the 1st of January, which gives us the 1st of February.

This can be a handy feature if you need to add days onto a date. Usually we'd have to take into account the number of days in the different months, and whether it's a leap year, if we wanted to add a number of days to a date, but it's much easier to use JavaScript's understanding of dates instead:

```
<html>
<body>
<script language="JavaScript">

  //ask the user to enter a date string
  var originalDate = prompt("Enter a date (month name, date, year)",
        "31 Dec 2003");
  //overwrite the originalDate variable with a new Date object
  var originalDate = new Date(originalDate);

  //ask the user to enter the number of days to be added, and convert to number
  var addDays = Number(prompt("Enter number of days to be added","1"))

  //set a new value for originalDate of originalDate plus the days to be added
  originalDate.setDate(originalDate.getDate() + addDays)

  //write out the date held by the originalDate object using the toString() method
  document.write(originalDate.toString())

</script>
</body>
</html>
```

If you enter 31 Dec 2003 when prompted, and 1 for the number of days to be added then the answer you'll get is *Thu Jan 1 00:00:00 UTC 2004*. Notice that we're using the `Number()` method of the Math object on the third line of the script. The program will still run if we don't, but the result won't be the same.

On the fourth line we set the date to the current day of the month, the `originalDate.getDate()` plus the number of days to be added, then comes the calculation and the final line outputs the date contained in the Date object as a string using the `toString()` method. If you're using IE5.5+ or Netscape 6+ then `toDateString()` produces a nicely formatted string using the date alone.

You can use the same methods for `get` and `set` if you're working with UTC time – all you need to do is add UTC to the method name. So `getHours()` becomes `getUTCHours()`, `setMonth()` becomes `setUTCMonth()`, and so on. You can also use the `getTimezoneOffset()` method to return the difference, in hours, between the computer's local time and UTC time. (You'll have to rely on the user having set their time zone correctly, and be aware of the differences in daylight saving between different countries.)

The Math Object

The Math object provides us with lots of mathematical functionality, like finding the square of a number, or producing a random number. The Math object is different from the Date and String objects in two ways:

- You can't create a Math object explicitly, you just go ahead and use it
- The Math object doesn't store data, unlike the String and Date object

You call the methods of the Math object using the format: `Math.methodOfMathObject(aNumber)`:

```
alert("The value of pi is " + Math.PI);
```

We'll look at a few of the commonly used methods next (you can find a complete reference by running a search at *http://developer.netscape.com*). We'll look at the methods for rounding numbers and generating random numbers here.

Rounding numbers

We saw earlier that the `parseInt()` function will make a fractional number whole by removing everything after the decimal point (so 24.999 becomes 24). Pretty often you'll want more mathematically accurate calculations, if you're working with financial calculations for example, and for these you can use one of the Math object's three rounding functions: `round()`, `ceil()`, and `floor()`. This is how they work:

`round()`: rounds a number up when the decimal is . 5 or greater

`ceil()`: (as in ceiling), always rounds up, so 23.75 becomes 24, as does 23.25

`floor()`: always rounds down, so 23.75 becomes 23, as does 23.25

Here they are at work in a simple example:

```
<html>
<body>
<script language="JavaScript">
  var numberToRound = prompt("Please enter a number","")
  document.write("round() = " + Math.round(numberToRound));
  document.write("<br>");
  document.write("floor() = " + Math.floor(numberToRound));
  document.write("<br>");
  document.write("ceil() = " + Math.ceil(numberToRound));
</script>
</body>
</html>
```

Even though we used `prompt()` to obtain a value from the user, which as we saw earlier returns a string, the number returned is still treated as a number. This is because the rounding methods do the conversion for us just so long as the string contains something that can be converted to a number.

If we enter 23.75 we get the following result:

round() = 24
floor() = 23
ceil() = 24

If we enter -23.75 we get:

round() = -24
floor() = -24
ceil() = -23

Generating a Random Number

You can generate a fractional random number between 0 and 1 using the Math object's `random()` method. Usually you'll need to multiply the number, and then use one of the rounding methods in order to make it useful.

For example, in order to mimic a dice throw we'd need to generate a random number between 1 and 6. We could create this by multiplying the random fraction by 5, to give a fractional number between 0 and 5, and then round the number up or down to a whole number using the `round()` method. (We couldn't just multiply by 6 then round up every time using `ceil()`, because that would give us the occasional 0.) Then we'd have a whole number between 0 and 5, so by adding 1 we can get a number between 1 and 6. This approach won't give you a perfectly balanced dice, but it's good enough for most purposes. Here's the code:

```
<html>
<body>
<script language="JavaScript">
  var diceThrow = Math.round(Math.random() * 5) + 1;
  document.write("You threw a " + diceThrow);
</script>
</body>
</html>
```

Arrays

JavaScript allows us to store and access related data using an **Array**. An array is a bit like a row of boxes (**elements**), each box containing a single item of data. An array can work with any of the data types that JavaScript supports. So, for example, you could use an array to work with a list of items that the users will select from, or for a set of graph coordinates, or to reference images.

Array objects, like String and Date objects, are created using the `new` keyword together with the constructor. We can initialize an Array object when we create it:

```
var preInitArray = new Array("First item", "Second item", "Third Item");
```

Or set it to hold a certain number of items:

```
var preDeterminedSizeArray = new Array(3);
```

Or just create an empty array:

```
var anArray = new Array();
```

You can add new items to an array by assigning values to the elements:

```
anArray[0] = "anItem"
anArray[1] = "anotherItem"
anArray[2] = "andAnother"
```

Once we've populated an array, we can access it through its index position (which, once again, is zero-based) using square brackets:

```
<html>
<body>
<script language="JavaScript">
  var preInitArray = new Array("First Item", "Second Item","Third Item");
  document.write(preInitArray[0] + "<br>");
  document.write(preInitArray[1] + "<br>");
  document.write(preInitArray[2] + "<br>");
</script>
</body>
</html>
```

Using index numbers to store items is useful if you want to loop through the array – we'll be looking at loops next.

You can use keywords to access the array elements instead of a numerical index, like this:

```
<html>
<body>
<script language="JavaScript">

  //creating an array object and setting index position 0 to equal the string
Fruit
  var anArray = new Array();
  anArray[0] = "Fruit";

  // setting the index using the keyword 'CostOfApple' as the index.
  anArray["CostOfApple"] = 0.75;

  document.write(anArray[0] + "<br>");
  document.write(anArray["CostOfApple"]);
</script>
</body>
</html>
```

Keywords are good for situations where you can usefully give the data labels, or if you're storing entries that are only meaningful in context, like a list of graph coordinates. You can't, however, access entries using an index number if they have been set using keywords.

We can also use variables for the index. We can rewrite the previous example using variables, (one holding a string and the other a number), instead of literal values:

```
<html>
<body>
<script language="JavaScript">
  var anArray = new Array();
  var itemIndex = 0;
  var itemKeyword = "CostOfApple";
  anArray[itemIndex] = "Fruit";
  anArray[itemKeyword] = 0.75;

  document.write(anArray[itemIndex] + "<br>");
  document.write(anArray[itemKeyword]);
</script>
</body>
</html>
```

Let's put what we've learnt about arrays and the Math object into an example. We'll write a script that randomly selects a banner to display at the top of the page.

We'll use an Array object to hold some image source names, like this:

```
var bannerImages = new Array();
bannerImages[0] = "Banner1.jpg";
bannerImages[1] = "Banner2.jpg";
bannerImages[2] = "Banner3.jpg";
bannerImages[3] = "Banner4.jpg";
bannerImages[4] = "Banner5.jpg";
bannerImages[5] = "Banner6.jpg";
bannerImages[6] = "Banner7.jpg";
```

Then we need six images with corresponding names to sit in the same folder as the HTML page. You can use your own or download mine from *www.glasshaus.com*.

Next we'll initialize a new variable, `randomImageIndex`, and use it to generate a random number. We'll use the same method that we used to generate a random dice throw earlier, but without adding 1 to the result because we need a random number from 0 to 6:

```
var randomImageIndex = Math.round(Math.random() * 6);
```

Then we'll use `document.write()` to write the randomly selected image into the page. Here's the complete script:

```
<html>
<body>

<script language="JavaScript">
```

```
    var bannerImages = new Array();
    bannerImages[0] = "Banner1.jpg";
    bannerImages[1] = "Banner2.jpg";
    bannerImages[2] = "Banner3.jpg";
    bannerImages[3] = "Banner4.jpg";
    bannerImages[4] = "Banner5.jpg";
    bannerImages[5] = "Banner6.jpg";
    bannerImages[6] = "Banner7.jpg";

    var randomImageIndex = Math.round(Math.random() * 6);
    document.write("<IMG src='" + bannerImages[randomImageIndex] + "'>");
  </script>
  </body>
  </html>
```

And that's all there is to it. Having the banner change will make it more noticeable to visitors than if you displayed the same banner every time they came to the page – and, of course, it gives the impression that the site is being updated frequently. It's not a good idea to speed up the changes so that they occur while the visitor is at the page, though: a banner spinning around at the top of the page can be really irritating.

The Array Object's Methods and Properties

One of the most commonly used properties of the Array object is the `length` property, which returns the index one count higher than the index of the last array item in the array. If, for example, you're working with an array with elements with indexes of 0, 1, 2, 3, then the `length` will be 4 – which is useful to know if you want to add another element.

The Array object provides a number of methods for manipulating Arrays, including methods for cutting a number of items from an Array, or joining two Arrays together. We'll look at the methods for concatenating, slicing and sorting next.

Cutting a Slice of an array

The `slice()` method is to an Array object what the `substring()` method is to a String object. You simply tell the method which elements you want to be sliced. This would be useful, for example, if you wanted to slice information being passed using a URL.

The `slice()` method takes two parameters: the first element of the slice, which will be included in the slice, and the final element, which won't be. To access the second, third, and fourth values from an array holding 5 values in all, we use the indexes 1 and 4:

```
<html>
<body>
<script language="JavaScript">
  //create and initialize the array
  var fullArray = new Array("One","Two","Three","Four","Five");
  //slice from element 1 to element 4 and store in new variable sliceOfArray
  var sliceOfArray = fullArray.slice(1,4);
  //write out new (zero-based) array of 3 elements
  document.write(sliceOfArray[0] + "<br>");
```

```
  document.write(sliceOfArray[1] + "<br>");
  document.write(sliceOfArray[2] + "<br>");
</script>
</body>
</html>
```

The new array stores the numbers in a new zero-based array, so slicing indices 0,1, and 2 gives us:

Two
Three
Four

The original array is unaffected, but you could overwrite the Array object in the variable by setting it to the result of the `slice()` method if you needed to:

```
fullArray = fullArray.slice(1,4);
```

Joining Two Arrays

The Array object's `concat()` method allows us to concatenate arrays. We can add two or more arrays using this method, each new array starting where the previous one ends. Here we're joining three arrays: `arrayOne`, `arrayTwo`, and `arrayThree`:

```
<html>
<body>
<script language="JavaScript">
  var arrayOne = new Array("One","Two","Three","Four","Five");
  var arrayTwo = new Array("ABC","DEF","GHI");
  var arrayThree = new Array("John","Paul","George","Ringo");

  var joinedArray = arrayOne.concat(arrayTwo, arrayThree);
  document.write("joinedArray has " + joinedArray.length + " elements<br>");
  document.write(joinedArray[0] + "<br>")
  document.write(joinedArray[11] + "<br>")
  </script>
</body>
</html>
```

The new array, `joinedArray` has twelve items. The items in this array are the same as they were in each of the previous arrays; they've simply been concatenated together. The original arrays remain untouched.

Sorting an Array

The `sort()` method allows us to sort the items in an array into alphabetical or numerical order:

```
<html>
<body>
<script language="JavaScript">
  var arrayToSort = new Array("Cabbage", "Lemon", "Apple","Pear","Banana");
  var sortedArray = arrayToSort.sort();
```

```
    document.write(sortedArray[0] + "<br>");
    document.write(sortedArray[1] + "<br>");
    document.write(sortedArray[2] + "<br>");
    document.write(sortedArray[3] + "<br>");
    document.write(sortedArray[4] + "<br>");

    </script>
  </body>
  </html>
```

The items are arranged like this:

Apple
Banana
Cabbage
Lemon
Pear

If, however, you lower the case of one of the letters – the `A` of `Apple`, for example – then you'll end up with a very different result, just as we did when we compared strings earlier on.

Making Decisions in JavaScript

Decision-making is what gives programs their apparent intelligence. You can't write a good program without it, whether you're creating a game, checking a password, giving the user a set of choices based on previous decisions they have made, or something else.

Decisions are based on conditional statements, which are simply statements that evaluate to true or false. This is where the primitive Boolean data type comes in useful. Loops are the other essential tool of decision-making, enabling you to loop through user input, or an array for example, and make decisions accordingly.

The Logical and Comparison Operators

There are two main groups of operators we'll look at:

- Data comparison operators: compare operands and return Boolean values
- Logical operators: test for more than one condition

We'll start with the comparison operators.

Comparing Data

These are some of the more commonly used comparison operators:

Operator	Description	Example
==	Checks whether the left and right operands are equal	123 == 234 returns false 123 == 123 returns true
!=	Checks whether the left operand is not equal to the right side	123 != 123 returns false 123 != 234 returns true
>	Checks whether the left operand is greater than the right	123 > 234 returns false 234 > 123 returns true
>=	Checks whether the left operand is greater than or equal to the right	123 >= 234 returns false 123 >= 123 returns true
<	Checks whether the left operand is less than the right	234 < 123 returns false 123 < 234 returns true
<=	Checks whether the left operand is less than, or equal to, the right	234 <= 123 returns false 234 <= 234 returns true

> Beware the == equality operator: it's all too easy to create errors in a script by using the assignment operator, =, by mistake.

These operators all work with string type data as well as numerical data, and are case-sensitive:

```
<html>
<body>
<script language="JavaScript">
  document.write("Apple" == "Apple")
  document.write("<br>");
  document.write("Apple" < "Banana")
  document.write("<br>");
  document.write("apple" < "Banana")
</script>
</body>
</html>
```

This is what you should get back:

true
true
false

The JavaScript interpreter is comparing the ASCII character set in which A is numerically represented by 65, B represented by 66, C by 67, and so on. So A and B are evaluated by the sum 65 < 66. The lowercase letter a has the code 97, so the evaluation a < B is evaluated as 97 < 66 and `false` is returned. You can do alphabetical comparisons using <, <=, >, >= operators. If you need to ensure that all the letters are of the same case then you can use the String object's `toUpperCase()` and `toLowerCase()` methods.

Comparison operators, just like the numerical operators, can be used with variables. If we wanted to compare `apple` and `Banana` alphabetically, we'd do this:

```
<html>
<body>
<script language="JavaScript">
  var string1 = "apple";
  var string2 = "Banana";

  string1 = string1.toLowerCase();
  string2 = string2.toLowerCase();
  document.write(string1 < string2)
</script>
</body>
</html>
```

There is something else you need to be aware of when you're comparing string objects using the equality operator, though. Try this:

```
<html>
<body>
<script language="JavaScript">
  var string1 = new String("Apple");
  var string2 = new String("Apple");
  document.write(string1 == string2)
</script>
</body>
</html>
```

You'll get *false* returned. In fact what we've done here is compare two String objects rather than the characters of two string primitives and, as the returned *false* indicates, two String objects can't be the same object even if they do hold the same characters. If you do need to compare the strings held by two objects, then you can use the `valueOf()` operator to do a comparison of the data values:

```
<html>
<body>
<script language="JavaScript">
  var string1 = new String("Apple");
  var string2 = new String("Apple");
  document.write(string1.valueOf() == string2.valueOf())
</script>
</body>
</html>
```

Logical Operators

Sometimes you'll need to combine comparisons into one condition group. You might want to check that the information users have given make sense, or restrict the selections they can make according to their earlier answers, for example. We can do this using the logical operators shown in the table below:

<table>
<tr><th>Operator</th><th>Description</th><th>Example</th><th></th></tr>
<tr><td>&&</td><td>And</td><td>123 == 234 && 123 < 20</td><td>(false)</td></tr>
<tr><td></td><td>Both conditions must be true</td><td>123 == 234 && 123 == 123</td><td>(false)</td></tr>
<tr><td></td><td></td><td>123 == 123 && 234 < 900</td><td>(true)</td></tr>
<tr><td>||</td><td>Or</td><td>123 == 234 || 123 < 20</td><td>(false)</td></tr>
<tr><td></td><td>Either or both of the conditions must be true</td><td>123 == 234 || 123 == 123</td><td>(true)</td></tr>
<tr><td></td><td></td><td>123 == 123 || 234 < 900</td><td>(true)</td></tr>
<tr><td>!</td><td>Not</td><td>!(123 == 234)</td><td>(true)</td></tr>
<tr><td></td><td>Reverses the logic</td><td>!(123 == 123)</td><td>(false)</td></tr>
</table>

Once we've evaluated the data, we need to be able to make decisions according to the outcome. This is where conditional statements and loops come in useful. You'll find that the operators that we've looked at in this chapter are most often used in the context of a conditional statement or loop.

Conditional statements

The `if...else` loop is used to test conditions, and looks like this:

```
if (condition)
{
  // execute code in here if condition is true
}
else
{
  // execute code in here if condition is false
}

// after if/else code execution resumes here
```

If the condition being tested is true then the code within the curly braces will be executed, but won't if it isn't. You can also create a final default block of code to execute by default, should none of the conditions set out be met, by using a final `else` statement.

Let's improve on the currency exchange converter we built earlier on in the chapter, and create a loop to deal with non-numeric input from the user:

```
<html>
<body>
<script language="JavaScript">
```

```
  var euroToDollarRate = 0.872;

  //try to convert the input into a number
  var eurosToConvert = Number(prompt("How many Euros do you wish to convert",""));

  //if the user hasn't entered a number then NaN will be returned
  if (isNaN(eurosToConvert))
  {
    //ask the user to enter a value in numerals
    document.write("Please enter the number in numerals");
  }
  //if NaN is not returned then we can use the input
  else
  {
    //and do the conversion as before
    var dollars = eurosToConvert * euroToDollarRate;
    document.write(eurosToConvert + " euros is " + dollars + " dollars");
  }

</script>
</body>
</html>
```

The `if` statement is using the `isNaN()` function which will return `true` if the value in variable `eurosToConvert` is a number.

Remember to keep error messages as polite and helpful as possible. Good error messaging helps make applications much more painless.

We can create more complex conditions by using logical operators and nesting `if` statements:

```
<html>
<body>
<script language="JavaScript">

  //ask the use for a number and try to convert the input into a number
  var userNumber = Number(prompt("Enter a number between 1 and 10",""));

  //if the value of userNumber is NaN then ask the user to try again
  if (isNaN(userNumber))
  {
   document.write("Please ensure a valid number is entered");
  }

  //if the value is a number but over 10 then ask the user to try again
  else
  {
    if (userNumber > 10 || userNumber < 1)
    {
    document.write("The number you entered is not between 1 and 10");
    }

   //otherwise the number is between 1 and 10 so write to the screen
   else
```

```
    {
        document.write("The number you entered was " + userNumber);
    }
    }

</script>
</body>
</html>
```

We know that the number is fine just so long as it is a numeric value, and is under 10.

> Note the layout of the code. We have indented the `if` and `else` statements and blocks so that it's easy to read and to see where code blocks start and stop. It's essential to make your code as legible as possible.

Try reading this code without the indenting or spacing:

```
<html>
<body>
<script language="JavaScript">
// ask for a number using the prompt()function and try to make it a number
var userNumber = Number(prompt("Enter a number between 1 and 10",""));
//if the value of userNumber is NaN then ask the user to try again
if (isNaN(userNumber))
{
document.write("Please ensure a valid number is entered");
}
//if the value is a number but over 10 then ask the user to try again
else {
if (userNumber > 10 || userNumber < 1)
{
document.write("The number you entered is not between 1 and 10");
}
//otherwise the number is between 1 and 10 so write to the screen
else
{
document.write("The number you entered was " + userNumber);
}
}
</script>
</body>
</html>
```

It's not impossible to read, but even in this short script it's harder to decipher which code blocks belong to the `if` and `else` statements. In longer pieces of code inconsistent indenting or illogical intending makes code very difficult to read, which in turn leaves you with more bugs and a harder job to do.

You can also use `else if` statements, where the `else` statement starts with another `if` statement, like this:

```
<html>
<body>
<script language="JavaScript">

  var userNumber = Number(prompt("Enter a number between 1 and 10",""));
  if (isNaN(userNumber))
  {
    document.write("Please ensure a valid number is entered");
  }
    else if (userNumber > 10 || userNumber < 1)
    {
     document.write("The number you entered is not between 1 and 10");
    }
    else
    {
    document.write("The number you entered was " + userNumber);
    }

</script>
</body>
</html>
```

The code does the same thing as the earlier piece, but uses an `else if` statement instead of a nested `if`, and is two lines shorter.

Breaking Out of a Loop

One more thing before we move on: you can break a conditional statement or loop using the `break` statement. This simply terminates the block of code running and drops the processing through to the next statement. We'll be using this in the next example.

We can have as many `if`, `else`, and `else if`s as we like, although they can make your code terribly complicated if you use too many. If there are a lot of possible conditions to check a value against in a piece of code then the `switch` statement, which we'll look at next, can be helpful.

Checking a Number of Conditions: the Switch statement

The `switch` statement allows us to "switch" between sections of code based on the value of a variable or expression. This is the outline of a `switch` statement:

```
switch (expression)
{
   case someValue:
   // code to execute if expression == someValue;
    break; // end execution
   case someOtherValue:
   // code to execute if expression == someOtherValue;
   break; // end execution
   case yesAnotherValue:
   // code to execute if expression == yetAnotherValue;
   break; // end execution
   default:
   // code to execute if no values matched
}
```

JavaScript evaluates `switch (expression)`, and then compares it to each `case`. As soon as a match is found, the code starts executing and continues through all the `case` statements. We're using `break` here to stop the code executing the current statement and move onto the next one. It's often useful to include a default `case` that will execute if none of the `case` statements match. This is a helpful tool for picking up on errors, where, for example, we expected a match to occur but a bug has prevented that from happening.

The values of the cases can be of any data type, numbers or strings for example. We can have just one or as many cases as we need. Let's look at a simple example:

```
<html>
<body>
<script language="JavaScript">
  // store user entered number between 1 and 4 in userNumber
  var userNumber = Number(prompt("Enter a number between 1 and 4",""));

  switch (userNumber)
  {
  // if userNumber is 1 write out and carry on executing after case statement
   case 1:
    document.write("Number 1");
    break;
   case 2:
    document.write("Number 2");
    break;
   case 3:
    document.write("Number 3");
    break;
   case 4:
    document.write("Number 4");
    break;
   default:
    document.write("Please enter a numeric value between 1 and 4.");
    break;
  }

  // code continues executing here
</script>
</body>
</html>
```

Try it out. You should just get the number that you've entered written out, or the sentence *Please enter a numeric value between 1 and 4*.

This example also illustrates the importance of the `break` statement. If we hadn't included `break` after each case then execution would have carried on within the block until the end of the `switch`. Try removing the `break`s and then enter 2. Everything after the match will execute, giving you this output:

Number 2Number 3Number 4please enter a numeric value between 1 and 4

You can use any expression inside the switch statement – a calculation for example:

```
  switch (userNumber * 100 + someOtherVariable)
```

You can also have one or more statements in between the case statements.

Repeating Things: Loops

In this section we look at how we can repeat a block of code for as long as a set condition is true. For example we might want to loop through each input element on an HTML form, or through each item in an array.

Repeating a Set Number of Times: the for Loop

The for loop is designed to loop through a code block a number of times, and looks like this:

```
for ( initialize statements; loop condition; increment statements)
{
  //
  // code to be repeatedly executed
  //
}

  // after loop complete execution of code continues here
```

You can pass three parameters into a for loop using the parentheses, each separated by a semicolon.

The first is the initialization: the code it contains will only run the first time the statement is run. It's frequently used to initialize new variables to help the loop run. If, for example, we wanted the loop to run 10 times then we might begin by creating a new variable and initializing it to 1:

```
for ( loopCounter = 1; loop condition; increment statements)
```

Then we'd increment loopCounter on each iteration of the loop, using the increment statement, and make the loop condition that the loop keeps running for as long as loopCounter is less than 10:

```
for ( loopCounter = 1; loopCounter =< 10; loopCounter++)
```

The loop keeps executing as long as the loop condition evaluates to true – for as long as loopCounter is less than or equal to 10. Once it hits 11 the looping stops and execution of the code continues at the next statement after the loop's closing parenthesis.

You can initialize more than one variable and increment statement by separating them with a comma:

```
for ( loopCounter = 1, var1 = 10, var2 = 5; loop condition; increment statements)
```

You don't have to initialize variables if you don't need them, but you do need to include the semicolon:

```
for ( ; loop condition; increment statements)
```

```
for ( variable, anotherVariable; loopCounter =< 10; variable++, anotherVariable--
)
```

Let's look at an example that uses the `for` loop to run through an array. We'll use a `for` loop to run through an array called `theBeatles`, using a variable called `loopCounter` to keep the loop running while the value of `loopCounter` is less than the length of the array:

```
<html>
<body>
<script language="JavaScript">
  var theBeatles = new Array("John","Paul","George","Ringo");

  for ( var loopCounter = 0; loopCounter < theBeatles.length; loopCounter++)
  {
   document.write(theBeatles[loopCounter] + "<br>");
  }
</script>
</body>
</html>
```

This example works because we are using a zero-based array in which the items have been added to the index in sequence. The loop wouldn't have run if we'd used keywords to store items in an array like this:

```
theBeatles["Drummer"] = "Ringo";
```

JavaScript also supports the `for..in` loop (which has been around since NN2, although IE has supported it only since IE5). Instead of using a counter the `for...in` loop runs though each item in the array using a variable to access the array. Let's create an array this way and see how it works:

```
<html>
<body>
<script language="JavaScript">
  // initialize theBeatles array and store in a variable
  var theBeatles = new Array();

  // set the values using keys rather than numbers
  theBeatles["Drummer"] = "Ringo";
  theBeatles["SingerRhythmGuitar"] = "John";
  theBeatles["SingerBassGuitar"] = "Paul";
  theBeatles["SingerLeadGuitar"] = "George";
  var indexKey;

  // write out each indexKey and the value for that indexKey from the array
  for ( indexKey in theBeatles)
  {
   document.write("indexKey is " + indexKey + "<br>");
   document.write("item value is " + theBeatles[indexKey] + "<br><br>");
  }
</script>
</body>
</html>
```

The results of the item key in `indexKey` at each iteration of the loop is written out alongside the value extracted from the array using that key in the same order as it occurs in the array:

indexKey is Drummer
item value is Ringo

indexKey is SingerLeadGuitar1
item value is John

indexKey is SingerLeadGuitar2
item value is Paul

indexKey is Bass
item value is George

Repeating Actions According to a Decision: the While Loop

The loops we have been working with so far take the instruction to stop looping from inside the script itself. There are likely to be times when you'll want the user to determine when the loop should stop, or for the loop to stop when a certain user-led condition is met. The `while` and `do...while` loops are intended for just this sort of situation.

In its simplest form a `while` loop looks like this:

```
while (some condition true)
{
  // loop code
}
```

The condition inside the curly braces can be anything you might use in an `if` statement. We could use some code like this to elicit numbers from a user until they enter the number 99, for example:

```
<html>
<body>
<script language="JavaScript">
  var userNumbers = new Array();
  var userInput = 0;
  var arrayIndex = 0;

//loop for as long as the user doesn't input 99
  while (userInput != 99)
  {
   userInput = prompt("Enter a number, or 99 to exit","99");
   userNumbers[arrayIndex] = userInput;
   arrayIndex++;
  }

</script>
</body>
</html>
```

Here the `while` loop's condition is that `userInput` is not equal to 99, so the loop will continue so long as that condition is true. When the user enters 99 and the condition is tested it will evaluate to false and the loop will end. Note the loop doesn't end as soon as the user enters `99` but only when the condition is tested again at the start of another iteration of the loop.

There is one small but significant difference between the `while` loop and the `do...while`: the `while` loop tests the condition before the code is executed, and only executes the code block if the condition is true, while the `do...while` loop executes the code block before testing the condition, only doing another iteration if the condition is true. In short, the `do...while` loop is useful when you know you want the loop code to execute at least once before the condition is tested. We could write our previous example with a `do...while` loop like this:

```
<html>
<body>
<script language="JavaScript">
  var userNumbers = new Array();

  //declare the userInput but don't initialize it
  var userInput;
  var arrayIndex = 0;

  do
  {
   userInput = prompt("Enter a number, or 99 to exit","99");
   userNumbers[arrayIndex] = userInput;
   arrayIndex++;
  } while (userInput != 99)


</script>
</body>
</html>
```

In this example we don't need to initialize the `userInput` variable because the loop code executes once before testing the value of `userInput` variable.

Continuing the Loop

As we've already seen, the `break` statement is great for breaking out of any kind of loop once a certain event has occurred. The `continue` keyword works very like `break`, except that it stops and re-tests the condition without dropping out of the statement altogether. Like the `break` statement, you can use `continue` with any of the loops we've worked with in this chapter.

Let's first alter the previous example so that if the user enters something other than a number, the value is not recorded and the loop finishes, using `break`:

```
<html>
<body>
<script language="JavaScript">
  var userNumbers = new Array();
  var userInput;
  var arrayIndex = 0;

  do
  {
  userInput = Number(prompt("Enter a number, or 99 to exit","99"));
  //check that user input is a valid number, and if not, break with error msg
  if (isNaN(userInput))
```

```
        {
        document.write("Invalid data entered: please enter a number between 0
        and 99 in numerals");
        break;
        }
        //if break has been activated, code will continue from here
        userNumbers[arrayIndex] = userInput;
        arrayIndex++;
      } while (userInput != 99)
      // next statement after loop
    </script>
    </body>
    </html>
```

Now let's change it again, so that we don't break out of the loop but instead just ignore the user's input and keep looping, using the `continue` statement:

```
<html>
<body>
<script language="JavaScript">
  var userNumbers = new Array();
  var userInput;
  var arrayIndex = 0;

  do
  {
   userInput = prompt("Enter a number, or 99 to exit","99");
   if (isNaN(userInput))
   {
    document.write("Invalid data entered: please enter a number between 0
    and 99 in numerals ");
    continue;
   }
   userNumbers[arrayIndex] = userInput;
   arrayIndex++;
  } while (userInput != 99)

   //next statement after loop

</script>
</body>
</html>
```

The `break` statement has been replaced with `continue`, so no more code will be executed in the loop and the condition inside the `while` statement will be evaluated again. If the condition is true then another iteration of the loop will occur, otherwise the loop ends.

Summary

We've covered a lot of ground in this chapter: most of the essentials of the JavaScript language in fact.

We've looked at how JavaScript handles data and seen that there are a number of data types: string, number, Boolean, and object as well as some special types of data like NaN. We saw that JavaScript supplies a number of operators that perform operations on the data, for example numerical calculations or joining strings together.

We then looked at how JavaScript allows us to keep a temporary note of data using variables. Variables last for the lifetime of the page, or the lifetime of the function if they are inside a user created function. We also looked at how to convert one type of data to another.

Next we worked with three of JavaScript's object: the String, Date, and Math objects. We saw that each of these provided useful functionality for manipulating strings, dates, and mathematical functions. We also looked at the Array object which allows a number of items of data to be stored in one variable.

We finished the chapter by looking at decision-making, the logic or intelligence of a programming language. We used `if` and `switch` statements to make decisions, for example using conditions to test the validity of data and act upon the findings. Loops also use conditions and allow us to repeat a block of code for a certain number of times or while a condition is true.

In the next chapter, we'll be finishing off our discussion of language essentials by creating and using our own functions, and seeing how this can help us create much more powerful code. We'll also check out some good coding practices that'll save you time and debugging effort if you implement them when you're writing code. Finally, we'll be looking at ways of storing useful libraries of code so that you can use them as and when you need them.

3

- Functions
- Good coding practice
- Creating and using JavaScript classes

Author: Paul Wilton

Functions and Code Design

In this chapter we'll be discussing functions, code design, `.js` modules, and creating custom JavaScript objects. In the last chapter we worked with some of JavaScript's many built in functions built, which allow us to do thing like converting a string data type to a number easily. As we start to do more sophisticated things with our JavaScript we'll find that the code becomes more complex. We'll also find the same functionality is needed again and again. This is where creating our own functions can really help: they save time, and make coding less complex.

Once we've covered functions, we'll look at designing code in a way that minimizes bugs. This allows us to get things done that much more efficiently. Something else that can help with making life easier by making coding easier is the `.js` file. This allows us to put JavaScript code, like a library of functions for example, into a single plain text file, and then insert it into pages as needed using the `<script>` tag and its `src` attribute.

Finally, we'll look at how to create our own specialized objects using JavaScript classes, which are also useful for efficient coding.

Functions

Functions allow us to wrap up code that performs a certain task into a convenient code block that we can reuse within web pages. For example, in the last chapter we coded a currency converter. We might want to wrap it up into a single function, and then put it in its own code library for use in other web pages. Functions are useful where we want to run, or call, the same bit of code again and again; if, for example, we had a button in an HTML form in our web page and we wanted it to perform the same task each time the button is clicked. So functions help us reuse our code and they make it more readable.

So when should we create a function? Creating a function is a good idea if we have some code that performs a useful, specific task that might be handy in lots of different web pages other than the one we are currently creating. Creating one is also a good idea if in the same web page we need to execute certain code more than once from different places on our page.

The important thing with functions is that they should do something efficiently. So that task might be dealing with the click of a button or it might be converting a temperature or detecting which browser the user has. It wouldn't be a great idea to try and make functions too general, for example detecting the user's browser and performing currency conversion!

We can pass information to functions using **parameters** (sometimes also called **arguments**). Examples of parameters are the number of degrees Celsius in a function that coverts temperatures from degrees Celsius to degrees Fahrenheit, the number of euros to be converted to dollars in a currency converting function. Functions can also return a single value to the code that called them, the **return value**. We'll learn more about parameters and return values shortly when we look at creating a function.

As with variables, it makes life easier if we give our functions descriptive names. For example names such as `doSomething()` and `f_c()` don't give any clues as to what the functions do, whereas `createDynamicMenu()` or `convertFahrenToCelsius()` do indicate the purpose of a function. If our functions do one task then naming them should be easy.

Let's look at how we create our own functions.

Creating a Function

To create a function we use the `function` keyword, followed by the name that we wish to give the function, and then, in parentheses, the list of parameters the function requires to be passed. An example function header is shown below:

```
function myFunctionName(firstParameter, secondParameter, anotherParameter)
```

Note the keyword `function` must be in lowercase.

The function name can be any word that is not a keyword used by JavaScript language such as `while` or `for`. It can contain numbers, alphabetical characters, and an underscore. However, it can only start with a letter or underscore, not a number. So these are valid names:

```
function displayShoppingBasket()
function notify_Error()
function notify101Error()
function checkValueWhileTimerRuns()
```

These aren't valid names:

```
function 1doSomething()    // number not allowed at start of name
function my Function()   // no spaces in function names
function while()    // while is JavaScript reserved word
```

Functions can have zero or more parameters. The limit on the number of parameters is really down to common sense rather than any actual maximum. Too many parameters, say more than 10, make the code difficult to read and the function difficult to understand, and are also an indication that your function is poorly designed. As with variables and function names, we should give our parameters descriptive names. If our function doesn't need any parameters, we must still put empty parentheses, `()`, after the function name.

Finally the code that our function will contain must be enclosed in curly braces, `{}`, beneath the function header. The curly braces enclose the "body" of the function:

```
function myFunctionsName(firstParameter, secondParameter, anotherParameter)
{
  //
  //   Function Code
  //
}
```

Variable Scope and Lifetime

In JavaScript, variables have something called **scope**. Scope dictates how much of the rest of the script, or even pages of an application, can access the variable. This is known as the **visibility** of the variable. Variables can be visible within certain code blocks in a page, to the complete page, or even to an application composed of many pages.

Closely linked to the concept of scope is the concept of a variable having a certain lifetime. Let's look at an example:

```
<html>
<body>
<script language="JavaScript">

  var myGlobalVariable = "GLOBAL";

  function myFunction()
  {
    var myLocalVariable = "LOCAL";
  }


</script>
</body>
</html>
```

We have two variables; the first is called `myGlobalVariable` and is inside the script block but outside the function block `myFunction`, while the second variable is called `myLocalVariable`, and lives inside the function `myFunction()`.

The scope of `myGlobalVariable` is the whole page. In other words, it can be accessed from anywhere within the page; even code inside functions can access this variable. Its lifetime is the duration the page remains loaded: as soon as the user navigates to another page or even refreshes this page then the variable's value is lost and the variable can no longer be accessed.

The scope of `myLocalVariable`, on the other hand, is limited to the function itself. It cannot be accessed by code outside of the function, and its lifetime is limited so that it only exists when the function call is made. Once the function has finished, then the variable ceases to exist.

So, why not just declare every variable as global if local variables are seemingly limited? Well, there are several good reasons for using local variables. Firstly, JavaScript variables take up memory, and by using local variables we can ensure that those resources are only used when necessary, because as a variable goes "out of scope", the memory can be released and reassigned to other variables.

Secondly, having local variables means that we can keep our functions self-contained, which makes them easier to reuse. Thirdly, as we have more and more global variables it becomes quite tricky to remember which function or code is using which variables. Even worse, we might end up with a global variable whose value we rely on in a number of different functions, but each function changes it. If we found that a global variable in function x doesn't have the value we expected, then we'd have to search though every possible function to find which ones access the global variable. This would make the code very difficult to maintain.

Using Functions

Let's start by creating a function. It has the same functionality as the currency converter that we saw in the last chapter:

```
<html>
<body>
<script language="JavaScript">

  function convertEuroToDollar(amountOfEuros)
  {

    var euroToDollarRate = 0.872;
    var dollars = amountOfEuros * euroToDollarRate;
    return dollars;
  }


  var eurosToConvert = Number(prompt("How many Euros do you wish to convert",""));
  if (isNaN(eurosToConvert))
  {
   document.write("Please ensure a valid number is entered");
  }
  else
  {
    var dollars = convertEuroToDollar(eurosToConvert);
    document.write(eurosToConvert + " euros is " + dollars + " dollars");
  }

</script>
</body>
</html>
```

Here's the function definition:

```
function convertEuroToDollar(amountOfEuros)
{
  var euroToDollarRate = 0.872;
  var dollars = amountOfEuros * euroToDollarRate;
  return dollars;
}
```

Our function is called `convertEuroToDollar()`. The function takes just one parameter, `amountOfEuros`. In the body of the function we use this parameter as the amount of Euros to be converted to dollars; we use this parameter just as if it was a variable we had declared. These parameters go out of scope when the function ends; we cannot access them with JavaScript from outside the function.

On the last line, we return the result of the calculation to the code that called the function by using the `return` keyword and the data to be passed back. We have passed the data contained in a local variable but it could have been literal data; `"some string"`, `123`. Note I use the word local variable; we declared `dollars` inside the function itself and so it is accessible and retains its value only inside the function while the function code executes. Just to prove a point we have declared global variables outside the function with the same names as the parameter and local variable, something we would avoid normally. The global variables bear no relation to the variables in the function and altering one will not affect the other.

Let's take a look at a more complex function (`fixnumber.htm`) in which we convert a number to a fixed number of decimal places. This is useful if, for example, we want to display money to the users of an e-commerce shopping cart: $1.20 rather than $1.2. In fact, we'll use this function in our e-commerce example later in the book. It's important that the user gets the sort of response they expect, if we displayed them as having a shopping cart with $23.45663 to pay, then they might start to have doubts about the quality of our web site!

```
<html>
<body>
<script language="JavaScript">
     function fixDecimalPlaces(fixNumber, decimalPlaces)
     {
       var digitSaver = Math.pow(10,decimalPlaces);

       fixNumber = new String((Math.round(fixNumber * (digitSaver)))/digitSaver);

       var zerosRequired;
       var decimalPointLocation = fixNumber.lastIndexOf(".");


       if (decimalPointLocation == -1)
       {
           fixNumber = fixNumber + ".";
           zerosRequired = decimalPlaces;
       }
       else
       {
          zerosRequired = decimalPlaces -
           (fixNumber.length - decimalPointLocation - 1);
       }


       for (; zerosRequired > 0; zerosRequired--)
       {
            fixNumber = fixNumber + "0";
       }

        return fixNumber;
```

```
    }

    var numberToFix;
    var decimalPlaces;

    do
    {
      numberToFix = Number(prompt("Please enter a number",""));

      if (!isNaN(numberToFix) && numberToFix != 0)
      {
        var decimalPlaces = Number(prompt("Please enter the number " +
                                          "of decimal places",""));

        if (!isNaN(decimalPlaces))
        {
          var htmlToWrite = numberToFix + " fixed to ";
          htmlToWrite += decimalPlaces + " decimal places is ";
          htmlToWrite += fixDecimalPlaces(numberToFix,decimalPlaces) + "<BR>";
          document.write(htmlToWrite);
        }
      }
    }
    while (confirm("Convert another number?"))

</script>
</body>
</html>
```

If we load the example into a browser we'll get two prompt boxes, the first to be shown is:

We can enter any number we like, let's say we enter *103.347*, then click *OK*. Then the following prompt box appears:

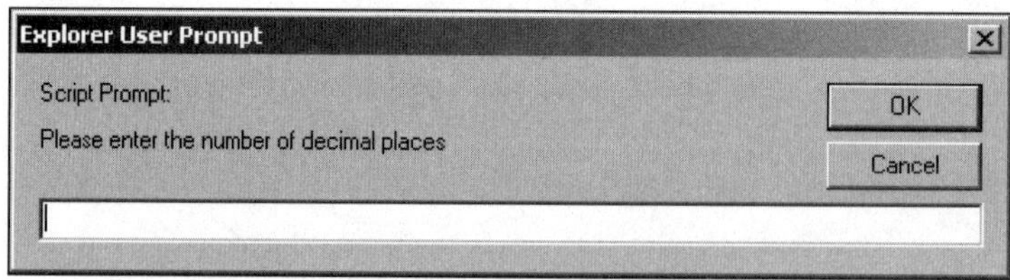

In here we enter the number of decimal places we want the number fixed to. For monetary values, this would be 2, so let's enter 2.

We click *OK* and then the result is shown as:

103.347 fixed to 2 decimal places is 103.35

And another box, called a confirm box, asks us if we want to continue and convert another number:

Let's look at how our page works. We'll start with the code that calls the function:

```
var numberToFix;
var decimalPlaces;

do
{
  numberToFix = Number(prompt("Please enter a number",""));

  if (!isNaN(numberToFix) && numberToFix != 0)
  {
    var decimalPlaces = Number(prompt("Please enter the number " +
                                      "of decimal places",""));

    if (!isNaN(decimalPlaces))
    {
      var htmlToWrite = numberToFix + " fixed to ";
      htmlToWrite += decimalPlaces + " decimal places is ";
      htmlToWrite += fixDecimalPlaces(numberToFix,decimalPlaces) + "<BR>";
      document.write(htmlToWrite);
    }
  }
}
while (confirm("Convert another number?"))
```

It looks like quite a lot of code, but it's actually fairly simple. It shows how even simple programs can get quite sizeable, which is why good formatting and variable names to improve readability is important.

The code, unlike the function, will start to execute as the page is loaded. We declare two variables at the top of the code, `numberToFix` and `decimalPlaces`, which will be used to hold the number to be fixed and the number of places to fix that number to.

Next we have the start of a `do...while` loop, which will keep looping so long as the user indicates they want to enter more numbers. Inside the loop's code block we start by prompting the user to enter a number, the number to be fixed to a certain number of decimal places. We store in the user's response in the `numberToFix` variable having first converted it to a number using the `Number()` function.

We then have an `if` statement:

```
if (!isNaN(numberToFix) && numberToFix != 0)
```

In the `if` statement there are two conditions, both of which must be true for the `if` statement's code block to execute; in other words, condition 1 must be true AND condition 2 must be true for an overall result of true.

In the first condition we use `isNaN()` function to check if `decimalPlaces` contains a number. We use the `!` operator to reverse the logic of the function, so instead of checking to see whether `decimalPlaces` is NaN (Not a Number), the JavaScript checks to see if it is a valid number. We don't want to try to fix the user's input to a certain number of decimal places if the user entered something invalid like "`asdsad`", which clearly can't be fixed to a certain number of decimal places!

The second condition in the `if` statement checks to see if `numberToFix` is not `0`, because if the user hit the *Cancel* button then an empty string will be returned and `Number()` converts that to `0`. If *Cancel* was hit then clearly the user doesn't want to continue to convert numbers.

Assuming a valid number was entered and the user didn't hit *Cancel* then the code in the `if` block goes on to ask the user how many decimal places they want the number fixed to. Again, we check that this is a valid number using `!isNaN(decimalPlaces)`. If it is valid, then we write out the results of fixing the number, using the `fixDecimalPlaces()` function we'll look at in a minute.

At the end of the `while` loop we ask the user if they want to convert more numbers; we use the `confirm()` function to get the users response. This built-in JavaScript function displays a text message that we pass it and the *OK* and *Cancel* buttons. If the user clicks *OK* then true is returned, if they click *Cancel* then false is returned. If the `while` condition is true, in other words, *OK* was clicked, then the loop goes round another time, otherwise it ends, which also means the end of the code. Ideally, *Yes* and *No* buttons would be better than *OK* and *Cancel* but the `confirm()` function doesn't give us that option. We'll see in Chapter 5, "*Windows and Frames*", how we can create our own designer pop-up boxes, which are more user-friendly.

Let's turn to the `fixDecimalPlaces()` function at the top of our code. The function header defines it as taking two parameters, `fixNumber` and `decimalPlaces`:

```
function fixDecimalPlaces(fixNumber, decimalPlaces)
```

The aim of the function is to round off any digits after the decimal place we don't want; in other words, any after the number specified by the `decimalPlaces` parameter. We can't just round the number as that would lose all the digits after the decimal point so we need to protect the digits we want by making them part of the whole number. We do that by multiplying the number by 10 to the power of the number of digits to be saved, which we calculate here:

```
var digitSaver = Math.pow(10,decimalPlaces);
```

So, let's say we want 2 decimal places. Our function multiplies this by 10 to the power of 2: 10 * 10 = 100, and the 100 is stored in the `digitSaver` variable. Now rounding the number won't remove the digits. This is the code that saves the digits:

```
Math.round(fixNumber * (digitSaver))
```

It belongs in this line:

```
fixNumber = new String((Math.round(fixNumber * (digitSaver)))/digitSaver)
```

so, for example:

23.412 * 100 = 2341.2
2341.2 rounded = 2341

But we obviously want the 2 digits back to the right of the decimal point which we do by dividing the number by the same number we multiplied it by:

```
Math.round(fixNumber * (digitSaver)))/digitSaver
```

which gives us the figure:

23.41

The full line, however, converts this result to a string, which may seem a little odd:

```
fixNumber = new String((Math.round(fixNumber * (digitSaver)))/digitSaver)
```

The reason is that for a number like 23.1 to be fixed to, say, 2 decimal places we need an extra zero to pad it out to 23.10. Adding the extra zeros required is the purpose of the remainder of the function. The first task is to work out how many, if any, zeros need to be added to the end of the number. For example 24.1 fixed to two decimal places needs one zero adding. We find out how many extra zeros are needed simply by counting how many digits there are currently after the decimal point and then subtracting this from the number of digits there should be after we've fixed the number, which is what these lines of code do:

```
var zerosRequired;
var decimalPointLocation = fixNumber.lastIndexOf(".");

if (decimalPointLocation == -1)
{
  fixNumber = fixNumber + ".";
  zerosRequired = decimalPlaces;
}
else
{
     zerosRequired = decimalPlaces - (fixNumber.length - decimalPointLocation -
1);
}
```

First, we find out where in the string containing our number digits the decimal place is. We use the String object's `lastIndexOf()` method which starts at the right-hand side of the string and works to the left until it finds the decimal point character. If it finds the character, it returns the character's index, or position, in the string counting from the left, or `-1` if the character is not found. In the case of 24.1 this would give 2 (remembering that string indexes start at zero), which is stored in `decimalPointLocation`.

Having found the location of the decimal point, assuming there is a decimal point, we then come to an `if` statement which checks if `decimalPointLocation` equals -1. What it is checking for is whether the floating point was found at all, if not then we need to add a decimal place and the number of zeros to be added is the same as the number of decimal places specified in variable `decimalPlaces`.

If a decimal point was found, then the `else` will execute. The number of zeros that the code needs to add is the number of decimal places required minus the number of digits currently after the decimal place. So, if the number is 24.1 and we want it fixed to 2 decimal places, the number of digits required (2) - number of digits currently (1) = 1 zero to be added. This is calculated by the following code:

```
zerosRequired = decimalPlaces - (fixNumber.length - decimalPointLocation - 1);
```

Variable `decimalPlaces` holds the number of decimal places. In parentheses, we have the length of the string. For 24.1, this will be 4, minus the character position index of the decimal point, which in this case is 2, then subtract 1. We subtract one because character index positions start at zero, so for 24.1 fixed to two decimal places the above works out as:

zerosRequired = 2 - (4 - 2 - 1)
zerosRequired = 2 - (1)
zerosRequired = 1

We have now worked out how many zeros need to be added. Now we need to actually add them to the end of the string, which is what the following code does:

```
for (; zerosRequired > 0; zerosRequired--)
{
    fixNumber = fixNumber + "0";
}
```

It loops round while `zerosRequired > 0`, so if no zeros were required in the first place then `zerosRequired` will be zero and the loop never executes. Otherwise it executes, and on each iteration of the loop it reduces `zerosRequired` by `1`. Each time the loop is executed, the string `fixNumber`, which holds our number as string characters, has a zero character added to the end.

On the last line of the code we return the value in `fixNumber`. It's now a String object; if we converted to a number, the zeros at the end would be removed automatically by JavaScript and the whole point of the function would be lost!

Optional Parameters

What if we want a function where some of the parameters are optional? For example, we might use the `fixDecimalPlaces()` function with 2 decimal places so often that we'd like the second parameter to be optional and default to two.

Well, JavaScript is quite relaxed about passing the correct number of parameters to a function, which can be a downside if we accidentally pass the wrong number of parameters when calling the function. However, this relaxed attitude does mean we can easily create functions with optional parameters. We need to make sure that our function checks for the existence of a value in a parameter, and if none passed we need to use a default. So, how do we check if a parameter has been passed?

If no value is passed then by default a parameter's value will contain no actual value. We can check for this by comparing the parameters value to the special JavaScript value of `null`:

```
if (decimalPlaces == null)
{
  decimalPlaces = 2;
}
```

We can add this to the very top of our `fixDecimalPlaces()` function and if the `decimalPlaces` parameter is not passed, then we set it to a default of two and no errors occur later in our code:

```
function fixDecimalPlaces(fixNumber, decimalPlaces)
{

   if (decimalPlaces == null)
      {
        decimalPlaces = 2;
      }
```

JavaScript will let us miss off the last parameters when calling the function, but if we try and call a function and miss off the first few parameters it'll get confused. For example:

```
fixDecimalPlaces(, 2)
someFunction(someParam1,,anotherParam,,,finalParam)
```

The above won't work because when we call the `fixDecimalPlaces()` function, we don't pass the first argument, but just leave it blank. When we call `someFunction()` we miss off arguments in the middle of the function call and leave them blank. Again, JavaScript won't let us do this. If we want to miss out parameters then we need to pass `null`. The following will work:

```
fixDecimalPlaces(null, 2)
someFunction(someParam1,null,anotherParam,null,null,finalParam)
```

That assumes that the functions have been designed to cope with parameters not being passed. It's better to make the optional parameters the last ones on the argument list.

Good Coding Practice

In this section, we'll summarize a few useful coding practices that if followed will help make creating JavaScript easier and reduce the number of bugs. In fact, most of them we have already covered as we have gone along.

The aim is for readable code because readable code is easier to debug and to change later on. So what about super-efficient code? Is that not important too? Well, it is, but in these days of super- fast computers it very unlikely that our code will be too slow. Exceptions include speed-critical applications like games, but JavaScript is unlikely to be the programming language of choice for the likes of Quake or Half Life! If we can improve code efficiency without affecting readability, then that's great, but otherwise, in most cases, it's readability that counts if our aim is to rapidly produce sophisticated and maintainable web sites. Most web sites are produced by teams, so it's vital that our code is readable for other programmers.

Let's run down a few ways we can improve our code.

Code Layout

Making sure our code is neatly laid out and well structured can really help to make code easily to read, and therefore reduce the number of bugs and the time spent fixing them.

The most important thing is the use of indenting to clarify code. For example, which of the following pieces of code is easier to understand? This one:

```
if (a == b)
{
if (a < 20)
{
a = 21;
}
else
{
if (b < 20)
{
b = 21;
}
}
}
else
{
a = 22;
if (b == 32)
{
b = 22;
}
else
{
a = 21;
}
}
```

or this one:

```
if (a == b)
{
  if (a < 20)
  {
    a = 21;
  }
  else
  {
    if (b < 20)
    {
      b = 21;
    }
  }
}
else
{
```

```
    a = 22;
    if (b == 32)
    {
      b = 22;
    }
    else
    {
      a = 21;
    }
  }
```

Hopefully you'll agree that it's easier with the second code block to identify the `if` and `else` code blocks. In the first one it would be very easy to forget a closing curly brace and then spend time trying to work out which brace goes with which `if...else`.

Indenting is useful with any situation where there is a code block in curly braces, such as with `do..while`, `while`, `for`, functions and `switch`:

```
for (a = 1; a < 10; a++)
{
  // indented code
  //
}

while (a < 10)
{
  //indented code
}

do
{
  // indented code
}
while (a < 10)

function myFunction()
{
  // indented code
}
```

There are different ideas on how to indent code, but the one above is quite simple to follow.

Comment Code

Adding descriptive comments to code makes it much easier to understand what the code is aiming to do. Comments should avoid being a reiteration of the code and aren't needed for every line. For example these sort of comments don't help:

```
// declare a variable to hold a value entered by the user
var myVariable = prompt("Enter a value","");

// is my variable 0?
```

```
if (myVariable == 0)
{

}
```

Comments should be more high-level than the code, explaining what is being done and why, like these:

```
// Ask the user what the value of their investments is currently
var myVariable = prompt("Enter a value","");

// if they don't have any investments then create a new portfolio
if (myVariable == 0)
{

}
```

Use Descriptive Names

Using descriptive names for variable names, function names, and function parameters is vital for making code easier to read. If we scan through some code and see a function called `doStuff()`, then we haven't a clue what it does and so need to spend a lot of time reading through it, running through the code in our mind to work out what it's trying to achieve. If it was called `calculateSalesTax()`, then we would have a pretty good idea what it does and only need to examine it further if it's something we are interested in. Our aim should be variable and function names that are as specific as possible but also give us good idea of what the variable or function is all about, without being overly long.

Function names usually start with a verb (for example, `calculate`, `write`, or `create`) then end with a descriptive word or two telling us what the action is operating on.

Variable and parameter names need to give an idea of what data they hold. For example, `cid` doesn't give many clues about the data, but `customerID` does. `user` is also a poor name, whereas `userFullName` makes it explicit as to what the variable contains. It's also worth trying to indicate what kind of data the variable or parameter contains. So `isUserIDValid` hints at the fact the variable contains a true or false type value.

Although optional, we may find using a naming scheme useful. For example, notice that all the function and variable names in our examples start with a lower case letter, then each word is made clear by starting it with a capital letter. This is a naming scheme known as camel casing:

```
isInvalidUserID
totalCostOfBasket
```

It helps with consistency if we stick with a naming scheme and consistency is another factor that takes the guesswork out of reading code.

Simplify Conditions

In loops and `if` statements things can get tricky to read when we have more than a couple of conditions. For example:

```
if ( (a == 10 && b < (c - 10) && d > (50 + f - g)) || (a + b == 50 && c > 100) ||
(d < 1000 || a > 1000))
{
  // some code
}
```

Apart from poor variable naming, we can also see it's getting a bit hard to work out what's going on with the conditions, whereas:

```
var isVersionOne = (a == 10 && b < (c - 10) && d > (50 + f - g)) ;
var isVersionTwo = (a + b == 50 && c > 100);
var isVersionThree = (d < 1000 || a > 1000);
if (isVersionOne || isVersionTwo || isVersionThree)
{
  // some code
}
```

There are more lines, and a bit more typing, but the code is a lot more readable.

Using variables with good names can also help clarify what the code is trying to do.

For example, what are we trying to do here?

```
if (basketTotalCost > 100 && country == "USA" && isPostalRateLocal == false)
{
  // code
}
```

Well, we might be able to guess, but this is even clearer:

```
var isFreeDeliveryAvailable  = (basketTotalCost > 100
              && country == "USA"
              && isPostalRateLocal == false)

if (isFreeDeliveryAvailable)
{
  // code
}
```

We may not want to use variables like this every time, but in situations where we have long and difficult to follow code it can really make life so much easier. There's no need to mentally work out the condition and think what it may relate to. It's clear that it's all about whether the customer gets free delivery.

Keep the Number of Exit Points to a Minimum

What we are talking about here is ending loops and functions prematurely. We can exit a loop using the `break` statement and we can exit a function early with the `return` statement. So why is this a negative thing to do? Well, it's surprisingly easy to miss a `break` or `return` statement embedded in a lengthy code section, and it breaks the natural flow of the code and makes it harder to work out where things start and stop. So, for example, in the code below the function can come to a premature end at one of 3 different places:

```
function isDataValid(dataToValidate)
{

if (someCondition)
{
  // lots of code
  return false;
}
else if (anotherCondition)
{
  // lots of code
  return false;
}
else if (yetAnotherCondition)
{
  // lots of code
  return false;
}

return true;
}
```

Rewritten, the function only ends in one place:

```
function isDataValid(dataToValidate)
{
var isValidData = true;
if (someCondition)
{
  // lots of code
  isValidData = false;
}
else if (anotherCondition)
{
  // lots of code
  isValidData = false;
}
else if (yetAnotherCondition)
{
  // lots of code
  isValidData = false;
}

return isValidData;
}
```

What we have done is use a variable to store the final value to be returned and then returned this variable at the end of the function.

Use Variables for Special Values

If we have a value that is unchanging but represents something specific then it can be handy to use a variable to represent it, especially where we use the variable a number of times in our code. For example:

```
var userIncome = 6000;
var totalTax = 0;
```

```
if (userIncome >= 5000 && userIncome <= 10000)
{
   totalTax = userIncome * 0.1;
   alert(totalTax);
}
```

This code is fine, but what do those 5000 and 10000 values represent? Are they important? Maybe as we write the code we'll remember what they mean, but we probably won't a year from now. Here's the same code rewritten:

```
var lowerTaxBandStart = 5000
var lowerTaxBandEnd = 10000;
var lowerTaxRate = 0.1;
var userIncome = 6000;
var totalTax = 0;

if (userIncome >= lowerTaxBandStart && userIncome <= lowerTaxBandEnd)
{
   totalTax = userIncome * lowerTaxRate;
   alert(totalTax);
}
```

Now it's clear what the values represent: tax bands. Another advantage of the second example is that it's easy to change the values. Let's say a year after we wrote the code the lower band changes from 5000 to 5150. In the first code example we'll need to carefully go through the code and change the 5000 to 5150 where it relates to the lower tax band. In our few lines of example code it's not a major task, but let's say that was 50 or 500 lines of code. Suddenly it becomes quite a task. With the second rewritten code we can simply change one line, the variable initialization, and that updates all our code.

Keep Related Code Together

If we keep lines of related code together we avoid having to make mental leaps throughout the code. It also means we are less likely to overlook something if we cut and paste the code elsewhere later. For example:

```
var degCelsius = prompt("Enter the degrees in Celsius",0);
...
...
// Lots of other code
...
...
var degFahrenheit = 9 / 5 * degCelsius + 32;
```

It would be very easy if the code was 50 lines for us to make changes to the `degCelsius` variable between its value being set ready for use and the line in which we actually first use it. Also, if we wanted to use the degrees Celsius to Fahrenheit code line, we could easily overlook the fact that the first line is also needed. What we should have done is this:

```
...
...
// Lots of other code
...
...
var degCelsius = prompt("Enter the degrees in centigrade",0);
var degFahrenheit = 9 / 5 * degCelsius + 32;
```

Minimize Variable Scope

We discussed earlier in the chapter that variables should be kept to where they are needed by limiting their scope. Variables should have local scope (be restricted to a function) unless there is a very good reason not to. If we need to pass data to a function it should be via the function's parameters and not via global variables.

Use Variables for Just One Purpose

It can be tempting sometimes to save on the number of variables in our code by using them again and again for different situations. This can either result in miscellaneous non-descriptive names like `tempNumber` or `tempVal`. It may seem a little wasteful to declare a variable for each different calculation but it does make our code more clear and easy to read.

For example:

```
var tempVal = prompt("Enter the degrees in Celsius",0);
tempVal = 9 / 5 * tempVal + 32;
```

What does the previous code do? The following code, despite no extra explanation, makes it clear:

```
var degCelsius = prompt("Enter the degrees in centigrade",0);
var degFahrenheit = 9 / 5 * degCelsius + 32;
```

We could have worked it out, but with the second version of the code we can see it is converting degrees Celsius into degrees Fahrenheit.

Another way in which it can be tempting to use variables for more than one purpose is flags. Let's say we have a variable that will contain a temperature measurement, except if it is –9999 when it flags up an error. For example, a function called `getTemperature()` returns the current outside temperature unless there is an error, in which case it returns `-9999`. We will probably remember this when we create the function but if we come back to it much later, or if someone else is altering the code, then it will be less obvious without looking at the function's code and reading it line by line to see what -9999 signifies.

Remove Unused Variables

It's good practice when changing code to remove any variables that are no longer used. If we don't do this and we come back to the code much later we find in lengthy pieces of code that we're never quite sure if a variable is still used. This means we leave it in just in case or even worse, we use it thinking it will have the value we expect.

Functions Should Do One Thing and Do it Well

We mentioned in the section on functions that we should design our functions to perform a specific task. Functions should also be cohesive, that is they should be self-contained. There should be no reliance on some external global variable. If a variable is needed, it should be passed as a parameter, that way we can all see what external information the function needs. It's easier to create cohesive functions if we use a divide-and-conquer approach when deciding what functions we need.

By this we mean split up the problem we have into smaller and smaller bits, until we get to the point where we have functions that just perform one task. For example, if we have an online banking system we might start by looking at what functionality we need. Let's say we decide we need the following functionality:

```
To Open and Close an account
To see the account balance
To view the last 10 transactions
To put money in and take money out
```

From this we can then subdivide further:

```
Function to open a new account
Function to close an account
Function to obtain account balance
Function to display account balance
Function to obtain last 10 transactions
Function to display last 10 transactions
Function to put money in
Function to take money out
```

We may want to split up these tasks even further. For example, creating a new account may involve a number of tasks, not only creating a new account but also checking to see if the customer is a new customer, and, if so, adding them to a central database and so on. With divide-and-conquer we keep dividing the problem into smaller chunks until we're happy we have the functionality down to nice cohesive functions, in other words, functions that perform one specific task. It makes it easier to identify what should be a function if we look at the verb and noun associations; for example 'open (verb) an account (noun)' will give us the function `openAccount()`, and 'close (verb) an account (noun)' will give us the function `closeAccount()`.

Organizing and Reusing Code

We'll find that as we develop web sites, the same required functionality pops up again and again. It might be routines to detect which browser the user has, routines for generating a shopping basket, and so on. We can just cut and paste code from our old web sites, but the potential problem with this is that the code may not have been designed to run on its own. There could be parts of other pages that our code uses. The other problem is finding the routine, as it can be quite hard to recall where it was that we used a function!

It would be much better if we could create libraries of useful code. For example, we could have a file that contained all the commonly required functions for an e-commerce shopping cart. We could be sure that simply by including the file on a web page we could call any of its functions. We could also make sure we have some documentation for the file to help us to use it later. Another advantage of code libraries or modules is that we can test and debug them thoroughly, and once we have them working they can be used many times without us needing to worry about bugs. If bugs do turn up over time, as is sometimes the case when we realize we missed something, we just have to fix the code in one place, our code module. We don't need to search different pages and web sites to amend and update the same functions. Putting JavaScript in code modules also has the advantage of splitting off the logic of our web pages, the code, from the presentation and content of the pages themselves, the HTML, which helps to keep our pages shorter and more manageable. In this section we'll be looking at how we can create files that contain just JavaScript code and then insert that code in a web page.

In the second part of this section we'll then turn our attention to how we can create our own JavaScript objects with their own methods and properties, just as JavaScript has built-in objects like the Math and String objects. We'll see that this can be a powerful way of programming, and make certain tasks easier and allow us to reuse code and therefore save time.

First, let's look at code modules.

Creating Code Modules with .js Files

Usually we include our JavaScript code inside the same page that is using it by using `<script>` tags. However, we can separate out the presentation and content part of the page, the HTML, from the logic, our JavaScript, by putting the JavaScript in a separate file. Doing this has the following advantages:

- It's easier to see what is code and what is HTML
- It's easier for one person to work on the code in the separate file without needing to touch the page
- Useful code can be placed inside a separate file and reused elsewhere
- Functions needed throughout our website can be placed in one separate file, which prevents duplication, and means that changes need only be made in one place

The actual file containing our code is simply a plain text file, normally saved with the `.js` extension. The extension just tells the computer's operating system, and anyone looking at the file, what is contained inside it. It's not compulsory to use the `.js` extension but that's the norm, so for consistency we should use it. Let's create a `.js` file, using any text editor or page editor, just as we have for been doing for HTML files, and put in it the `fixDecimalPlaces()` function that we looked at earlier in the chapter:

```
function fixDecimalPlaces(fixNumber, decimalPlaces)
{
  var digitSaver = Math.pow(10,decimalPlaces);

  fixNumber = new String((Math.round(fixNumber * (digitSaver)))/digitSaver);

  var zerosRequired;
  var decimalPointLocation = fixNumber.lastIndexOf(".");


  if (decimalPointLocation == -1)
  {
      fixNumber = fixNumber + ".";
      zerosRequired = decimalPlaces;
  }
  else
  {

     zerosRequired = decimalPlaces -
      (fixNumber.length - decimalPointLocation - 1);
```

```
    }

    for (; zerosRequired > 0; zerosRequired--)
    {
         fixNumber = fixNumber + "0";
     }

    return fixNumber;

}
```

There's no need for the code to be inside a `<script>` tag, it simply exists inside the .js file on its own. Save the file as `MathFunctions.js`. We can paste other functions into the `.js` file, too, to create a whole library of useful functions

We have our `.js` file but how can we insert it into a web page and use it? It's actually very easy, we use the `<script>` tag and its `src` attribute to include the code in the page. Let's amend the example page we created earlier for the `fixDecimalPlaces()` function:

```
<html>
<head>
<script language="JavaScript" src="MathFunctions.js"></script>
</head>
<body>
<script language="JavaScript">

    var numberToFix;
    var decimalPlaces;

    do
    {
      numberToFix = Number(prompt("Please enter a number",""));

      if (!isNaN(numberToFix) && numberToFix != 0)
      {
        var decimalPlaces = Number(prompt("Please enter the number " +
                                          "of decimal places",""));

        if (!isNaN(decimalPlaces))
        {
          document.write(numberToFix + " fixed to ");
          document.write(decimalPlaces + " decimal places is ");
          document.write(fixDecimalPlaces(numberToFix, decimalPlaces) + "<br>")
        }
      }
    }
    while (confirm("Convert another number?"))

</script>
</body>
</html>
```

We have included our MathFunctions.js file into this page by using the line:

```
<script language="JavaScript" src="MathFunctions.js"></script>
```

inside the page head, though the code can be included anywhere so long as it's not called before it has been included in the page.

The src attribute uses the same syntax as the src attribute for an <img> tag. This means we can use relative paths if we want and have different web sites point to the same code library:

```
<script language="JavaScript"
        src="../MyWebsites/CodeLibrary/MathFunctions.js"></script>
```

The actual path will change depending on where the page that uses the file is and where the code file is.

The code later on in the page doesn't need to be changed at all; it works just as if the code was in the page rather than included using the src attribute.

Creating our own Objects with JavaScript Classes

We've seen that JavaScript provides its own objects; for example, the String object and the Math object. As well as providing built-in own objects JavaScript allows us to create our own objects. Creating our own objects is useful where we want to model a real world situation. For example, we could have an object representing a shopping cart. Creating our own type of objects is especially useful where we have data and functionality combined. A shopping cart is a good example, because we have lots of data (items in the cart, data about each item) and we also need functionality such as displaying the shopping cart to the user. Objects can also be useful where we have a number of different items, each with a number of pieces of data; for example items in the shopping basket which have properties such as price, item name, etc. Where we have no need to store data but simply want functionality, such as our fixDecimalPlaces() function we saw before, then it's generally easier not to create a special object, but just have a code library.

Just as a builder of a house needs architect's plans to know what to build and how it should be laid out, when creating our own objects we need to provide blueprints telling JavaScript what our object should look like. The key to this is the JavaScript **class**, which is essentially a template for the object, like the architect's drawings are the template used to build a house. Before we can use our new object type we need to define its class, its methods, and its properties. The important distinction is that when we define our class, no object based on that is created. It's only when we create an instance of our class using the new keyword that an object of that class type, based on our class blueprint, or **prototype**, is created.

A class consists of three things:

- A constructor
- Method definitions
- Properties

A **constructor** is a method called every time one of our objects based on this class is created. It's useful for where we want to initialize properties or the object in some way. We need to create a constructor even if we don't use it. As with functions, a constructor can have zero or more parameters.

We're familiar with the methods of JavaScript's built-in objects, but now we get the chance to define our own methods for performing specific tasks. Our class will specify what methods we have and the code that they execute. We can also define our own properties. However, unlike other programming languages, although we *can* declare our class's properties, we don't need to – we can simply go ahead and use properties without letting JavaScript know in advance.

It's a good idea to put the code for a class definition inside a `.js` file. If we include classes with the same purpose, for example classes for converting exchange rates, in one file it can makes it easier to work out which classes are defined in which files.

Let's create a simple class based on the real-world example of an item in a user's shopping basket. We'll put this in a `.js` file called `ShoppingBasketClasses.js`.

Defining a Class

Let's start by creating a class for a shopping item. Our class will be called the `ShoppingItem` class. The first thing we need to do is create the class constructor:

```
function ShoppingItem(itemDesc, itemPrice, itemQty)
{
   this.itemDesc = itemDesc;
   this.itemPrice = itemPrice;
   this.itemQty = itemQty;
}
```

The first thought might be that what we have here is simply a function, and you'd be right. It's not until we start defining the `ShoppingItem` class's properties and methods that it becomes a class. This is in contrast to other programming languages, which have a more formal way of defining classes.

Looking at the code, the important thing to note is that the constructor function's name must match that of the class we are defining, in this case the `ShoppingItem` class. That way when a new instance of our class as an object, termed an **object instance**, is created this function will be called automatically. Note we have three parameters for our class and these are used inside the class itself, but note that we use the `this` keyword, for example:

```
this.itemDesc = itemDesc;
```

Inside any class method, the `this` keyword will refer to that object instance of our class. Here we refer to the `itemDesc` property of this class object and we set it to equal the `itemDesc` parameter. If you have used other object-oriented programming languages you might wonder where we defined the `itemDesc` property. The answer is that we didn't; when we access the property JavaScript creates it for us. There is no check that the property exists, JavaScript creates it as it needs to. The same is true if we use the object with a property never mentioned in our class definition. All this free property creation might sound great, but it has drawbacks, the main one being that if we accidentally misspell a property name then JavaScript won't tell us; it'll just create a new property with the misspelled name, something that can make it difficult to track bugs. One way around this problem is to create methods that **get** a property's value and others that allow us to **set** a property's value. This may sound like hard work, but it can reduce bugs, or at least make them easier to spot. Let's create a few property get/set methods for our `ShoppingItem` class:

```
ShoppingItem.prototype.getItemDesc = function()
{
  return this.itemDesc;
}

ShoppingItem.prototype.setItemDesc = function(itemDesc)
{
  this.itemDesc = itemDesc;
}

ShoppingItem.prototype.getItemPrice = function()
{
   return this.itemPrice;
}

ShoppingItem.prototype.setItemPrice = function(itemPrice)
{
   this.itemPrice = Number(itemPrice);
}

ShoppingItem.prototype.getItemQty = function()
{
  return this.itemQty;
}

ShoppingItem.prototype.setItemQty = function(itemQty)
{
  this.itemQty = Number(itemQty);
}
```

What we have done above is define a set and get method for each of our classes' three properties, `itemQty`, `itemPrice` and `itemDesc`. Let's look at how we created one of the methods, the `setItemQty()` method:

```
ShoppingItem.prototype.setItemQty = function(itemQty)
{
  this.itemQty = Number(itemQty);
}
```

The first thing we notice is that it's a very odd way of defining a function. On the left we set the class's `prototype` property's `setItemQty` to equal a function, which we then define immediately afterwards. In fact, JavaScript supplies every object with a `prototype` property, which allows new properties and methods to be created. So, whenever we want to create a method for our class we simply write:

```
className.prototype.methodName = function(method parameter list)
{
  // method code
}
```

We've created our class, but how do we now create new objects based on that class?

Creating and Using Class Object Instances

We create instances of our classes just the same way we created instances of built-in JavaScript classes, using the `new` keyword.

So, to create a new instance of our `ShoppingItem` class we'd write:

```
var firstShoppingItem = new ShoppingItem("Shoes","29.00",2);
var secondShoppingItem = new ShoppingItem("Video Game","49.00",3);
```

Here, just as with a String object, we have created two new objects and stored them in variables `firstShoppingItem` and `secondShoppingItem`. This time it's a new object based on our class.

Let's call the `getItemQty()` method of the first object:

```
document.write(firstShoppingItem.getItemQty())
```

And we'll see 2 written into the page, which was the quantity set when we called the constructor. As we've put our class code in a `.js` file to use it in a web page we need to include it with the `src` attribute of a `<script>` tag, as in the example page below (`ShoppingBasketExample.htm`):

```
<html>
<head>
<script language="JavaScript" src="ShoppingBasketClasses.js"></script>
</head>
<body>
<script language="JavaScript">

var firstShoppingItem = new ShoppingItem("Shoes","29.00",2);
var secondShoppingItem = new ShoppingItem("Video Game","49.00",3);
document.write(firstShoppingItem.getItemQty() + "<br>")
document.write(secondShoppingItem.getItemDesc())

</script>
</body>
</html>
```

If you run this code you should get the output:

2
Video Game

At the top of the page inside the `<head>` is our `<script>` tag, which imports the class defining code into the page, which our code later on needs to create one of our class objects. We need to include this in every page that uses our class. The `src` attribute points to the URL of our class, which in this case assumes that the class's `.js` file is in the same directory as our page.

In the second script block we create two objects based on our class, as we saw earlier, then use their `getItemQty()` and `getItemDesc()` methods.

An Array of Items

So far we have a class for items we can put in a shopping basket, but no class representing a shopping basket. A shopping basket can have zero or more items inside it. How can we create a shopping basket class that supports the storage of zero or more items? The answer is by using arrays, which we discussed in Chapter 2.

Let's start by defining our class, which we'll call the `ShoppingBasket` class. We'll add the code to the `ShoppingBasketClasses.js` file:

```
function ShoppingBasket()
{
   this.items = new Array();
}
```

Here we define the constructor. Inside the constructor we initialize the `items` property that will hold all the `ShoppingItem` class objects.

Next we need to add a way of putting items into the shopping basket; for this we create the `addItem()` method:

```
ShoppingBasket.prototype.addItem = function(itemDesc, itemPrice, itemQty)
{
  this.items[itemDesc] = new ShoppingItem(itemDesc,itemPrice,itemQty);
}
```

The method takes 3 parameters, which are the details needed to create a new shopping basket item. Then inside the method we create a new object of type `ShoppingItem`. A reference to this object is stored inside our `items` array, using the `itemDesc` to associate the place the new object is stored.

So let's look at how we can access the items in the array. In the method below called `getTotalCost()` we go through each item in the shopping basket and calculate the total cost of the basket:

```
ShoppingBasket.prototype.getTotalCost = function()
{
  var basketItem;
  var basketTotalCost = 0;

  for (basketItem in this.items)
  {
    basketTotalCost = basketTotalCost
    +
    this.items[basketItem].getItemQty()
    *
    this.items[basketItem].getItemPrice();
  }

  return basketTotalCost;
}
```

We can access each item by its description but what we want to do is simply loop through the whole basket, so we use a `for...in` loop that loops through each item in the `items` array. Each time the loop executes, `basketItem` will be set by JavaScript to contain the `itemDesc` of the next item; it doesn't contain the item itself but its associated keyword.

As we have the associated keyword we can access the item objects in the array like this:

```
this.items[basketItem]
```

Remember the `this` keyword refers to this object instance of our class. We then use the `ShoppingItem` objects `getItemQty()` and `getItemPrice()` methods to calculate the total cost for those items ordered and add that to the total cost of the shopping basket.

On the last line we return the total cost of the basket to the calling code.

Save the `ShoppingBasketClass.js` file and let's see this working in practice by creating a simple test page (`ShoppingBasketExample2.htm`):

```
<html>
<head>
<script language="JavaScript" src="ShoppingBasketClasses.js"></Script>
</head>
<body>
<script language="JavaScript">

var customerBasket = new ShoppingBasket();
customerBasket.addItem("DVD Recorder","500",1);
customerBasket.addItem("512mb RAM","50",2);
customerBasket.addItem("LCD Monitor","200",3);
document.write("Your shopping basket's total cost is $"
         + customerBasket.getTotalCost());

</script>
</body>
</html>
```

If you view this page in your web browser, you should see the output:

Your shopping basket's total cost is $1200

At the top the `<script>` tag imports the `.js` file containing our class definition code.

In our main script block further down the page we start by creating a new object based on our `ShoppingBasket` class. This will automatically call our class constructor function that initializes this object, in this case creating an `items` property containing an `Array` object.

In the next three lines we add items to our basket using the `addItem()` methods. We use this method to make it easier to debug the code when things go wrong, because we can just look through our own class methods to see why the `items` property doesn't contain what we expect, rather than having to go through that code and all code on our web page that might access it. As with variables we should limit where they are accessed from to make tracking bugs and modifying code easier.

On the final line we write out the total cost of the basket using the `getTotalCost()` method to return the total cost of the basket.

Our shopping basket class objects are quite rudimentary, but using the principles we have learned here we'll be looking in the last three chapters of this book at a sophisticated set of shopping basket classes and creating a full e-commerce application.

Summary

In this chapter we started by looking at functions. We saw that functions allow us to wrap up frequently used code and put it into a single place that we can call again and again in our pages. As an example, we converted the currency conversion example from the last chapter into a function. We saw that we should give the function any information that it might need by using parameters, which we can pass to the function when calling it. Functions can also return a value or they may choose to return no values at all. If we want to return multiple values we could use an array, but this is only a good idea when the data is related. We also saw how we could make our parameters optional by checking for whether they have been passed or not.

We then looked at some ways of making our coding easier to debug and amend later if we need to. We saw that one of the keys to creating easy to maintain code was readability. If code is easy to read then it's easier to spot bugs and to change. Just by making code layout logical, indenting code blocks like those associated with loops and `if` statements, we make life much easier for ourselves. We also saw that using descriptive names for variables and functions can help greatly.

Our next topic was how to organize and reuse code. We found that the need for certain functionality, for example a math function or shopping basket functionality, appears in many of our web sites. We saw that by using `.js` files, we could put useful and related routines into one file and then use them in different pages, even different web sites. It saves time because we don't need to reinvent the wheel every time, and because if we spot a bug in a routine we can fix it in one place and all the web pages and sites that use it also benefit. We saw that to include one of our `.js` files in a web page we needed to use the `<script>` tag and its `src` property.

Finally, we looked at how we can create our own types of objects with JavaScript. We saw how these could be used to model real-world entities in a programming language. We gave as an example a shopping basket and items inside a shopping basket. We created classes that objectified these real-world things so we could create a shopping item object and a shopping basket object.

We have now covered most of the essential JavaScript language so in the next chapter we can start applying it to the web browser and seeing how JavaScript and the web browser interact.

4

- Modifying the page with JavaScript
- Events
- Browser detection

Author: Paul Wilton

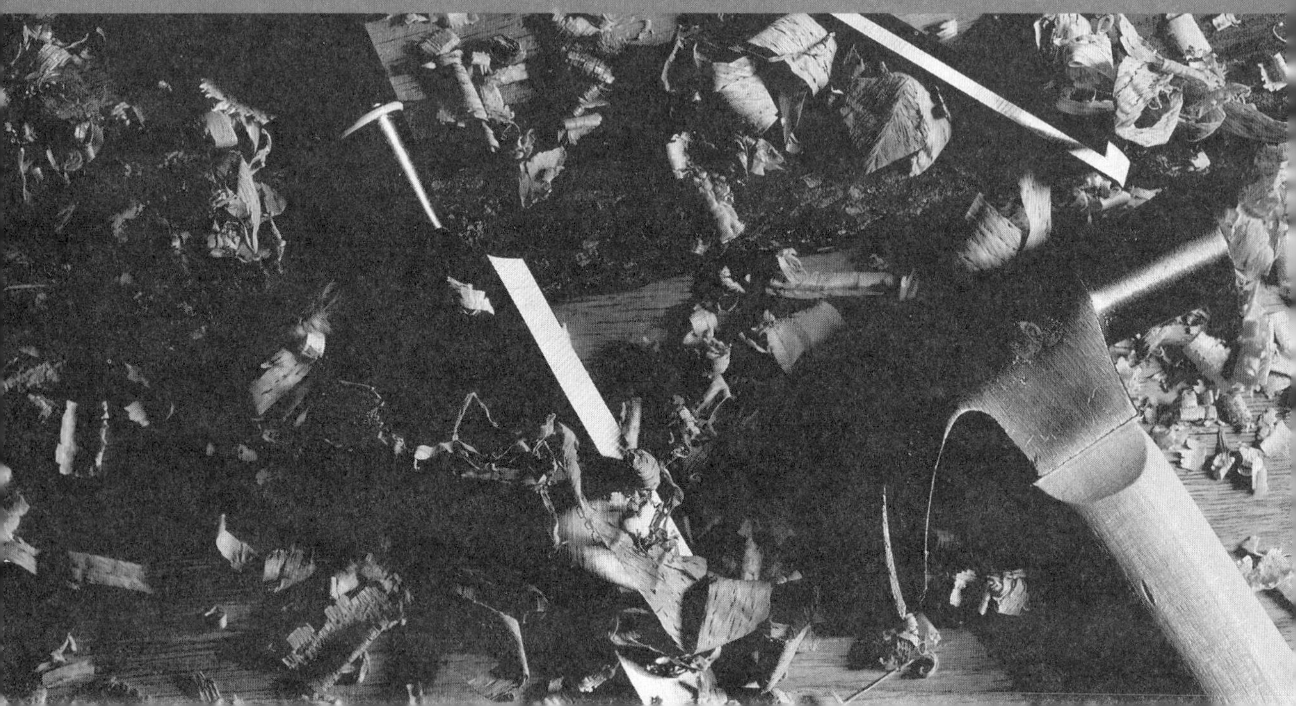

Interacting with the Web Browser

After the first three chapters, we should have all the essential JavaScript under our belts. In this chapter, we'll be looking at how we can use it to interact with the browser. By our interaction, we mean the way we can change how a web page looks as it is downloaded and after it has been downloaded, and how the browser lets us interact with the user of the page.

We'll concentrate on some of the objects that the browser makes available to our JavaScript code, how we can access and use HTML forms with JavaScript, and finally how to capture events (for example, the user clicking the mouse button or pressing a key on the keyboard). At the end of the chapter, we'll also look at how we can detect which browser the user is viewing our web pages with – this is necessary since different browsers make different objects available to our code. While in this chapter we'll be sticking to JavaScript that will work with all IE3+ and NN3+ browsers, we'll look at how IE and NN differ in the following two chapters.

Browser Objects

We've already seen in Chapter 2 that JavaScript includes built-in objects such as the String object, Date object and Math object. This is JavaScript's way of providing functionality specific to certain types of data, like characters and dates. The Math object is slightly different in that there is only one Math object and it's already created for us by JavaScript – we simply use the mathematical functionality it provides via its methods and properties.

However, JavaScript wouldn't be that useful on its own. It's a fine language, but it's JavaScript's ability to interact with its host environment that makes it really useful. What do I mean by **host environment**? Well, we learned in Chapter 1 that JavaScript is available not just in the web browser, but also on some web servers, in Adobe's PDF file format, and even for scripting tasks in Windows. Each of these contexts plays host to JavaScript and allows JavaScript to manipulate the host, whether it's a window or a web page. In each case, the JavaScript language is more or less the same, but the host environment is quite different. The question is, "how do we interact with the host?" Well, each host provides a set of objects that it makes available to JavaScript, just as the Math object is automatically created and made available to our code.

For this book, the host environment we are interested in is the web browser. When a web page is loaded, the browser looks at the page and creates objects representing different elements in the page. Some objects will always be available. For example, every page makes available a `window` object representing the browser window it is contained in, and a `document` object representing the page itself. Other objects are only available if the corresponding HTML element is contained in the page. For example, if we have three `<img>` elements in our page, then the browser creates three corresponding `Image` objects. Each object is accessible to JavaScript, much as String and Date objects are available to it. However, not every HTML element will have an object created for it – the earlier browsers, like IE3 and NN3, only made a limited number of the elements on a page accessible as objects. In contrast, modern browsers, like NN6 and IE5, make virtually all elements available to JavaScript as objects.

Although each browser makes some elements available to JavaScript as objects, the way of accessing them varies between browsers. The good news is that NN6+ and IE5+ have adopted standards that make coding for both browsers easier, which we'll discuss in Chapter 7.

The browser organizes all the objects it makes available to JavaScript in a tree-like hierarchy. The `window` object contains all the other objects and is at the top of the hierarchy. Contained inside the window is our page, represented by the `document` object. Inside the `document` object are the objects representing the HTML elements in the page. We could represent it in a tree diagram like this:

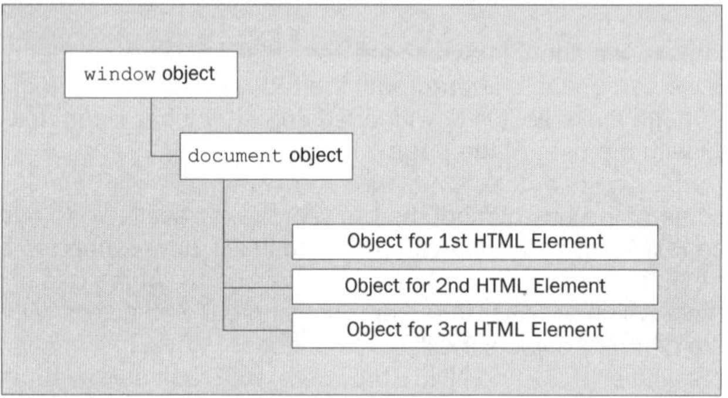

The hierarchy of objects representing HTML elements or page objects within the document is called the **Document Object Model** (DOM). The DOM is rather like a road map, but instead of telling us what cities are available and how to get to them, the DOM determines which of the HTML elements will be made available to JavaScript as objects and how we can access them.

While early browsers (such as IE3 and NN3) had similar DOMs, they were most definitely not identical. This does, of course, cause problems for developers trying to write JavaScript code that runs on both browsers. In an effort to solve this problem, the web standards organization, the World Wide Web Consortium, or W3C (*http://www.w3.org/*), has set various standards for what a DOM should contain and how its objects should be accessible to the browser. Modern browsers, like IE5+ and NN6+, have adopted the W3C DOM level 1 standard to varying degrees and, to a lesser extent, the W3C DOM level 2.

In this chapter we'll look at the objects of the DOM that have been supported by browsers since IE3 and NN3. This means that most of the code in this chapter will work on most browsers, even older ones. We'll turn to an investigation of how the IE4 and NN4 DOMs work in Chapter 6. In Chapter 7, we'll be looking at the W3C DOM and its support by IE5+ and NN6+.

Let's start by briefly looking at the key browser objects and how we use them.

Key Browser Objects

The key objects when programming the browser are the `window` and `document` objects.

The `window` object represents the browser window itself. For example, it provides information about the screen, the browser version, which pages have been visited by the user, and much more. This information is usually provided through various other objects that are accessed as properties of the `window` object, namely the `location`, `screen`, and `navigator` objects.

The `document` object, which itself is accessed as a property of the `window` object, deals with the HTML page itself. For example, it allows us to access HTML forms and images within the page, and even to write new information to the page.

The diagram below shows how the above objects are linked – note that it's from the `window` object that all the other objects can be accessed. The `document` object also contains our `forms`, `images`, and `links` arrays, which are available as its properties.

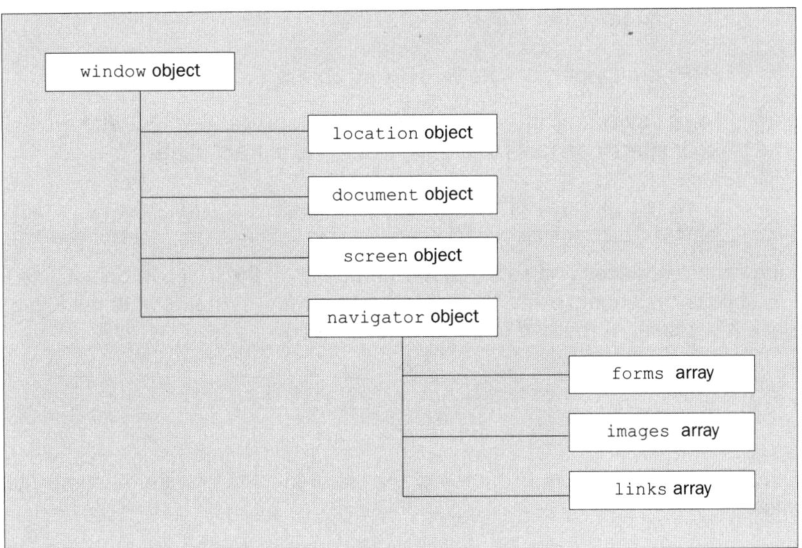

The table below summarizes the objects we've met so far:

Object	Description
`window`	Represents the browser window or frame.
`navigator`	Provides information about the browser, for example, the browser version. This is a property of the `window` object.
`location`	Provides information about the location (the URL or file path) of the currently loaded page. This is a property of the `window` object.

Object	Description
`screen`	Provides details of the user's screen, for example, the number of colors supported or screen resolution. This is a property of the `window` object.
`document`	Represents the HTML page within the browser window or frame. Allows us to access HTML elements inside the page. This is a property of the `window` object.
`forms`	An array containing all the `form` objects (representing `<form>` elements) inside the current page. This is a property of the `document` object.
`images`	An array containing all the `Image` objects (representing `<img>` elements) inside the current page. This is a property of the `document` object
`links`	An array containing all the link objects (representing `<a>` and `<area>` elements that specify an `href` attribute) inside the current page. This is a property of the `document` object.

Strictly speaking, when we access objects that are properties of the `window` object, like the `location` and `document` objects, we should prefix their object name with `window` (we should also prefix `alert()` in this way, since it is actually a method of the `window` object):

```
window.document.write("<strong>some html</strong>");
window.alert (window.location.href);
```

However, since the `window` object is at the top of the hierarchy, the browser assumes its use by default, so we can write:

```
document.write("<strong>some html</strong>");
alert(location.href);
```

with no need to put `window` in front.

Note that, to avoid bugs, it's better if we don't declare variables with the same names as browser objects. For example, if you declared a variable called `location`, then in the following code JavaScript will assume that you are accessing your variable rather than the `location` object property of the `window` object:

```
var location;
alert(location.href);
```

Modifying our Page with JavaScript

Now that we've met the key browser objects, we'll start looking at how we can use them to alter how our web page looks when it's downloaded by the user. The important thing to note is that the actual page (the one we type out and save as a file onto the server) is not altered at all. The only page that is altered is the one that it held in the memory of the user's computer. Dynamically changing the page (by moving elements or altering their color, etc.) after the page has been sent to the browser is referred to as **Dynamic HTML** or **DHTML** for short. Purists may argue that, strictly speaking, only some aspects of changing a page after it has loaded are DHTML, but here we'll use it to refer to any changes made using JavaScript.

Changing the Page as it Downloads

In this section we're going to see how to use the `write()` method of the `document` object to change the page as the browser loads and interprets it. This technique for changing the page has been around since IE3.02 and NN2, and so has the advantage of being cross-browser compatible. It's also quite simple to use. However, except in NN4 with a `<layer>` element, it's not of much use once the page has finished loading (although, of course, we can always reload the page).

We can use `document.write()` to write any HTML to the page that would be valid at that point. As far as the browser is concerned, it's pretty much the same as if the HTML had been included in the original page on the server. Inside the parentheses after the method name, we place the HTML or plain text that we want to write. Note that the display of any added HTML is effected by the page content around it. For example, we may write some text into the page within a formatting element:

```
<strong>
  <script>
    document.write("This will be effected by the strong element");
  </script>
</strong>
```

Let's look at a common example of writing HTML into the page. In this page, *greeting_example.htm*, the web site's greeting varies depending on the time of day:

```
<html>
<body>
<h1>My Heading</h1>
<div id="welcomeMessageDiv">
  <script language="JavaScript">
    var hourOfDay = new Date();
    hourOfDay = hourOfDay.getHours();
    var greetingMessage = " and welcome";

    if (hourOfDay >= 0 && hourOfDay < 12)
    {
      greetingMessage = "Good morning" + greetingMessage;
    }
    else if (hourOfDay < 17)
    {
      greetingMessage = "Good afternoon" + greetingMessage;
    }
```

```
      else
      {
        greetingMessage = "Good evening" + greetingMessage;
      }

      document.write(greetingMessage);
    </script>
  </div>
  </body>
  </html>
```

The code obtains the current time from the clock on the user's computer, and then checks the current hour against certain criteria, creating the message string accordingly. This message is then written to the page.

Let's look at the code in more detail. At the top of the script block, the `hourOfDay` variable is set to the current hour. The way that we've done this is to create a new Date object, and then use its `getHours()` method to retrieve the current hour.

The next few lines are a series of `if...else` statements, which decide, based on the value in `hourOfDay`, what greeting should be displayed to the user. If the hour is between midnight and midday, a "Good morning" greeting is added to the `greetingMessage` variable storing the message to be displayed. If the hour is between midday and 5pm (which is 17:00, as JavaScript works on a 24-hour clock), a "Good afternoon" message is displayed. Otherwise, it's assumed the hour is in the evening and an appropriate message is created.

On the final line of the script block, the `document` object's `write()` method is used to write the value contained in variable `greetingMessage` into the page. The message is placed in the same position as the code is in the page – it will be written inside the `<div>` element that contains the script block. In this case, we just write plain text with no HTML tags to the page, but if, for example, the last line of the script block had been:

```
      document.write("<strong>" + greetingMessage + "</strong>");
```

then this HTML would have been processed and rendered just as if the HTML had been there in the original page all along (that is, the greeting message would have been displayed in bold font).

Changing the Page after it has Downloaded

Since NN2, it's been possible to use JavaScript to make some changes to a page's content and format after it's been downloaded and displayed by the browser. For the early browsers, they were just simple changes, for example switching the image that was loaded. However, modern browsers allow a wide range of changes to be made after the page has completed loading.

In this chapter, we'll cover DHTML that works with version 4+ browsers and some version 3 browsers. They may be older techniques, but they are still very useful, even on modern browsers. Let's start by looking at image swapping, which is available with NN3+ and IE4+.

Swapping Images

As we saw earlier, the `document` object has the `images` array property, each element of which contains an `Image` object, one for each `<img>` element of the page. The most useful property of the `Image` object is the `src` property – we can use this to change the image file to be displayed, even after the page has completed loading into the browser. We may use this to change a displayed banner advertisement while a user is looking at a page, or to create a menu with an image that changes depending on the menu option that the user's mouse hovers over.

Let's take a look at a very simple example where we change an image by clicking on a hyperlink.

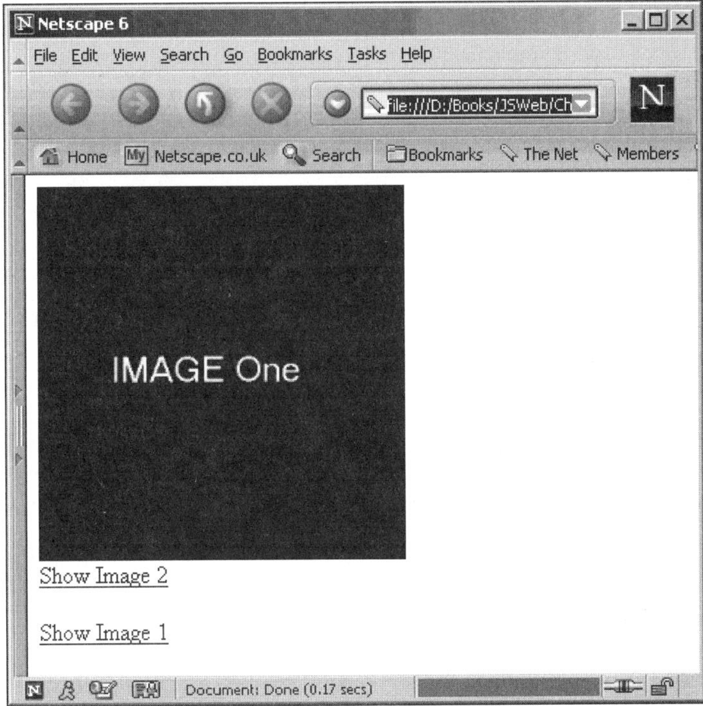

When the page initially loads, `Image1.jpg` is shown. However, when the *Show Image 2* hyperlink is clicked, `Image2.jpg` will be loaded into the page. When the *Show Image 1* link is clicked, `Image1.jpg` is reloaded.

The example is called `SwapImage.htm`:

```
<html>
<head>
  <script language="JavaScript">
    function loadNewImage(imgSrc)
    {
      document.images['SwapImg'].src = imgSrc;
    }
  </script>
</head>
```

```
<body>
<img src="Image1.jpg" name="SwapImg">
<br>
<a href="javascript: loadNewImage('image2.jpg')">Show Image 2</a>
<br><br>
<a href="javascript: loadNewImage('image1.jpg')">Show Image 1</a>
</body>
</html>
```

The `Image1.jpg` and Image2.jpg files can be found in the code download for this book.

Let's look first at the two hyperlinks. Normally, a hyperlink takes us to another page, but they can also be set to different protocols, for example `mail:`, `ftp:`, or, as in our case, `javascript:`. The `javascript:` protocol tells the browser to expect some JavaScript code to execute rather than a URL to navigate to. It's important to remember not to include a space between `javascript` and the colon (`:`) or it won't work.

```
<a href="javascript: loadNewImage('image2.jpg')">Show Image 2</a>
<br><br>
<a href="javascript: loadNewImage('image1.jpg')">Show Image 1</a>
```

The JavaScript code calls a function that was created earlier in the page: the `loadNewImage()` function.

As an aside, note that if the code in the function had been included in the link directly like this:

```
<a href="javascript: document.images['SwapImg'].src = 'image2.jpg';">
  Show Image 2
</a>
<br><br>
<a href="javascript: document.images['SwapImg'].src = 'image1.jpg';">
  Show Image 1
</a>
```

then, instead of swapping the images, in some browsers we'd just see the text `image2.jpg` or `image1.jpg` displayed instead. Putting the same code inside a function fixes this bug.

When either of the links is clicked, the `loadNewImage()` function is called. The value of the `imgSrc` parameter passed to the function depends on which link was clicked. This parameter determines which new image will be loaded.

The `loadNewImage()` function contains just one line:

```
document.images['SwapImg'].src = imgSrc;
```

This is where the actual image swapping is done. Each `<img>` element in the page has an associated `Image` object, which can be found as an element of the `images` array property of the `document` object. The `Image` objects in the array can be accessed either by a numerical index or using the `name` attribute value given to the `<img>` element. In the example above, the name of the `<img>` element, `SwapImg`, has been used. However, we could instead have used a numeric index like this:

```
document.images[0].src = imgSrc;
```

The order of the `<img>` elements in the page's code determines their order in the `images` array. The first `<img>` in the page is the first in the array and has an index value of `0`; the second would have an index of `1`, the third `2` and so on. As it's the first `<img>` element in the page (in fact, here it is the only `<img>` element in the page), its index is 0.

Accessing via the index rather than name is useful where you want to loop through all the `Image` objects in the `images` array.

Back to our code, we could actually have accessed the `images` array using the `name` of the `<img>` element directly without the square brackets. So:

```
document.images.SwapImg.src = imgSrc;
```

is exactly the same as:

```
document.images['SwapImg'].src = imgSrc;
```

Image Rollovers and Caching

A trick that's been available since NN3 and IE4 is image rollovers. This happens when the user's mouse rolls over an image, changing it to a different image. When the mouse moves off the image, it changes back to the original image. There are a lot of variations on this theme, for example using image rollovers for menus, but the principles are the same.

> *Note that we should be careful when using image rollovers not to hide information that users might want to see without having to search for it. Expandable menus, for example, might not be particularly helpful if the user has to rollover various site elements before finding what they are looking for.*

One problem image rollovers (and image swaps, as in the previous example) suffer from is the time taken to load the images from the server when they are first needed. The resulting pause may leave the page looking less than smooth and professional. To ensure the image changes right away, we need to have it preloaded into the browser's cache. We do this by loading *all* the necessary images into the browser as the page loads, even if only some of the images are initially shown. We can do this by:

- Using `<img>` elements with the `width` and `height` attributes set to 1 so they are not visible.
- Creating a new `Image` object for each image we want to load, and setting the object's `src` property to the file we want cached.

Let's look at an example of the latter technique. This page is called `ImageRollOver.htm`. (As usual, the image files are available within the code download.)

```
<html>
<head>
  <script language="JavaScript">
    var imgLinksOver = new Image();
    imgLinksOver.src = 'LinksButton_Over.jpg';

    var imgLinksOut = new Image();
```

```
      imgLinksOut.src = 'LinksButton_Out.jpg';

      var imgAboutOver = new Image();
      imgAboutOver.src = 'AboutButton_Over.jpg';

      var imgAboutOut = new Image()
      imgAboutOut.src = 'AboutButton_Out.jpg';

      function swapImage(imgSrc, imgName)
      {
        document.images[imgName].src = imgSrc;
      }
    </script>
  </head>
  <body bgcolor="white">
  <a href="Links.htm"
     onmouseover="swapImage(imgLinksOver.src, 'imgLinks')"
     onmouseout="swapImage(imgLinksOut.src, 'imgLinks')">
       <img src="LinksButton_Out.jpg" name="imgLinks" border=0></a>
  <br>
  <a href="About.htm"
     onmouseover="swapImage(imgAboutOver.src, 'imgAbout')"
     onmouseout="swapImage(imgAboutOut.src, 'imgAbout')">
       <img src="AboutButton_Out.jpg" name="imgAbout" border=0></a>
  </body>
  </html>
```

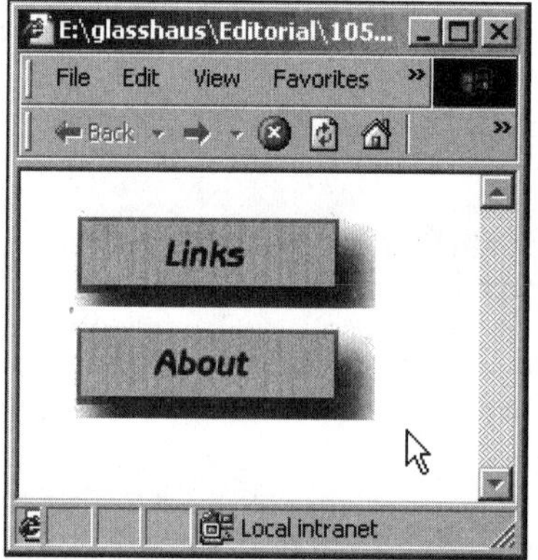

When the mouse is no longer over the *About* image, it returns back to its original state.

Now let's look at the page source. At the top of the page is a script block containing the code that causes the images to be cached and also the function that does the image swapping.

There are obviously two images involved for each button – the image for when the mouse is not over the image and the image for when it is. It's necessary to create `Image` objects for each of these images. First the *Links* button is dealt with:

```
var imgLinksOver = new Image();
imgLinksOver.src = 'LinksButton_Over.jpg';

var imgLinksOut = new Image();
imgLinksOut.src = 'LinksButton_Out.jpg';
```

A variable `imgLinksOver` is declared and assigned a reference to a new `Image` object. Then, on the second line, the `src` property of that `Image` object is set to the location and filename of the image to be cached. Here we are caching `LinksButton_Over.jpg`. The image will be loaded by the browser, but not initially displayed.

On the next two lines the same thing is done for the `LinksButton_Out.jpg` image, which is the default image displayed when the user's mouse is not over the image.

The next four lines in the script block do the same thing (cache the over and out images) for the *About* button.

All the caching code is in a script block right at the top of the page, outside of any function, so it will be executed before the main body of the page, in particular before the `<img>` elements are reached. By the time the browser comes to load the default images into the `<img>` elements, they are already in the cache and can be displayed as soon as the user rolls their mouse over the image.

At the end of the script block we have our function, `swapImage()`, which (surprise, surprise!) does the image swapping. It takes two parameters: the new location of the image to be displayed (`imgSrc`) and the `name` of the `<img>` element whose image needs to be swapped (`imgName`). It then uses the following code to set the `src` property of the relevant `Image` object to the location of the new image:

```
document.images[imgName].src = imgSrc;
```

The function won't be executed as soon as it's loaded into the browser – it's called when the mouse rolls over or off an image. The question is, "how is it called?" The answer is in the `<a>` element definitions:

```
<a href="Links.htm"
   onmouseover="swapImage(imgLinksOver.src, 'imgLinks')"
   onmouseout="swapImage(imgLinksOut.src, 'imgLinks')">
     <img src="linksbutton_out.jpg" name="imgLinks" border=0></a>
```

Notice that, as well as the normal `href` attribute definition, the `<a>` element also has `onmouseover` and `onmouseout` attributes defined. These are **event handlers** – they tell the browser to look out for the mouse rolling on or off the hyperlink, and their values tell JavaScript what to do when these events occur. We take a little more detailed look at event handlers later on in the chapter.

You may wonder why the event handler attributes have been added to the `<a>` element rather than the `<img>` element. This is a trick we're using – in older browsers, such as NN3 and NN4, the `<img>` element didn't support the `onmouseover` or `onmouseout` attributes. In modern browsers, such as IE4+ and NN6+, it does, but as this chapter caters for older browsers as well as the modern ones, we will use the `<a>` element to do the event capturing. The `<img>` element is inside our `<a>` element, so if the mouse is over or off the `<a>` element, then it's also over or off the `<img>` element.

> *Notice that the closing `</a>` tag is placed on the same line as the `<img>` tag. This is to stop NN browsers from displaying little lines after the image, which it will do if the `</a>` tag is on a different line.*

The event handler attributes define what code should be executed if the event the attribute deals with occurs. In our example, on the event of the mouse rolling over our `<a>` element, the `onmouseover` attribute specifies the following code that should be executed:

```
swapImage(imgLinksOver.src, 'imgLinks')"
```

In this instance, it calls the `swapImage()` function we discussed above. It passes `imgLinksOver.src` as the location of the image to be displayed and `imgLinks` as the `name` of the `<img>` element that needs its `src` attribute changing. Remember that `imgLinksOver` is the global variable we declared at the top of the page – it was set to reference an `Image` object that we created. Why use this? Why not just pass the actual file name and location? We could have done that without any problem, but it would mean that if the file location changed we'd have to change it in two places in our code (where the global variable is defined *and* in the `<a>` element's attribute). By using the global variable, we just have to change it in one place. It's amazingly easy to miss something like this when altering some code.

It was mentioned in the last chapter that you should be careful when using global variables – if your code will work with local variables, then it is probably best to stick to them. However, here we have a good reason for using global variables, since we wish to keep the value of the variable outside the function it is used in.

Note that it doesn't have to be a function that's called in the event handler attributes – it can be any JavaScript code. Each statement of the code should be separated by semi colons, as we have here:

```
onmouseover="alert('Hello'); alert('Another statement');
             document.write('More code')"
```

The technique of rollovers and image caching can also be used for animation, though animated gifs or Flash movies may be a better option. JavaScript has the advantage over Flash of widespread support and no need for a plugin. Although the browsers I use have Flash built in as standard, it's amazing how many times I go to a web site to find I have an out-of-date plugin and have to spend time downloading the new one. Remember that users hate to wait on the Web – a plugin that takes even just a few minutes to download is enough to drive a lot of users to other web sites, so unless your web site has details of next week's winning lottery number, it's best to be judicious with the use of content requiring the very latest plug ins! Although animations used in the right place can look great, it's also good practice not to overuse them. Users may be impressed the first time they see them, but on the second or third visits the animation can become annoying and distracting.

Dynamically Changing Links

All the `<a>` and `<area>` elements that have `href` attributes are accessible via the `links` array property of the `document` object. There is one main difference between this array and the `images` array – elements of the `links` array can only be accessed via index values, not using their element's `name` attributes.

Let's look at a simple example of an image map with four clickable areas defined. In the browser, it looks like this:

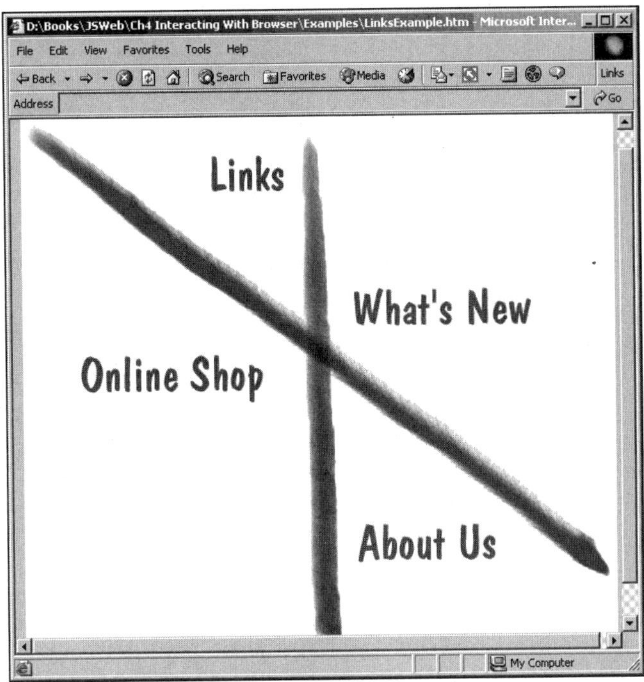

Imagine that the web site caters to both business and consumer users, and we want to vary the pages that the links take the user to depending on the type of user. In our example, the type of user accessing the page is preset, but in reality it would be based on cookies and preferences set by the user or by some other means.

This example is called *LinksExample.htm*.

```
<html>
<head>
  <script language="JavaScript">
    function window_onload()
    {
      // For the example isBusinessUser is always set to true but
      // in the real world it would be acquired via some other means, for example
      // previously selected by the user and stored as a preference
      var isBusinessUser = true;

      // If a business user, then change the links hrefs to appropriate pages
      if (isBusinessUser)
      {
        document.links[0].href = "businessLinks.htm";
        document.links[1].href = "businessWhatsNew.htm";
        document.links[2].href = "businessAboutUs.htm";
        document.links[3].href = "businessShop.htm";
      }
    }
  </script>
```

```
</head>

<body onload="window_onload()">
<map name="SiteLinksMap">
  <area href="link.htm" shape="polygon"
        coords="276, 200, 10, 4, 273, 5"
        name="areaLinks">
  <area href="WhatsNew.htm" shape="polygon"
        coords="305, 218, 293, 4, 575, 3, 575, 408"
        name="areaWhatsNew">
  <area href="AboutUs.htm" shape="polygon"
        coords="313, 511, 305, 262, 573, 460, 575, 518"
        name="areaAboutUs">
  <area href="areaShop.htm" shape="polygon"
        coords="282, 521, 8, 520, 3, 36, 278, 238"
        name="areaShop">
</map>
<img border="0" src="SiteImageMap.jpg" usemap="#SiteLinksMap">
</body>
</html>
```

Create simple HTML pages for the eight pages referenced in this page – or download our versions with the code download. Then, on loading this page, you'll discover that clicking on any of the four links will take you to a business-user page. However, if you change the value of the `isBusinessUser` variable (defined in our function above as `true`) to `false`, the four links will take you to consumer-user pages.

The important part of the code is the `window_onload()` function defined in the script block. This is called when the page loads by the `window` object's load event, which will be discussed in more detail later in the chapter. The `onload="window_onload()"` attribute added to the `<body>` element connects the `window` object's load event to the `window_onload()` function.

The `window_onload()` function first checks to see what type of user is viewing the main page, that is whether they are a business or consumer user. In our example, this is artificially set by hard coding the value of the `isBusinessUser` variable. In reality, it would be decided by some other means, for example by the user selecting preferences in an earlier part of the web site and this being recorded using cookies. (You'll learn more about cookies in Chapter 9.)

If it is a business user (that is, if `isBusinessUser` is `true`), then the `href` attributes of all the links in the page specified by the `<area>` elements are changed to point to links of the same topic, but with a business-based slant. For example, *links.htm* is the default for the first link, but is changed to *businessLinks.htm* if the user is a business user.

Accessing Forms

Similar to the `images` and `links` arrays, the `document` object has a `forms` array property that stores each `form` object corresponding to a `<form>` element in the page. As well as accessing each form object via its array index or via the name of the form, it's also possible to use the name of the form element directly. For example, imagine we had a form like this:

```
<form name="myForm">
  <!-- form elements go here -->
</form>
```

Assuming it's the first form in the page, it can be accessed in any one of the following three ways:

```
document.forms[0]
document.forms['myForm']
document.myForm
```

The first way is useful if there are a number of forms in the page and we wanted to loop through each of them in turn. However, generally, the third way is the easiest to use if no looping is needed.

Accessing the form itself is just the start of JavaScript's form functionality. More useful in client-side processing is being able to access the form elements (such as textboxes, radio buttons, and checkboxes) inside the form. The `form` object has an `elements` array, which contains the objects corresponding to each form element within the form. We can use this to access each element, using either an index or the element's name. However, it's also possible to access the element directly, just using its name. For example, imagine we had an HTML form and form element (a textbox) as defined below:

```
<form name="myForm">
  <input type="text" name="myTextBox">
</form>
```

We can access the form element in any one of the three ways shown below:

```
document.myForm.elements[0]
document.myForm.elements['myTextBox']
document.myForm.myTextBox
```

As expected, if we want to loop through the elements in a form, then the first way is the option we need. If we just want to access a specific form element by name, then the third method is generally easiest.

Accessing the value of a form element is generally a matter of accessing the `form` object's `value` property. However, for some form elements, it's more complex than that. Below, we'll look at each form element type in turn. The radio buttons and select control elements are more complex than the other elements – we'll look in more detail at each.

Button Elements

The value of a button element corresponds to the text displayed on the button face. For a button called `myButton` in `myForm`, the following code will change the button's displayed text to *somevalue*.

```
document.myForm.myButton.value = 'somevalue';
```

Reset Button

Accessing the value of a reset button again allows us to change what is displayed on the button face.

```
document.myForm.myResetButton.value = 'somevalue';
```

Note that the `form` object has a `reset()` method that has the same effect as clicking this button – it resets all values in the form back to their default values.

Submit Button

Accessing the value of a submit button again allows us to change what is displayed on the button face.

```
document.myForm.mySubmitButton.value = 'somevalue';
```

Note that the `form` object has a `submit()` method that has the same effect as clicking this button – it sends all values in the form to the server for processing.

Checkbox Elements

The value of a checkbox (that is, the text displayed beside it) is generally not as important client-side as whether or not the user has checked the checkbox. The code below uses the `checked` property of the checkbox object, and stores the value `true` in variable `isChecked` if the checkbox was checked or `false` otherwise.

```
var isChecked = document.myForm.myCheckbox.checked;
```

Textbox Elements

We can access the value written inside a textbox using the `value` property:

```
var enteredValue = document.myForm.myTextbox.value;
```

Hidden Elements

This element is similar to a textbox element, but is not visible to the user. We'll see it in use in Chapter 9 where we pass data between web pages, without the user knowing. We access its value using its `value` property.

```
var elementValue = document.myForm.myHiddenTextbox.value;
```

Password Elements

A password element is like a textbox element, but displays its contained value (whether typed by the user or added using JavaScript) as * characters rather than the actual characters, meaning that no one can look over the user's shoulder and steal their password. We access its value using its `value` property.

```
var elementValue = document.myForm.myPassword.value;
```

Text area Elements

A text area control is really just a multi-line textbox. We access the value inside a text area using its `value` property

```
var enteredValue = document.myForm.myTextArea.value;
```

Radio Buttons

Radio buttons are put into groups (out of which the user can only select one button) by giving them the same name. For example, below are two groups of radio buttons, one group called `group1` and the other called `group2`:

```
<form name="form1">
  <input type="radio" name="group1" value="A">
  <input type="radio" name="group1" value="B">
  <input type="radio" name="group1" value="C">

  <input type="radio" name="group2" value="V">
  <input type="radio" name="group2" value="W">
  <input type="radio" name="group2" value="X">
  <input type="radio" name="group2" value="Y">
</form>
```

Each radio button group is accessible via the group name (`group1` and `group2` in the example above). The object this name references is an array: each member of the array is an individual radio button from the group. As with any array, these can be accessed using the index value. In the line below, the variable `radio1Val` is set to the value (`A`) of the first radio button in `group1`:

```
var radio1Val = document.form1.group1[0].value;
```

However, what we're really interested in is usually the value of the particular radio button that the user has selected. To get this value, we need to loop through the radio button's group array, look at each radio button to see if it's checked, and if so then obtain its value. This is what the function below does:

```
function getSelectedRadioValue(radioGroup)
{
  var selectedRadioValue = "";
  var radIndex;

  for (radIndex = 0; radIndex < radioGroup.length; radIndex++)
  {
    if (radioGroup[radIndex].checked)
    {
      selectedRadioValue = radioGroup[radIndex].value;
      break;
    }
  }

  return selectedRadioValue;
}
```

This function takes one parameter, namely the radio button group whose selected radio button value we want to obtain.

In the first line, the variable `selectedRadioValue` is initialized to an empty string. If no radio button is selected, then this empty string will be returned by the function.

The `for` statement, which follows, iterates through each radio button by looping through the `radioGroup` array. The number of radio buttons in the group can be determined using the `radioGroup` array's `length` property. In each iteration of the loop, the `if` statement checks to see whether the radio button has been checked by the user. If it has, `selectedRadioValue` is set to the selected radio button's value. If a selected radio button was found, then we break out of the loop with the `break` statement – as there can only be one selected, there is no need to look for more.

On the final line, we return the value in `selectedRadioValue`, which will either be an empty string if no button was selected or the value of the selected radio button.

Select Elements

The select element is similar to a group radio button, in that it provides a group of values that the user can choose from (albeit in a different format). However, with a select element, it is sometimes possible to choose more than one option.

The `select` object corresponding to a `<select>` element has an `options` array property, much as the radio button group has a `group` array property. Each member of the `options` array is one of the possible values the user can choose from, corresponding to an `<option>` element specified within the `<select>` element.

If only one value from the options can be selected (in other words, if the `<select>` element's `multiple` attribute is not set, or is set to `false`), then the code to find the selected value is fairly easy:

```
var element = document.myForm.mySelectElement;
enteredValue =  element.options[element.selectedIndex].value;
```

The first line sets variable `element` to the `select` object corresponding to the `<select>` element with name `mySelectElement` within `myForm`. We do this to make accessing the element easier in code – instead of having to write `document.myForm.mySelectElement` every time, we just need to use `element`.

The second line uses the `select` object's `selectedIndex` property to find out which option the user has selected. We use that value to access the selected `option` object in the `options` array property of the `select` object, and extract its value using its `value` property.

This code is fine if only one option can be selected, but if the `multiple` attribute of the `<select>` element is set to `true` and the options of the select control are displayed as a list (which happens when the `size` attribute of the `<select>` element is greater than 1), then it's much trickier to extract the options the user has selected. It's necessary to create a function to extract all the values selected. We'll look at an example, *SelectWithMultipleChoiceOption.htm*, that uses such a function:

```
<html>
<head>
  <script language="JavaScript">
    function getSelectedOptionValues(optionsArray)
    {
      var selectedOptionsValues = new Array();
      var optIndex;
      var selectedOptionsValuesIndex = 0;

      for (optIndex = 0;
           optIndex < optionsArray.length;
           optIndex++)
      {
        if (optionsArray[optIndex].selected)
        {
          selectedOptionsValues[selectedOptionsValuesIndex] =
            optionsArray[optIndex].value;
          selectedOptionsValuesIndex++;
```

```
        }
      }

      return selectedOptionsValues;
    }

    function showSelectedValues()
    {
      var selectedValues =
        getSelectedOptionValues(document.form1.select1.options);
      var selectedValuesList = "";

      for (var arrayIndex = 0; arrayIndex < selectedValues.length; arrayIndex++)
      {
        selectedValuesList += selectedValues[arrayIndex] + "\n";
      }

      document.form1.textResults.value = selectedValuesList;
    }
  </script>
</head>
<body>
<form name="form1">
  <select size="7" name="select1" multiple>
    <option value="Opt 1">Option 1</option>
    <option value="Opt 2">Option 2</option>
    <option value="Opt 3">Option 3</option>
    <option value="Opt 4">Option 4</option>
    <option value="Opt 5">Option 5</option>
    <option value="Opt 6">Option 6</option>
    <option value="Opt 7">Option 7</option>
  </select>
  <textarea rows="20" cols="40" name="textResults">
  </textarea>
  <br>
  <input type="button" value="Show Selected Values"
         onclick="showSelectedValues();"
         name="button1">
</form>
</body>
</html>
```

This creates a page in the browser like that below:

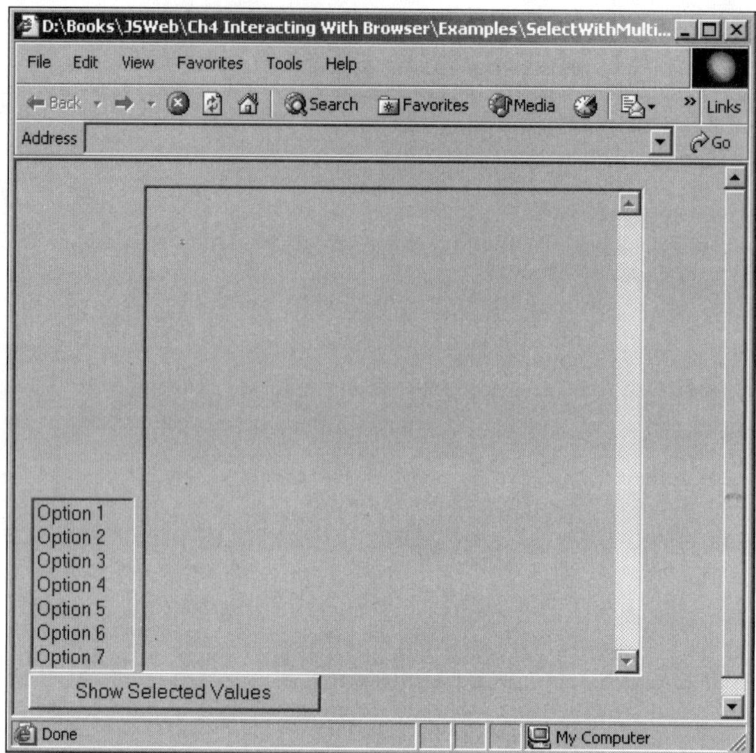

If you select one or more options from the select control, and then press the *Show Selected Values* button, the values of the options selected will be listed in the text area box. Note that the values of options are not the displayed values (for example, *Option 1*), but the value set in each `<option>` element with the `value` attribute (for example, *Opt 1*).

Let's start by looking at part of the `<select>` element definition:

```
<select size="7" name="select1" multiple>
```

The number of list options shown at any one time is determined by the `size` attribute, and the ability of the user to select one or more options is due to the inclusion of the `multiple` attribute.

The button in the page has an event handler, `onclick`, added to it, which will call the `showSelectedValues()` function created in the script block at the top of the page whenever the button is clicked. (We'll look at event handlers in detail later in the chapter.)

```
function showSelectedValues()
{
  var selectedValues =
    getSelectedOptionValues(document.form1.select1.options);
  var selectedValuesList = "";
```

```
  for (var arrayIndex = 0; arrayIndex < selectedValues.length; arrayIndex++)
  {
    selectedValuesList += selectedValues[arrayIndex] + "\n";
  }

  document.form1.textResults.value = selectedValuesList;
}
```

This function uses the `getSelectedOptionValues()` function to extract the values of the selected options, and places them in an array stored in variable `selectedValues`. Then, the `for` loop iterates through each item in the array and adds its value to the string in the `selectedValuesList` variable. (The addition of `\n` between values causes each value to be displayed on its own line.) On the last line the `textResults` text area control has its value set to this string to show the values extracted.

Let's turn to the `getSelectedOptionValues()` function which extracts the values of the selected options from the select control.

```
function getSelectedOptionValues(optionsArray)
{
  var selectedOptionsValues = new Array();
  var optIndex;
  var selectedOptionsValuesIndex = 0;

  for (optIndex = 0;
       optIndex < optionsArray.length;
       optIndex++)
  {
    if (optionsArray[optIndex].selected)
    {
      selectedOptionsValues[selectedOptionsValuesIndex] =
        optionsArray[optIndex].value;
      selectedOptionsValuesIndex++;
    }
  }

  return selectedOptionsValues;
}
```

You may notice that the function is remarkably similar to the function we saw earlier that extracted the value of the selected radio button from a radio button group.

The function starts by creating a new Array object and storing it in variable `selectedOptionsValues`, which will be used to store each of the values extracted from the select control's `options` array.

The `for` loop then iterates through each `option` object in the `options` array and checks whether the option is selected. If it is, then its value is added to the array in `selectedOptionsValues`.

Finally on the last line we return our array to the calling function.

Reacting to Events

This section will look at how we can react to the user's actions, in terms of key presses, mouse clicks, and mouse movements. The generic term for these types of actions is **events**.

There are significant differences between browsers in how they capture events, so in this section only IE3+ and NN3+ compatible code will be covered. Chapters 6 and 7 will cover the specifics of IE4, NN4, and later browsers. Having said that, the simple event handling covered in this chapter is still very useful, even in modern browsers, and is probably the main technique for capturing events that you will use, unless you have more advanced needs. It is also an advantage if we can write code that doesn't exclude browsers – only resort to code that limits the browser compatibility where it's really necessary.

Just to clarify the terminology used here, **events** occur when the user is interacting with the browser, for example clicking a button causes a click event. An **event handler** is a way of capturing an event and making specific code execute. The event handler's name is the same as the event, except that we add `on` in front, for example `onclick`.

There are two main cross-browser techniques for specifying an event handler:

- Add the event handler as an attribute of the element whose event we want to capture.
- Use the event handler properties of the object corresponding to the element whose event we want to capture.

For example, if we have an `<a>` element in the page and we wanted to capture its click event, we could add the `onclick` event handler as an attribute:

```
<a href="somepage.htm" onclick="myEventHandlerFunction()">Link</a>
```

Alternatively, we could use the `a` object's `onclick` property to specify a function to be called when the click event occurs. (Note the use of the `links` array to retrieve the `a` object – we assume that the `a` object is the first in the page.)

```
<script>
  document.links[0].onclick = myEventHandlerFunction;
</script>
```

Note also that this only works on NN3+ and IE4+ browsers.

It's important that this code should not execute before the `<a>` element has been loaded into the page or before the function (`myEventHandlerFunction()`) used for the event handler is created. The following page, *EventsNoError.htm*, works fine:

```
<html>
<head>
  <script language="JavaScript">
    function myEventHandlerFunction()
    {
      // some code
    }
```

```
  </script>
</head>
<body>
<a href="somepage.htm" name="myLink">Link</A>
<script>
  document.links[0].onclick = myEventHandlerFunction;
</script>
</body>
</html>
```

The <a> element and the function are both defined before the code specifying the event handler property. The following, *EventsError.htm*, won't work:

```
<html>
<head>
  <script language="JavaScript">
    function myEventHandlerFunction()
    {
      // some code
    }
  </script>
</head>
<body>
<script>
  document.links[0].onclick = myEventHandlerFunction;
</script>
<a href="somepage.htm" name="myLink">Link</a>
</body>
</html>
```

Now the script block defining the event handler code is before the <a> element in the page – the script is parsed by the browser before the a object exists, and so will cause an error.

We'll see shortly that the window object's load event, which fires after the page parsing and loading is complete, is a good place to put event handler code as we can be sure the page is fully loaded and parsed.

In the next sections, we'll be looking at the events linked with the browser window itself, the document, individual HTML elements, and finally with forms and the form elements they contain.

Window Events

Window events are events that happen to the browser window as a whole rather than to any specific part of the page that is loaded. Some of the events only really prove useful when new browser windows are opened, such as the focus event, which occurs (or **fires**) when the user makes a window the focus of their actions.

The two most commonly used window event handlers are onload and onunload.

Load and Unload Events

The load event fires when a window or frame has completely loaded a page. It's a good place to put **initialization code** – that is code we need to run before the user plays with the page, but after the page has loaded. We'll see in the next chapter that, when used with multiple frame pages, we need to be careful about the order in which the load events fire.

The unload event fires when the page is unloaded, either because the user has navigated to a new page or has closed the browser altogether. Note that NN3 and NN4 won't display alerts if they are in the `onunload` event handler code.

The easiest way to add event handlers for these events is by adding attributes to the `<body>` element, as shown below:

```
<body onload="callSomeFunction()" onunload="callSomeOtherFunction()">
```

The following example page, *AdvertChangeExample.htm*, uses the window's load event to initialize a timer that is used to change the loaded banner advert every few seconds:

```
<html>
<head>
  <script language="JavaScript">
    var timerID;
    var advertIndex = 0;
    var advertImgSrcs = new Array("firstAd.jpg","secondAd.jpg",
      "ThirdAd.jpg","FourthAd.jpg");

    function swapAdImg()
    {
      advertIndex++;
      if (advertIndex > advertImgSrcs.length -1)
      {
        advertIndex = 0;
      }

      document.images['imgMainAdvert'].src = advertImgSrcs[advertIndex];
    }

    function window_onload()
    {
      timerID = window.setInterval("swapAdImg()", 4000);
    }
  </script>
</head>
<body onload="window_onload()">
  <img name="imgMainAdvert" src="firstAd.jpg">
</body>
</html>
```

The `<body>` element contains the `onload` event handler, which calls the function `window_onLoad()` when the window's load event fires. The `window_onLoad()` function is defined in the script block in the head of the page:

```
function window_onload()
{
  timerID = window.setInterval("swapAdImg()", 4000);
}
```

It contains just one line, which uses the `window` object's `setInterval()` method to start a timer going in the page. The method `setInterval()` takes two parameters – the first is the code to be called each time the timer fires, and the second is the interval that should occur between each firing of the timer, which is measured in milliseconds. In our example, every 4000 milliseconds, or 4 seconds, the function `swapAdImg()` will be called.

The `setInterval()` method returns a value which is a unique timer id. We can have more than one timer going in a page if we want, and the timer id allows us to reference each individual timer. The main reason for referencing the timer again is to stop it using the `clearInterval()` method, if this is necessary before the browser is closed or a new page is loaded. In the example we don't stop the timer, but if we did want to the code would be:

```
window.clearInterval(timerID);
```

The function that is called every 4 seconds and does the image swapping is `swapAdImg()`:

```
function swapAdImg()
{
  advertIndex++;
  if (advertIndex > advertImgSrcs.length -1)
  {
    advertIndex = 0;
  }

  document.images['imgMainAdvert'].src = advertImgSrcs[advertIndex];
}
```

First the global variable `advertIndex` declared earlier in the page is incremented. It's been made a global variable even though it's only used inside this one function so that the variable retains its value – a local variable would lose its value once the function ends.

All the image `src` values are stored in the array `advertImgSrcs`, which we've also declared as a global variable. The `advertIndex` variable holds the index in this array of the currently loaded image's `src`. If, after variable `advertIndex` is incremented, its value is greater than the number of `src` values in the `advertImgSrcs` array, we set it back to zero. We check this by comparing the value `advertIndex` to the length of the array -1, because array index values start at zero.

In the final line, the `Image` object representing the `<img>` element that displays our advert has its `src` property set to the new advert image source.

Document Events

The `document` object has a number of events dealing with user interaction with the page, for example `click`, `dblclick`, `keydown`, `keypress`, `keyup`, `mousedown`, and `mouseup`. Unfortunately, details of what key or mouse button the user pressed are obtained using different techniques depending on whether the user has a Netscape and Microsoft browser. There is even some difference in the technique between NN4 and NN6 browsers. In Chapters 6 and 7 we'll discuss code that is specific to these browsers, but here we'll stick to code that works for NN4+ and IE4+.

Let's look at an example using the click event, which works for all version 4 browsers and later. Here is the `ClickExample.htm` page:

```
<html>
<head>
  <script language="JavaScript">
    function document_onclick()
    {
      alert('CLICK');
    }

    document.onclick = document_onclick;
  </script>
</head>
<body>
  <p>Document Click Example - Click Anywhere</p>
</body>
</html>
```

We create the function that'll be executed when the document is clicked, the `document_onclick()` function. I've chosen this name to give away its purpose, but it doesn't have to be called this. Then we tell the browser that when the document is clicked the `document_onclick()` function should be executed by setting the `document` object's `onclick` property to reference the function we just created. Note that it's important that the function should exist before the line that sets this property. However, in the case of document, we don't have to worry about where we put the event handler code as we did when setting event handlers for page elements that weren't yet loaded.

In Chapters 6 and 7 when we look at browser specific event handling we'll see how we can access details such as the position of the mouse when the user clicked.

HTML Elements and Events

In older browsers, such as NN4 and IE3, the number of HTML elements that have associated objects and events is quite limited. In Chapters 6 and 7 we'll see that with modern browsers, such as IE4+ and NN6+, most elements have associated objects and events.

Apart from form elements, which we'll be looking at shortly, the element with the most associated events is the `<a>` element. Its events include:

- click (not available in IE3)
- dblclick (not available in IE3 or NN3)
- mouseover
- mouseout (not available in IE3)
- mousedown (not available in IE3 or NN3)
- mouseup (not available in IE3 or NN3)

The good thing about the <a> element is we can wrap it around other elements that don't support events, like the <img> element. We saw this used earlier in this chapter in the rollover and swap image examples.

Let's see the <a> element in use with an example that creates a button based on the <img> element:

```
<html>
<head>
  <script language="JavaScript">
    function imgButton_onmousedown()
    {
      document.images['imgButton'].src = 'DownButton.jpg';
    }
  </script>
</head>
<body>
  <a href="javascript: void(0);"
     onmousedown="imgButton_onmousedown()"
     onmouseup="document.images['imgButton'].src = 'UpButton.jpg'">
  <img src="UpButton.jpg"
       border=0
       name="imgButton"></a>
</body>
</html>
```

Save this as ImgButton.htm. The page looks like that on the left by default. When the button is clicked, the page changes to that shown on the right until the user lets go of the mouse button, when it returns to its default image.

Look at the <a> and <img> element definitions:

```
<a href="javascript: void(0);"
   onmousedown="imgButton_onmousedown()"
   onmouseup="document.images['imgButton'].src = 'UpButton.jpg'">
<img src="UpButton.jpg"
     border=0
     name="imgButton"></a>
```

The <img> element doesn't have the events we need, so we simply wrap it inside an <a> element, which does. The <a> element is only there so we can use its events – we don't want the link to be followed, so we have set the href attribute to javascript: void(0);, which basically does nothing. We could alternatively have used <a href="#"> or <a href="javascript:myFunction();return false;"> for the same effect.

The <a> element has two event handler attributes defined, namely `onmousedown` and `onmouseup`. When the mousedown event fires, the function `imgButton_onmousedown()` is called, which changes the image's `src` property to the *Clicked* image. Although that's the only code I have put in the function, there would normally also be the code associated with the task to be performed when clicking the button. For example, if the button was labeled *view shopping basket*, then the code that showed the shopping basket would be placed here.

The code attached to the `onmouseup` event handler attribute simply swaps the *Clicked* image for the *Click Me* image once the user's mouse button is released.

Note that if we put an `alert()` function in the `imgButton_onmousedown()` function, it would have caused problems. The button remains in the *Clicked* state, because the focus of events now switches away from the element to the alert box that has appeared, so the `onmouseup` event handler code won't get called. Adding the `onmouseout` event handler to the <a> element and setting it to do the same as the `onmouseup` event handler can fix this. It ensures that the button will return to its *Click Me* state.

```
<a href="javascript: void(0);"
   onmousedown="imgButton_onmousedown()"
   onmouseup="document.images['imgButton'].src = 'UpButton.jpg'"
   onmouseout="document.images['imgButton'].src = 'UpButton.jpg'">
```

Form Element Events

The `form` object representing the <form> element has two events, submit and reset – we'll take a look at submit shortly. However, even in older browsers such as NN3+ and IE3.02+, the form elements contained within a <form> element have numerous associated events. The table below lists some of the more common event handlers they can have:

	onclick	**onfocus**	**onblur**	**onchange**	**onselect**	**onkeydown**	**onkeypress**	**onkeyup**
button	X	X	X					
checkbox	X	X	X					
hidden								
option								
password		X	X					
radio	X	X	X					
reset button	X	X	X					
select		X	X	X				
submit button	X	X	X					
text		X	X	X	X			
text area		X	X	X	X	X.4	X.4	X.4

An X indicates that the event handler is available with that form element. If the X has a number after it, the number indicates the browser version it is supported from (by default, the event handlers are available with version 3 browsers onwards).

As with the events we have looked at previously, they can be captured by adding an event handler attribute to the element definition. For example, to capture the `onclick` event of a button, we would write:

```
<input type="button" value="Click Me" onclick="someFunction()">
```

We'll look at the `onkeydown`, `onkeypress` and `onkeyup` events in Chapters 6 and 7 (covering browser-specific code) because they are of more use to us when we want to obtain the key that was pressed. For now, we'll look at the slightly less obvious events, starting with the form's submit event.

Submit Event

The submit event is the most important event for an HTML form. This event fires when a form is submitted by the user, either by clicking a submit button or by pressing *Enter* while in a textbox. However, this event doesn't fire if the form is submitted by using the `form` object's `submit()` method in your code.

The submit event is a great place to put final form checking code before a form is sent to the server, because the form's submission can be cancelled if necessary. It can be cancelled simply by having the event handler (or a function it calls), return the value `false`.

In the example below, *FormSubmitEvent.htm*, the user is asked to enter a number between 1 and 10 in the textbox. If they don't do that, we cancel the form submission:

```
<html>
<head>
  <script language="JavaScript">
    function isFormValid()
    {
      var numberEntered = document.form1.txtNumber.value;

      var isValidNumber = !isNaN(numberEntered);
      var isWithinRange = numberEntered >= 1  && numberEntered <= 10;
      var isFormOk = isValidNumber && isWithinRange;

      if (!isFormOk)
      {
        alert("Please ensure you enter a valid number between 1 and 10");
      }

      return isFormOk;
    }
  </script>
</head>
<body>
<form action="somePage.htm"
      method="POST" name="form1"
      onsubmit="return isFormValid()">
  Enter a number between 1 and 10:<br>
  <input type="text" name=txtNumber>
  <input type="submit" value="Submit">
</form>
</body>
</html>
```

Let's start with the <form> element's definition:

```
<form action="somePage.htm"
      method="POST" name="form1"
      onsubmit="return isFormValid()">
```

The action attribute is set to *somePage.htm*, which you should create a plain HTML page for (or download the page with the code download). Usually, of course, this would be a page with some server-side processing, such as an .asp page, but since we don't deal with server-side processing in this book, we've stuck with an HTML page.

The onsubmit event handler attribute has been added and returns a value from the function isFormValid(), which is created at the top of the page. This function returns either true if the form is valid or false otherwise. If a true value is returned to the event handler, the submit continues as normal, but if it's false the form submission is canceled to give the user the opportunity to correct the form. This is good because it reduces the load on the server and it is also quicker for the user. If the form was only checked on the server, then the user would have to wait while the page was submitted, then checked on the server, and then be redirected to a page telling them they have made an error.

We'll now turn to the function that does the checking when called by the onsubmit event handler:

```
function isFormValid()
{
  var numberEntered = document.form1.txtNumber.value;

  var isValidNumber = !isNaN(numberEntered);
  var isWithinRange = numberEntered >= 1  && numberEntered <= 10;
  var isFormOk = isValidNumber && isWithinRange;

  if (!isFormOk)
  {
    alert("Please ensure you enter a valid number between 1 and 10");
  }

  return isFormOk;
}
```

The variable numberEntered is set to the value in the textbox txtNumber – this is the value we are checking. Then the variables isValidNumber and isWithinRange are set to the results of two expressions, which will be either true or false. These expressions check that the user's input is a number and that it's within range. Using variables like this rather than if statements, which is another way of doing the same thing, makes the code much more readable. The final result of whether the input is valid is placed in the isFormOk variable, which will contain true only if the number is valid *and* the number is within range.

In the if statement, we check if the form is OK, and let the user know if data was invalid. On the final line we return isFormOk – if it contains true, then the form post will continue.

Focus and Blur Events

These events occur when a form element gets the focus of a user's input and when the focus is moved off an element to another part of the page.

The example below, saved as `Focus_BlurEvents.htm`, demonstrates when these events fire.

```
<html>
<body>
<form name="form1">
  <input type="text"
         onfocus="this.value = 'onfocus fired';"
         onblur="this.value = 'onblur fired';">
  <input type="text"
         onfocus="this.value = 'onfocus fired';"
         onblur="this.value = 'onblur fired';">
  <input type="button" value="Button">
</form>
</body>
</html>
```

If you click on (or tab to) either of the two textboxes, the textbox's focus event fires and *onfocus fired* is displayed in the textbox. If you remove the focus from that textbox (by clicking on, or tabbing to, the other textbox), then the blur event fires and *onblur fired* displays in the textbox.

Note the use of the `this` keyword in the code. Inside an event handler it always references the object corresponding to the element the event handler is an attribute of.

The focus can be removed from a textbox by clicking elsewhere in the page, for example on another form element or on the page itself. The focus is also lost if the user switches from the browser window to another window or running program. The blur event can be useful for checking data when the user leaves a form element, but it's important to be careful. Firstly, users often like to fill in forms in the order of information they know, not in the order the elements appear. For example, on an e-commerce form, they may fill in their name and address and skip over the credit card details until later when they have their card to hand. If they tab through each form element and try and go past the card details, then a blur event will occur for these textboxes. If the `onblur` event handling code stops the user from continuing until a valid card number is entered, then this will be inconvenient for the user. Generally, it's much better to check the form just before it's going to be submitted.

Note that unlike the submit event we looked at above, the focus and blur events fire even when the focusing or blurring was due to the use of JavaScript and the element's `focus()` or `blur()` methods.

Change Event

The change event fires when the focus is moved away from a form element, if the entered or selected value has changed since the last time it lost focus.

The example below, *ChangeEvent.htm*, helps demonstrate when the change event fires:

```
<html>
<head>
  <script language="JavaScript">
    function addEventToList(eventText)
    {
      document.form1.txtEventList.value += eventText;
    }
  </script>
</head>
<body>
<form name="form1">
  <input type="text"
         onchange="addEventToList('textbox onChange fired\n')">
  <select size="4" name="select1"
          onchange="addEventToList('select onChange fired\n')">
    <option value="Opt 1">Option 1</option>
    <option value="Opt 2">Option 2</option>
    <option value="Opt 3">Option 3</option>
    <option value="Opt 4">Option 4</option>
    <option value="Opt 5">Option 5</option>
  </select>
  <textarea rows="20" cols="40" name="txtEventList"></textarea>
</form>
</body>
</html>
```

This creates a page with three form elements – a textbox, a select control, and a text area:

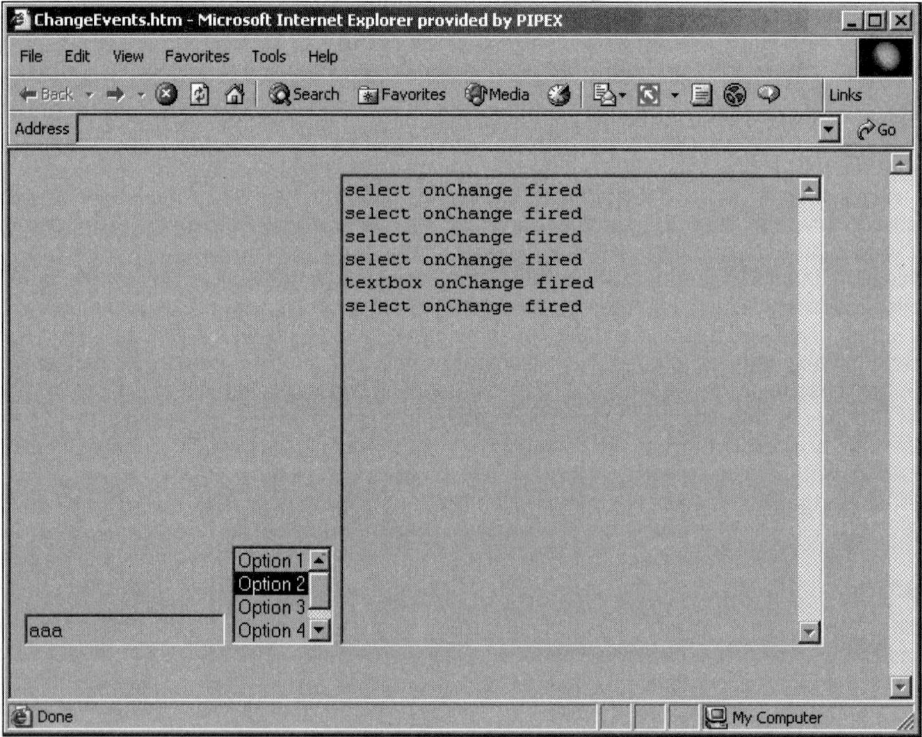

When the textbox or select control's change event fires, it's noted in the text area on the right of the page. Notice that the textbox change event only fires when focus is moved away from the textbox, but the select change event occurs as soon as a new option is chosen.

The `<select>` element has an `onchange` attribute, which calls the `addEventToList()` function to do the actual listing of the event in the text area:

```
<select size="4" name="select1"
        onchange="addEventToList('select onChange fired\n')">
```

The same applies to the textbox, which also has the `onchange` event handler:

```
<input type="text"
       onchange="addEventToList('textbox onChange fired\n')">
```

The function that both of these call is:

```
function addEventToList(eventText)
{
  document.form1.txtEventList.value += eventText;
}
```

This simply adds the string in parameter `eventText`, to the end of the value in the `txtEventList` text area box.

Select Event

The select event fires when the user selects text inside either a textbox or a text area. It fires each time the text that has been selected changes.

Checking the User's Browser

We've discussed the fact that different browsers support, not only different versions of JavaScript, but also different levels of access to the browser objects. Some browsers, like IE4+ and NN6+, allow access to most of the page content. In comparison, IE3.0 provides very limited access to anything more than the form elements and a few other elements, such as `<a>`.

It's therefore very useful to be able to detect the type and version of the browser that the user is viewing our web page with. There are two main techniques of doing this: browser detection and object detection.

Browser Detection

Browsers provide information about themselves via properties of the `navigator` object, which is a property of the `window` object. Its most useful properties are `appName`, which returns a string indicating the name of the browser, and `appVersion`, which returns a string indicating the version of the browser. The *BrowserDetection.htm* page below causes the value of these two properties to be displayed in the page.

```
<html>
<body>
  <script language="JavaScript">
```

```
    document.write(navigator.appName + "<br>");
    document.write(navigator.appVersion);
  </script>
</body>
</html>
```

Try this out in a few browsers if you can. The name of the browser is displayed as:

User's Browser	appName Display in Page
IE3+	*Microsoft Internet Explorer*
NN2+	*Netscape*
Opera 3+	*Opera/Netscape/Microsoft Internet Explorer*

The last one is particularly confusing. Opera actually allows the user (under *Preference / Connections*) to set whether the browser is identified as Opera, Netscape, or Microsoft Internet Explorer.

The version of the browser may be displayed as:

User's Browser	appVersion Display in Page
NN6.1	5.0 (Windows; en-GB)
IE6.0	4.0 (compatible; MSIE 6.0; Windows NT 5.0; UUNET; Q312461)
IE3.02	2.0 (compatible; MSIE 3.02; Update a; Windows 95)
NN3.03	3.03 (Win95; I)
Opera 3.6	3.03 (Win95; I)

You can see that the variations are quite extensive. NN2.0-4.x supplies the exact version number, while NN6.x just shows 5.0. IE seems to supply the version of NN that it is most compatible with – from IE4.0 onwards, only the version number 4.0 is given.

In conclusion, using the `appVersion` and `appName` properties to determine the version and type of browser is quite error prone.

Object Detection

An alternative to browser detection is to check to see if the browser supports the object we need for our code to work.

In Chapter 6 we'll see that various properties of the `document` object such as `all` and `layers` are commonly needed for DHTML in version 4.x browsers. However, only IE4+ supports `document.all` and only NN4 supports `document.layers`. Code such as in *ObjectDetection.htm* below can be used to check whether an object is available to us before we use it:

```
<html>
<body>
  <script language="JavaScript">
    if (document.all)
    {
      // Code using document.all goes here
    }
    else if (document.layers)
    {
      // Code using document.layers goes here
    }
  </script>
</body>
</html>
```

Note that this page won't execute any code for some Opera browsers an NN6, which don't support `document.layers` or `document.all`. (Opera 5.0+ browsers whose `appName` property returns *Microsoft Internet Explorer* support `document.all`.)

We'll see more of this technique in Chapter 6.

Summary

In this chapter we've covered the basics of how JavaScript can access various parts of the browser and various HTML elements within the page. Most of what has been covered in this chapter will work even on older browsers, like NN3 and IE3, though it still proves useful with modern browsers too.

We saw that the browser makes itself accessible to the web programmer via various objects, which can be used in JavaScript. The hierarchy and order of these objects is determined by the Document Object Model (DOM) of the browser version in question. We looked at the basic DOM that is supported by both older and newer browsers. This DOM is simple, and quite limited when compared to the sophisticated DOMs supported by IE4+ and NN6+. We saw that the browser window is represented by the `window` object, and the page inside the window by the `document` object. It's via properties of the `document` object that we can access a limited number of HTML elements including forms, form elements (such as textboxes), images, and links.

In the second half of the chapter, we looked at a means of interaction with the user via browser events. Many of the browser objects we encountered in the first half of the chapter have events we can connect code to. This allows us to react when a user clicks a button, loads a page, and so on.

We concluded the chapter by looking at some basic browser checking techniques.

In the next chapter, we'll be looking at how to open new browser windows and manipulate them with JavaScript. We'll also see how we can code across frames in a browser.

5

- Built-in windows
- Creating your own windows
- Frames and framesets
- Image Viewer Application: Part 1

Author: Stephen Williams

Windows and Frames

Windows in the real world provide viewing ports that allow us to look out of buildings and view the outside world, or inside to view the contents. In the same way windows in programming provide view ports so content can be displayed, or viewed, by the user. Similarly, the browser window allows us to see the contents of an HTML document.

Traditionally when you click on a hyperlink to open, retrieve, and view a new document it will be displayed within the same window. However, documents can be presented in multiple views; HTML allows different documents to be presented in the same window (by replacing a previous document), or independently in sub-windows. Multiple views offer designers a way to keep certain information visible, while other views are scrolled or replaced. For example, within the same window, one frame might display a static banner, a second a navigation menu, and a third the main document that can be scrolled through or replaced by navigating in the second frame.

In this chapter, we'll start by looking at some of the built-in mechanisms for displaying information. Then we'll look at how we can present documents in other windows, commonly known as the pop-up window, and how to write JavaScript to communicate between different windows. Finally we'll look at frames, which are sub-windows within a window, and allow multiple documents to be viewed adjacent to one another simultaneously.

Basic Built-In Dialog Windows

The browser provides JavaScript with three different built-in popup windows, which are the alert, confirm, and prompt modal dialog windows. Modal dialog windows are windows that open on top of a parent window and remain above the parent window until closed; the user cannot interact with the parent window until the dialog window is closed.

These three built-in dialog windows do not have any available properties for you to change the appearance of the dialogs. So, basically you're stuck with the way they look and function, or are you? Well, yes, if you want to use the built-in dialogs; however, these dialog windows are useful for many situations. As we'll see shortly, there are ways that you can create your own alternatives. First, though, let's take a closer look at the built-in dialogs.

The Alert Dialog

The alert dialog is the simplest and most often used of the common built-in dialogs. Its intended use is to provide warning information, or hints, to a user, often informing them that something is not quite right and an error is possibly about to occur or an intended action can not be completed.

Its use is very straightforward:

```
window.alert("Hello World!! ");

// Alternative shorter form
alert("Hello World!!");
```

The example above shows two ways in which you can create an alert box. The `alert()` method is a method of the `window` object and so can be called as such. However, the `window` object is the top-level object within a browser window and methods and properties of the `window` object do not always need the `window` reference when calling them, as the browser automatically infers it. Hence the second alternative, which is more commonly used to create pop-up windows.

When creating the alert dialog we simply call the `alert()` method and pass it a single parameter that is a string to be displayed. The figure below shows an example of an alert dialog created using either of the statements above.

The alert dialog is very useful when it comes to debugging your JavaScript code. Instead of passing an actual string of characters as the parameter, it is equally valid to pass a variable. JavaScript will attempt to convert the variable to a string value and display that string. In the following section of sample code, each iteration of the loop calls the `alert()` method and passes `i` as the argument.

```
for (var i = 0; i < 5; i++)
{
  alert(i);
}
```

Each time the `alert()` method is called, JavaScript converts the value of `i` to a string and displays a string representation of that variable's value. As soon as the `alert()` method is reached within a section of code, the alert dialog is displayed with its message, and processing of the script halts. In this example, the `for` loop stops executing at the point at which the `alert()` method is called and any lines that follow the `alert()` method will not be executed.

The alert dialog remains on screen, and script processing halted, until a user clicks the *OK* button. When the user clicks the button, the dialog disappears and the remaining JavaScript continues to be processed. In this example it means when the alert dialog is closed the `for` loop continues to execute immediately after the line containing `alert()` method.

If the alert dialog didn't halt the script when it was created, then the example above would create and display 5 alert boxes in rapid succession. In this case, that wouldn't be too much of a problem, but you could imagine in loops that consist of 15 iterations, let alone several 10s or 100s of iterations, this could be a problem as they would appear quicker than the user could close them.
Placing `alert()` statements strategically in your code whilst developing it allows you to check the values of variables and hopefully identify any rogue values that are causing your script problems. One point to note, though, is if you use this method to aid debugging scripts, watch out when you place alerts inside loops.

If a loop iterates more than about 15 times it can be very tedious looking at the variable's value each time. In these cases, "wrap" the `alert()` statement inside an `if` statement that will allow the alert dialog to be called only for the first few iterations of the loop; often five or less times is enough. The same is true for users of your web pages; they will loose patience very quickly if they are hit with lots of alert dialog boxes. On live web pages use the alert dialog very sparing and only where absolutely necessary.

The Confirm Dialog

The confirm dialog is intended to be used to ask a user a question and therefore make a decision. This dialog provides a user with a message and two button: *OK* and *Cancel*.

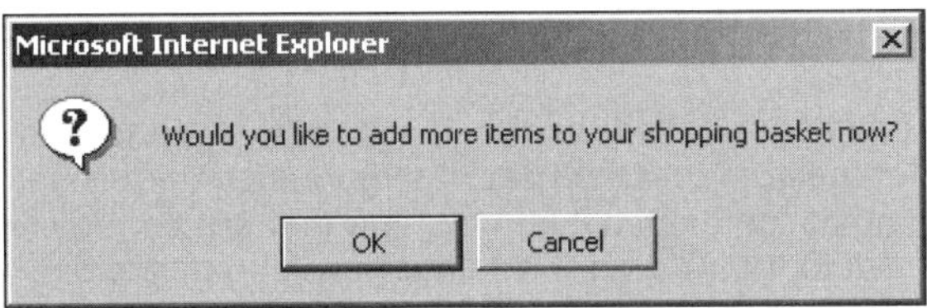

To create a confirm dialog use the `confirm()` method and pass a single string parameter (the message to be displayed), similar to the `alert()` method:

```
var msg = "Would you like to add more items to your shopping basket now?";
if (confirm(msg))
{
  // Code to allow user to select more items
  alert("Clicked OK button.");
}
else
{
  // Code to allow user to pay for items in basket now
  alert("Clicked Cancel button.");
}
```

When the user clicks on either the *OK* or *Cancel* button the `confirm()` method returns a Boolean value. Clicking on *OK* returns `true`, while clicking on *Cancel* returns `false`. The returned value can then be captured and used in an `if...else` statement to execute appropriate code based on a user's decision.

The Prompt Dialog

The final built-in dialog is the prompt dialog window. Calling the prompt method displays a dialog with a message, an input field, and two buttons (*OK* and *Cancel*). Use the `prompt()` method to display a dialog so that the user can input a value. This value is then returned when the user clicks the *OK* button.

The sample code below shows how the prompt dialog could be used to request from a user what quantity of a particular item they require.

```
function requestQuantity(item)
{
  var msg = "How many " + item + " would you like?";
  var x = parseInt(prompt(msg, "1"));
  if (isNaN(x) || x < 0)
  {
    if (confirm("Value entered was not a valid number! Try Again?"))
    {
      x = requestQuantity(item);
    }
    else
    {
      x = 0;
    }
  }
  return x;
}

var qty = requestQuantity("Apples");
```

In this piece of code a function is called, `requestQuantity()`, and a single parameter is passed that is the string name of the item that the user has requested (in this case "`Apples`"). The function accepts the argument and concatenates it into a string that will be the message to the user. The second line makes the call to the `prompt()` method, passing to it two arguments: the first argument is the message to be displayed, and the second is a default value for the input box. If you do not specify an initial value for the input box, the dialog box displays *undefined*; but in this instance we have provided a default value of 1.

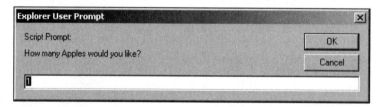

When the user clicks the *OK* button, the value of the input box is returned (pressing the *Cancel* button returns `null`). Incidentally if you do not want the default value of *undefined* displayed when no second argument is passed, use `""` as the second argument:

```
var x = prompt(myMsg, "");
```

Our `requestQuantity()` function passes the return value from the prompt dialog to the `parseInt()` method, which attempts to convert the returned value to a whole number and stores the result in the variable `x`. If `x` is not a number `parseInt()` returns a value of `NaN` (Not a Number). Note that `x` is also tested to make sure it is not less than 0, as in this case you cannot have a negative number of apples!

The subsequent code within the function then tests the value stored in `x`. If a valid number has not been supplied the user is shown a confirm dialog to ask them to enter a valid number. If they enter a valid number, `x` is returned from our function. If the user decides they don't wish to try again `x` is set to 0. Finally, once the checking has been completed the function exits by returning the value stored in `x`.

Creating New Browser Windows

In the previous chapter, we saw that the `window` object is the top-level object for each HTML document, which represents a browser window. The JavaScript runtime engine within the browser creates a new `window` object for each document opened. You can open a new pop-up window by calling the `open()` method of the `window` object. Each new window opened is capable of being sized, positioned on screen, and a number of decorative features enabled or disabled. A pop-up window is independent of the window that opened it, the **opener** window (we'll talk more about the opener window later in the chapter). As each new window opened is independent of the opener window, a parent-child hierarchical relationship does not exists between the windows and therefore the opener window can be closed without automatically closing the newly opened window. Therefore you should be aware that if a user closes the opener window, the pop-up window could remain open. This can be a problem, especially if the pop-up window attempts to communicate back to the opener window as it could throw JavaScript errors. As we will see later in the chapter there are ways to prevent the errors from being raised.

The open method accepts three optional arguments, so in its simplest form a new window can be opened by calling the following line of code:

```
window.open();
```

and because `open()` is a method of the `window` object the reference to the `window` object can be left off, simplifying further to give:

```
open();
```

In this instance, a call to the `window` object creates a new empty window. In its own right this piece of code is pretty useless – a blank empty window is created. No page is loaded, its size and appearance is dependent on the default values of the browser being used, and its properties cannot be altered. As we will see shortly we can add a number of items to this code to make the opened window more useful.

Note that although the ability to use the shorter form to open a window (that is without specifying the reference to the `window` object) can help to make your code smaller and simpler, if someone else wants to make changes to a page that you have coded, it can make your code difficult to read. So it's usually better to use the fully qualified form.

As I mentioned above, the `open()` method allows three optional arguments to be specified. These arguments can determine the location of newly opened windows, their target name, and the features that will be displayed within them. We will look at setting the windows' features in the next section.

The first argument provided is a string specifying the URL to open in the new window, and the second argument is a string specifying the window name to use in the `target` attribute of a `<form>` or `<a>` tag. Like JavaScript variables, the window's `name` must only contain alphanumeric or underscore (_) characters.

The following simple HTML document (helloPopup.html):

```
<html><body>Hello World! I'm in a Popup Window.</body></html>
```

can be displayed in a pop-up window called helloWin using the following line of code:

```
window.open("helloPopup.html", "helloWin");
```

If the window name is not supplied, and you do not supply the third argument for the window features (as in this example above) all of the browser window's features are displayed by default; in other words, all of the menus, toolbars, and other features. So this example will open a new window that will look identical to the browser window that opened it, with the exception that the hello.html document is displayed in it.

Once the new pop-up window is opened, the window name, specified by the second argument, can be used in other browser windows to target new documents to be displayed in this pop-up window. To do this, you need to add the target attribute to an <a> tag and give it the value of the window name:

```
<a href="myDoc.html" target="helloWin">View My Doc</a>
```

Later in the chapter we will see how JavaScript can be used to change the document displayed in the window.

A new window can be opened directly from an event handler; in order to do this though you must specify the reference to the window object. In fact, this is true for any of the methods and properties of the window object, inside event handlers always use a reference to the window object.

```
//This will open a new window
<a href="#" onclick="window.open('hello.html', 'helloWin')">Click Me</a>

// This does not open a new window
<a href="#" onclick="open('hello.html', 'helloWin')">Click Me</a>
```

In JavaScript, a call to open() without specifying an object name is equivalent to document.open(), when used directly inside the event handler. Again we see how using the fully-qualified code is more beneficial than using a shorter form, in this case the reasons being even more extreme as the example will not work using the shorter coding form.

An alternative approach to circumvent this issue is to call a function from the event handler and in the body of the function you can make a call to the open() method.

```
function createWindow()
{
   open("hello.html", "helloWin");
   // Additional code after opening a new window
}

// This is fine to open a new window, as the open method
// is called from inside a function
<a href="#" onclick="createWindow()">Click Me</a>
```

Using a function in this way to create a new pop-up window has the added benefit in that you can add extra code after the window is open that is easier to read than if the code was all included in the event handler.

Window Chrome

Browser windows come with a variety of features, such as menus, toolbars and scrollbars; these features are sometimes known as decoration or **chrome**. We can specify which of these features are displayed in the window by using the third argument of the `open()` method. This third argument is a string of comma-delimited name-value pairs (in other words *`name=value,name=value`*), where the name is the name of the feature that is to be set.

It is important to note that this string should not contain any spaces. If spaces are included the newly opened window may not display as expected; features listed after the space may not be applied. Some of the latest browsers, notably IE5+ and Netscape 6+, are a bit more lenient on the matter – older browsers are not.

The example below shows the call we made earlier to open a new window displaying the `hello.html` document. This time, though, we have added the third argument to specify the width and height on the new pop-up window:

```
window.open("hello.html", "helloWin", "width=200,height=200");
```

Executing this statement produces a small browser window, which is 200 pixels wide and 200 pixels high:

Notice now that when the third argument is supplied to the `open()` method all other features and properties are removed, except for those explicitly specified in the `open()` method's parameters. Therefore you do not have to explicitly turn features off, only turn them on.

In addition to setting the width and height features shown above there are a number of other features that can be included in the make-up of the third argument string. Some of these features are browser-specific, whereas others are more generic and can be used in most browser. The table below details the main features that can be set in both Internet Explorer and Netscape version 4+ browsers.

Window Feature	Description
`directories`	If `yes`, creates the standard browser bookmark directory button bar (such as What's New and What's Cool? with Netscape browsers and Channel Guide with Internet Explorer).
`height`	Specifies the height of the window in pixels.

Table continued on following page

Window Feature	Description
`location`	If `yes`, creates the location bar in the new window.
`menubar`	If `yes`, creates the menu at the top of the window.
`resizable`	If `yes`, allows a user to resize the window.
`left`	Specifies the distance the new window is placed from the left-hand side of the screen in pixels.
`top`	Specifies the distance the new window is placed from the top of the screen in pixels.
`scrollbars`	If `yes`, creates horizontal and vertical scrollbars when the document grows larger than the window dimensions.
`status`	If `yes`, creates the status bar at the bottom of the window.
`titlebar`	If `yes`, creates a window with a title bar.
`toolbar`	If `yes`, creates the standard browser toolbar, with buttons such as *Back* and *Forward*.
`width`	Specifies the width of the window in pixels.

It's important to note that once a new pop-up window is created with certain features enabled or disabled, these features cannot be altered and are fixed for the lifetime of the window. The exceptions to this rule are the window position and size, as we will see in the next section.

With IE4+ browsers, a fourth optional argument can be supplied to the `open()` method, which has a Boolean value; either `true` or `false`. This argument determines whether the URL of a document that is loaded into the new window should create a new entry in the window's history or replace the current entry.

By setting this fourth argument to `true`, when the window is opened the current history entry is overwritten by the new page being loaded. If you use this fourth argument, be aware that the user will not be able to navigate back to a previous page in the pop-up window because the history no longer has a reference to it – users can find this very irritating.

Creating Dependent Pop-up Windows

Earlier I mentioned that pop-up windows are created independently of the opener. This need not necessarily be true; it is possible to create pop-up windows that are dependent on the opener window. In this instance, closing the opener window will automatically close the pop-up window too.

With Netscape 4+ browsers you can include a proprietary feature name, called `dependent`, that will create a pop-up window and is dependent on the opener window. In this case, closing the opener widow will cause the popup window to close too. In Netscape 6+ browsers you can also add a second proprietary feature name, called `modal`, when the pop-up window is displayed, which prevents the user from interacting with, or switching to, the opener window until the pop-up window is closed.

```
var helloWin = window.open("hello.html", "helloWin",
"width=200,height=200,dependent=yes,modal=yes");
```

These two features are not supported by Internet Explorer browsers, instead with Internet Explorer version 4+ browsers a new type of pop-up window is available for creating modal windows, through the use of the `showModalDialog()` method. Also, the loading of new pages and script execution in the opener window is halted when the modal window is opened until the user closes it.

The `showModalDialog()` method accepts three arguments. The first is required and is the URL of a document to be loaded and displayed. The second and third arguments are both optional, so in its simplest form the following statement can be used to create a modal dialog window:

```
showModalDialog("hello.html");
```

The second argument specifies the variables that can be used in the document displayed. This argument can be passed any type of value, including an array of values. Scripts running in the page loaded into the dialog box can extract the values passed by the caller from the `dialogArguments` property of the window object. So if we opened a modal dialog window as follows:

```
showModalDialog("hello.html", "modal example");
```

In the page loaded in the modal dialog window, we could obtain the value of the second argument using the following:

```
var inArg = window.dialogArguments;
alert(inArg);
```

This would then display an alert box with the message *modal example*.

Finally, the third argument is a string that specifies the window features for the dialog box, using a list of semicolon-delimited name-value pairs. The following line creates a modal dialog window 350 pixels high and 300 pixels wide, which is resizable and has no status bar.

```
showModalDialog("hello.html", "modal example", "dialogHeight:250px;
dialogWidth:300px; resizable:yes; status:no;");
```

By default, modal dialogs windows, created with the `showModalDialog()` method, are centred on screen. This can be overridden using the `dialogLeft` and `dialogTop` properties to position the dialog relative to the top left corner of the window. The following table lists the different features that can be used, with their possible values and their default value.

Feature Name	Values	Default	Description
`dialogHeight`	Height in pixels		Sets the height of the dialog window. Minimum is 100 pixels.
`dialogLeft`	Left in pixels		Sets the left position of the dialog window relative to the upper-left corner of the desktop.
`dialogTop`	Top in pixels		Sets the top position of the dialog window relative to the upper-left corner of the desktop.

Table continued on following page

Feature Name	Values	Default	Description
dialogWidth	Width in pixels		Sets the width of the dialog window. Minimum is 100 pixels.
center	yes/no/1/0/on /off	yes	Specifies whether to center the dialog window within the desktop.
edge	sunken/raised	raised	Specifies the edge style of the dialog window.
help	yes/no/1/0/on /off	yes	Specifies whether the dialog window displays the context-sensitive Help icon.
resizable	yes/no/1/0/on /off	no	Specifies whether the dialog window has fixed dimensions.
scroll	yes/no/1/0/on /off	yes	Specifies whether the dialog window displays scrollbars.
status	Yes/no/1/0/on /off	Varies	Specifies whether the dialog window displays a status bar.

The `showModalDialog()` method also returns a value. However, there would be little point in returning a reference to a window object as the script in the opener window is halted until the user closes the modal dialog window. Instead the window returns a value from the `returnValue` property of its `window` object. Before closing the window, JavaScript can set this property and when the window closes send the value back to the opener window.

So, in its entirety, you can open a modal dialog using code similar to the following:

```
var returnedValue = showModalDialog("hello.html", "modal example",
"dialogHeight:250px; dialogWidth:300px; resizable:yes; status:no;");
alert(returnedValue);
```

When the dialog window is closed, script execution in the opener window will continue and the alert box will display the value that was returned, from the window object `returnValue` property.

Positioning and Sizing a Window

When the `open()` method of the `window` object is called, the new window opens, and the method returns a reference to the newly opened window. Note that, in contrast to the built-in dialog, the execution of scripts in the opener window continues once the pop-up window is open. The window reference returned from the `open()` method can be stored in a variable and used at a later point to access methods and properties of the new window.

```
var helloWin = window.open("hello.html", "helloWin", "width=200,height=200");
```

Sometimes it is more striking to a user to move the pop-up window to the center of the screen. To do this, we need to know the width and height of the user's display, which can be obtained from the screen object, as well as the width and height of the pop-up window. The example below shows how you can achieve this.

```
// Center a popup window on screen
var w = 200;
var h = 200;
var x = (screen.width - w) / 2;
var y = (screen.height - h) / 2;
var chrome = "width=" + w + ",height=" + h + ",left=" + x + ",top=" + y;
var helloWin = open("hello.html", "helloWin", chrome);
```

The width and height of the pop-up window are stored in the w and h variables, respectively. The x and y co-ordinates are calculated for the windows top left corner, in order to position the window in the center of the screen. The next line creates a string for the features argument of the open() method and stores it in the chrome variable. Finally, the next line creates the pop-up window.

A useful method when a new window is opened is the focus() method of the window object. When one or more pop-up windows are opened often these additional windows can become hidden behind one another. Use the focus() method to navigate to a specific window or frame, and give it focus.

```
var helloWin = open("hello.html", "helloWin", "width=200,height=200");
hellowWin.focus();
```

Giving focus to a window brings the window to the top of all the windows on the screen.

Updating a Window's Content

Once the pop-up window has been opened you will, at some point, want to change the document of that window. With JavaScript there are two ways that you can do this: by changing the location to view a different HTML document, or by writing the document dynamically.

Window objects possess a `location` property that can be used to point the window to a new document location. Setting this property to a new URL will cause the browser to retrieve a new document and display it in the window, as you can see below.

```
var helloWin = open("hello.html", "helloWin", "width=200,height=200");
helloWin.location = "goodbye.html";
```

In the previous chapter you saw the `document` object and its `write()` method for changing the contents of a page as the page is downloading. Every window possesses a `document` object and the `write()` method can be used to write new content to the window. When the `write()` method is used in this situation a completely new document is created, replacing the document that was present.

There are at least two good reasons why you would want to write a new HTML document with JavaScript.

- The HTML is small and web connections can be slow
- The HTML depends on some other data currently stored within the browser

So, let's have a look at how you would write a new document within a window.

```
var htmlStr = "<html><body>JavaScript says 'Hello World'</body></html>"
var helloWin = open("hello.html", "helloWin", chrome);

helloWin.document.open();
helloWin.document.write(htmlStr);
helloWin.document.close();
```

Before JavaScript can write a new document, the `open()` method of the `document` object must be called. This prepares the browser to remove the current document and create a new document. After the call to the `open()` method, content can be written using the `write()` method. Finally, the `document.close()` method has to be called, which closes the open document and prevents any more data being written to the newly created document.

Repositioning and Resizing a Window

A problem that you may encounter is that you can't guarantee that the window is visible to the user. For example, they may have moved the window off to the side of the screen at an earlier point in time. Window objects have a method called `moveTo()`, which allows JavaScript to move the window to a location on screen.

```
var helloWin = open("hello.html", "helloWin", "width=200,height=200");
hellowWin.moveTo(100, 200);
```

The `moveTo()` method accepts two arguments, the x and y coordinate values of the window, in pixels, of the browser window's top left corner. The example above moves the `helloWin` window to a position 100 pixels from the left-hand side of the screen and 200 pixels from the top of the screen.

There is probably a good chance that if you have given the focus to a window, and repositioned it on screen for the user's attention, the content of the pop-up window will have changed too. In this case you may want to resize the window, especially if you have made the window non-resizable. It is possible to do this by using the `resizeTo()` method of the `window` object.

```
helloWin.location = "goodbye.html";
var width = 300;
var height = 200;
helloWin.resizeTo(width, height);
```

Netscape 6+ browsers make the job of resizing pop-up windows even easier. The `window` object in this browser has a new method called `sizeToContent()`. By calling this method, on the pop-up window, you don't even have to calculate the dimensions to set the window to; simply call the method and the browser will do all the work for you!

```
helloWin.sizeToContent();
```

The use of the methods we've seen so far in this section have been used to reposition and resize the pop-up window from another window, by using a reference to the window and calling the methods for that window. Depending on your needs it maybe more advantageous to call the methods from inside the pop-up window itself after the document has loaded. To do this, simply create a function, which in this example is called `reposition()`, and call the function after the documents has loaded.

```
// Resize and Center a pop-up window on screen
function reposition()
{
   var w, h;
   if (window.sizeToContent)
   {
      sizeToContent();
      w = outerWidth;
      h = outerHeight;
   }
   else
   {
      if (document.width)
         w = document.width
      else if (document.body.scrollWidth)
         w = document.body.scrollWidth + 5
      else if (document.documentElement.scrollWidth)
         w = document.body.scrollWidth + 5
      else
         w = screen.width / 3;

      if (document.height)
         h = document.height
      else if (document.body.scrollHeight)
         h = document.body.scrollHeight + 20
      else if (document.documentElement.scrollHeight)
         h = document.body.scrollHeight + 20
      else
         h = screen.height / 3;

      resizeTo(w, h);
   }
   var x = (screen.width - w) / 2;
   var y = (screen.height - h) / 2;
   moveTo(x, y);
}
```

The first part of the function calculates the width and height of the window and stores the values in the `w` and `h` variables. An `if...else` statement is used to determine if the browser has the `sizeToContent()` window object method available (as with Netscape 6+ browsers) or not. If it is, then we call the `sizeToContent()` method and then obtain the `width` and `height` properties of the window, using the `outerWidth` and `outerHeight` properties respectively, after the window has been resized.

If the browser does not support the `sizeToContent()` window object method, we have to obtain the dimensions of the document and manually resize the window using the `resizeTo()` window method. A set of `if...else` blocks are used to obtain the document width and another to obtain the document height.

The `width` and `height` properties of the `document` object provide the values for the width and height to set the window to in Netscape 4 browsers. The `scrollWidth` and `scrollHeight` properties of the `document.body` object provide the values of the width and height in Internet Explorer 4.x and 5.x browsers, and these properties of the `document.documentElement` object in Internet Explorer 6+ browsers. Note also an extra value has been added to both the width and height with Internet Explorer browsers to take into account the window frame dimensions itself. Finally, the `else` block terminates with a call to the `resizeTo()` method.

Once the window has been resized properly the location to place the window at on screen can be calculated, the values stored in the x and y variables, and the function exits after a call to the moveTo() method.

One final point to note: for Netscape 4 browsers to be resizable you will need to set the resizable feature to yes. If the feature is not set, it will be by default set to no, and a call now to resizeTo() will do nothing.

Communicating Between Windows

So far, we have seen how to create a new window and access the built-in methods and properties of that window from the window that opened it. If you include your own custom functions and variables within a document, they can be accessed from the opener window in the same fashion as the built-in methods and properties:

```
var winName = window.open("someDoc.html", "winTargetName",
"width=300,height=200");

// Call a function in another window
winName.customFunctionName()

// Obtaining the value of a variables from another window
var obj = winName.variableName

// Setting a variables value in another window
winName.variableName = obj
```

Let's have a look at an example of this. Imagine the someDoc.html file used in the above example contains a form that is named userDetails. The opener window opens a pop-up window with the page loaded and wants to set the values of some of the fields within the form. The following code shows how you might achieve this using object properties:

```
var popupForm = winName.document.userDetails;
popupForm.age.value = "15";
popupForm.city.value = "London";
```

A reference to the form within the document loaded in the pop-up window is first created and stored in the popupForm variable. We have used popupForm to store a reference to the form to make our subsequent code smaller and easier to read. Then the values of two fields, named age and city, within the form are set.

The only drawback with the example above is that you have to know the name of the form and the fields within the form in advance. Any changes made to the form or renaming of elements would mean you would also have to make changes in the opener window too. To avoid this problem it can be far easier to include in the someDoc.html file a function that we can pass the form field values to from the opener window. This function can take care of setting the values of the form fields for use, and the opener window does not need to know anything about the form in the pop-up window. The example below shows this alternative, using a method.

```
var popupForm = winName.document.userDetails;
popupForm.setFormDetails(15, "London");
```

Well, this is good, but you're probably now wondering about communicating between windows in the opposite direction – from the pop-up window back to the opener window. It is no coincidence that I have been calling the window opening the pop-up window the "opener" window. The `window` object has a property called `opener` and this property stores a reference back to the window that opened it, which means methods and properties in this opening window can be accessed in the exact same way:

```
// Call a function in the window that opened this window
opener.customFunctionName()

// Obtaining the value of a variables from the window that opened this window
var obj = opener.variableName

// Setting a variables value in the window that opened this window
opener.variableName = obj
```

So, for example, if you wanted to set the value of a form text field from a pop-up window, after the user has completed some interaction with the pop-up window, you could use the following piece of code within the pop-up window:

```
var ageValue = winName.document.userDetails.age.value;

// Setting a form field value in the window that opened this pop-up window
opener.document.masterDetails.age.value = ageValue
```

where `masterDetails` and `age` are the names of the form and the text (or hidden) field control in the opener window.

As you can see from these example the only difference when communicating back and forth between the windows is the window reference itself; obtaining and setting property values and using methods is the same.

Closing Windows

You may have now realised closing pop-up windows can cause problems to occur. What if the user has closed a window and JavaScript wants to access its properties or methods? We know what our code is doing and therefore if the window should be open or not, but we cannot guarantee what the user does with the window. Thankfully, window objects come equipped with the `closed` property, which we can use for an occasion such as this:

```
if (windowRef && windowRef.closed)
{
   alert("Doh! The window has been closed.")
}
else
{
   windowRef.someMethod()
}
```

If the window object is not present, or the window has been closed, and we don't check that this is the case before trying to use a method of the window object, JavaScript will throw an error because the window object or the method will not be available.

Once a pop-up window has been opened it is nice to provide your users with a sensible and easy to use means to close the popup window. The window object provides a method, called `close()`, that allows you to do just this.

```
// Close a window from a function
function destroy(windowRef)
{
   if (windowRef && !windowRef.closed)
      windowRef.close()
}
```

The `destroy()` function above allows you to close a window safely. The function accepts as a parameter a reference to a window object. It then tests the window exists and is not closed before invoking the window's `close()` method.

We can now use this `destroy()` function to close a window, which can be either the opener or a pop-up window, by passing to the function a reference to the window object that needs to be closed.

```
// Close the window using a link
<a href="javascript:destroy(window.myWin); return false;">Close Window</a>

// Close a window using a form button
<form>
  <input type="button" value="Close Window" onclick="destroy(window.myWin)">
</form>

// Close the window containing this form is located in
<form>
  <input type="button" value="Close Window" onclick="destroy(window)">
</form>
```

Finally, we should mention the `onunload` event handler. This event handler can be included in the `<body>` tag of a document and fires after the window has been requested to close. JavaScript code can be attached to this event handler that cleans up before the window is completely destroyed.

```
<html>
<head>
<script language="JavaScript">
function destroy(windowRef)
{
   if (windowRef && !windowRef.closed)
      windowRef.close()
}

function sendData()
{
   var userAge = document.fData.age.value
   if (window.opener)
      window.opener.document.fData.age.value = userAge
}
</script>
```

```
</head>
<body onunload="sendData()">
   Example of using the unload event handler
<form name="fData">
   Enter Your age: <input type="text" name="age" value="0" size=2><br>
   <input type="button" value="Close Window" onclick="destroy(window)">
</form>
</body>
</html>
```

The example code above would be used in a pop-up window; the user can enter a value for their age in the form text field and then click on the button to close the window. When the pop-up window closes, the `onunload` event handler triggers calling the `sendData()` function. This function obtains the value of the text field and returns it to a field in the form, with the same names, in the opener window.

Although this example is a bit simplistic, you can see how this technique can be very useful – it allows data that is stored in a pop-up window to be returned back to the opener window before it is lost completely.

Custom Dialog Windows

We've now covered most of what you need to know about creating new windows and how to communicate between the different windows. Earlier in the chapter, I mentioned that you could use these techniques to replace the built-in dialogs. In this final section about pop-up windows we will see how to create your own pop-up window to replace the alert dialog.

To create our own custom alert dialog the dialog must contain a place to display the alert message and a button so that the user can close the dialog after reading the message. The following HTML page (`alertWin.html`) does exactly this:

```
<html>
<head>
<title>Custom Alert Example</title>
<script language="JavaScript">
<!--
var dlgAlert = null

function showAlertDialog(width, height, msg)
{
  var isOpen = (dlgAlert && !dlgAlert.closed)
  if (!isOpen)
  {
    var x = (screen.width - width) / 2;
    var y = (screen.height - height) / 2;
    var chrome = "width=" + width + ",height=" + height
                      + ",left=" + x + ",top=" + y;
    dlgAlert = open("about:blank", "dlgAlert", chrome);
  }

  var htmlStr = "";
  htmlStr += "<html><head><title>Alert</title></head><body>";
  htmlStr += "<form><table>";
```

```
    htmlStr += "<tr><th>Alert Message</th></tr>";
    htmlStr += "<tr><td>" + msg + "</td></tr>";
    htmlStr += "<tr><td><input type='button' value='OK'";
    htmlStr += "onclick='window.close()'></td></tr>";
    htmlStr += "</table></form>";
    htmlStr += "</body></html>";

    dlgAlert.document.open();
    dlgAlert.document.write(htmlStr);
    dlgAlert.document.close();

    dlgAlert.focus();
}
// -->
</script>
</head>

<body
<form>
   <input type="button" value="Show Alert"
        onclick="showAlertDialog(200, 150, 'This is a custom Alert Dialog
Window')">
</form>
</body>
</html>
```

The code produces a fairly innocuous page, with only a simple button presented. When the button is clicked, the `onclick` event handler of the form button fires the `showAlertDialog()` function. This function is solely responsible for creating a custom alert dialog window. It accepts three parameters: the width of the window (in pixels), the height of the window (in pixels), and a string that represents the message to be presented to the user.

The first line of the `showAlertDialog()` function checks to see if the alert dialog window is already open and stores a Boolean value in `isOpen`. If the window isn't already open, the function creates a pop-up window, sized using the values of width and height arguments and centered on the screen. A reference to the newly opened window is stored in the global `dlgAlert` variable. In this example, instead of using a URL to open an HTML document in the pop-up window `about:blank` is used, which informs the browser to open a window with a blank document.

Testing the pop-up window is already open is required in case the `showAlertDialog()` function was called before the pop-up window is closed. Trying to open a window that is already open will cause JavaScript errors to be raised.

Once the pop-up window is open, a string is built that contains the HTML source for the document, and with it the alert message to the user from the `msg` parameter, to be displayed in the pop-up window. The HTML formatted string stored in the `htmlStr` variable is then used to create a new document to be displayed in the pop-up window. Note that we have built up a string rather than call the `document.write()` method multiple times. Finally the `focus()` method is called to make sure the window is the topmost browser window bringing the custom alert dialog window to the attention of the user.

As a simple example this works very well. There are several things you can do to improve the example for your own needs.

The string built up to produce the source for the HTML document to be displayed has not been styled. You can add extra information to format the document so that it will integrate with the design of your web site or web application.

The pop-up window is not a modal window, but adding the `dependent` feature when creating the pop-up window will automatically allow the pop-up window to be closed when the opener window is closed in Netscape 4+ browsers. Also adding the `modal` feature will prevent the user from switching back to the opener window before the pop-up window is closed in Netscape 6+ browsers. Of course, Internet Explorer 4+ browsers do not support the `dependent` and `modal` window features, but instead support their own mechanism to create a modal window through the use of the `showModalDialog()` method.

You should now be able to go on and create your own custom dialogs to replace the built-in confirm and prompt dialogs, as well as creating other custom dialogs as necessary.

Windows within Windows

So far in this chapter we have looked at windows that exist outside other windows. However, a window can also exist inside another window. These types of windows are known as **frames**. Frames have been available since Netscape Navigator version 2 and Internet Explorer version 3 and allow multiple documents to be viewed at the same time, independently of each other, within a single browser window. Each document can load or modify the documents in other frames and this allows you to overcome some of the limitations of a single page. For example, once a page has been loaded, many parts of that page cannot be modified without reloading the whole page or getting heavily in to the document object model (DOM, see Chapter 7), which is not only distracting but it can cause the loss of existing information, such as data stored in memory in JavaScript variables. Loading only a portion of the page in a different frame can provide the flexibility that is needed for many applications.

Matters were complicated somewhat with the advent of the version 4 browsers when both browsers introduced their own additional proprietary mechanisms for incorporating a document viewing system within another document. Netscape introduced the `<layer>` and `<ilayer>` tags, which were buggy and, therefore, often difficult to script. Internet Explorer introduced the `<iframe>` tag (an inline frame), which was much more friendly to use and easier to script. Of course, with both techniques available and neither browser supporting the other's tags, JavaScript coders were given a lot of headaches trying to support both systems.

Thankfully, the release of the HTML 4 standard included support for the `<iframe>` element, which Netscape 6 supports. As the `<layer>` and `<ilayer>` tags are now deprecated (which means that they are no longer supported in the HTML standard) I won't discuss them and instead concentrate on the `<iframe>`.

In the remaining half of this chapter we'll look first at the `<iframe>`, and then discuss frames and how JavaScript can be used to control them.

Documents within Documents

The `<iframe>` is particularly handy, defining a frame within a document, and acts very similar to having a window within the document. We can expect all modern web browsers to support it, as it is part of the HTML 4 specification. By using stylesheet information it can be positioned on the page and different documents can be loaded into it via targeted links or by using JavaScript to change the window's `location` property.

Consider a page that contained an `<iframe>` and used the following HTML code:

```
<iframe src="hello.html" name="hello" width="200" height="200"></iframe>
```

A page loaded with this code will produce an iframe that is 200 pixels wide by 200 pixels high. The `src` attribute dictates which HTML document will be loaded into the iframe. The `name` attribute is used to allow us to write JavaScript that can easily access the iframe from the parent frame. Remember this example will only work with Internet Explorer 3+, Netscape 6+, and HTML 4 compliant browsers. It will not work with Netscape 4 or earlier browsers, as they do not support the `<iframe>` tag.

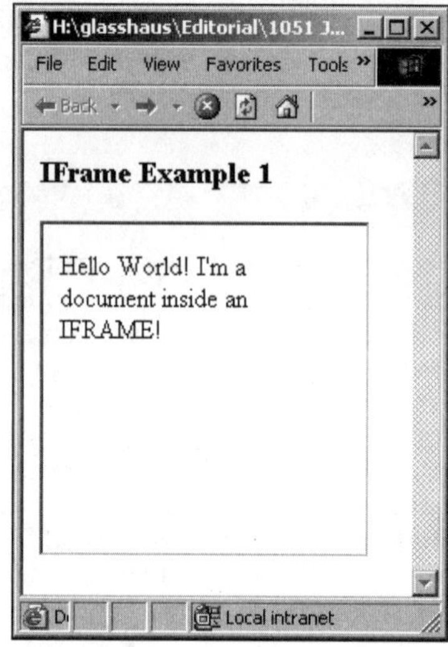

To access the properties and variables of the iframe, we need to first create a reference to it. The iframe is an inline frame existing within the document, but is not a property of the document as one might initially think. Instead, it is a property of the window that contains the document. Note that windows can contain other windows and documents, whereas documents only contain content. The `window` object has a `frames` property, which is an array of references to the frames that exist within the window and by using this frames property we can obtain a reference to the iframe. There are three different ways that a reference to an iframe can be achieved:

```
var ifHello = window.frames[0]
var ifHello = window.frames['hello']
var ifHello = window.hello
```

The first example obtains the frame reference by its order within the page. As `frames` is an array the first frame will have an index of `0`. Alternatively, we can use the iframe's name, instead of its index number. In the final example, we've simply used the name of the iframe itself without using the `frames` property.

Having obtained a reference to the iframe, we can now communicate with it as we would with any other type of window, calling methods and properties of the iframe itself, custom variables and functions, or the document inside the iframe.

```
// Obtain a reference to the iframe
var ifHello = window.hello;

// Call a method within the iframe
if (ifHello && ifHello.SomeFunction)
    ifHello.someFunction();

// Obtain the value of a property within the iframe
if (ifHell && ifHello.someVariable)
   var myVar = ifHello.someVariable;

// Obtain a reference to the documents within the iframe
if (ifHello && ifHello.document)
   var helloDoc = ifHello.document;
```

You will notice in the examples above that each time you want to call a method in the iframe the reference to the iframe is tested to see if it is not `null` (that is, it exists) and the iframe has the particular named function. We do this because if the iframe reference is wrong, or for some reason the page doesn't contain the method we want to use, JavaScript will throw an error. Testing in this way will make sure we can safely call the iframe method and if we cannot then JavaScript simply does nothing and no error is raised. We do the same when obtaining and setting the properties of an iframe.

Hierarchical Relationship

When we created and opened a new window there was no direct relationship between the window. The pop-up window has the `opener` property that allows JavaScript to obtain a reference back to the window that opened it. Iframes are related to the window in which they are contained, but do not have the `opener` property. Instead, a direct hierarchical relationship exists between the containing window and the iframe located inside it; closing the containing window also closes the iframe window. The containing window is known as the parent window, and the iframe is known as a child window of the parent window.

To access the parent window from the child iframe, the iframe window object has a property, called `parent`, which stores a reference to the parent window in which it is contained.

```
// Access the properties and methods within the iframe's parent window
var myVar = parent.someVariable
parent.someFunction()

// Obtain a reference to the document within the iframe's parent window
var parentDoc = parent.document
parentDoc.bgColor = "red"
```

Here we can see how to call up to the parent window and change the background colour of the page to red.

Multiple Windows within Window

As we have seen throughout this chapter, a browser is able to have more than one window open at any one time. Each window can contain either an HTML document with a `<body>` tag or a `<frameset>` tag. A frameset comprises of 1 or more frames within a single browser window, and hence you can have multiple windows existing within a single window.

Each frame is a window that contains a document and has a window object associated with it. These windows all exist within a top-level window that constructs the frame set. Therefore each time a frameset is used there are n+1 windows open, where n is the number of frames.

Frames, like iframes, are containers for documents and don't have the same properties as a whole window – that is, they have no menus or toolbars. A number of properties can be specified, though, such as a name, size, and position.

Framesets

Framesets have been available since Netscape version 2 and Internet Explorer version 3 browsers. They enable multiple documents to be viewed at the same time, independently of each other. A common usage of framesets is to define a frame that contains an often-static page with a list of links, in the form of a menu, and another frame that is updated to view different documents. The following code (SimpleFrameset.html) shows an example of the HTML code that could be used to create such a two-paneled frameset.

```
<html>
<frameset cols="30%,70%">
   <frame src="left.html" name="frLeft">
   <frame src="right.html" name="frRight">
</frameset>
</html>
```

The frameset defines 2 frames, laid out in columns, with the left-hand side occupying 30% of the browser width and the right-hand side occupying the remaining 70% of the browser width. The rows and cols attribute on the <frameset> element divide the screen into rows and columns. Both of these attributes take a comma-delimited list of values, where numbers are interpreted in percentages or pixels (if no percent symbol is used) and are based on available space within the browser window. Optionally, instead of calculating the size of each frame you can use a * symbol for one of the frame sizes, which means take up any remaining space. So the <frameset> tag could have been defined using:

```
<frameset cols="30%,*">
```

or:

```
<frameset cols="*,70%">
```

For each frame to be included within the frameset a <frame> tag is used to define the frame, and the src property of this tag informs the browser as to which document to display within the frame. In our example, the HTML documents to be displayed in each frame are located within the same directory as the frameset document. The name attribute is optional and provides a destination for any navigational targeting by links. That is, links in other frames can be instructed to open files in a named frame, rather than obeying their default behavior (which generally means opening in the frame where the link is located).

In this example the source for the left-hand frame (left.html) is:

```
<html>
<body>
   <h3>This is the left frame.</h3>
</body>
</html>
```

and the right-hand frame (`right.html`) is:

```
<html>
<body>
   <h3>This is the right frame.</h3>
</body>
</html>
```

If you now load this example up within you browser you should see something similar to the following screenshot.

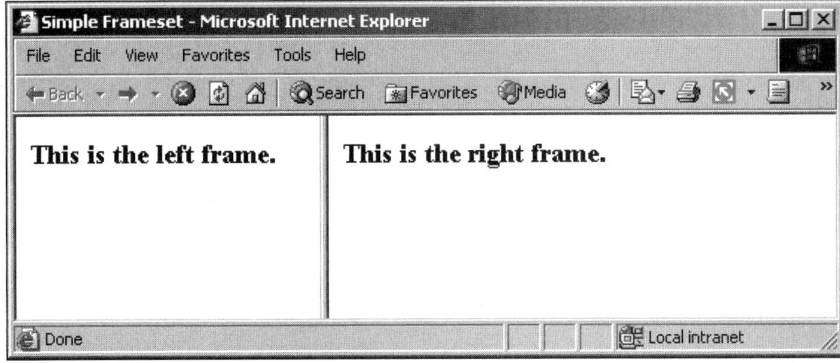

Each of the frames within a frameset are independent of each other. A document displayed by a frame can be viewed, resized, scrolled, and updated without affecting the contents of the other frames.

Frameset Hierarchy

Frames can be arranged in a hierarchical structure. At the top of the structure is the parent window and below all the child windows (frames). The parent window is only visible in terms of any decoration that maybe visible such as menus and toolbars, instead we only see the frames that exist inside it.

The following diagram shows the hierarchy of the frames within the frameset defined within the `SimpleFrameset.html` file, described above.

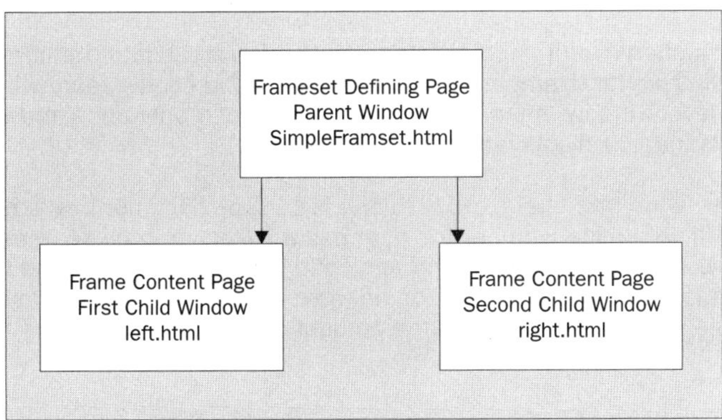

Note the order of the child frames is related to the order in which the `<frame>` tags are defined within the frameset.

Accessing frames

Each frame can be accessed from the top-level parent window using the `frames` array, in a similar manner to accessing iframes from a parent window. Remember that all arrays are zero-based; they start at `0` and count upwards. So, to access the first child frame in our example with JavaScript located in the parent window, you would use:

```
var leftFrame = window.frames[0]
```

And to access the second child window:

```
var rightFrame = window.frames[1]
```

However, you can also reference a child window by using the name of the subframe within the `frames` array, rather than its index number.

```
var leftFrame = window.frames["frLeft"]
var rightFrame = window.frames["frRight"]
```

Or easier still, simply use the frame name without the need for referencing the `frames` array at all – this is the most common and preferred approach by JavaScript developers.

```
var leftFrame = window.frLeft
var rightFrame = window.frRight
```

This last way to access frames directly just by using their names is so much easier than counting frames that it almost makes it mandatory to include the `name` attribute with the `<frame>` tag.

When trying to access the parent top-level window object from any of the child frames you can use the parent property, again as we saw with iframes:

```
var parentWindow = parent
```

Within framesets it's often useful to place variables and functions that are common and often used within the parent window, for example, browser detection and cookie read/write scripts. Placing code like this in the top-level window means that the code is loaded only once and can be used by many different documents that are displayed within the frameset.

For example, below is the frameset `SimpleFrameset.html` document, which now has a simple function in it that will determine whether the user has a Netscape browser (see Chapter 4 for more information on browser detection). Including this code in the frameset means that any documents loaded into the frames within the frameset do not have to have their own browser detection code. This reduces the file sizes, which reduces the amount of coding required.

```
<html>
<script language="JavaScript">
function isNS()
```

```
{
   return (document.layers && navigator.appName == "Netscape")
}
</script>
<frameset cols="30%,70%">
   <frame src="left.html" name="frLeft">
   <frame src="right.html" name="frRight">
</frameset>
</html>
```

Note checking the value of the `navigator` object property `appName` is not sufficient to identify whether the browser is Netscape or not, as the Opera browser can also use this value. So in this case we have included the object test `document.layers` too.

Any document loaded in a frame within this frameset can then use the following line of code to identify if the browser in use is a Netscape browser or not:

```
var usingNetscape = parent.isNS();
```

Note that as well as functions being stored in the frameset, you can store data in variables in the parent frameset window object.

You should now be asking yourselves a question, what if you want to access one child frame from another child frame though? For instance, in the example we've been using here you might want to change the document being displayed in the right-hand frame by using JavaScript in the left-hand frame.

We now know how to call down to a child window from the parent and how to call up from the child to the parent. So, combining these actions together allows JavaScript to call from one frame to another.

In the example below we can see just this. The HTML document for the left-hand frame has been modified so that the page now has a link included and can be used to navigate forward through a series of presentation pages (like a slideshow).

```
<!-- left.html -->
<html>
<head>
<script language="JavaScript">
var currPage = 0;
var defaultName = "slide";

function showNextSlide()
{
   var url = defaultName + currPage + ".html";
   var rightFrame = parent.frRight;
   rightFrame.location = url;
   currPage++;
}
</script>
</head>
<body>
   <h3>This is the left frame.</h3>
   <a href="JavaScript:showNextSlide(); return false;">Show Next Side</a>
</body>
</html>
```

Clicking on the link calls the showNextSlide() function, which loads a new document into the right-hand frame. The first line of the function builds a string to represent the URL of the HTML document to be loaded. In this example, the series of pages will have URLs that take the form of slide0.html for page 1, slide1.html for page 2, slide2.html for page 3, and so on.

Next, a reference to the right-hand frame is obtained by calling up to the parent window and back down to the other child window, and is stored in the rightFrame variable. Then this variable is used to access the location property on the frame's window object, and change it to the new URL that was built dynamically and stored in the url variable. Finally, the currPage counter variable is incremented so that the next time the function is called, the next slide in the series will be displayed.

So the code above shows how JavaScript can traverse the frame structure and change the document currently being displayed in the right-hand frame.

Complex Framesets

The last example, updating a frame with a new document from a different location, presents a potential problem for communicating between frames. If the right-hand frame displays a new document which itself contains a frameset, this can cause problems if the frames within this frameset need to access the top-level window that contains the left-hand and right-hand frames.

Consider that the right-hand frame is updated with the following HTML file (RightFrameset.html):

```
<html>
<frameset rows="40%,*">
   <frame src="TopRight.html" name="frTopRight">
   <frame src="BottomRight.html" name="frBottomRight">
</frameset>
</html>
```

This frameset creates two frames positioned vertically in rows. The TopRight.html file has the following code:

```
<html>
<body>
   <h3>This is the top right frame.</h3>
</body>
</html>
```

and the BottomRight.html file has this code:

```
<html>
<body>
   <h3>This is the bottom right frame.</h3>
</body>
</html>
```

The screenshot below shows how this example would look when loading this frameset within the right-hand frame:

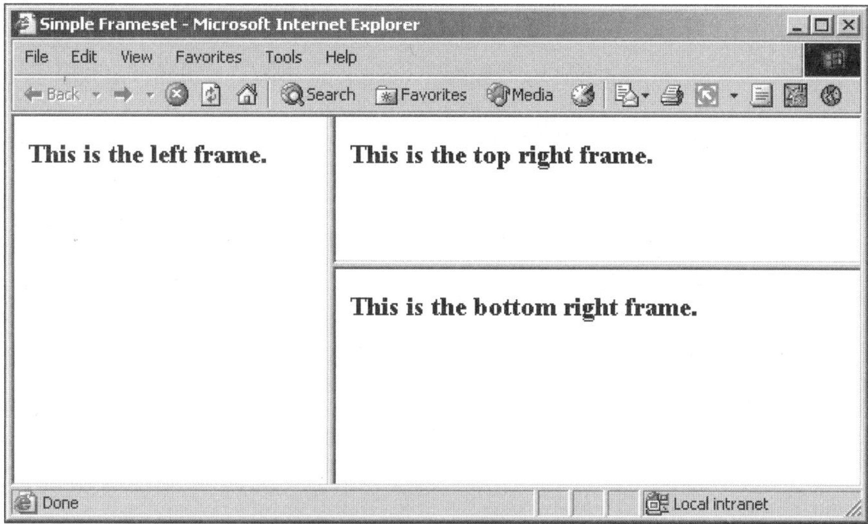

In this scenario, the `parent` properties of the top-right frame and the bottom-right frame no longer reference back to the same top-level window as in the simpler frameset of the previous example. If you take a look at the new hierarchical relationships between each of the windows you will be able to see the problem more clearly.

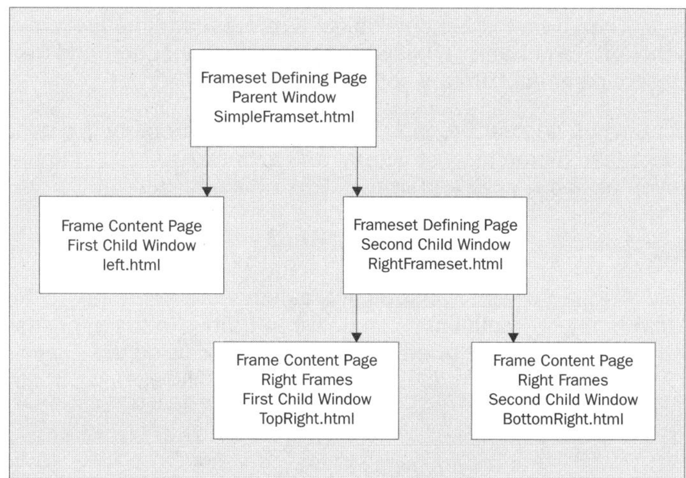

We can see here that the top part of the hierarchy structure is the same as in the previous example. The top level of the structure contains two child windows. The difference this time is that the second child window is now itself a parent of two further child windows.

The `parent` property of the `window` object only refers to the direct parent window that contains the child windows. So the `parent` property of either of the right-hand frame's child windows is the second child window of the topmost window in the hierarchy. For the right-hand frame's child windows to access the topmost window, you first need to reference the parent frameset of these child frames:

```
var rightWindow = parent
```

Next we can reference the topmost window by accessing the parent property of this window.

```
var topWindow = rightWindow.parent
```

Or simply combining these two calls will give:

```
var topWindow = parent.parent
```

You can imagine that quite quickly these calls can become long and awkward to understand when trying to traverse up and down the hierarchical structure. It can become even more complicated if, for example, one of the right-hand frame's child frames itself contains an iframe. To access the top most frame from inside the iframe will require extending the chain another level (to give `parent.parent.parent`!) So to minimize these problems and to make your code clearer, it is often useful to store a reference to long object reference chains in another variable, like the `topWindow` variable above, and then use the object reference in the variable in subsequent code:

```
// Change the colour of the left frame background to red
// from the bottom right frame
var topWindow = parent.parent
var leftFrame = topWindow.frTopRight
leftFrame.document.bgColor = "red"
```

In the code block above, from the bottom right-hand frame a reference to the top-level window (the frameset) is obtained. Then from this window object a reference to the first child frame of the frameset, which is the left-hand frame. Finally the reference to the left-hand frame window object is used to change the document background color to red.

The `window` object contains another property called `top`. This property is a synonym for the topmost window in any frame-based hierarchical structure, and acts like a shortcut to the top-level window, making our code much easier to write and use.

```
var topWindow = top
```

From any of the child 'Frame Content' windows you can use the `top` property to gain access to the topmost window. Unfortunately, communication between frames in the opposite direction is not as simple. You have to extend the object reference chains further using the `frames` property of the right child window, or the frame names, to reach the bottommost child windows in the hierarchy from the topmost window.

```
var rightTopWindow = top.frRight.frTopRight
var rightBottomWindow = top.frRight.frBottomRight
```

Image Viewer Application – Part 1

Over the next three chapters we will use the knowledge presented in each chapter to build an Image Viewer application. The purpose of this application is to allow different sets of images, such as a photo-album or gallery, to be viewed. The application will draw mainly on knowledge discussed in this and the following two chapters and require some of the fundamentals of JavaScript language that are presented in the earlier chapters of this book.

When the application is finished it should look like the following screenshot:

Application Outline

The application consists of three areas. On the left-hand side is a navigation menu (Area 1), which can be used to select which set of images a user would like to view. When a user selects a set of images, thumbnails of each image in the collection are displayed, in a scrollable area, in the center of the window.

The thumbnails in the central strip (Area 2) are flanked at the top and bottom by two arrowhead images. JavaScript captures mouse click events on these images and the thumbnail images can be scrolled up and down if the total height of the images is greater than the height of the iframe itself.

When the user moves their mouse over the thumbnail images, the style properties of the images will change to allow a highlighted border to appear, providing a visual cue to the user that they can click on the image. When the user clicks on a thumbnail, the image to be viewed is displayed full size in a viewing area on the right-hand side of the screen (Area 3). The diagram below depicts the three main areas created by the iframes within the application.

Building the Application

So to create this application, where do we start? From the graphic above we know that we need three areas within our main page. Two areas the user will be able to interact with (navigation and thumbnail selection) and a third area to simply display content. For this we will create a single page with three <iframe> elements, each area being contained within an <iframe>. JavaScript will capture the user's mouse actions and communicate the user's intentions between the frames.

The HTML source code for the imageViewer.htm page is detailed below:

```
<html>
<head>
<title>Image Viewer</title>
</head>
<body>
<iframe name="categoryFrame" id="categoryFrame" src="CategoryIndex.htm"
        scrolling="auto" frameborder="none">
</iframe>
<img src="ScrollUp copy.gif" id="scrollUpImg" width="142" height="38"
     onclick="scrollThumbnailUp_onclick()"
     alt="Scroll Thumbnails Up">
<iframe name="thumbnailFrame" id="thumbnailFrame" src="DefaultThumbnailImage.gif"
        scrolling="no" frameborder="none" marginwidth="0">
</iframe>
<img src="ScrollDown copy.gif" id="scrollDownImg" width="142" height="38"
     onclick="scrollThumbnailDown_onclick()"
     alt="Scroll Thumbnails Down">
<img src="ImageLoadingAnimation.gif" id="imageLoadingAnimation"
      width="150" height="40"
     alt="Loading Image...please wait">
<iframe name="mainImageFrame" id="mainImageFrame" src="DefaultMainImage.gif"
        scrolling="auto" frameborder="none" marginheight="0 marginwidth=0"
        onload="hideImageLoadingImage()">
</iframe>
</body>
</html>
```

Each HTML tag has been provided with an id attribute so that we reference each element within the page easily with JavaScript. The iframe's categoryFrame and mainImageFrame have their scrolling attribute set to auto so that if the contained documents are larger than the dimensions of the iframe the browser will add scrollbars automatically.

Conversely the iframe for displaying the thumbnails, thumbnailFrame, has its scrolling attribute set to no so that the browser will not display scrollbars. In this instance we are going to use JavaScript to create the scrolling effect. To do this two <image> tags are added, the arrowheads in the earlier screenshot, which will be positioned above and below this second iframe. These two images have onclick event handlers, which will capture the user's mouse click action and call a function that will perform the scrolling action within the iframe. So we must remember to create two functions for the onclick event handlers; we will come back to these shortly.

A third <image> tag has been added, with the id attribute of imageLoadingAnimation. This image is an animated gif file that will be displayed when the user clicks on a thumbnail to view an image and is hidden after the image has loaded.

Image Loading...

When the application is first loaded there will be no thumbnails visible and so there is no need for this image to be visible either. We will apply a stylesheet to this page shortly and set the `visibility` property for this image to `hidden`, so that it is not visible. To make the image visible again we will therefore require a function that will toggle the `visibility` style property of this image between visible and hidden. You will see how to code this effect in Chapter 6.

The second and third iframes each have an image referenced by the `src` attribute. These images are sized to the same dimensions as the iframes themselves and simply inform the user what to do to view an image fully. The first iframe references an HTML file that will display the tree view navigation system. We will look at this file later in the *Navigation System* section.

If you copy the above code, save it in a file called `ImageViewer.htm`, and test it, you will find it doesn't look too inspiring. All the elements are positioned and sized by the browser using its normal flow layout. A JavaScript error is raised because of the `onload` event handler associated with the third frame, which is the main image viewing frame.

Stylizing the Application

We already know that a stylesheet is required to set the `visibility` property of the `imageLoadingAnimation` image and the position of the arrow images above and below the second iframe. We will also use a stylesheet to position each element on the page and provide them with the correct dimensions.

```
<style>
   body { background-color:black; }
   img, iframe { position:absolute; }

   iframe { top:50px; height:480px; margin:0px; border-style:none; }
   iframe#categoryFrame { left:10px; width:210px; }
   iframe#thumbnailFrame { left:125px; width:190px; background-color:black; }
   iframe#mainImageFrame { left:320px; width:640px; border:5px ridge #c0c0c0; }

   img#scrollUpImg { left:150px; top:10px; }
   img#scrollDownImg {   left:150px; top:535px; }
   img#imageLoadingAnimation { left:320px; top:10px; visibility:hidden; }
</style>
```

Copy the stylesheet above into the `<head>` section of the `ImageViewer.htm` file. The stylesheet gives the page a black background. All image and iframe elements are set to absolute positioning by default. All iframes by default are positioned 50 pixels from the top of the page, set to be 480px high, with no margins and no borders.

The remaining style properties are applied specifically to each element by attaching style properties to each element via its `id` attribute. For each iframe, the position of its x coordinate is supplied by the `left` property and given a width. Similarly the x coordinate and y coordinate is supplied to position each image precisely on the page. The background colour of the `thumbnailFrame` has been set to black and a ridge border property is added to `mainImageFrame`, overriding the default of no border set earlier in the style sheet. Finally, the `imageLoadingAnimation` image has its visibility set to `hidden` so that it is not displayed when the page loads.

Preventing JavaScript Errors

If you try loading this page now, you will find it looks similar to the screenshot shown previously. However, we still have the JavaScript error. So let's add some JavaScript to fix this problem. In this chapter we will simply include empty functions; we'll define the functions but we won't add statements to the function body. When JavaScript makes a call to these functions, the functions will do nothing and exit silently without raising an error.

The JavaScript that's causing the error when the page first loads is a call to a nonexistent `hideImageLoadingImage()` function. We need to create an empty function for this and also include functions for the `onclick` event handlers of the image elements that will be used to cause the document in the thumbnail iframe to scroll up and down.

```
<script language="JavaScript">
function hideImageLoadingImage()
{
   // add code here
}

function scrollThumbnailUp_onclick()
{
   // add code here
}

function scrollThumbnailDown_onclick ()
{
   // add code here
}
</script>
```

If you now copy this script block and add it to the header section of the page, the JavaScript error will not be raised anymore. In addition, clicking on the arrowheads at the top and bottom of the thumbnail iframe will silently execute and not raise a JavaScript error.

Allowing for Smaller Screens

If you look carefully at the style properties for the `mainImageFrame` iframe, which is used to display the full image, you will be able to calculate that the right-hand side of the iframe is located 960 pixels (left + width = 320+460 = 960) from the left-hand side of the browser window. For many users this may be too wide for their monitor screen. There are still many people who have monitors that are capable of 800x600 pixels or less. It would be good therefore to create an interface so that these users can use the application, and see the navigation panels and whole image at the same time.

The amount of work involved to do this is remarkably small. Only a few properties in the stylesheet need change as you can see in the alternative stylesheet below.

```
<style>
  body { background-color: black; }
  img, iframe { position:absolute; }
  iframe { top:50px; height:360px; margin:0px; border-style:none; }

  iframe#categoryFrame { left:0px; width:210px; }
  iframe#thumbnailFrame { left:120px; width:190px; background-color: black; }
```

```
    iframe#mainImageFrame { left:310px; width:455px; border:5px ridge #c0c0c0; }

    img#scrollUpImg { left:140px; top:10px; }
    img#scrollDownImg { left:140px; top:425px; }
    img#imageLoadingAnimation { left:310px; top:10px; visibility:hidden; }
  </style>
```

If you look carefully and compare this stylesheet with the previous one, you will notice the only differences exist for the location properties (`left` and `top`) and the dimension properties (`width` and `height`).

Create a copy of the `ImageViewer.htm` file created previously and rename this file `ImageViewer_smallscreen.htm`. Then remove the stylesheet within this new file and copy the stylesheet above in its place. You now have two files: one for users with small screens and one for users with large screens.

So far so good, but it would be better if the application was intelligent, capable of calculating the user's screen size and automatically redirecting them to the page that best suits their needs.

JavaScript is able to perform this testing easily. The following section of code uses an `if` statement that tests the available height of the browser window, which is the height of the browser window available to display content, without the extra decorations such as menus, toolbars, and status bar.

If the available screen height is less than 700 pixels the browser is redirected to the `ImageViewer_smallscreen.htm` file by passing the name of the file to the `replace()` method of the window's `location` object. The `replace()` method loads the specified URL over the current history entry. After calling the `replace()` method, the user cannot navigate to the previous URL by using browser's *Back* button.

```
// cope with 800 * 600 or less
if (screen.availHeight < 700)
{
  window.location.replace("ImageViewer_smallscreen.htm");
}
```

If you copy and paste this code into the script block of the `ImageViewer.htm` file, the JavaScript interpreter will execute this code as the page loads and automatically redirect the browser to the page suited to users with the smaller screen size.

Navigation System

The first stage to building our application is now nearly completed. The final piece to slot into place is the HTML file for Area 1, the tree-view navigation panel. Clicking on an option in this panel will display a set of thumbnail images in the central iframe. If an option has a + graphic next to it and it is clicked, rather than show a set of thumbnails, a set of associated menu options will be displayed between this and the next menu option and indented.

The screenshot above shows all of the menu options that are available. Top-level menu options are in a bold font and options in a sub list are indented slightly in a normal font. An option that has been clicked on has been highlighted with a grey background and when the mouse is positioned over an option, the text label is highlighted in a yellow font.

An HTML file, called `CategoryIndex.htm`, needs to be created that will be displayed in the first iframe on the left-hand side of the page. In the body section a single `<div>` element encapsulating some textual content will be created for each menu option. Mouse event handlers are added to capture when the mouse is out or over, or if the mouse is clicked on, the `<div>` element. The mouse over/out events will be used to change the style properties of the element, highlighting and dimming the menu option to give a visual cue to the user as to whether the element is clickable. The mouse click event will be used to either show the associated set of thumbnails or drop down a sub-list of menu options.

```
<!-- Pics of Flowers -->
    <div onmouseover="OnMouseOverHeading(this);"
        onmouseout="OnMouseOutHeading(this);"
        onclick="loadNewImageCategory(this, 'FlowersThumbnails.htm')"
        class="Heading">Flowers</div>
```

The code snippet above shows the HTML to create the first top-level menu option for showing pictures of flowers. Three separate functions are attached to each of the mouse events and again in this chapter we will simply create empty functions to prevent JavaScript error messages popping up. Each function is passed a reference to the `<div>` element, and the `loadNewImageCategory()` function accepts as a second argument the name of the file to display in the middle thumbnail iframe. For this and each of the other menu options the files, for each set of thumbnails, will be created in the next chapter. Styling is applied to the element by attaching the stylesheet `Heading` class.

The second top-level option uses this code too but the third option needs to be modified as this option causes a sub-list to drop down. The modified code can be seen below:

```
<!-- Landscape Photos -->
    <div onmouseover="OnMouseOverHeading(this);"
        onmouseout="OnMouseOutHeading(this);"
        onclick="switchDisplay('trLandscapes','imgLandscapes')"
        title="Click for further details"
        class="Heading">Landscapes<img src="plus.gif" id="imgLandscapes"></div>
```

In this `<div>` element a `title` attribute is supplied, which will cause a ToolTip to display the value of the attribute if the user hovers their mouse over the element. An image is supplied after the menu option label that shows a plus sign to indicate it has an associated sub-list. This image will be changed dynamically to one that displays a minus sign after the option has been clicked.

The `onclick` event handler is attached to a fourth function, `switchDisplay()`, which accepts two arguments. The first argument is the name of a `<div>` element that will contain the sub-list of menu options associated with this option. This container `<div>` element will initially have a `display` style property set to `none` so that it is not rendered when the page initially loads. The function will then toggle the display property between `block` (to allow the `<div>` element to be rendered) and `none`. The second argument is the `id` name given to the `<img>` element of this menu option, which will be used by the function to toggle the image's `src` property between an image showing a plus symbol and one showing a minus symbol. Again, we'll simply be using an empty function for the moment in this chapter.

We can now create the full HTML code for the body section, which can be seen below:

```
<h5 style="color:goldenrod; font-size:9pt;">Photo Index</h5>
<!-- Pics of Flowers -->
   <div onmouseover="OnMouseOverHeading(this);"
        onmouseout="OnMouseOutHeading(this);"
  onclick="loadNewImageCategory(this, 'FlowersThumbnails.htm')"
  class="Heading">Flowers</div>
<!-- Pics of Katie -->
   <div onmouseover="OnMouseOverHeading(this);"
        onmouseout="OnMouseOutHeading(this);"
        onclick="loadNewImageCategory(this, 'KatieThumbnails.htm')"
        class="Heading">Katie</div>
<!-- Landscape Photos -->
   <div onmouseover="OnMouseOverHeading(this);"
        onmouseout="OnMouseOutHeading(this);"
        onclick="switchDisplay('trLandscapes','imgLandscapes')"
        title="Click for further details"
        class="Heading">Landscapes<img src="plus.gif" id="imgLandscapes"></div>
      <div id="trLandscapes" class="dropLevel">
         <!-- UK Photos -->
         <div onmouseover="OnMouseOverHeading(this);"
              onmouseout="OnMouseOutHeading(this);"
              title="Click for further details"
              onclick="switchDisplay('trUKPics','imgUKPics')"
              class="SubHeading">UK Towns<IMG src="plus.gif" id="imgUKPics"></div>
            <div id="trUKPics" class="dropLevel">
               <!-- Huntingdon -->
               <div onmouseover="OnMouseOverHeading(this);"
                    onmouseout="OnMouseOutHeading(this);"
                   onclick="loadNewImageCategory(this,
'HuntingdonThumbnails.htm')"
                    class="SubHeading">Huntingdon</div>
               <!-- Keele -->
               <div onmouseover="OnMouseOverHeading(this);"
                    onmouseout="OnMouseOutHeading(this);"
                    onclick="loadNewImageCategory(this, 'KeeleThumbnails.htm')"
                   class="SubHeading">Keele</div>
               <!-- Chester -->
               <div onmouseover="OnMouseOverHeading(this);"
                    onmouseout="OnMouseOutHeading(this);"
                    onclick="loadNewImageCategory(this, 'ChesterThumbnails.htm')"
                    class="SubHeading">Chester</div>
               </div>
         <!-- Sunsets Pics -->
         <div onmouseover="OnMouseOverHeading(this);"
              onmouseout="OnMouseOutHeading(this);"
              onclick="loadNewImageCategory(this, 'SunsetThumbnails.htm')"
              class="SubHeading">Sunsets</div>
      </div>
   </div>
```

Take note of the `<div>` tags with the `id` attribute of `trLandscapes`. This `<div>` has a stylesheet class, `dropLevel`, applied. This is the class that initially sets the `<div>` element to have a display property set to `none` and allows the sub-list of `<div>` elements to be indented relative to its parent. Similarly, a `<div>` tag with the `id` attribute of `trUKPics` is used as a container for a further sub-list that provides menu options for the UK Photos collection with the `dropLevel` stylesheet class applied.

After inserting the code for the body section we can add the style sheet information, which can been seen below:

```
<style>
body { background-color:black; font:8pt verdana; color:darkorange; }

.Heading, .SubHeading
   {
      font-weight:bold;
      margin:0px; margin-top:5px;
      cursor:pointer; cursor:hand;
   }
.SubHeading { font-weight:normal; }
.dropLevel { margin-left:10px; display:none; }
</style>
```

The `<body>` element has been provided with a background color of black and a default font and colour for the textual content. The `<div>` elements will inherit the font and color style properties for text elements from the `<body>` element. The three classes provided the extra styling required for each of the `<div>` elements. Note the `Heading` and `subHeading` classes have the `cursor` property defined twice. This is because there is a compatibility issue between Netscape and Internet Explorer with this property. Netscape and Internet Explorer version 6+ browsers accept the Cascading Style Sheet Level 2 `pointer` value for the cursor property to change the mouse cursor to a hand. Microsoft version 4.x and 5.x browsers do not; instead they opt for a Microsoft proprietary value of `hand`.

Finally, we have to add the empty functions that are attached to the event handlers of the `<div>` elements. Including the script block below in the header section will prevent any JavaScript errors being raised when the mouse is moved over/out of, or clicked on, the `<div>` elements.

```
<script language="JavaScript">
function OnMouseOverHeading(thisTag)
{
   // add code here
}

function OnMouseOutHeading(thisTag)
{
   // add code here
}

function switchDisplay(tagId, branchImage)
{
   // add code here
}

function loadNewImageCategory(menuElementClicked, categoryURL)
{
   // add code here
}
</script>
```

You should now copy each of the three sections above into the `CategoryIndex.htm` file. With all the initial pieces of the application in place, if you try to view the application you should see something like the following screenshot.

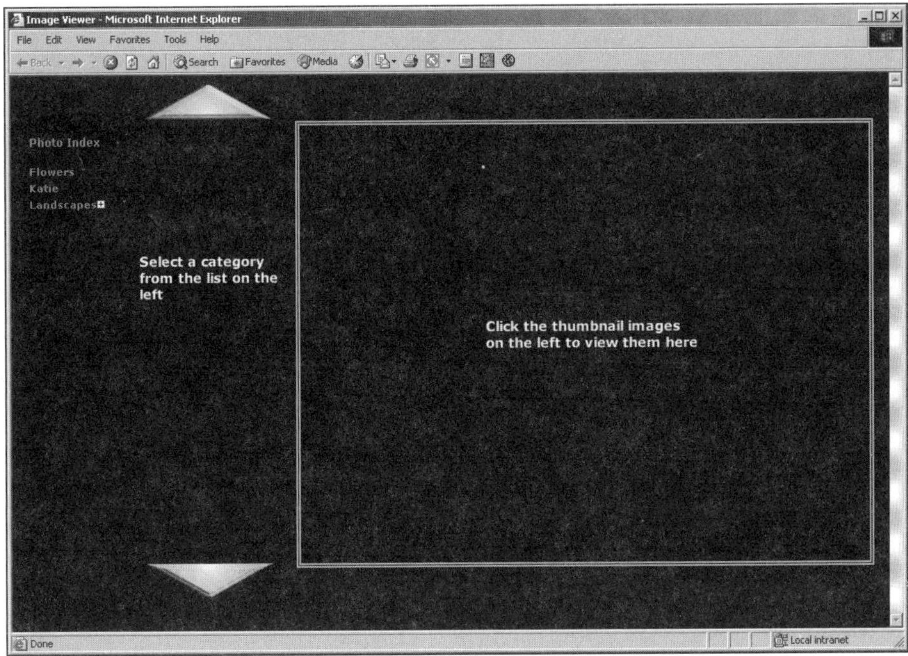

Although the application is not functional yet, we have come a long way with relatively little coding. In the next chapter we will add JavaScript DHTML code to the empty functions that we created here and create other additional functions required to make this application functional.

Summary

This chapter has covered the most important features that you should know when it comes to using JavaScript with windows and frames. With the exception of the iframe, you have learnt that cross-browser JavaScript coding with the two major browsers is fairly consistent and not too difficult.

We've seen how to obtain references to windows, and frames, and from that reference gain access to their methods and properties. Furthermore, the `window` reference allows us access to the document contained within the window, or frame, and we can obtain a reference to the document object within the window and manipulate it using standard DHTML techniques. The following chapter will discuss these DHTML techniques.

You should now have enough information to go and create you own pop-up windows to provide additional information to a user, or request additional information from the user, and obtain that information for use within your own web site or web application.

In the next chapter you will learn how to access the document properties and methods and use DHTML to alter the properties of elements within the document. If you combine knowledge gained in this chapter with the next you will be able to fully manipulate the windows and frames and the documents they contain.

The Image Viewer application will be extended further in the next chapter, adding functionality to the application that is presently missing. The empty functions that have been included here will be fleshed out making use of JavaScript that is covered in this and the next chapter.

6

- CSS
- IE 4 DHTML
- Netscape 4 DHTML
- Writing cross-browser DHTML
- Image Viewer Application: Part 2

Author: Sing Li

DHTML for IE4 and NN4

DHTML (Dynamic HTML) is a marketing term that describes the ability to dynamically change the appearance of an HTML page after it has been loaded and displayed. Throughout the evolution of the Internet Explorer and Netscape browsers, DHTML has been used (and sometimes misused) to refer to many specific competitive features of different level browsers. As the era of the browser war approaches its end, browser features with respect to Dynamic HTML are finally converging (as we shall see in the later chapters with 6.x version browsers), making the variety of browsers more compatible, and the life of a web designer considerably easier.

In this chapter, we revisit the early days of DHTML, the height of the browser war era. The two browsers that we're focusing on here, Internet Explorer 4.x and Netscape Navigator 4.x, (both still in use by a sizable base) are as incompatible as browsers have ever been. In the days when these were the principal browsers, DHTML loosely meant changing an HTML document while it's being viewed in the browser, whether in response to user interactions or by using some preprogrammed JavaScript code.

While the browser vendors battled it out, implementing different approaches to achieve the same dynamic behavior, webmasters and designers had to accommodate a large number of incompatible browsers, and have to even today. In this chapter, we will explore this formative stage of DHTML development, focusing on the following topics:

- Cascading Style Sheets (CSS) and their relationship with DHTML
- Manipulating CSS with JavaScript to create dynamic changes
- IE4.x specific DHTML features
- NS4.x specific DHTML features
- Cross-browser DHTML code

We'll put some of these new concepts into practice, and see how they fit into the ImageViewer application.

> Please note that the focus of this chapter will be on two older legacy browsers – Netscape Navigator 4.x and Internet Explorer 4.x. (Although these browsers are no longer in mainstream circulation, the user base of both browsers remains significant, and webmasters and designers still need to create pages that are compatible with them.) Due to the quirks of these older browsers, the web pages in this chapter may or may not be compatible with newer browsers. While every effort has been made to ensure that the pages, while not compatible, will not create errors in the latest browser version, we will be accomplishing the same Dynamic HTML effects (and more) with the latest browsers in later chapters.

One of the early features common to both IE and NN versions of DHTML is CSS (Cascading Style Sheets). We will see what problem CSS attempts to solve, and learn how to work with the NN4.x and IE4.x implementation next.

The Need for Cascading Style Sheets (CSS)

Anyone who creates and maintains a web site containing more than a couple of web pages will testify to the difficulty in maintaining the consistency of appearance across the web pages. While you can get around some of these problems using frames, changes to the appearance of your pages will still require some painstaking editing on every one of the affected pages.

This problem exists because HTML does two things at once: it controls both the **structure** and **appearance** of a document. HTML's structural control, for example, is implemented through the elements that control paragraphs `<p>`, lists `<ul>`, different heading levels `<h1>`, images `<img>`, tables `<table>`, and more:

```
<html>
  <head></head>
  <body>
    <h1>Main Heading</h1>
    <p>This is the first paragraph.</p>
    <p>This is the second paragraph.</P>

    <table >
      <tr><th>Cell 1</th></tr>
      <tr><td>Value 1</td></tr>
    </table>
  </body>
</html>
```

This HTML document contains one heading, two paragraphs, and a table with two cells. Note that even though the document will take on the default appearance as defined by the browser, we have not tried to control how it will appear in any way. The structure of the document can only be seen through the default formatting applied by the browser. If you load this page (called `structure.html` in the code distribution) it should look something like this:

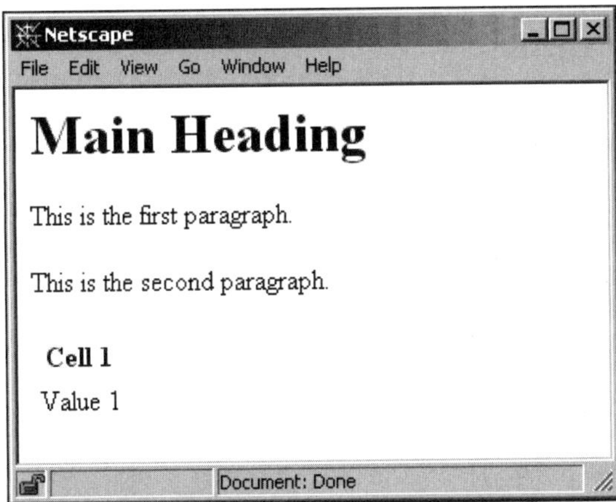

The browser's default formatting has revealed the general structure of the document, using relative font size and emphasis. The next figure shows the conceptual structure that the page depicts:

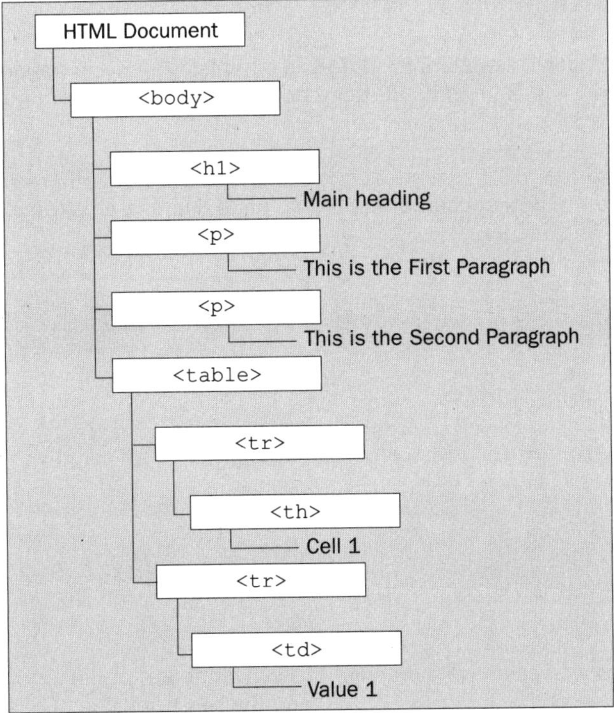

Some HTML tags and attributes are also used to affect the **appearance** of the page. Tags like `<center>`, `<strong>`, and `<font>`, for example. We also have **attributes** such as the `bgcolor` attribute of the `<body>` tag.

Since HTML pages often intermix both document structure tags and appearance control tags/attributes in unpredictable ways, any change to the appearance of the document – even if the structure is left alone – can require painstaking editing.

CSS attempts to solve this problem by factoring out the control over the appearance of the document, and isolating them all in one place: in the Stylesheet.

What is CSS?

In its simplest form, a CSS stylesheet defines the appearance of standard HTML structural tags for a particular document. It does this by declaring a number of rules, each one in the form of:

```
selector { list of style declarations }
```

The following stylesheet (`myStyle.css`) describes the appearance of various HTML elements in the document:

```
body { background-color:black; color:white; }
h1   { font-size:28pt; font-family:Arial; font-weight:bold; }
th   { color:lightblue; font-size:18pt; font-family:arial; font-weight:bold; }
td   { color:red; font-size:12pt; font-family:arial; font-style:italic; }
div  { font-size:18pt; font-style:italic; color:yellow; }
```

The selectors in this example are standard HTML elements: `<body>` is defined as being white text on a black background, `<h1>` is defined as 28-point bold type in the Arial font family, and `<th>` is defined as light blue in color, and so on.

You can include an external CSS stylesheet into the HTML file that you are working on using the `<link>` element in the `<head>` section of the HTML page. Here is an example:

```
<html>
     <head>
     <link rel="stylesheet" href="myStyle.css" type="text/css">
     </head>
     <body>
        <h1>Main Heading</h1>
        <p>This is the first paragraph.</P>
        <p><div>This is the second paragraph.</div></P>
        <table>
          <tr><th>Cell 1</th></tr>
          <tr><td>Value 1</td></tr>
        </table>
     </body>
 </html>
```

The `<link>` element specifies the relationship (the `rel` attribute) of the external link, in this case the stylesheet, and the `type` of the link (`text/css`), and the `href` link itself (`myStyle.css`). (I've also added in a `<div>` element around the second paragraph to demonstrate the effect of the stylesheet on this element.)

If you load this page (`styled.html`) in a CSS compliant browser such as IE4.x or NN4.x, you should see the page styled like this:

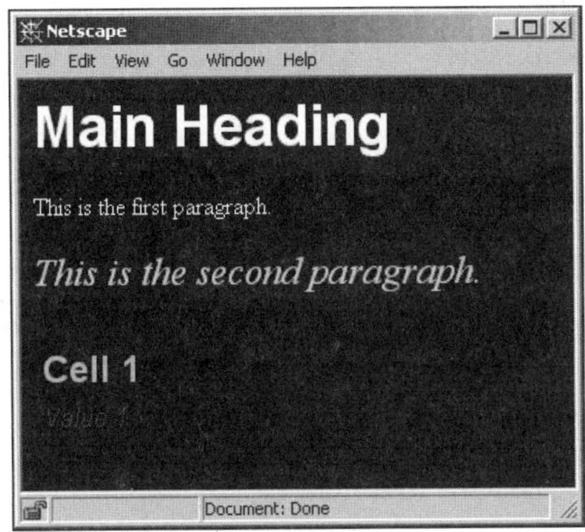

Using a CSS stylesheet we can maintain style changes throughout an application with minimum editing, no matter how many web pages are linked to the external stylesheet. This is one of the main advantages of separating the appearance from the structure, and, of course, of CSS stylesheets.

Using CSS to Position Elements

The CSS provided with a 4.x level browser is an attempt to implement some features of CSS1 together with positioning functionality. Positioning can be used to place visual element at a precise position on the web page, or it can even be used to implement limited animation (by changing the position via a script). Although positioning is a standard feature of CSS2, this later version of CSS didn't come into existence until after the 4.x series of browsers.

Let's look at an example. We'll use CSS inside an HTML page to set the exact pixel positioning of two `<div>` elements, using two `id`s in the head of the document: `magicRegion`, placed at (20, 100), and `changeRegion`, at (90, 80). These are set using the `position`, `top`, and `left` CSSP style definitions. Here's `cssp.html`:

```
<html>
  <head>
  <style type="text/css">

    #magicRegion { position:absolute; top:20px;
                   left: 100px; width: 200px;
                   color:yellow; background-color: black;
                   font-size:24pt; font-family:Arial; }
    #changeRegion { position:absolute; top:90px;
                    left: 80px; width: 500px;
                    color: red; background-color: blue;
                    font-size:48pt; font-family:Times; }
  </style>
  </head>
  <body>
    <div id="magicRegion">Magic Region</div>
    <div id="changeRegion">
       This will change!
    </div>
  </body>
</html>
```

We're placing the elements at absolute coordinates using `position: absolute;`. You can set relative coordinates using `position: relative;` which specifies the position with respect to where the element would have been placed by the normal layout of the page.

As expected, if you load the page using IE, the two positioned `<div>` elements are clearly visible at their specified position:

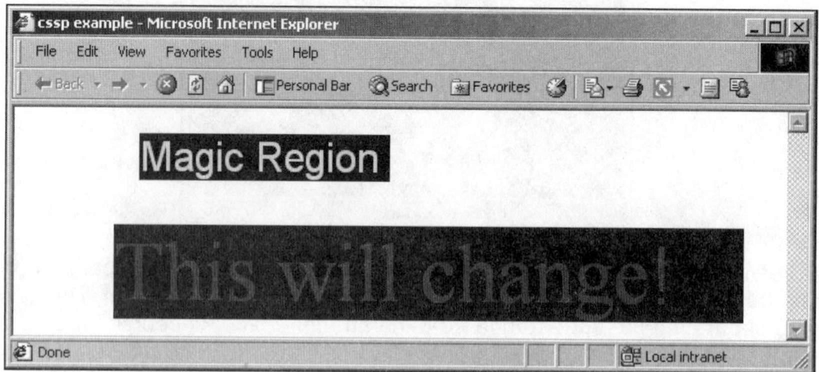

You may have noticed that we also set the width of the two `<div>` elements explicitly in this example. If we don't specify the width explicitly, the `<div>` will appear quite differently across NN4.x and IE4.x. NN4.x will display the background color behind the text, while IE4.x will show the same color for the entire `<div>`. This is one problem that often occurs when writing code that must work on multiple browsers. We will explore many more such problems in the next sections.

> The background color behavior inside a `<div>` element with text is different in IE4 and NN4, so you should always explicitly specify width using `<div>` to achieve a compatible effect.

Manipulating CSS with JavaScript

As we've seen so far, DHTML deals with the dynamic change in the appearance of a displayed HTML page, and the appearance of an HTML page can be controlled using CSS. So, we need only to modify the style attributes in the CSS stylesheet in order to make changes to the HTML, and we can do that using JavaScript together with the DHTML support built into the browser.

IE4.x supports dynamic manipulation of many CSS/CSSP properties using JavaScript, while NN4.x supports only a few. There are a lot of differences in the syntax though, and a large number of bugs in each browser's DHTML support. You have to be extremely careful when you're creating pages for these browsers, and make sure that new designs are tested on all target browsers.

Let's begin by looking at the built-in DHTML support provided by each browser in turn.

DHTML in IE 4

Let's modify the previous example, cssp.html so that the color of the text in changeRegion changes whenever the user passes the mouse over the magicRegion. We'll need to make two changes to the file. Let's begin by using a JavaScript function to change the color of changeRegion. We need to put this between the <script> tags within the <head> element of the page. Here's the beginning of jscssp.html:

```
<html>
  <head>
    <script>
      function changeIt(changeColor) {
        document.all.changeRegion.style.color = changeColor;
      }
    </script>
    <style type="text/css">
```

Note that we test for, and use, the document.all collection here. This collection is always available to JavaScript programs using the IE4+ browsers. The document.all collection contains every named element on the current document in the order that they are defined. We can access the collection using the index of the element:

```
document.all(1)
```

or using the id of the element as an index:

```
document.all("changeRegion")
```

or using the syntax above we used in jscssp.html. This is the most commonly used syntax:

```
document.all.changeRegion
```

It provides a very easy way to locate any element in the document. The document.all collection does not exist on NN or most other browsers, so code that uses it won't be compatible with those browsers. We'll look at ways of dealing with this incompatibility a little further on.

In the code above we are referencing the style object associated with the changeRegion element. The style object exposes many visual properties of the displayed elements, and a JavaScript program can modify a lot of these properties. We are using the color property in this case. You can find a comprehensive list of all available properties here:

http://msdn.microsoft.com/workshop/author/dhtml/reference/objects/obj_style.asp

Next, we need an onmouseover and onmouseout event handler inside the magicRegion <div> element:

```
<body>
  <div id="magicRegion" onmouseover='changeIt("white");'+
       onmouseout='changeIt("red");'>Magic Region</div>
  <div id="changeRegion">
  This will change!
```

This page will only work in IE (we'll show how it's done in NN4 later on in the chapter), so you'll need to test it in that browser. When you move your mouse over the *Magic Region*, the JavaScript function `changeIt()` is called and the color of the text '*This will change!*' goes white:

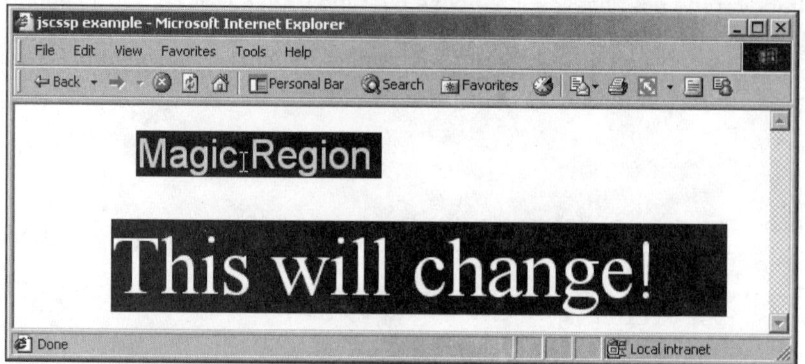

Color is only one of the properties of the `style` object that we can change dynamically using JavaScript. As an exercise, you may want to modify the `changeIt()` method to dynamically change the font family, weight, or even the CSSP positioning of `changeRegion`. In fact, by changing the CSS position of an element using JavaScript, we can code simple element animations using DHTML (at least we can in the IE4+ browsers).

Microsoft's Internet Explorer 4.x is a very popular series of browsers. As a result, today's web developers still need to cater for the sizable population of users using this series of browsers.

How IE4 Deals with DHTML

One of the principal differences between IE4 and its Netscape counterpart is that the IE4 web browser immediately updates and 're-renders' the display as soon as an HTML element is modified. This means that the browser has to render the entire web page as soon as the HTML is modified. This is a very powerful DHTML feature, because it allows us to literally change the HTML on the fly. Furthermore, IE4 enables modification to almost all the CSS properties associated with any HTML element – except HTML's `id` element and position.

Let's create a new file, `ie4dhtml.html.`, to demonstrate what we can do with DHTML support in IE4.

This page shows the text *Free membership!* in the `changeRegion <div>` element. When you move the mouse over the *Apply Today* text in the `magicRegion <div>`, the *Free membership!* text will change to a membership application form in the `changeRegion <div>`. You might find this kind of effect used as a recruitment advertisement.

This magic is done using the `innerHTML` property of IE4. The `innerHTML` of an element is the HTML text within the tag. Here we're using it to access the HTML within the `changeRegion <div>` element, so we've simply put the new HTML code right into the `changeRegion <div>` element. Here's `ieDhtml.html`:

```
<html>
  <head>
  <link rel="stylesheet"  type="text/css" href="dhtmlPages.css">
```

```
<script language="JavaScript">
  var changed = false;

  //creating the form and saving it in a variable
  var formHTML = "<form class='changeFormStyle'>Name: <input type='text'><BR>" +
       "Address: <input type='text'><br>" +
       "<input type='submit' value='submit'></form>";

  //change the "Free membership!" text dynamically to the application form
  function changeIt() {
    if (!changed) {
      document.all.changeRegion.innerHTML = formHTML;
        changed = true;
    }
  }
</script>
</head>
<body>

<div id="magicRegion" onmouseover='changeIt("in");'>Apply Today!</div>
<div id="changeRegion">
 Free membership!
</div>
</body>
</html>
```

Then all we need is the CSS stylesheet to go with it. Here's `dhtmlPages.css`, which is a modification of the stylesheet we used in `jscssp.html`:

```
#magicRegion { position:absolute; top:20px; left: 100px; width:200px;
               color:yellow; background-color: black;
               font-size:24pt; font-family:Arial; }
#changeRegion { position:absolute; top:90px;
                left: 80px; width: 500px;
                color: red;  background-color: blue;
                font-size:48pt;  font-family:Times; }
.changeTextStyle { color: red;
                   background-color: blue;
                   font-size:48pt; font-family:Times; }
.changeFormStyle { color: black; font-size:12pt;
                   font-family:Arial;  font-weight:bold;}
```

We're using two new styles, both beginning with a dot: `.changeTextStyle` and `.changeFormStyle`. These selectors are classes. A class is associated with an element by setting the `class` attribute within the tag. In the previous example we could have used the `class` attribute set to `changeFormStyle`:

```
<form class="changeFormStyle">
  …
</form>
```

So as you can see in these simple examples, IE 4's DHTML support enables us to create all sorts of interactions and transformations on a web page. You can use it to dynamically modify many of the CSS attributes of an HTML element, and replace any HTML fragment on the displayed page using the `innerHTML` property. For more extensive information on the `innerHTML` property, you may want to consult the following URL:

http://msdn.microsoft.com/workshop/author/dhtml/reference/properties/innerhtml.asp?frame=true

Unfortunately, Netscape Navigator 4.x does things quite differently.

DHTML in NN4

The NN4 series of browsers cannot dynamically re-render an HTML page incrementally, as IE4 can, so you can't change an area of a page and see the result immediately. Instead, DHTML interactions rely on a completely different mechanism: positioning, visibility control, and document rewrite, using a new layer element in NN4.

Because of the display engine limitation, it is not possible to have an `innerHTML` property to dynamically affect the web page. What's more, most of the accessible CSS style properties in NN4 are read only; you can't modify them because the browser can't display the changes immediately.

Instead of CSS property changes, or `innerHTML` property, most of the dynamic features in NN4 are enabled through the introduction of the layer element. A layer is like an overlay HTML page: it can be positioned dynamically over the page being displayed. And since it is an independent HTML page, one can also "open" its document and re–rewrite the content. In fact, NN4 treats any positionable element that uses `position:absolute` as a layer.

Theoretically, multiple layers can be made visible or invisible at any time, but we can't use the visibility toggle for most dynamic interaction, because some versions of NN4 only allow a layer to be made visible once.

When you're writing JavaScript to use with NN4, you can access the `document.layers` collection. This collection contains all the layers defined within the document. This will include any `<div>` (or other position elements such as `<span>`, `<p>`, etc.) that has `position:absolute` specified as a style – because NN4 treats them as layers.

> NN4 and IE4 difference: IE4 uses `innerHTML` to dynamically re-render portions of an HTML page. NN4 uses a new layer tag that displays an HTML page over the existing page, the content of this page can be rewritten using JavaScript during runtime.

Let's look at how we can achieve an effect like the dynamically changing DHTML page we created earlier for NN4.

Note that we need to use JavaScript code to assign the `onmousever` event handler. Assigning this handler inline, with the `<div>` element as we have done in the IE4 version, doesn't work in some versions of NN4. Here's the code for the NN4 compatible page (`nn4dhtml.html`):

```
<html>
  <head>
  <link rel="stylesheet"  type="text/css" href="dhtmlpages.css">
  <script language="JavaScript">
    var formHTML = "<form class='changeFormStyle'>Name: <input type='text'><br>"+
        "Address: <input type='text'><br>" +
        "<input type='submit' value='submit'></form>";
    var changed = false;
      function changeIt() {
        if (!changed) {
          var tp = document.changeRegion.document;
          tp.open();
          tp.write(formHTML);
          tp.close();
        changed = true;
        }
      }
  </script>
```

Because NN4's `<layer>` contains an independent HTML document, we will see shortly that the `changeRegion` `<div>` is treated exactly like a layer object by NN4.

Note that the two `<div>` elements in the highlighted code below are being positioned absolutely by the CSS because absolutely positioned `<div>` elements are treated like layers in NN4 and layers are complete HTML documents that can be positioned over one another. This is why the JavaScript code:

```
document.changeregion.document
```

refers to the HTML text inside the `changeRegion` `<div>`. The first document is the HTML document itself; the second document is the document inside the `changeRegion` `<div>` – acting like a layer. This is why the `document.open()` and `document.write()` works on the `<div>` for replacing content.

Here's the rest of the code:

```
</head>
  <body>
    <div id="magicRegion" >Apply Today!</div>

    <div id="changeRegion">
     Free membership!
    </div>
```

The following JavaScript will set the event handler when the mouse is moved over the `magicRegion` `<div>`.

```
  <script>
    document.magicRegion.onmouseover = changeIt;
  </script>
</body>
</html>
```

Using <layer>, or an absolutely positioned <div> element (which is treated identically to a <layer> object), it is possible to create similar effects to those enabled by the innerHTML and the dynamic rendering engine of the IE4+ series of browser. NN4's DHTML model, although slightly different, is still very capable of creating a compelling dynamic web experience for the user.

The real irony, though, is that the layer tag is no longer supported by NN6. Instead, the NN6 browser supports DHTML through something called the W3C DOM (Document Object Model). More about this in Chapter 7.

So we've looked at writing distinct DHTML for NN4 and IE4, but we haven't yet seen how to put these two together in a page that works for both. We'll look at that next.

Writing Cross-Browser DHTML

Because of the incompatibility of DHTML across the IE4.x and NN4.x series of browser, and even further incompatibility with the IE5.x, IE6.x and NN6.x series of browsers, writing HTML code that is cross-browser can be a pretty convoluted process.

If we restrict our DHTML coding to simply accessing and manipulating CSS attributes, and confine our dynamic changes to the common set of attributes between the two series of browser, then we can write DHTML code that works on both IE4 and NN4. However, this approach won't give us much to work with, since the DHTML support in the two browsers have very little in common. Even when our goal is the most minor dynamic interaction, there are still significant differences between the two browser series that we must be very careful about.

You need to be careful how you try to access the CSS property of an element that you want to change using JavaScript. This how you'd access most CSS properties in IE4+:

```
document.all.<element id>.style.<attribute>
```

Note that, in IE4, all access to CSS properties of an element must go through the style object associated with the element. In NN4, however, we need to use the precise hierarchy to locate an element and its attribute:

```
document.<element hierarchy>.<element id>.<attribute>
```

The document.all collection does not exist in NN4. We have to navigate through the element relationship hierarchy to locate a specific element. NN4 does, though, allow JavaScript CSS property syntax, which means that we can access a CSS property without referring to an associated style object (as is required in IE4).

So as we've already seen, you can write DHTML code that involves moving elements dynamically, or modify the HTML that is displayed dynamically, using the layer tag in NN4 (or absolutely positioned <div>, <span>, <p>, etc). IE4, on the other hand, is able to re-render dynamically – so you can use the innerHTML property to replace any HTML fragment for dynamic changes. Here are some more crucial differences:

Version	Specifics
IE4, IE5, IE6	`document.all.<element id>` works
	Can modify most CSS style attributes and have immediate re-rendering
	Dynamically animated movement of HTML elements is possible by changing its CSSP positioning
	HTML of page can be modified and re-rendered using `innerHTML` property
	`Onmouseover` and `onmouseout` attributes can be used to configure mouse over event handlers
NN4	Need to traverse the hierarchy of the element to access it
	Can only modify very few CSS attributes using DHTML
	Animated movement of HTML element is supported via layer tag, and dynamic positioning of layers
	Modification of HTML can only be performed on layer, by opening the layer's document and re-writing its HTML
	JavaScript can be used to assign `onmouseover` and `onmouseout` handler for maximum compatibility
NN6, IE6	Supports W3C DOM access for uniform DHTML
	Supports most of CSS1 for consistent CSS behavior

Due to the very large number of bugs in all versions of browsers relating to DHTML and CSS rendering, it's impossible to give an exhaustive list of incompatibilities that you might face when you're creating cross-browser DHTML code. For more information on creating cross-browser DHTML code, you may want to visit Netscape's Dynamic HTML developer's site at the following URL:

http://developer.netscape.com/tech/dynhtml/dynhtml.html

Whatever you're working with, though, you'll need to test diligently against all the versions of all the browsers that you intend to support.

The Difficulties with Cross–Browser DHTML

Given all differences we just looked at, even the most minimal cross-browser DHTML page often requires two distinct flows of DHTML logic for the NN4 and IE4 series of browser. When you're tackling the problem using this approach you'll need to be tolerant of slight differences between layout and interaction of the two browsers – this is how web professionals typically deal with the issues. The goal should be to attain a similar effect, and not an exact replica. We need to strike this compromise because the mechanism to support DHTML is totally different on the two legacy series of browsers.

Once you've resigned yourself to writing DHTML for each browser, the only remaining problem is how to determine the browser that is currently accessing the page. There are quite a few solutions to this problem.

We'll begin by modifying the DHTML page we have already worked with to make it cross-browser compatible. This is `xbdhtml.html`:

```
<html>
  <head>
  <link rel="stylesheet"  type="text/css" href="dhtmlpages.css">

  <script language="JavaScript">
  var formHTML = "<form class='changeFormStyle'>Name: <input type='text'><br>" +
      "Address: <input type='text'><br>" +
       "<input type='submit' value='submit'></form>";
  var changed=false;
    function changeIt() {
      if (!changed) {
        if (document.all) {
          document.all.changeRegion.innerHTML = formHTML;
          changed = true;
        } else {
          if (document.layers) {
            var tp = document.changeRegion.document;
            tp.open();
            tp.write(formHTML);
            tp.close();
            changed = true;
          }
        }
        }
      }
  </script>
</head>
  <body>
    <div id="magicRegion" >Apply Today!</div>
    <div id="changeRegion">
    Free membership!
    </div>
    <script>
      if (document.all) {
        document.all.magicRegion.onmouseover = changeIt;
      }
      else {
        document.magicRegion.onmouseover = changeIt;
      }
    </script>
  </body>
</html>
```

Inside the `changeIt()` function, we check for the existence of the `document.all` collection to determine if the browser being used is IE4+. If we detected IE4, we can go ahead and use the simple `document.all.<element name>` indexing in the code to address the `changeRegion <div>`, and we can also use the `innerHTML` property to perform dynamic changes.

Otherwise, we check to see if the `document.layers` collecton exists because this will tell us if the browser is NN4.x. If it is, we must address the element through its hierarchy and rewrite the content of the layer (absolutely positioned).

In fact, `xbdhtml.html` is essentially a merge of `iedhtml.html` and `ns4dhtml.html`. If you load it up using NN4, it looks like this:

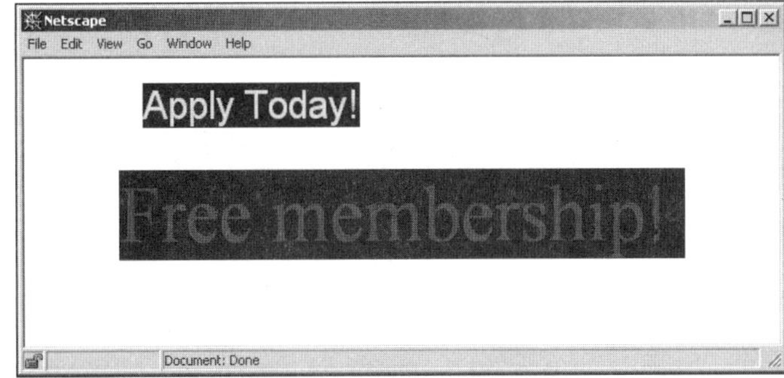

If you pass the mouse over the *Apply Today!* text, an application form will appear:

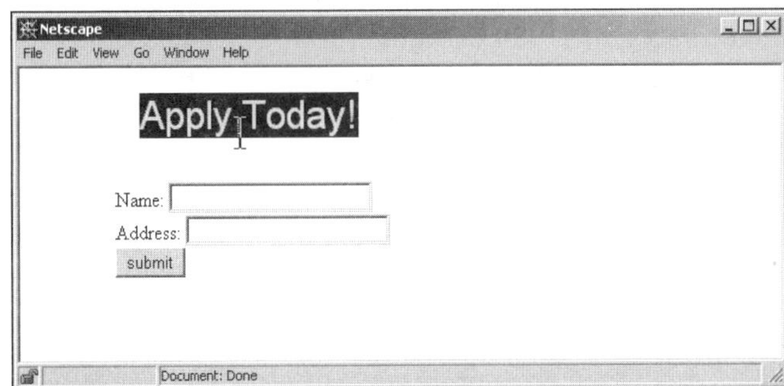

When you access the same `xbdhtml.html` using IE4, and passing the mouse over the *Apply Today!* text, you will see the page change like this:

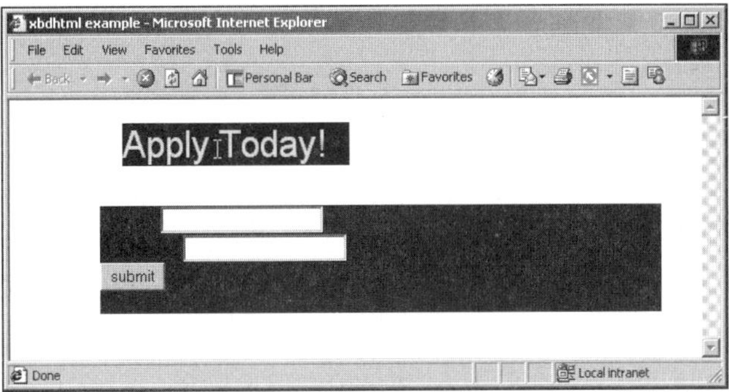

The two resulting screens do not look exactly the same. Different spacing, fonts, bugs in style inheritance for the various elements, and more contribute to the slightly different output.

> When you're creating cross-browser DHTML pages, you'll often need to settle for similar looking output that will work across the target browsers. Attempts to create results that are exactly identical are often futile, and can consume a lot of resources, energy, and time for very little return.

In the above example, we have used two different techniques to determine the browser that is being used: the `document.all` collection test (which tests for the object's existence), and the `document.layers` collection test. We'll recap these techniques here, and demonstrate a third technique for achieving browser identification.

Technique 1: Using document.all Collection Test

This technique is illustrated in the following code fragment:

```
if (document.all) {
   //IE4+ browser compatible code…
}
else
{
    //code for other browsers…
}
```

This technique is good for checking if we're in a Microsoft IE4 or higher version browser, because it looks for the existence of the `document.all` collection. Where this exists, we can be quite certain that we are in an IE4 or higher (or a compatible browser like Opera). This technique is fast, and is useful to determine if we can code IE4 style DHTML.

Technique 2: Using the document.layers Collection Test

This technique is useful when we need to determine if the browser is an NN4.x browser. The NN4.x browser series alone exposes the `document.layers` collection to JavaScript programs, so we can check for it in order to isolate coding appropriate for NN4 browsers alone:

```
if (document.layers) {
    //NN4 browser compatible code…
}
else
{
    //code for other browsers…
}
```

Techinque 3: Using a Browser Sniffer

This is a substantially more comprehensive technique. While it involves a little more work, it gives very detailed information about the vendor and browser version accessing the web page. Browser sniffers are specialized JavaScript programs that you can incorporate into your web page to "sniff out" the browser that is accessing the page.

Browser sniffers tend to use a myriad of techniques to achieve positive browser identifications (including the two techniques mentioned above). The owners of these programs update the sniffer code whenever a new browser is released to ensure its usefulness.

Using a browser sniffer makes determination of browser vendor and version quite simple. However, due to the complexity of these programs, it will introduce a lot of code into your web page, which can mean that it executes a little slower.

One very popular browser sniffer, the *Ultimate JavaScript Client Sniffer*, can be found here:

http://www.mozilla.org/docs/web-developer/sniffer/browser_type.html

At the time of writing, the most current version is 3.03 and it will detect IE 3,4,5,5.5,6, Netscape 2,3,4, and 6, Opera3, 4, and 5, and HotJava 3 on Win32, Mac, Linux, and SunOS.

All you need to do to use the sniffer is include the JavaScript code from this URL into a `<script>` element in the `<head>` section of your page. You then have a series of predefined Boolean flags, named `is_???` that you can code with. You can write code that test these flags like this:

```
if (is_nav4) {
      //NN4 only coding, such as layer tags...
}

if (is_nav4up) {
     //NN4+ coding ...
}

if (is_ie4) {
     //IE4 only coding...
}

if (is_ie4up) {
     //IE4+ coding...
}
```

ImageViewer: Part 2: Adding DHTML and CSS

Let's start further analysis of the ImageViewer application that we have started in the last chapter, and apply some of the new concepts we have explored in this chapter.

Applying CSS/CSSP Stylesheets

A CSSP Stylesheet is being used in the `ImageViewerMain.html` to regulate the consistent formatting of the display. Drawing from our earlier discussion of CSS, we can see that this stylesheet is included as part of the web page. Of course, we could have linked to an external CSS stylesheet like this:

```
<link rel="stylesheet" type="text/css" href="viewerstyle.css">
```

All we need to do is ensure that the above `<link>` element is placed within the `<head>` element of the `ImageViewer.htm` file.

You can see the formatting and positioning specified by the application designer in this stylesheet. Let's tabulate those decisions here, and show the segments of code responsible for the format:

```
<style>
  body { background-color:black; }

  img, iframe { position:absolute; }
  iframe { top:50px; height:480px; margin:0px; border-style:none; }

  iframe#categoryframe
  {
```

```
    left:10px; width:210px;
  }

  iframe#thumbnailframe
  {
    left:125px; width:190px;
    background-color:black;
  }

  iframe#mainimageframe
  {
    left:320px; width:640px;
    border:5px double #c0c0c0;
  }

  img#scrollupimg
  {
    left:150px; top:10px;
  }

  img#scrolldownimg
  {
    left:150px; top:535px;
  }

  img#imageloadinganimation
  {
    left:320px; top:10px; visibility:hidden;
  }

</style>
```

Positioning iframes and imgs with CSS

Let us analyze this CSS Stylesheet selector-by-selector. First, we define the presentation of the standard `<body>` element. Recall that CSS Stylesheet helps us to separate the presentation from the structure.

```
body { background-color:black; }
```

This CSS rule sets the background color black, which is exactly what we see when we load `ImageViewer.htm`.

Next, we define the presentation of the `iframe` tag. Remember that this `iframe` tag is used of three times in our application, in each of the three areas of the application. The first selector specifies that the CSSP positioning code that we specify in `iframe` and `img` selectors will be absolute positioning.

```
img, iframe { position:absolute; }
```

The next selector sets the default appearance of our `iframe`(s). It is positioned 50 pixels from the top of the page, and has a height of 480 pixels. We also make the `iframe` margin and border invisible by setting them to 0 and style 'none' respectively.

```
iframe { top:50px; height:480px; margin:0px; border-style:none; }
```

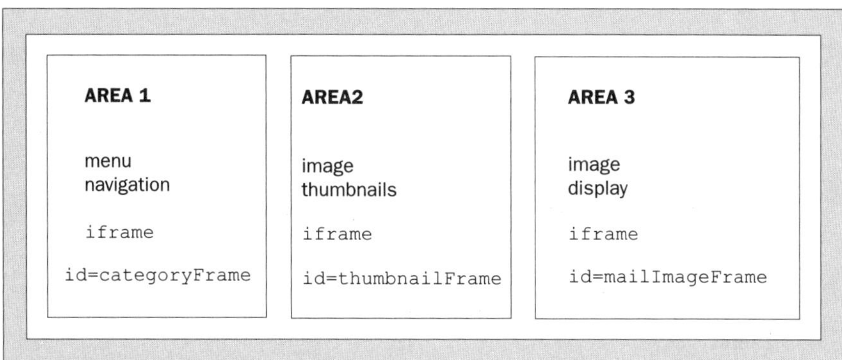

Note that the `iframe` selector will affect all three `iframe`s on the page. We also want to define the appearance of individual `iframes`. This happens in the next selector, which refines the general `iframe` format above, using a specialized `id` called `categoryFrame` (the `iframe#categoryFrame` selectors. Here, we set the `categoryFrame` 10 pixels from the left of the page (remember that we have already set positioning to absolute) and gives this instance of `iframe` a width of 210 pixels:

```
iframe#categoryFrame
  {
    left:10px; width:210px;
  }
```

The next two selectors perform the same specialized positioning function, but this time for the `thumbnailFrame` (Area 2) and `mainImageFrame` (Area 3) respectively:

```
  iframe#thumbnailFrame
  {
    left:125px; width:190px;

  }
iframe#mainImageFrame
  {
    left:320px; width:640px;
    border:5px double #c0c0c0;
  }
```

There is a gray double border of 5 pixels wide in the `mainImageFrame`. This gives a "framed" look for Area 3, where the image will be displayed.

The last set of CSS styles is used to position the two scroll button images at the top and bottom of the `tumbnailFrame`, as well as an animated *loading...* image that is only used on IE browsers.

```
IMG#scrollUpImg
{
  left:150px; top:10px;
}
```

```
IMG#scrollDownImg
{
  left:150px; top:535px;
}

IMG#imageLoadingAnimation
{
  left:320px; top:10px; visibility:hidden;
}
```

Applying DHTML

There's a lot that goes on in the `ImageViewer` application when users start clicking on the different areas. All of this, of course, is accomplished using JavaScript and DHTML.

In order to understand how the code in `ImageViewerMainCode.js` works, we need to have a bigger picture of how Area 1 (the navigation) and Area 2 (the thumbnails) work together:

```
ChesterThumbnails.htm
FlowersThumbnails.htm
HuntingdonThumbnails.htm
```

One of the thumbnails will be loaded into Area 2 (thumbnails) depending on the category selection that the user clicked on.

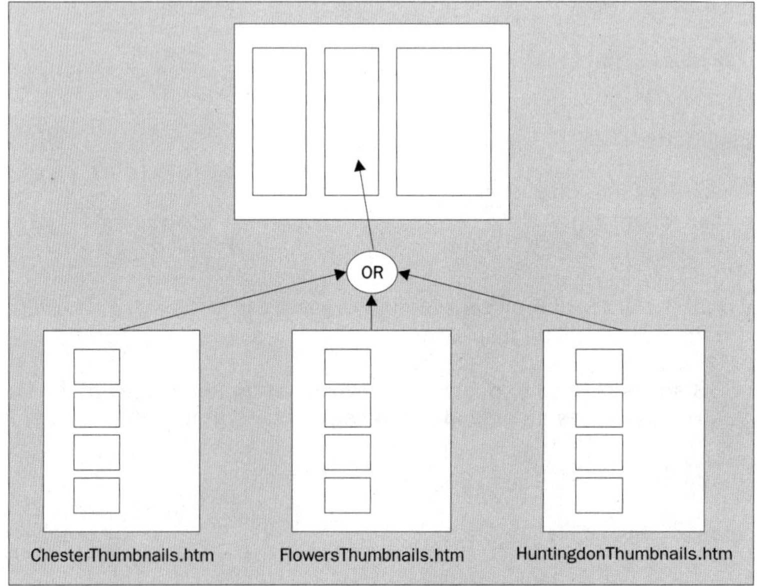

This selection is made through the collapsible list displayed in Area 1 (navigation). The collapsible list makes heavy use of DHTML in controlling the CSS Display property. Let's look at this in detail next.

The Collapsible List Implementation

We'll analyze the content of `CategoryIndex.htm` which controls the CSS Elements using DHTML. The `iframe` in Area 1 provides a collapsible list of choices.

First, there is the CSS stylesheet that specifies the format for the `<body>` tag. In this case, we're using the tiny 8-point font in dark orange, with a background set to black. The `<div>` tag is given a margin of 0 pixel, so that there is no extra space around it.

We then define two classes, `.Heading` and `.SubHeading`. This uses the same size font as the body, but with `bold` for the font weight. Defining CSS specialization as a class like this enables us to use the class attribute later on in an HTML tag like this:

```
<div class="heading">…</div>
```

The `.Heading` class CSS specialization will then be applied to this `<div>` element. The top margin for these specializations is set at 5 pixels.

```
<html>
<head>

<style>
body { font:8pt verdana; background-color:black; color:darkorange; }
div { margin:0px; }
.Heading, .SubHeading
  {
    font-size:8pt; font-weight:bold;
    cursor:pointer; cursor:hand; margin:0px; margin-top:5px;
  }
```

Note how we immediately override the font-weight of the `.SubHeading` class, sending it back to normal. We also define a class of `.dropLevel`, which isn't rendered at all initially:

```
.SubHeading { font-weight:normal; }
.dropLevel { margin-left:10px; display:none; }
</style>
```

DHTML MouseOver Highlighting

The code illustrates `mouseOver` animation. In this case, the style of the text label is changed when the cursor moves over the label. When the mouse is over the label, the text color turns from dark orange to gold, and the text is underlined. When the mouse cursor goes outside of the label, the dark orange text is restored.

```
<script language="JavaScript">
var previousMenuElementClicked;

function OnMouseOverHeading(thisTag)
{
```

```
    thisTag.style.textDecoration = 'underline';
    thisTag.style.color = 'gold';
  }

  function OnMouseOutHeading(thisTag)
  {
    thisTag.style.textDecoration = 'none';
    thisTag.style.color = 'darkorange';
  }
```

Hiding DIV Elements : The Illusion of a Collapsible Menu

The collapsible menu is implemented by toggling the display of nested `<div>` elements.

Writing Cross-browser DHTML

The `getTagById()` function is a cross-browser DHTML function that wraps up the different ways to access an element, given its tag `id`. It is a utility function that is called by other functions on this page. We can see simple browser detection using the `document.all` collection test technique in its logic. This code basically distinguishes between IE4+ browsers and other browsers. However, the `document.getElementById()` method used in the other branch makes this function compatible to only NN6 browsers or above.

```
function getTagById(tagId)
{
  var selectedTag;
  if (document.all)
  {
    selectedTag = document.all.item(tagId);
  }
  else
  {
    selectedTag = document.getElementById(tagId);
  }

  return selectedTag;
}
```

The `switchDisplay()` function is used to toggle the display of the two hidden nested `<div>`s that comprise the collapsible part of the list. It takes two arguments, the first one is the `<div>` that needs to be displayed (`expand`) or not displayed (`collapse`). The second argument takes the `<img>` tag that displays the addition (+) or minus (-) sign depending on whether the branch is expanded or collapsed.

The logic is quite interesting: it checks to see if the `<div>` is now displayed or not. In order to determine this, the `display` property may return `""` (the very first time because the inline style object does not yet have the display property assigned) or `"none"` (subsequently, once the `display` property has been assigned). If it is being displayed then it is removed from sight and the `<img>` is set to the plus icon, indicating a collapsed state. If it is not being displayed, then it is displayed and the `<img>` is set to the minus icon, indicating an expanded state.

```
function switchDisplay(tagId, branchImage)
{
  var tagToSwitch = getTagById(tagId);
  var imgToSwitch = getTagById(branchImage);
  if (tagToSwitch.style.display == "" || tagToSwitch.style.display == "none")
  {
    tagToSwitch.style.display = "block";
    imgToSwitch.src = "minus.gif";
    if (document.all)
    {
      tagToSwitch.scrollIntoView();
    }
  }
  else
  {
    tagToSwitch.style.display = "none";
    imgToSwitch.src = "plus.gif"
  }


}
```

The `loadNewImageCategory()` function is called when one of the leaf elements of the collapsible list is clicked. It causes a new thumbnail page, one of the three listed above, to be loaded into the thumbnails area (Area 2). It takes two arguments, the first one is the leaf `<div>` element that has been clicked by the user, and the second is the URL of the thumbnail page that should be displayed in Area 2.

The actual loading of the thumbnail into Area 2 is performed by a function that is located in the parent frame of the `ImageViewer.htm`, and called `loadNewCategoryThumbnails()`. The rest of the logic is used to reset the color of the previously clicked menu item to black, and set the currently selected one to gray.

```
function loadNewImageCategory(menuElementClicked, categoryURL)
{
  parent.loadNewCategoryThumbnails(categoryURL);
  if (typeof(previousMenuElementClicked) == "object")
  {
    previousMenuElementClicked.style.backgroundColor = "black";
  }

  previousMenuElementClicked = menuElementClicked;
  previousMenuElementClicked.style.backgroundColor = "gray";
}
</script>
```

Laying out the Nested DIV Elements

The nested <div> elements are manually laid out within the HTML page itself. You can find the code in the <body> section of the categoryindex.htm page. This image is of the <div> elements and their nesting, each level associated with an index number.

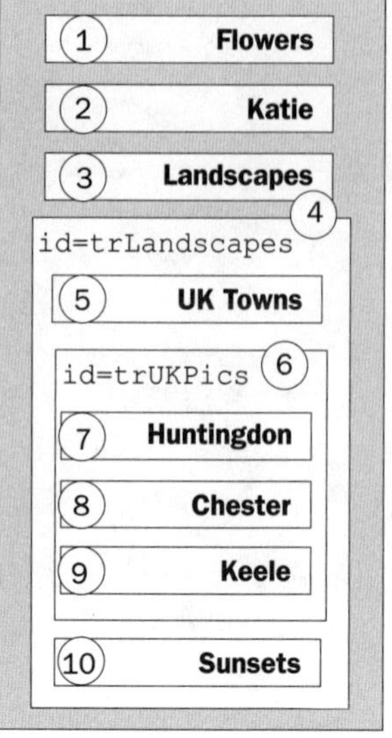

The code that creates this nesting is shown below, with the corresponding index number marked for each div element that is created:

```
</head>
<body>
<H5 style="color:goldenrod; font-size:9pt;">Photo Index</H5>
<!-- Pics of Flowers -->
      <!-- index 1 —>
      <div OnMouseOver="OnMouseOverHeading(this);"
         OnMouseOut="OnMouseOutHeading(this);"
         onclick="loadNewImageCategory(this, 'FlowersThumbnails.htm')"
         class="Heading">Flowers</div>
<!-- Pics of Katie -->
      <!-- index 2 —>
      <div OnMouseOver="OnMouseOverHeading(this);"
         OnMouseOut="OnMouseOutHeading(this);"
         onclick="loadNewImageCategory(this, 'KatieThumbnails.htm')"
         class="Heading">Katie</div>
```

Thus far, the layout has been straightforward, since the elements are all visible. In the next set of <div> definitions, though, we can see that the trLandscapes <div> has a dropLevel class, which will render it initially invisible. This means that only the preceding unnamed <div> will be visible. This unnamed <div> has an onclick() handler that will call the switchDisplay() function and toggle the visibility of the hidden trLandscapes <div>.

```
<!-- Landscape Photos -->
      <!-- index 3 —>
      <div OnMouseOver="OnMouseOverHeading(this);"
         OnMouseOut="OnMouseOutHeading(this);"
```

```
         onclick="switchDisplay('trLandscapes','imgLandscapes')"
         title="Click for further details"
         class="Heading">Landscapes<IMG src="plus.gif" id="imgLandscapes"></div>
      <!-- index 4 —>
      <div id="trLandscapes" class="dropLevel">
```

The same technique is used in a nested and unnamed <div> (meaning that there is no associated id attribute), the initially invisible `trUKPics` <div> will be expanded when the user clicks on the unnamed preceding <div>, and the `switchDisplay()` function is called.

```
   <!-- UK Photos -->
      <!-- index 5 —>
      <div OnMouseOver="OnMouseOverHeading(this);"
         OnMouseOut="OnMouseOutHeading(this);"
         title="Click for further details"
         onclick="switchDisplay('trUKPics','imgUKPics')"
         class="SubHeading">UK Towns<IMG src="plus.gif" id="imgUKPics"></div>
      <!-- index 6 -->
      <div id="trUKPics" class="dropLevel">
      <!-- Huntingdon -->
      <!-- index 7 -->
      <div OnMouseOver="OnMouseOverHeading(this);"
         OnMouseOut="OnMouseOutHeading(this);"
         onclick="loadNewImageCategory(this, 'HuntingdonThumbnails.htm')"
         class="SubHeading">Huntingdon</div>
   <!-- Keele -->
      <!-- index 8 -->
      <div OnMouseOver="OnMouseOverHeading(this);"
         OnMouseOut="OnMouseOutHeading(this);"
         onclick="loadNewImageCategory(this, 'KeeleThumbnails.htm')"
         class="SubHeading">Keele</div>
   <!-- Chester -->
      <!-- index 9 -->
      <div OnMouseOver="OnMouseOverHeading(this);"
         OnMouseOut="OnMouseOutHeading(this);"
         onclick="loadNewImageCategory(this, 'ChesterThumbnails.htm')"
         class="SubHeading">Chester</div>
      </div>
   <!-- Sunsets Pics -->
      <!-- index 10 -->
      <div OnMouseOver="OnMouseOverHeading(this);"
         OnMouseOut="OnMouseOutHeading(this);"
         onclick="loadNewImageCategory(this, 'SunsetThumbnails.htm')"
         class="SubHeading">Sunsets</div>
    </div>
   </body>
   </html>
```

So the collapsible part of the list is actually two hidden <div>s, one called `trLandscapes`, and another called `trUKPics`, and the application toggles between visible and invisible via the `switchDisplay()` function.

Taking a look at the leaf elements of the collapsible list, we can see that they are in this general form:

```
<div OnMouseOver="OnMouseOverHeading(this);"
     OnMouseOut="OnMouseOutHeading(this);"
     onclick="loadNewImageCategory(this, 'associated thumbnail page')"
     class="SubHeading">Category of thumbnails</div>
```

While the `OnMouseOver` and `OnMouseOut` handlers provide the mouse-over highlighting effect for the list item, the `onclick` handler is the one that will load a new associated thumbnail page into the Area 2, the thumbnail area. The user can click on the visible *Category of thumbnails* description, and the `loadNewImageCategory()` function will be called to load the required thumbnail into Area 2.

So that's how the collapsible list is created, and how the appropriate thumbnail page is loaded into Area 2 depending on user selection. We can now proceed back to the main `ImageViewer.htm` page and fill in those empty JavaScript functions that we have left in the last chapter.

Back to the Main Page

Look into `ImageViewer.htm`, right after the inline CSSP stylesheet, and you'll find the following lines that read in and process the JavaScript code in the `ImageViewerMain.js`:

```
<script language="JavaScript" src="ImageViewerMainCode.js">
</script>
```

To keep things tidy and modular, all of the JavaScript coding has been contained in this externally included `.js` file.

Let 's take a look at the `ImageViewerMain.js` file and see how it handles the various user interactions with JavaScript and DHTML. Here, we can fill in the logic of some of the JavaScript functions.

In our examination of the `CategoryIndex.htm` page and its collapsible list, we saw that it depended on a `loadNewCategoryThumbnails()` function in its parent frame to update the thumbnail in Area 2. It is in `ImageViewerMainCode.js` where we find this function.

The `loadNewCategoryThumbnails()` function is called whenever a leaf `<div>` of the collapsible list is clicked. The URL of the thumbnail page to load is supplied as an argument. This function simply locates the Area 2 `iframe`, and changes its `href` property to the argument URL, causing the thumbnail page to load into the `iframe`.

```
function loadNewCategoryThumbnails(categorySrc)
{
  // use function rather then access direct from other page
  // makes it easier to change id of frame

  var mainImgFrame = window.frames["thumbnailFrame"];
  mainImgFrame.location.href = categorySrc;
}
```

The two scroll buttons at the top and bottom of Area 2 depends on the next two functions, `scrollThumbnailUp_onclick()` and `scrollThumbnailDown_onclick()` for proper operation. Each function simply locates the `iframe`, and then calls its `scrollBy()` method to perform the scrolling.

```
function scrollThumbnailUp_onclick()
{
  var thumbnailIFrame = window.frames["thumbnailFrame"];
  thumbnailIFrame.scrollBy(0,-95);

}

function scrollThumbnailDown_onclick()
{
  var thumbnailIFrame = window.frames["thumbnailFrame"];
  thumbnailIFrame.scrollBy(0,95);
}
```

The only other function that we have not covered is the `loadNewMainImage()` function. This function is called directly from one of the thumbnail pages, and it simply replaces the `href` of the Area 3 `iframe` (the image display area) with the JPG file URL supplied as the argument.

Note that on IE4+ browsers, it also detects using the `document.all` collection test and then shows the animated icon while the JPG file is loading into the Area 3 `iframe` (just in case the user is on a slow link and waiting for the image to load completely).

```
function loadNewMainImage(imgSrc)
{
  // use function rather than access direct from other page
  // makes it easier to change id of frame

  var mainImgFrame = window.frames["mainImageFrame"];
  if (document.all)
  {
    document.all.imageLoadingAnimation.style.visibility = "visible";
  }

  mainImgFrame.location.href = imgSrc;

}
```

The last function that we cover is called from the `onLoad` handler of the Area 3 `iframe`. Its main purpose is to hide the animated icon upon the completion of the picture download.

```
function hideImageLoadingImage()
{
  // load event not supported by Netscape once frame loaded
  if (document.all)
  {
    document.all.imageLoadingAnimation.style.visibility = "hidden";
  }
}
```

A Final Word on ImageViewer Application and Browser Compatibility Issues

While the ImageViewer application works reasonably well across IE4.x, IE5.x, IE6.x, and NS6.x browsers, it doesn't work on NN 4.x browsers because it depends heavily on the unsupported `iframe` construct. This again reinforces the difficulty in creating cross-browser compatible DHTML code.

Summary: The Early Days of DHTML

In this chapter, we had a look at the beginnings of Dynamic HTML (DHTML): the ability to cause dynamic changes to a web page after it is displayed. We explored the fascinating world of Cascading Style Sheets, discovered that CSS can help to separate the appearance aspects of a web page from the structure of the page – enabling easy maintenance and modifications of a large body of web pages. Furthermore, combining the programming power of JavaScript with the appearance control of CSS gives us a great way to dynamically cause change in the resulting HTML document.

Using the DHTML support of IE4+ browsers, we learned that its display engine is capable of dynamically re-rendering a web page incrementally. This allows most CSS attributes to be changed via JavaScript and redisplayed immediately. We also experimented with the highly versatile `innerHTML` property that enables segments of HTML code to be changed completely and re-displayed without reloading the HTML page.

NN4's support for DHTML is quite different than IE4. While supporting CSS, the CSS properties exposed for programmatic access via JavaScript is limited; almost all properties are read only ones. Instead, NN4 relies on a new tag called `<layer>` that enable layers of HTML content to be positioned, made visible/invisible, and dynamically rewritten under programmatic control. Creating a `<div>` (or other elements that can be positioned) with absolute positioning is equivalent to creating a layer.

The different DHTML support provided by NN4 and IE4 creates major problems when writing cross-browser DHTML code. While it is possible, true cross-browser DHTML code is very restrictive in terms of expressiveness and capability. Instead, it is very common to test for the browser being used, and then execute browser specific DHTML code. We examined three different techniques for browser detection, and discuss the pros and cons of using each one.

Finally, we continued our analysis of the ImageViewer application, and applied our knowledge of CSS, DHTML, and cross-browser DHTML programming to explain the various elements of the application – including a collapsible list created using DHTML coding.

The widespread complaint from the web design community about the terrible incompatibilities between the 4.x browsers did not fall on deaf ears. By the next generation, IE 6.x and NN 6.x, compatibility of DHTML support has reached an all time high – thanks to a large part to a new object model standard from W3C, known as the W3C Document Object Model (DOM). We'll look at the DOM in the next chapter.

7

- The DOM
- Manipulating the page with the DOM
- DOM events
- Image Viewer Application: Part 3

Author: Stephen Williams

The DOM: DHTML for the Latest Browsers

In Chapter 4 we met some of the objects that most browsers make available to JavaScript. These include the `window` and `navigator` objects, which can be used to identify the browser environment an HTML page exists in and navigate the Internet using JavaScript. The chapter also looked at the simple document object model (DOM) that exists in the IE4 and NN4 browsers and how it can be used to access parts of the document, such as images and form elements.

In Chapter 6 we went on to look at how we can use DHTML to effect changes within the document. The ability to cause these changes can vary greatly between IE4 and NN4 browsers and the chapter explored the ways in which the object support of IE4 and NN4 differs. Here, we'll complete our investigation of browser objects by looking at the W3C DOM, which defines objects that it is hoped present and future browsers will all support, making browser compatibility problems much less of an issue.

The Document Object Model (DOM) developed by the W3C defines a platform- and language-neutral application programming interface (API) that allows programs and scripts to dynamically access and update the content, structure, and style of HTML and XML documents.

Browsers that support the ECMAScript binding of DOM methods and properties to objects allow JavaScript to use these DOM methods and properties rather than a browser-specific API. This increases the cross-browser/platform compatibility of the JavaScript code. The aim, therefore, is to allow code scripted using the DOM API to be written once and work across different browsers with no, or a limited number of, modifications.

In reality, the level of support for the DOM APIs is mixed. The two main browsers Internet Explorer 5+ and Netscape 6+ both have the highest level of support for the DOM. However, they have only implemented parts of the DOM, and not necessarily the same parts. This chapter will focus only on the important parts of the DOM that have been implemented and are similar in both browsers.

Overview of the DOM

The goal of the DOM specification is to define a programmatic interface for XML and HTML documents. With the DOM, programmers can navigate the document structures, and add, modify, or delete elements and content.

The DOM is separated into four different levels – 0, 1, 2, and 3. Levels 1, 2, and 3, which are under the realm of the W3C, can be found at *http://w3c.org/dom/domtr*.

Functionality equivalent to that exposed in Netscape Navigator 3.0 and Microsoft Internet Explorer 3.0, such as the browser objects described in Chapter 4, is referred to informally as "**DOM Level 0**". However, there is no W3C specification for this Level. *DOM Level 0* is sometimes referred to as the HTML DOM, which forms part of the *DOM Level 1* specification.

The **DOM Level 1** is a recommendation of the W3C that can be separated into two parts: DOM Core objects and DOM HTML objects.

- The **DOM Core** provides a set of fundamental objects that can represent any structured document. The methods and properties of the DOM Core objects represent the functionality used for XML documents, and also serve as the basis for DOM HTML objects.

- The **DOM HTML** objects build upon and extend the DOM core objects, providing additional methods and properties that produce a more convenient view of an HTML document.

Any compliant implementation of the DOM HTML should implement all of the fundamental DOM Core objects as well as the HTML objects.

The DOM Level 1 specification has been intentionally limited to those methods needed to represent and manipulate document structure and content. The **DOM Level 2** specification, another recommendation of the W3C, extends and builds on DOM Level 1. As of DOM Level 2, the DOM has been modularized into eight different modules: Core, HTML, Views, StyleSheets, CSS, Events, Traversal, and Range. Prior to this in DOM Level 1, the Core and HTML interfaces existed in one single specification.

The diagram below shows how these modules relate to each other. Modules included in DOM level 1 are located within the gray box. Note that XML 1.0 is not actually a module, but is included in the diagram because support for XML 1.0 documents is provided by parts of the Core module. Arrows indicate modules that extend other modules.

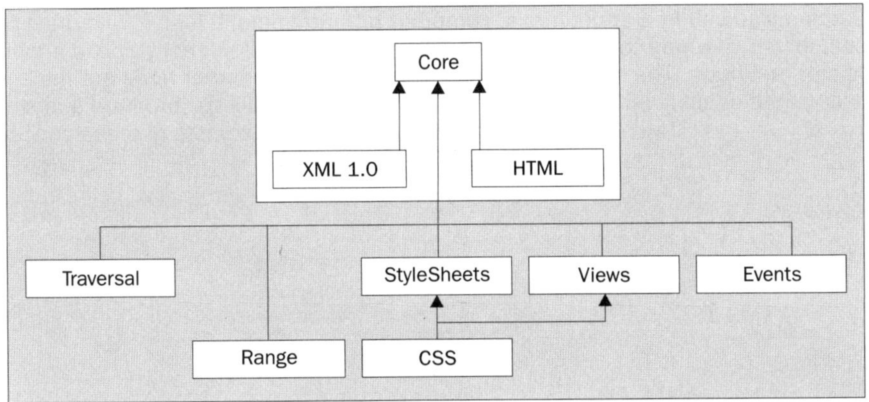

The Traversal and Range modules add enhancements to the ability of traversing the document structure provided by DOM Level 1. The StyleSheets, CSS, and Views modules add enhanced support for altering document presentation. The last additional module, Events, adds support for user interface events, such as mouse events, and document structure manipulation events, such as moving an element from one part of the document to another part.

DOM Level 3 is a work in progress at the time of writing. It extends DOM Level 2 to include further support for event handling, loading and saving external XML-based documents, and a path-based mechanism for automatically finding nodes within the document structure. This chapter won't discuss DOM Level 3 any further, since its support in browsers is virtually non-existent at the time of writing. You should visit the W3C web site at *http://www.w3.org/DOM/* for more information and the full detailed specification on DOM.

So how much support for the DOM is there at present? The Level 1 DOM is supported to some extent by NN6.0+ and IE5.0+ browsers. Support is greatest in NN6.0+; IE5.x browsers only partially implement Level 1 DOM.

If you are trying to learn about DOM, NN6 or IE5.5 are probably the best to experiment with. Version 4 and earlier browsers are not suitable – the examples in this chapter will not work with them. Note also that the Windows and Macintosh versions of Internet Explorer differ considerably, so you cannot be certain that scripts developed on one platform will work properly on the other.

To discuss the whole of DOM in detail would require a whole book in itself. This chapter will concentrate on the DOM Level 1 functionality, which is primarily concerned with traversing, accessing parts of, and manipulating the document structure. Later in the chapter we'll look at a few very useful aspects of DOM Level 2 for which support exists. Before this though, let's look at how a document is structured and represented by the DOM.

DOM Structure

As its name suggests, the DOM is a mechanism for closely modeling the structure of a document using objects. All DOM documents, such as XML and HTML documents, have a defined structure that is very much like a tree structure. This document structure consists of **nodes** that are organized in a tree-like hierarchy. Each node in the tree represents either a different type of content or a different structural element.

If you are unfamiliar with tree structures in computer programming, it is useful to draw analogies with family trees, as this is where they borrow their terminology. A node directly above another node in the tree is a parent node. The nodes one level directly beneath another node are the children of that node. Nodes at the same level, and with the same parent, are siblings (brothers and sisters). Let's have a look at a simple HTML document, which we'll use as an example of these concepts.

```
<html>
   <head>
      <title>DOM Structure</title>
   </head>
   <body>
      <h3>Hello World!</h3>
      <p>This is a <b>simple</b> example of a <i>DOM model.</i></p>
   </body>
</html>
```

A document such as this can be represented using a tree structure model as depicted in the following diagram:

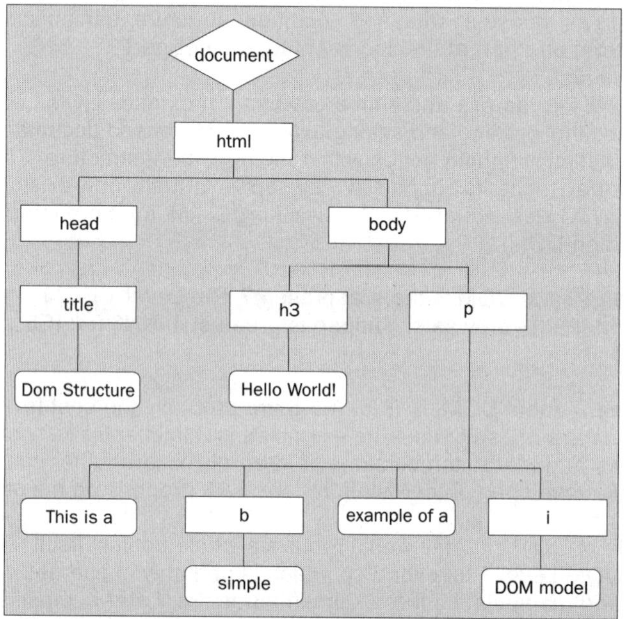

At the top of the tree structure is the `document` object, being the root to the whole tree. Beneath this is the `<html>` element, which is the root element of the document. The elements and text contained within the document spread out under the `<html>` element within the tree structure. The rounded boxes represent terminal "leaf nodes" that contain textual content (known as **text nodes**). The square boxes represent "branch nodes" that may contain zero or more child nodes (known as **element nodes**). These child nodes may themselves be branch nodes or leaf nodes.

Here we have seen examples of text and element nodes, but there are many others, for example comment nodes. It will be no surprise that the DOM represents each type of node with a different object, and these objects have different properties and methods. These derive from the interfaces that the object implements, a topic that we'll look at next.

DOM Interfaces

As we saw in Chapter 3, within the world of object-oriented programming, objects are constructed from instructional sets of data called classes. A class is very much akin to the architect's design blueprints for constructing a building, defining the properties and methods an object will possess when created from the class.

Classes can extend other classes, building upon the properties and methods already present in a base class. Again if we look at the building analogy, it's similar to starting with plans for a two-bedroom house, and extending the plans to give a three-bedroom house. This form of extending classes is known as **inheritance**; the extended class contains the methods and properties of the base class as well as its own specific methods and properties.

Classes can implement abstract data types known as **interfaces**. Interfaces define methods and properties that a class must define. For example, imagine an interface called Biped that defines left leg and right leg properties, and the methods walk, run, and jump. All classes that implement this interface must contain the interface properties and methods. A Human class could implement the Biped interface and so could the Bird class – two different classes that are used to create two different types of objects, both containing the same properties and methods. Without needing to know anything about the Human or Bird class, we could refer to both objects as if they were the same types of object, that is both Biped objects.

Just as classes can extend each other so can interfaces. A class that implements an extended interface must implement all the methods and properties of the extended interface, as well as the base interfaces from which the extended interface is derived. With our Biped analogy, we could create a Primate interface that extends the biped interface. The Primate interface could define the properties body, left arm, right arm, hair, and head, and the methods turnBody and bendOver. A Human class implementing the Primate interface would have to contain all these properties and methods, as well as those defined by the Biped interface that Primate extends.

Note interfaces do not define how a method actually functions – only that it must exist. Creating interfaces and extending them in this way creates a framework of how objects within a system are related to one another and the properties and methods these objects possess. This is in essence how the DOM interfaces work. The DOM interfaces define properties and methods that objects within a program (the browser in this case) must implement to represent and manipulate the document structure. The DOM defines many interfaces and this chapter will concentrate mainly on a few of the key interfaces from the DOM Core module.

Core DOM Interfaces

The most fundamental DOM interface is the **Node** interface – this is the primary (or base) datatype for the entire document object model, defined within the DOM Core module. It represents a single node in the document tree structure, and is implemented by all node objects within the document.

The Node interface defines many methods and properties, including those for dealing with child nodes. While all objects that implement the Node interface must expose all these properties and methods, not all objects will have children. For example, Text nodes are not allowed to have children as they exist at the terminus of the branches in the document structure, and adding children to such nodes results in an error being raised.

In the previous diagram showing a representation of a simple HTML document, the branch nodes all corresponded to HTML elements, which are objects that are derived from the **HTMLElement** interface of the DOM HTML module. The interfaces for all HTML elements are derived from this base interface. The HTMLElement interface itself is derived from the **Element** interface, which is in turn derived from the Node interface, within the DOM Core module. We know that elements may have attributes associated with them – there are methods of the Element interface that retrieve an attribute value by name.

The terminal leaf nodes are Text node objects that implement the **Text** interface. The Text interface inherits from the **CharacterData** interface, which in turn inherits from the Node interface. No DOM objects correspond directly to CharacterData, so we won't delve into that interface here. HTML Comments exist within the document structure too and are nodes derived from the **Comment** interface, which is also an extended interface of the CharacterData interface.

If there is no markup inside an element's content, the text is contained in a single object implementing the Text interface that is the only child of the element. If there is HTML markup, it is parsed into the information items (such as elements and comments) and text nodes that form a list of child elements.

The **Document** interface represents the entire HTML or XML document. Conceptually, it is the *root* of the document tree, and provides the primary access to the document's data. Since elements, text nodes, etc. cannot exist outside the context of a document, the Document interface also contains methods needed to create these objects.

The **DocumentFragment** interface represents a minimal document object that extends the Node interface. It is common to want to be able to extract a portion of a document's tree or to create a new fragment of a document, and the document fragment object can be useful to store such fragments. When a document fragment is inserted into a Document (or indeed any other Node that may take children) the children of the document fragment and not the document fragment itself are inserted into the document structure. This makes the document fragment very useful when the user wishes to create nodes that are siblings; the document fragment acts as the parent of these nodes so that the user can use the standard node properties and methods to manipulate the fragment.

The diagram below shows the relationship between the main interfaces described above and how they are extended from the Node interface.

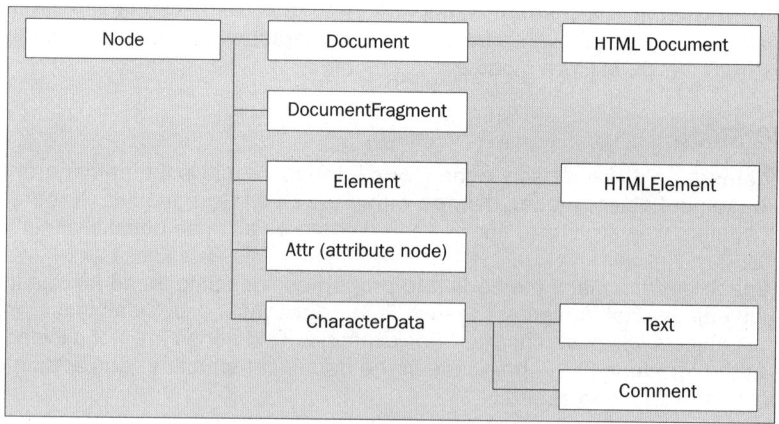

Over the next few sections we will look at the more useful methods and properties that these interfaces define and how they can be used to manipulate the document.

Accessing Parts of a Document

The DOM Level 1 specification is primarily concerned with traversing the document structure and manipulating that structure.

Accessing Elements

Traditionally the browser provides a number of collections that allow JavaScript to access parts of the document so that DHTML can be used to manipulate the properties of the document. Collections are a convenient means to access a set of nodes within the document structure and the items within the collection can be accessed using array notation. For example, to access an image we would use the `document.images` array, or the `document.forms` array to access the forms within our document.

Internet Explorer 4 moved beyond these simple collections available with IE3.0 and NN4 by including the `document.all` collection. This is a useful array, which stores references to all the elements in the document. It can be used to create your own custom collections, for example:

```
var collDivs = document.all.tags("div"); // Collection of div elements
var collForms = document.all.tags("form"); // Collection of form elements
var collBolds = document.all.tags("b"); // Collection of b elements
```

The `tags()` method searches the elements referenced in the `all` collection and returns a collection of elements with the same name as the string value supplied as the parameter.

Unfortunately, NN4 does not have the capability to create custom collections like this – it's one of the many reasons why NN4 browsers are less flexible than IE4 browsers. Moving onwards, DOM Level 1 provides a method that allows JavaScript to create custom collections by using the `document.getElementsByTagName()` method defined in the Document interface:

```
var collDivs = document.getElementsByTagName("div");
var collForms = document.getElementsByTagName("form");
var collBolds = document.getElementsByTagName("b");
```

Both NN6+ and IE5+ browsers have implemented this method, though IE5+ browsers also still support the `document.all` collection property to provide backward compatibility with the earlier version 4 browsers.

Being able to create your own custom collections is great if you need to loop through all the elements of a particular type and perform some operation on them. For example, you could create a script that will iterate through every <b> element in a document and change the styling properties of the element in response to a user action. The sample code below does exactly this:

```
var collBolds = document.getElementsByTagName("b");

for (var i = 0; i < collBolds.length; i++)
{
  collBolds[i].style.color = "red"
}
```

A collection of all the <b> elements in the document is created, and stored in the `collBolds` variable. The `for` loop then iterates through each item in the collection and sets its `color` style property to be red. You should already be familiar with setting style properties in this way from Chapter 6, since this is how IE4+ browsers change style properties. NN6 browsers now support this technique of manipulating style properties, because this approach has been adopted by the DOM Level 2 CSS module.

For mass extraction, the `getElementsByTagName()` method is very powerful. However, it's not so useful if you want to access a single specific element within a document. In its IE5 browser, Microsoft introduced the `getElementById()` method of the `document` object to perform this task. If you supply the `id` of an element as a parameter to the method, it will return a reference directly to that element. This method is part of the DOM Level 1 specification, and so is available in Netscape 6.0+ browsers.

The `getElementById()` method was defined initially by the HTMLDocument interface in DOM Level 1 and is now defined in the Document interface in DOM Level 2; it's therefore automatically available to HTMLDocument objects in DOM level 2 as the HTMLDocument interface is extended from the Document interface.

If you imagine a document containing an element (it can be virtually any type of element, such as a <span>, <div>, or <td>) that has an `id` attribute set to equal `"nickname"`, you can access that element directly using the `getElementById()` method. This is illustrated in the following example, `GetElementById.htm`:

```
<html>
<head>
<title>Obtaining an Element By ID</title>
<script>
function highlightElement(elem)
{
  var el = document.getElementById(elem);
  el.style.color = "red"
  el.style.fontWeight = "bold"
}
</script>
</head>
<body>
  <span id="nickname">Bilbo Baggins</span>
  <form>
    <input type="button" value="Highlight"
onclick="highlightElement('nickname');">
  </form>
</body>
</html>
```

In this example, clicking the button calls the `highlightElement()` function and passes the string id name of the element to be highlighted (the <span> element in this case) to it as an parameter. The `highlightElement()` function obtains a reference to the named element using the `document.getElementById()` method.

Once a reference has been acquired for the element, DHTML can be used to change the properties of this element. In the example above, we have simply changed the textual content of the element to be colored red and provided it with a bold font.

The two DOM methods we've met so far can also be used in combination, providing an even more powerful mechanism for accessing elements within the document structure. The `getElementsByTagName()` method is available to both Document and Element type objects. Therefore, when you obtain a reference to an element using the `getElementById()` method, the returned element has the `getElementsByTagName()` method available to it. If this element is a root node to a substructure, then the `getElementsByTagName()` method can be used to create a collection of elements from within that substructure. For example, a collection of `<b>` elements could be obtained from a specific paragraph using the following code sample:

```
// Obtain a reference to a paragraph
var paraEl = document.getElementById("myParagraph");

// Obtain a collection of bold elements within the paragraph
var paraBolds = paraEl.getElementsByTagName("b");
```

The converse of this task is to obtain a reference to an element from within a collection of elements. This is possible by treating the collection of elements as an array that is indexed by the id values of its elements:

```
// Obtain a collection of bold elements
var collBolds = document.getElementsByTagName("b");

// Obtain a reference to an element from within the collection
var theElement = collBolds["myElementIdName"];
```

In this example a collection of `<b>` elements is created. We then use the string name of the `id` attribute to directly obtain a reference to the element with the same id name from the `collBolds` collection.

The following example, `collection.htm`, alters our previous example to show a simple web page that uses a collection to obtain a reference to an element from its `id` name.

```
<html>
<head>
<title>Obtain an Element By ID from a Collection</title>
<script>
  function highlightElement(idName)
  {
    var collBolds = document.getElementsByTagName("b");
    var theElement = collBolds[idName];

    if (theElement != null)
    {
      theElement.style.color = "#ff0000";
      theElement.style.fontSize = "14pt";
    }
  }
</script>
</head>
<body>
  <span id="username">
    <b id="firstname">Bilbo</B> <b id="surname">Baggins</b>
```

```
    </span>
    <form>
      <input type="button" value="Highlight"
onclick="highlightElement('firstname')">
    </form>
</body>
</html>
```

Clicking on the button in this example will simply highlight the word *Bilbo*, which is found in the first <b> element, by setting the font color to red and the font size to 14pt.

Traversing the Document Structure

As we saw earlier, the document structure is represented within a browser as a tree structure comprising many different nodes. The two DOM methods discussed in the previous section provide high-level functionality to search the document structure, find particular HTML elements within the structure, and return references to them. The DOM also provides low-level properties to traverse the document structure and access the nodal elements within. By using these lower-level properties you can 'walk' through the tree structure node by node, either vertically or horizontally depending on your needs.

Often, when using the low-level node traversal properties, you will first obtain a reference to a parent node. For any parent node, there may be zero or more child nodes. (Note, however, not all child nodes may have children, for example text nodes are nodes that terminate the branches of the tree structure and therefore have no child nodes. In these instances the traversal properties have a `null` value.) Node objects have three properties that provide access to the children of a parent. The first of these is the `childNodes` property, which stores a list of the child nodes. The elements of the list can be accessed in a similar way to an array. Loops can be used to iterate through each of the nodes in succession and perform some operation on or with them.

```
var children = someNode.childNodes;

for (var i= 0; i < children.length; i++)
{
  var child = children[i];
  //do something with the child node
}
```

Note that there is a major inconsistency here – the NN6 and IE5+ browsers for the same document build different `childNodes` collections, since they treat white space in the document differently. White space characters can be line breaks, carriage returns and tabs. For example, consider the following page `childnodeProblem.htm`:

```
<html>
<head>
<title>childNodes problem</title>
</head>
<body onload="alert(document.body.childNodes.length);">
<p id="p0">a paragraph</p>
<p id="p1">a paragraph</p>
</body>
</html>
```

Before and after the two paragraphs a white space character exists, creating new lines for each piece of the HTML source. This white space character is converted to a child node in NN6 browsers, whereas in IE browsers the white spaces are ignored. Hence, running this piece of code in IE5+ browsers produces an alert box with a value of 2, whereas in NN6+ browsers a value of 5 is returned. Obviously, this is a serious problem and shows that, even with the DOM being standardized, the way the browsers interpret the specifications to implement the DOM, allows inconsistencies to arise. This fact highlights a difficulty in producing successful cross-browser code, when using the properties of Nodes that we will look at next for traversing the document structure.

From time to time, you will probably want to inspect only the first or last child nodes of a parent. Of course, you could do this easily with the `childNodes` property as follows:

```
var first = someParentNode.childNodes[0];
var last = someParentNode.childNodes[someParentNode.childNodes.length-1];
```

However, it is much easier to use two other properties, `firstChild` and `lastChild`, which directly reference the first and last child nodes respectively.

```
var first = someParentNode.firstChild;
var last = someParentNode.lastChild;
```

We've now seen how to traverse the tree structure in a downwards direction, but what about going back up? From each child node you can directly reference the parent node using a single property called `parentNode`, as can be seen below.

```
var parent = someChildNode.parentNode;
```

As well as traversing up and down the nodal structure, we can also traverse from side to side, that is from one child node to the next. Nodes possess two properties that allow this mode of traversing: `nextSibling` and `previousSibling`. As their names suggest, `nextSibling` references the next node along from a particular node with the same parent, and `previousSibling` references the node prior to the current node (again with the same parent).

```
var next = someChildNode.nextSibling;
var previous = someChildNode.previousSibling;
```

By using the `firstChild` and `nextSibling` properties, we can loop sideways through each of the children of a parent node, rather than using the `childNodes` property that we saw previously:

```
for(var n = someParentNode.firstChild; n != null; n = n.nextSibling)
{
  //do something with the n child node
}
```

The loop initializes a variable `n` to the first child node of a parent. Then, after each successive pass through the loop, `n` is set to the next child node until there are no more child nodes and `n` equals `null`. At this point, the loop exits.

The diagram below summarizes the important properties of nodes that allow you to traverse the nodal structure of a document in either the up, down, or side-to-side directions.

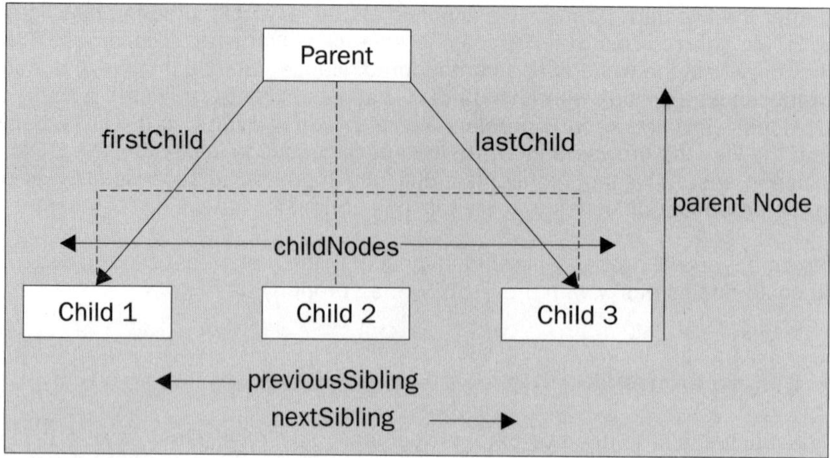

In this section we've seen how to traverse the nodal structure of the document, but we don't know much about the nodes themselves. As we move through this chapter you will learn more about the nodes, how to manipulate them, and how important traversing is.

Identifying Nodes

As we touched on earlier, different types of objects represent different nodes within the document structure. Within the DOM, all nodes are derived from a base interface called Node, which defines all the common methods and properties that nodes should possess. The Node interface is extended by other interfaces (such as Element and Text interfaces) to provide more specific properties for the different types of objects that can exist. Two properties (`nodeType` and `nodeName`) are defined by the Node interface to allow JavaScript to determine the type of node that is currently being interrogated.

All nodes have a particular type, which can be queried using the `nodeType` property. This property stores a constant numeric value – a different value is stored for each node type. By traversing through the document and testing the type of each node, JavaScript can selectively identify similar groups of nodes. The constant numeric values for each type of node are summarized in the table below.

Node Type	Node Type Constant Value	Node Name
ELEMENT_NODE	1	Element name
ATTRIBUTE_NODE	2	Attribute name
TEXT_NODE	3	#text
COMMENT_NODE	8	#comment
DOCUMENT_NODE	9	#document
DOCUMENT_FRAGMENT_NODE	11	#document-fragment

The third column of the table indicates the names that the different nodes may have, stored in the nodeName property. For most types of node, this property is not particularly useful. However, with element and attribute nodes, the value of nodeName allows us to differentiate between nodes. Objects that represent HTML elements are extended from the DOM Element interface – the value of nodeName for this type of node is equal to the name of the HTML element. Similarly, for attribute nodes the nodeName equals the name of the attribute, equivalent to the name of an attribute within an HTML element.

Knowing this information, we can now traverse the document structure identifying different node types as we go. Let's have a look at an example – consider the following section of HTML source code:

```
<p id="test">Here is a <b>paragraph</b> with some text in it. Using the
<b>traversal properties</b> discussed in the previous section and <b>node type</b>
JavaScript can identify the number of <b>HTML elements</b> within this paragraph.
</p>
```

The following recursive function can be used to count the number of HTML elements within the paragraph above.

```
function countHTMLElements(node)
{
  var sum = 0;
  if (node.nodeType == 1) /* Element Node test */
    sum++;
  for(var i=0; i < node.childNodes.length; i++)
  {
    sum += countHTMLElements(node.childNodes[i]);
  }
  return sum;
}
```

The function accepts a node object as a parameter and examines it and all of its children, counting the number of Element nodes (that is, HTML elements), and returning the number of elements encountered.

```
var count = countHTMLElements(document.getElementById("test"))
```

This statement will return the number of HTML elements in the previous HTML source code and stores the value in the count variable. In this instance, the value returned is 5 since there are five HTML elements within the source code above.

Changing the function so that the if statement tests whether the nodeType is equivalent to 3 (that is, a text node), the modified form of the function will return a value of 9, indicating that there are 9 text nodes within the HTML fragment. With respect to text nodes, it is useful to know about another property called nodeValue.

The nodeValue property of text nodes is a reference to the actual string value that is displayed on a page. The property can be accessed to find the textual value of the node, or set to change the text displayed on a page.

Modifying the countHTMLElements() function above to include the nodeValue property, we can transform the function into one that will return the complete textual content within an element.

```
function getText(node)
{
  var txt = "";
  if (node.nodeType == 3) /* Text Node test */
    txt += node.nodeValue;
  for(var i=0; i < node.childNodes.length; i++)
  {
    txt += getText(node.childNodes[i]);
  }
  return txt;
}
```

You should be able to see that the nodeValue of each text node is concatenated into a string stored in the txt variable, and the resultant string is returned. If used with the HTML Source fragment above, all the text of the paragraph is return without any of the HTML tags.

Using the nodeValue property, we can also change the text that is displayed within a document. The uppercase() function below obtains the string value of the node passed as a parameter, converts it to uppercase, and resets the nodeValue to the equivalent uppercase string.

```
function uppercase(node)
{
  if (node.nodeType == 3)
  {
    node.nodeValue = node.nodeValue.toUpperCase();
  }
}
```

You may have used or seen the innerText property that is available for obtaining and setting the textual content within an HTML element. This is a proprietary Microsoft Internet Explorer property, available with its version 4+ browsers. It is not a part of the DOM specification, and is not available in other browsers, such as Netscape Navigator. So, if you want to change the text within an element with code that works across browsers that use DOM, then it is better to use the nodeValue property of the text node within an HTML element.

When used in combination with attribute nodes, the nodeValue property allows us to read or set the value of the attribute. We will learn more about this later in this chapter.

Manipulating the Document

The ability to change the nodeValue of a text node is a very useful feature in its own right, allowing textual content within the document to be changed dynamically, without altering the document structure itself. However, to mutate the document structure itself, we use various other methods that the DOM interfaces define. This, in combination with what has already been discussed, is where DOM really becomes powerful.

Mutating the Document Structure

The Node interface defines several methods for node manipulation, allowing nodes to be removed from and appended to the document structure. One of these methods is the `removeChild()` method that accepts a node as an parameter (a child to the node the method is called from), removes the child node, and returns a reference to the removed node.

```
var n = parentNode.removeChild(childNode);
```

Note that if the node to be removed also contains child nodes, they too are removed. However, they can still be accessed using the removed node reference returned from the `removeChild()` method.

We can easily create an operation that removes all the content from an element by using a loop to iterate through a list of child nodes, passing each as a parameter of this method:

```
function clearElement(node)
{
  while (node.hasChildNodes())
  {
    node.removeChild(node.firstChild);
  }
}
```

The `clearElement()` function above removes the nodal structure below a parent node, which is passed as its parameter. Instead of using a `for` loop to iterate through each of the child nodes, a `while` loop is used. This loop tests to see whether the node contains any child nodes by using the `hasChildNodes()` method, from the Node interface, which returns `true` if the node does have child nodes and `false` if not. Each pass through the loop removes the first child, until there are no more child nodes to be removed.

Nodes can also be added back into the structure through the use of the `appendChild()` method. This method appends a node to the end of a list of child nodes, thus also making the node the last child node of the parent. If the node already exists, it is first removed before being appended as the last child node.

The `reverse()` function below uses the `appendChild()` method to reverse the order of the nodes below a parent node.

```
function reverse(node)
{
  var i = node.childNodes.length - 1
  while (i >= 0)
  {
    node.appendChild(node.childNodes[i]);
    i--
  }
}
```

This function loops backwards through each of the child nodes, successively removing and appending the nodes, reversing their order. Note there is no need to use code to remove the child node before appending it back to the list of child nodes, as the `appendChild()` method does this for us.

In a similar operation to appending nodes back into a list of child nodes, the `replaceChild()` method can be used to replace one child node with another. This method accepts two parameters: the first is the new node and the second is the old node. If the new node already exists as a child node of a parent, it is first removed. We will see a use for this in the next section.

Creating New Nodes

Being able to mutate the document structure is starting to add a whole new dimension to DHTML and open up a whole host of new possibilities. In this section, we'll see that the Document interface provides methods for the creation of new HTML elements and Text nodes. These nodes can then be inserted into the document at specific points using the methods and properties of nodes described above.

Recall the `getText()` function, defined earlier; the function returns the string value of all the text nodes contained within a node and its child nodes (if they exist). The following example shows a function, `setText()`, which will allow you to set the text of an element.

```
function setText(node, txt)
{
  clearElement(node);
  var txtNode = document.createTextNode(txt);
  node.appendChild(txtNode);
}
```

The function first removes all the child nodes using the `clearElement()` function defined earlier. A new text node is then created using the `createTextNode()` method of the `document` object, and appended to the specified parent node using the `appendChild()` method we have already seen. The `createTextNode()` method accepts a single parameter, namely the string value of the text node.

We now have two functions, `getText()` and `setText()`, that use the DOM API, are cross-browser compatible, and completely remove the need to use the Internet Explorer specific `innerText` property.

As well as creating new text nodes, new HTML elements can be created using the `createElement()` method, also defined by the Document interface. This method accepts a single parameter that is the string name of the HTML element to be created.

The next example, `Embolden.htm`, uses a function that creates a `<b>` element using the `createElement()` method, and re-parents a node so that it and all its descendants are displayed in a bold font within an HTML page.

```
<html>
<head>
<script>
function convertToBold(node)
{
  var boldElement = document.createElement("b");
  var parent = node.parentNode;
  parent.replaceChild (boldElement, node);
  boldElement.appendChild(node);
}
</script>
</head>
<body>
```

```
    <p id="makeMeBold">Here is a simple paragraph</p>
    <form>
      <input type="button" value="Make Bold"
             onclick="convertToBold(document.getElementById('makeMeBold'))">
    </form>
  </body>
  </html>
```

If you try this example in your browser, clicking on the form button will cause the text in the paragraph to become bold. The displayed paragraph becomes the equivalent of the HTML source code below:

```
<b><p id="makeMeBold">Here is a simple paragraph</p></b>
```

Note that some HTML elements cannot be re-parented by certain other HTML elements. Therefore, there is a need to be careful when using this type of functionality.

Modifying Attributes

Adding attributes to HTML elements can have marked effects on how content within the document is displayed. The Element interface defines two methods for retrieving and setting the values of attributes.

The `getAttribute()` method accepts as a parameter the string name of an attribute, and returns the value of the named attribute if it exists or an empty string if not. Note that some attributes, such as the `<input>` element's `type` attribute, have a default value if one is not set. The method may return a default value instead of an empty string for an attribute, even if the attribute is not set in the source.

The example below shows how you can obtain the value of the horizontal alignment attribute (`align`) of an element. In this case, we are using the paragraph with the `id` name equal to `makeMeBold` from the previous example.

```
var elem = document.getElementById('makeMeBold');
var alignment = elem.getAttribute("align");
```

The `setAttribute()` method adds a new attribute and value to an element. It accepts two parameters – the first is the name of the attribute to set and the second is the value of the attribute. If an attribute with that name is already present in the element, its value is changed to that given in the value parameter. The example below, again using the paragraph from the previous example, shows how you can set the horizontal alignment attribute of an element to be centered.

```
var elem = document.getElementById('makeMeBold');
elem.setAttribute("align", "center");
```

A useful effect in browsers that have implemented HTML 4 is to use the `title` attribute of an element to supply extra information to a user in the form of a ToolTip when their mouse cursor is positioned over it. For example, it could be used when acronyms appear within a document so that the `title` attribute supplies the expanded meaning of the acronym. Below is the HMTL source code of an example acronym that may be used within a web page.

```
<acronym title="DOM (Document Object Model)"
         style="cursor:pointer;"
         onclick="expandAcronym(this)">DOM</acronym>
```

The `<acronym>` element in this example has an `onclick` event handler that calls a function called `expandAcronym()`, passing as a parameter a reference to the element itself. When called, the function swaps back and forth the text value of the element and the value of the `title` attribute.

```
function expandAcronym(el)
{
  var elTxt = getText(el);
  var titleTxt = el.getAttribute("title");
  setText(el, titleTxt);
  el.setAttribute("title", elTxt);
}
```

The `expandAcronym()` function obtains the text from the element by using the `getText()` function defined earlier and the value of the `title` attribute using the `getAttribute()` method. The text of the element is set to the text value that was previously stored in the `title` attribute using the `setText()` function that, again, we defined earlier. Finally, the value of the `title` attribute is set to the original text of the element using the `setAttribute()` method.

This effect can be seen in the screenshots below. Clicking on the `<acronym>` element expands the text content to the value of the `title` attribute, and a second mouse click returns the text back to its original value. Note the ToolTip changes too, as we change the value of the `title` attribute.

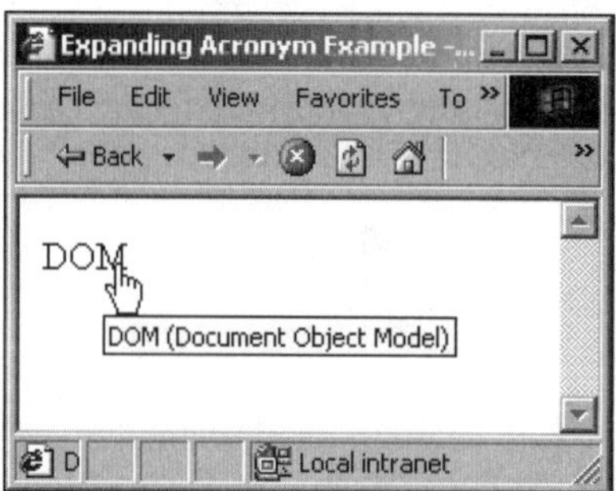

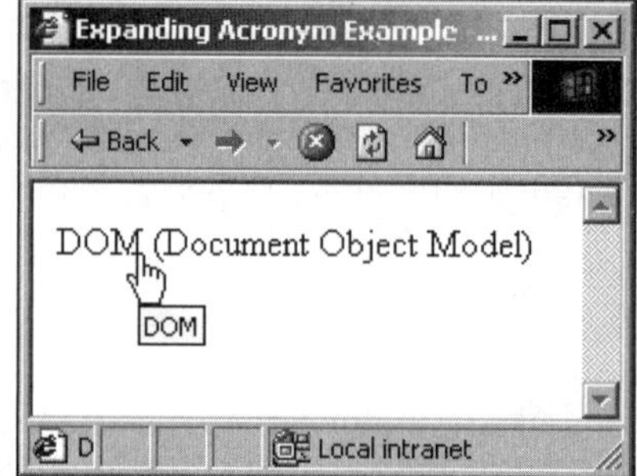

DOM Compatibility

If you try to run any of the scripts within this chapter, you will usually run into problems in browsers that don't comply with the DOM (that is, version 4 browsers and earlier). Worse still, the browser that has implemented DOM may not have implemented the full specification. This latter issue is not such an issue when considering a vast amount of the DOM Level 1 specification, but is important when DOM Level 2 is taken into account. This raises compatibility issues; one way around these issues is to know which browsers implement what features of the DOM and use a client sniffer every time you want to use DOM features (see Chapter 6 for more discussion of client sniffers).

A simple and easy technique that does not involve client sniffers is to test that a particular object or method exists before using it. We saw this technique in use in Chapter 4 and Chapter 6.

The example below defines a function that tries to use the `getElementById()` function:

```
function doSomething(id)
{
  if (document.getElementById)
  {
    var el = document.getElementById(id)
    // some code
  }
  else
  {
    alert("DOM getElementById feature not available")
    // do some other code
  }
}
```

This function tests to see if the `document` object possesses the `getElementById()` method and, if it does, it knows it can safely use the method in the `if` block. If not, the code in the `else` block is used.

As a web developer, you will undoubtedly come across many issues with DOM support. One of the best web resources that detail whether many of the features are supported can be found at *http://www.xs4all.nl/~ppk/js/* in the *DOM Compatibility Table* page.

Netscape 6.0 support was good, but 'flaky' in some respects. The Netscape 6.1+ browsers resolved many issues, having the best support for DOM level 1 and much of the DOM Level 2 specification. These browsers are probably the best place to test your scripts first.

Support for DOM level 1 within IE5.x is good, albeit incomplete. However, DOM level 2 is not supported, except for the ability to manipulate the CSS properties of elements (this is very useful, as many DHTML applications depend on this ability). IE6 has improved the DOM level 1 support, but still has not embraced DOM level 2 wholly.

DOM Compliance Test

The DOMImplementation interface is defined as part of the DOM Level 1 core module – this is one of the few interfaces that do not extend another interface. The Document interface defines an `implementation` property that is an object with a DOMImplementation type, available from the `document` object. This `implementation` object has the `hasFeature()` method, which can be used to determine whether a DOM module is supported.

> *Note that any implementation that conforms to the DOM Level 2 or any DOM Level 2 module must conform to the Core module by default.*

The `hasFeature()` method accepts two string parameters: the first is the name of the module, for example "HTML", and the second is the DOM version, for example "2.0". It returns a value of `true` or `false` to indicate whether the module is supported. As no browser yet supports DOM Level 3, the function can only possibly return `true` if the second parameter has a value of "1.0" or "2.0".

The following lines of code show how to use the `hasFeature()` method. In this case we are testing to see if the DOM HTML Level 2 module has been implemented.

```
var hasDomHtml = false;
if (document.implementation)
  hasDomHtml = document.implementation.hasFeature("Html", "2.0")
```

Before the `hasFeature()` method is used, the `if` statement tests whether the `implementation` object has been implemented as a property of the `document` object. If we didn't do this and the `document.implementation` property didn't exist, then neither could the `hasFeature()` method and a JavaScript error will result when an attempt to call the method occurs.

The following table shows the DOM Level 1 and 2 modules and their conformance within Netscape Version 6.1 and 6.2 browsers:

Module Feature Name	**Supports Dom**		**Description**
	Level 1.0	**Level 2.0**	
Core	Yes	Yes	
HTML	Yes	Yes	DOM HTML module support
XML	Yes	Yes	DOM XML module support
Views	–	Yes	DOM Views Module support
StyleSheets	–	Yes	DOM StyleSheets module support
CSS	–	Yes	DOM Cascading StyleSheets module support
CSS2	–	No	DOM Cascading StyleSheets Level 2 module support
Events	–	Yes	DOM Events module support
UIEvents	–	No	DOM User Interface Event module support
MouseEvents	–	Yes	DOM Mouse Event module support
HTMLEvents	–	Yes	DOM HTML Event module support
MutationEvents	–	No	DOM Document Structure Mutation Event module support
Range	–	Yes	DOM Text Range module support
Traversal	–	No	DOM Document Traversal module support

As you can see, the latest Netscape browsers conform to much of the DOM 2 specification. However, according to the DOM specifications, the UIEvents module must be implemented to have correctly implemented the MouseEvents module. Thus NN6 wrongly claims here to have the MouseEvents feature. Similarly, although a `true` value is returned from the `hasFeature()` method for the Range module, you may find that some of the module has not been fully implemented.

Unfortunately IE5 browsers have not implemented the DOMImplementation interface so their DOM conformance cannot be tested. Hence, as in the example piece of code above, testing the `document.implementation` property is important if you use it within IE5 or earlier browsers. IE6 has implemented the interface, but the `hasFeature()` method only returns `true` for the HTML module feature, and only for version 1.0.

Importing XML Documents

Importing new content into a web page without loading a whole new document has long been a problem for web developers. Version 4 browsers went some way towards fixing this problem by including the `<iframe>` and `<layer>` elements. (NN6 browsers do not support the `<layer>` element, which was introduced with NN4 browsers, because the `<iframe>` element is part of the HTML 4 specification). These elements, which we covered in Chapter 5, allow new documents to be loaded into parts of a main page.

Part of the DOM Level 2 allows us to move away from this mechanism of loading new documents into a frame to view supplementary content. Instead, IE5+ and NN6+ browsers allow XML documents to be imported directly into an HTML page. Using the methods and properties discussed earlier in this chapter, JavaScript can traverse the XML document, extract content, and insert the new content into the HTML document at specific points.

If you have ever visited the Microsoft MSDN Library web site, you will have seen the left-hand frame that contains a TreeView style navigation menu system. If haven't seen this yet, point your browser to the URL *http://msdn.microsoft.com/library/* to have a look. (Note that it works best using an IE5.0+ browser.) Clicking on a menu option in the left-hand pane allows a sub-list of menu options to be displayed. As it does this, an option drops down that says '*Loading...*'. At this point, the browser is requesting an XML file that will contain the sub-menu options. Once the XML document has been retrieved, JavaScript extracts the content and builds the new sub-menu, replacing the '*Loading...*' visual cue.

In this section we will have a look at how we might do something similar. The aim is to create a simple TreeView menu navigation system using data imported from an XML document to create the menu options and their actions. The screenshot below shows how this menu will look:

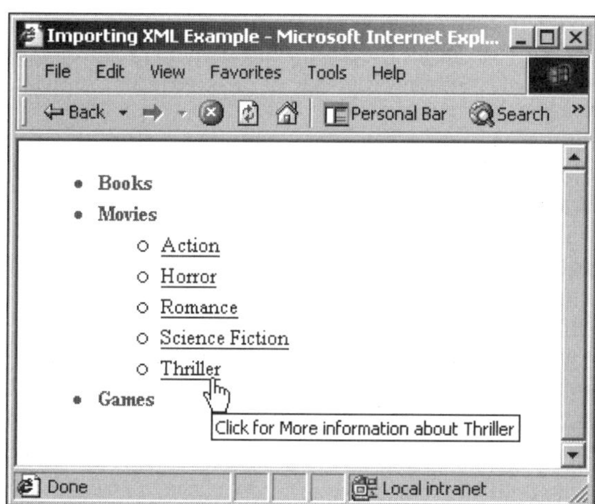

The top-level menu items are colored red and use a bold font. The sub-level menu items are colored blue and underlined. Each menu and menu item has a `title` attribute that pops up a ToolTip when the mouse cursor is placed over it.

To start this example, a simple HTML document needs to be created, called `Importing_XML.htm`, as below. We'll add to this as we build up the menu.

```
<html>
<head>
<title>Importing XML Example</title>
<style>
  <!--
  #menubar { width:180px; height:150px; }
  #menubar LI { font-size:10pt; cursor:pointer; cursor:hand; }
  .sublist { display:none; }
  .menu { font-weight:bold; color:#dd3030; }
  .menuitem { color:#0000ff; text-decoration:underline; }
  // -->
</style>
<script language="JavaScript">
  <!--
  function winload()
  {
    importDoc('menu.xml', xmlHandler)
   // Any other initialization code goes here...
  }
  // -->
</script>
</head>
<body onload="winload()">
  <div id="menubar">Menu is Loading...</div>
</body>
</html>
```

The body of the page contains a single `<div>` element, which will act as the container element for the menu. The `id` attribute of the `<div>` element allows some style properties to be applied to it within the `<style>` element at the top of the page (giving the size and background color of the menu) and allows JavaScript to access the element easily. The `<style>` element contains several other classes and properties that will be applied to the elements of the navigation system when they are created later.

The `onload` event handler has been added to the `<body>` element, so that the `winload()` function is called after the page has loaded. The `winload()` function can be used to initialize any variables required in the page or to call functions needed to set up the page correctly after the page has loaded. In this instance, it calls the `importDoc()` function, passing two parameters: the string name of the XML file to import (`menu.xml`) and a reference to a function that will handle the processing of the XML document (`xmlHandler`).

With NN6 browsers, importing XML documents is available using the `createDocument()` method of the `document.implementation` object. IE5+ browsers use an alternative approach of a proprietary ActiveX COM object instead, to achieve the same result. We add this to our page within the `importDoc()` function:

```
<script language="JavaScript">
  <!–
  // Script for IE5+ and NS6 browsers
  function importDoc(url, handler)
  {
    var xmldoc = null
    /* Use the standard DOM Level 2 technique, if supported
       Else use the MS proprietary ActiveX method, if supported
       Else do something else, if neither import technique works
    */
    if (document.implementation && document.implementation.createDocument)
    {
      xmldoc = document.implementation.createDocument("", "", null);
      xmldoc.onload = function()
      {
        handler(xmldoc);
      }
    }
    else if (window.ActiveXObject)
    {
      xmldoc = new ActiveXObject("Microsoft.XMLDOM");
      xmldoc.onreadystatechange = function()
      {
        if (xmldoc.readyState == 4)
          handler(xmldoc);
      }
    }
    else
    {
      // Add code here for browsers that
      // do not support importing xml documents
    }
    if (xmldoc != null)
      xmldoc.load(url);
  }

  function xmlHandler(doc)
  {
  }

  function winload()
  {
    importDoc('menu.xml', xmlHandler)
    // Any other initialization code...
  }
  // -->
</script>
```

The `importDoc()` function above uses an `if...else` statement to check whether the DOM mechanism is available to import the XML document. If not, then it checks to see if the Microsoft ActiveX control is available. If neither of these options is available, other code can be included in the final `else` statement.

Netscape 6+ browsers will create an empty XML document by calling the `createDocument()` method. A function is then attached to the `onload` event handler of the XML document. This function is used to pass the XML document to the `handler` function passed as the second parameter to the `importDoc()` function. (Recall that when we call `importDoc()` in our `winload()` function, we specify the function `xmlHandler()` as this parameter.)

The operation is similar in IE browsers – a new ActiveX `XMLDOM` object is created and a function is added to the `onreadystate` event handler (equivalent to `onload`).

The last part of the `importDoc()` function checks to see if an object has been created and stored in the `xmldoc` variable. If so, the `load()` method of the object is used to load the XML file that was passed as the first parameter to the `importDoc()` function.

The XML `handler` function has to be added to the event handler of the XML document object, because the `importDoc()` function doesn't know when the document will have finished loading. The event handler is automatically activated when the document finishes loading, and concomitantly a reference to the XML document object is passed to the `handler` function.

The previous code block shows an empty function for the `xmlHandler()` function – this is the function that will handle the processing of the XML document. Before we can use the XML document, we need to know what it is we are processing. Below we can see an example of an XML file (`menu.xml`) that we will use in this example.

```
<?xml version="1.0" ?>
<menubar>
  <menu label="Books">
    <menuItem label="Biographies" url="biog_buk.html" />
    <menuItem label="Educational" url="educt_buk.html" />
    <menuItem label="General Fiction" url="genfic_buk.html" />
    <menuItem label="Romance" url="romance_buk.html" />
    <menuItem label="Science Fiction" url="scifi_buk.html" />
  </menu>
  <menu label="Movies">
    <menuItem label="Action" url="action_mov.html" />
    <menuItem label="Horror" url="horror_mov.html" />
    <menuItem label="Romance" url="romance_mov.html" />
    <menuItem label="Science Fiction" url="scifi_mov.html" />
    <menuItem label="Thriller" url="thriller_mov.html" />
  </menu>
  <menu label="Games">
    <menuItem label="Platform" url="platform_gam.html" />
    <menuItem label="Role Playing" url="rpg_gam.html" />
    <menuItem label="Educational" url="educat_gam.html" />
    <menuItem label="Multi-Player" url="multiplay_gam.html" />
    <menuItem label="Classics" url="classic_gam.html" />
  </menu>
</menubar>
```

As you can see from the XML data above, three custom elements have been defined. The `<menubar>` element is used to simply group all the menu options and acts as the top-level root node to the document. A `<menu>` element defines each top-level menu option, and the `label` attribute value supplied will be used for the text on the page. Each top-level menu option contains one or more menu items defined by the `<menuItem>` element. Again, the value of the `label` attribute supplied will be used for the text on the page and the value of the `url` attribute will be used in the action of clicking on a menu item. With this in mind, we can now complete the code for the `xmlHandler()` function as below.

```
function xmlHandler(doc)
{
  var topLevel = document.createElement("ul");
  var menus = doc.getElementsByTagName("menu");

  //Outer loop to generate Menus
  for (var i = 0; i < menus.length; i++)
  {
    var m = createMenu(i, menus[i].getAttribute("label"));
    topLevel.appendChild(m);
  }
  var menubar = document.getElementById("menubar");
  menubar.removeChild(menubar.childNodes[0]);
  menubar.appendChild(topLevel);
}
```

It is important to note that now we have two documents in existence: the HTML document displayed in the browser window and an XML document that exists within memory. Navigating and manipulating the document structure of both documents uses the methods defined by the DOM Level 1 core module. The XML document is used as a data store – as we navigate its document structure, the structural elements are identified and content is extracted. This information is then used to build a sub tree structure of HTML elements and text nodes, which can then be inserted in to the HTML document at the required place.

This `xmlHandler()` function uses many of the DOM methods that we have already seen throughout this chapter. First, the function creates an unordered list element (`<ul>`) that is stored in the `topLevel` variable. Next, a collection of `<menu>` elements is obtained from the XML document using the `getElementsByTagName()` method, and stored in the `menus` variable. A `for` loop is used to iterate through each of the elements in this `menus` collection.

The value of the `label` attribute and the loop index number for each `<menu>` is passed to a function called `createMenu()`, which we'll create a little later. This will return a `<li>` element, which is appended to the `<ul>` element stored in the `topLevel` variable, building up the HTML for the menu. Finally, once all the menus have been added, the `for` loop will exit and all that remains is to remove the text node with the contents "*Menu is loading...*" and append the text stored in the `topLevel` variable to the menubar `<div>` element in the page.

This code is sufficient for the top-level menus, but what about the `<menuItem>` elements associated with each top-level menu option? The function needs to be extended to include an inner `for` loop that will perform a similar operation to the outer `for` loop in creating the menus. Let's have a look:

```
function xmlHandler(doc)
{
  var topLevel = document.createElement("ul");
  var menus = doc.getElementsByTagName("menu");

  //Outer loop to generate Menus
  for (var i = 0; i < menus.length; i++)
  {
    var m = createMenu(i, menus[i].getAttribute("label"));
    topLevel.appendChild(m);
```

```
        var subLevel = document.createElement("ul");
        subLevel.className = "sublist";
        var menuItems = menus[i].getElementsByTagName("menuItem");

        //Inner loop to generate MenuItems
        for (var j = 0; j < menuItems.length; j++)
        {
          var mi = createMenuItem(menuItems[j].getAttribute("label"),
            menuItems[j].getAttribute("url"));
          subLevel.appendChild(mi);
        }
        topLevel.appendChild(subLevel);
      }

      var menubar = document.getElementById("menubar");
      menubar.appendChild(topLevel);
    }
```

Each set of `<menuItem>` elements will populate an unordered list (`<ul>`), just like the top-level menus. Outside the inner `for` loop, a `<ul>` element is created and a reference to it is stored in the `subLevel` variable. Style properties are added to the element, setting the `className` attribute and the `sublist` class defined in the `<style>` element at the top of the page. The `sublist` stylesheet class will set the `display` property of the `<ul>` element to none, so that the element is not rendered when the menu is first rendered on the page.

The `getElementsByTagName()` method of each `<menu>` element is used to generate a collection of menuItems. An inner `for` loop is used to iterate through the collection; with each pass, the values of the `label` and `url` attributes of each `<menuItem>` element are obtained and passed as parameters to a function called `createMenuItem()`, which, again, we'll create later. This function, similar to the `createMenu()` function, returns a `<li>` element which is then appended to the unordered list referenced by the `subLevel` variable. Finally, when the inner loop exits, the `subLevel` element is appended to the element referenced by the `topLevel` variable.

Having completed the code for the XML document `handler` function, the two helper functions, `createMenu()` and `createMenuItem()`, need to be coded. Both functions create and return an `<li>` element, which is appended as a child to one of the `<ul>` elements created in the `xmlHandler()` function. Appended to the `<li>` elements is a text node, which stores the text label of each menu option that is displayed. The `className` attribute of each `<li>` element is set to either `menu` or `menuitem` to apply the style properties of each element, and the `title` attribute is set to provide a useful ToolTip to the user when they place their mouse cursor over the element.

```
    function createMenu(lvl, lbl)
    {
      var li = document.createElement("li");
      var txtNode = document.createTextNode(lbl);
      li.appendChild(txtNode);
      li.className = "menu";
      li.title = "Click for More options";
      li.onclick = function()
      {
        showList(lvl)
      }
```

```
    return li;
  }

  function createMenuItem(lbl, uri)
  {
    var li = document.createElement("li");
    var txtNode = document.createTextNode(lbl);
    li.appendChild(txtNode);
    li.className = "menuitem";
    li.title = "Click for More information about " + lbl
    if (uri != null)
    {
      li.onclick = function()
      {
        window.location = uri;
      }
    }
    return li;
  }
```

Before exiting and returning an `<li>` element, each function attaches a function to each element's `onclick` handler. The `createMenu()` function attaches a function that calls another function called `showList()`. We will come to this function a bit later – its purpose is to display the menu items associated with a menu, and hide all other menu items. The function attached to the `onclick` event handler of the `<li>` element created in the `createMenuItem()` function is used to change the window's `location` property and allow the browser to jump to a new URL.

The code is now nearly complete for the TreeView menu navigation system. All that remains for this example is to create the `showList()` function that is used within the `onclick` event handler of the top-level menu options.

```
  function showList(whichSubList)
  {
    var menus = document.getElementById("menubar").childNodes[0];
    var lists = menus.getElementsByTagName("ul")
    if (lists[whichSubList])
    {
      if (lists[whichSubList].style.display != "block")
        lists[whichSubList].style.display = "block"
      else
        lists[whichSubList].style.display = "none"
    }
  }
```

The first statement of the `showList()` function creates a reference to the first child node of the menubar `<div>` element, which is the `<ul>` element containing the top-level menu options. A collection of the `<ul>` elements that exist within the top-level `<ul>` element is then created. The first `if` statement tests whether a `<ul>` element exists at the index within the collection with the same value as the `whichSubList` parameter. If it does, an inner `if...else` statement is used to toggle visibility of the sub-menu for the menu clicked. If the `display` property is not equal to `block`, then it's assumed to be invisible. In this case the `display` property is set to `block` allowing the sub-list to be rendered and hence displayed on the page. Otherwise, the property is set to `"none"`, meaning that the sub-list will not be displayed.

One last point to note – importing XML documents into Macromedia Flash is very similar to importing XML into an HTML page. Flash uses a scripting language called **ActionScript**, which is based on JavaScript. Similar properties exist within Flash to extract and manipulate the XML data. This presents an interesting scenario: both a Flash- and an HTML-based web site could be designed to co-exist, the Flash package and HTML pages acting as presentation templates, both deriving content from the same XML documents.

I think you'll agree that the ability to import XML data directly into a web page and use of the DOM to manipulate it offers a powerful tool for creating web functionality, but as yet the potential has been little realized. In the future, as more people using the web have DOM-compliant browsers, you can expect to see XML-based web pages becoming more and more widespread.

DOM Event Model

Events have been around since the earliest browsers started using JavaScript, allowing scripts to be executed in response to an action. Actions that can raise events are generated from a variety of different sources, including the mouse, keyboard, and HTML elements.

In Chapter 4 we first encountered event handling, looking at events that were common to both IE4 and NN4 and how user mouse interactions can raise events. To handle the events, JavaScript code and functions were attached to event handlers, either as properties of objects representing HTML elements or as attributes of the elements themselves. With NN4 browsers, event handlers can only be added to certain elements, but IE4+ browsers allow event handlers to be added to all HTML elements within the body of the document.

Here, we'll look at events in a bit more detail, and see how they are handled in the latest browsers.

Event Flow Systems

The NN4 and IE4+ browsers implemented two different event models that allowed the event to flow up or down the document structure.

The event flow systems were introduced because of the way that information is represented in a browser web page. You know that content within a document can be encapsulated by a variety of elements – for example, a piece of text can be located within a bold element, that is located within a paragraph. If you click on the text, what receives the mouse click event? Is it the text node, the bold element, the paragraph element, two of the three, or all three? The answer is that it could be any of these options. Using an event flow system, the event is passed from one element (or node) to the next along an ancestral chain until it encounters an object that is capable of handling the event.

There are two main event flow systems: event capturing and event bubbling.

Event Capturing

The event capturing system operates by an event being raised from the top of the document model and flowing down through the structure until it reaches the intended target. On its way down through the document structure, any ancestor nodes that are registered to receive the same type of event as the target are able to capture the event before the target receives it.

Event capturing was introduced with NN version 4 browsers, but is not true event capturing as described above. Not all objects in the ancestral hierarchy are exploited when an event flows through the structure. In NN4 browsers, only top-level objects, such as windows, documents, and layers, get a chance to handle the event before the intended target. In general, the event is directed directly to the target. Each time an event is raised, a new `event` object is created and passed automatically to the event handler functions.

Event Bubbling

The IE4+ browser adopted the event bubbling system. In these browsers, a single global `event` object is created, so that only one `event` object exists at any one time. As new events are raised, they are held in a queue until the event currently being processed has been completely handled. As the `event` object exists as a global object, the event handler functions when triggered must obtain a reference to the `event` object from the `window` object.

Event bubbling is the symmetrical opposite of event capturing. When an event is raised, it is dispatched to its intended target, triggering the event handlers of the target if they exist. Once dispatched to the target, the event bubbles up through the parent chain to the top of the document structure, triggering event handlers attached to the parental ancestor nodes that are registered to handle events of the same type.

The DOM Dual Approach to Event Handling

The DOM Level 2 events model provides a common subset of both the capture and bubbling events systems in use and thereby attempts to provide interoperability with existing scripts. The DOM events module has been designed to produce an event model system that allows:

- The binding of event handlers to all nodes, not only HTML elements, as in NN4 and IE4.x/5.x browsers.
- Event flow through the document structure that can either flow up or down the ancestral chain.
- Contextual information for each event, for example where on the page the event occurred and the type of event that occurred.

Currently only Netscape 6+ browsers use the DOM events model. Like the Netscape 4 browsers, for each new event raised a new `event` object is created and it is automatically passed as a parameter to the event handler functions.

Event Binding

Event binding is the process of registering a function as being responsible for handling an event of a particular type for a particular HTML element. When the element receives an event, the bound function handles the event (if it is of the correct type), and once the event is dealt with, it propagates through the document structure depending on the event flow system deployed by the browser.

Event handling via functions attached to an element by the event handler attribute of an HTML element is known as **inline binding**. This has the advantage of allowing you to pass parameters to the event handler's function easily. It is one of the simplest, most common, and backward-compatible methods for event binding. Indeed, we have already seen several examples within this chapter, such as the `onload` attribute added to the `<body>` element in the *Importing XML Documents* example and the `onclick` attribute added to the `<acronym>` HTML element in the *Modifying Attributes* section.

You should be aware that all functions within JavaScript exist as objects and, as such, can be referenced by their name as you would any other object. The DHTML technique of **object binding** allows a function object to be attached to event handlers directly through statements within a script, as can be seen below:

```
function evtHandler(evt)
{
  // Do something
}

var myElement = document.getElementById("myElementId");
myElement.onclick = evtHandler;
```

Note that DOM Levels 1 and 2 do not define object binding of functions to event handlers. IE and NN browsers have implemented this technique, but DOM is silent on this issue.

With Netscape browsers, a reference to an `event` object raised is passed automatically as a parameter to the event-handling function; hence we have supplied a single parameter `evt` for the function. Binding function objects to element event handlers in this fashion does not allow parameters to be passed to the function. However, there is a trick to getting around this problem by wrapping the event handler within an anonymous function:

```
myElement.onclick = evtHandler(evt)
{
  //some code here to handle the event object and perform some work if necessary.
  spanEvtHandler(arg1, arg2);
}
```

Note that, when using object binding, the name of the event handler is case sensitive and you should always use lowercase names for maximum compatibility across different browsers.

The inline binding and object binding methods for attaching event-handling functions to event handlers were both seen extensively in Chapter 4. Here, however, we come to a parting of the ways and with it an added complication. Internet Explorer 5+ and Netscape 6+ have implemented two additional types of event binding. Internet Explorer 5+ browsers use a non-standard technique that was implemented before the W3C DOM Events standard was completed. Netscape 6+ browsers, however, use the technique defined by the DOM events model.

With Internet Explorer 5+ browsers, every HTML element and `document` object possesses an `attachEvent()` method, as the example below shows:

```
function evtHandler()
{
  // Do something
}

var myElement = document.getElementById("myElementId");
myElement.attachEvent("onclick", evtHandler);
```

The `attachEvent()` method accepts two parameters. The first is the string name of the event handler and the second is an object reference to the event-handling function.

The W3C DOM Events approach deployed by Netscape 6+ is similar to Internet Explorer's `attachEvent()` method. The DOM approach uses a method called `addEventListener()`, which can be used with any node within the document structure. This means that all text nodes can use this method, as well as all HTML element nodes. The `addEventListener()` method uses the following syntax:

```
nodeRef.addEventListener(eventType, listenerReference, captureFlag);
```

The first parameter to the method is the string name of the event, without the `on` preposition (for example, click or load). The second parameter is the object reference to the event-handling function. Finally, the third parameter is a Boolean value that determines at which point in the event flow an event handler is triggered. As mentioned previously, DOM events have produced a system that uses common elements from both the capture and bubbling event flow systems.

Setting the `captureFlag` parameter to `true` will indicate that the function wishes to initiate capture. After initiating capture, the event will be dispatched to the event-listener function before passing down the document structure to any descendants registered to receive events. A value of `false` for the `captureFlag` parameter indicates that the event handler should only be triggered during the bubbling event flow system. Events bubbling up the document structure will not trigger event listeners designated to use capture. In Netscape 6+ browsers, our example will now look like this:

```
function evtHandler(evt)
{
  // Do something
}

var myElement = document.getElementById("myElementId");
myElement.addEventListener("click", evtHandler, false);
```

With object binding, applying a new function to an event handler will remove the previous function from handling the event. An advantage of event binding using the `attachEvent()` or `addEventListener()` methods is that multiple event-handler functions can be registered with an element to handle the same event.

Choosing an Event Binding Method

With so many techniques for event binding, you are probably now a bit confused as to which binding method to use. The answer simply is "it's up to you".

If you have to support Internet Explorer, then the W3C `addEventListener()` method is out of the question. Furthermore, if you have to support Internet Explorer 5 on the Mac, then you can forget about the `attachEvent()` method too – it is not supported on this platform. Similarly, if you have to support the Netscape 4 browser, you can forget both of these methods.

If you do have to be compatible with the above browsers, your choice becomes limited to inline binding or object binding. These choices provide the best support across multiple platforms, with old and new versions of the same browser.However, there is a problem even with these forms of binding too. Like IE4+ browsers, NN4 will allow event handlers to be added to all elements, but unlike IE4+, NN4 does not support event handling on all elements. This means that no event-handler function will be triggered for most elements, even though they are bound to events in the HTML source. Worse still, object binding of functions to event handlers will work only on links, form elements, or positioned elements.

The Event Object

Event objects expose a number of properties that describe the event that occurred, such as the type of event, where on screen, and over which element it occurred. As mentioned earlier, event-handling functions with Netscape browsers are automatically passed a reference to an `event` object, whereas Internet Explorer creates a global `event` object. The first task, therefore, when creating an event-handling function is to obtain a reference to the `event` object for the correct browser in use. The following function shows one such way of obtaining a reference to the `event` object:

```
function document_mouseover(evt)
{
   var eventObj = null;
   if (evt)
   {
      // try to use NN event object
      eventObj = evt;
   }
   else if (window.event)
   {
      // try to use IE event object
      eventObj = window.event;
   }
   else
   {
      // Event not found handling code
   }
   // other event-handling code
}
```

In this example, the function has been named as if it were to be used to handle a mouseover event on the document. A single parameter to the function is defined for Netscape browsers. The first line may be a bit confusing at first, but really it's quite simple. A variable `eventObj` is declared and an `if...else` statement block is used to try to obtain the correct reference to the `event` object raised. First we try to set the variable to the `evt` parameter for NN browsers. If it does not exist, we try using the `window.event` object as in IE browsers. Otherwise, we do something else to handle the fact that we cannot obtain a reference to an `event` object.

Having obtained the correct reference to the `event` object, you can now use that object to find out more about the event raised and handle the event in the appropriate manner. The table below shows some of the more common and useful properties that `event` objects possess.

Netscape 6 (4.x)	**Internet Explorer 4.0**	**W3C DOM**	**Description**
type	type	type	The name of the event type
target	srcElement	target	The node that the event originated from
cancelBubble (no equivalent)	cancelBubble	stopPropagation()	Prevent event from propagating further through the document structure

Netscape 6 (4.x)	Internet Explorer 4.0	W3C DOM	Description
button (which)	button	button	Integer value depicting which mouse button changed state
charCode (which)	keyCode		Integer value depicting which keyboard key was pressed. Use with the `String.fromCharCode()` method to convert the integer code value to the character
x	x		X coordinate of the event relative to the element that the event occurred over
y	y		Y coordinate of the event relative to the element that the event occurred over
screenX	screenX	screenX	X coordinate of the event relative to the screen
screenY	screenY	screenY	Y coordinate of the event relative to the screen
clientX (layerX)	clientX	clientX	X coordinate of the event relative to the browser
clientY (layerY)	clientX	clientY	Y coordinate of the event relative to the browser
altKey (modifiers)	altKey	altKey	Boolean value, `true` if *Alt* key is depressed
ctrlKey (modifiers)	ctrlKey	ctrlKey	Boolean value, `true` if *Ctrl* key is depressed
shiftKey (modifiers)	shiftKey	shiftKey	Boolean value, `true` if *Shift* key is depressed

Note that with the Netscape 4.x browsers there are a number of differences (specified in parentheses). The `cancelBubble` property, which we'll discuss shortly, does not exist. The `button` property is known as the `which` property; Netscape 6 browsers maintain the `which` property for backwards compatibility. The `modifiers` property was used to determine if any of the *Alt*, *Shift*, or *Ctrl* keys were depressed during the event and holds a string rather than a Boolean, with values such as `ALT_MASK`, `CONTROL_MASK`, and `SHIFT_MASK`.

Being able to identify the element that raised the event is very useful. The `target` property (for Netscape browsers) and the `srcElement` property (for Internet Explorer browsers) provide a reference to this element. Note that with Netscape 6 browsers the target is often a text node and in this instance you probably wish to return a reference to the parent node of the text node.

```
function getEventSource(evt)
{
  if (evt != null) // Netscape and DOM
  {
    if (evt.target.nodeValue && evt.target.nodeValue == 3) // NN6 and DOM
        return evt.target.parentNode;
    else // NN4
        return evt.target;
  }
  else // Internet Explorer
  {
    return window.event.srcElement;
  }
}
```

The `getEventSource()` function above shows how you may obtain a reference to the source element, across different browsers. Once a reference has been obtained, you can change the properties of that element, for example to move, or resize it. Netscape 4 browsers, with weak DOM support, do not allow you to do too much, but Internet Explorer 5+ and Netscape 6+ do. For example, using the DOM property `nodeType`, seen earlier in the chapter, the element's type can be identified. If it is of a certain type, then we can choose to do something with it or ignore it.

Canceling Event Propagation

As you have learned, once raised, events are dispatched to an element or other node and then, by default in the latest browsers, bubble up the document structure. If at any point they reach a node with an event handler registered, the bound function will be triggered. These functions will then do some work and, once finished, the event will continue to travel up the parental chain to the top of the document structure. This can be useful, but also detrimental.

If an event has been handled early in the parental chain, we may not need the event to travel any further. If it does, it may trigger event handlers we don't want it too. The `cancelBubble` property, described in the table above, can be set to `true` to prevent the `event` object from propagating further. The DOM event model does not define the `cancelBubble` property, but rather supplies the `stopPropagation()` method to achieve the same result and more; in fact it prevents the event from flowing in either the capturing or bubbling flow system.

The following example shows us where in the DOM an event is first handled and how it flows through the document structure. The HTML source code, `eventFlow.htm`, below creates a simple page with an image located inside a `<div>` element. The style properties are added to make the `<div>` element bigger than the image. Also a table is defined with three headings in the head section and an empty body section. This table will be use to dynamically write data to rows within the body section showing how the event flows through the document.

```
<html>
<head>
<title>Event Flow Example</title>
<script>
</script>
</head>
```

```
<body onload="winload(document)">
<div id="thediv"
  style="width:230px; height:230px; background-color:#e0e0e0; text-align:center;">
  <img src="blackbox.gif" id="dbgImg" width="176" height="112" vspace="30">
</div>

<table cellspacing="10">
  <thead>
    <tr><th>Target</th><th>Current Target</th><th>Phase</th></tr>
  </thead>
  <tbody id="debugList"></tbody>
</table>
</body>
</html>
```

The `onload` event handler has been set in the `<body>` element to trigger the `winload()` function. This function will attach an event-handling function to the `onclick` event handlers of the document and all the nodes below the document root. This can be seen in the following code, which should be placed in the script block in the header section of the document.

```
function winload(n)
{
  n.addEventListener("click", clickHandler, false)
  n.addEventListener("click", clickHandler, true)

  for (var i = 0; i < n.childNodes.length; i++)
  {
    winload(n.childNodes[i])
  }
}
```

In this example we will only use the DOM method `addEventListener()` to attach the event-handling function, `clickHandler`, to the objects within the document. This means that this is a NN6-only example. This function is registered to receive events in both the capturing and bubbling phase. The event-handling function, `clickHandler`, is defined below:

```
function clickHandler(evt)
{
  var tNode, cell;
  var row = document.createElement("tr");

  cell = document.createElement("td");
  tNode = document.createTextNode(evt.target.nodeName);
  cell.appendChild(tNode);
  row.appendChild(cell);

  cell = document.createElement("td");
  tNode = document.createTextNode(evt.currentTarget.nodeName);
  cell.appendChild(tNode);
```

```
    row.appendChild(cell);

    var cell = document.createElement("td");
    var phase;
    if (evt.eventPhase == Event.BUBBLING_PHASE)
      phase = "Bubbling";
    else if (evt.eventPhase == Event.CAPTURING_PHASE)
      phase = "Capturing";
    else
      phase = "At Target";
    tNode = document.createTextNode(phase);
    cell.appendChild(tNode);
    row.appendChild(cell);

    document.getElementById("debugList").appendChild(row);
  }
```

This `clickHandler()` function creates a new table row element to which the function will append table cell elements. Each time a new table cell element is created, a text node is created, containing the debug information, and appended to the table cell element. Each newly created table cell element is then appended to the table row element.

The first table cell element will contain the DOM name of the target element, which is obtained from the `nodeName` property of the node referenced by the `target` property of the `event` object.

The second cell contains the DOM name of the element that is currently handling the `event` object, referenced by the `currentTarget` property of the `event` object.

To create the text data for the third cell a set of `if...else` statements are used to test the current flow phase of the `event` object. The `event` object possesses an `eventPhase` property that stores an integer value indicating the current phase state. A global `Event` object exists in NN6 that possesses properties that define what the integer values mean. Testing the `eventPhase` property of the `event` object against the defined term from the `Event` object allows us to determine which phase the event is in and set the `phase` variable to a particular string value, which is then used to initialize the text node of the third cell.

Finally, the last statement appends the table row element to the table body.

Loading this page and clicking on the black image produces an output similar to the following screen shot:

From this figure you can see that clicking on the black image creates a set of data that populates the table. The first column shows the element that was clicked on, in this case the <img> element. The second column shows each of the nodes that handled the event in the document structure. As you notice the event flows from the document root, down to the target <img> element, and then returns back up the document structure to the root. The third column indicates the flow phase that the event is in – we can see that the event flow begins in the capture phase, until it reaches its target, and then leaves the target <img> element in the bubbling phase.

If we had clicked on the <div> element, the data displayed would have show *DIV* in the first column, the rows with *Current Target* equal to *IMG* would be missing, and the *Phase* column would have displayed *At Target* for the *DIV* elements.

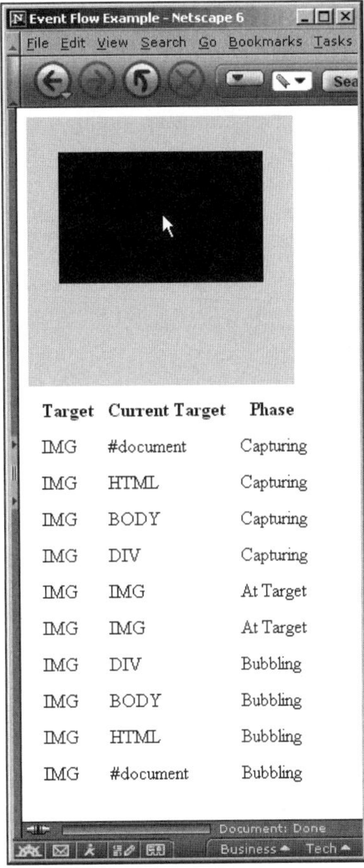

Event Flow Example - Netscape 6
File Edit View Search Go Bookmarks Tasks
Target Current Target Phase
IMG #document Capturing
IMG HTML Capturing
IMG BODY Capturing
IMG DIV Capturing
IMG IMG At Target
IMG IMG At Target
IMG DIV Bubbling
IMG BODY Bubbling
IMG HTML Bubbling
IMG #document Bubbling
Document: Done
Business Tech

To investigate how stopping the propagation at a particular place within the document structure works, we can now include the following function:

```
function cancelEvent(evt)
{
  evt.stopPropagation();
  clickHandler(evt);
}
```

This function simply stops the event object from propagating any further. The event is then passed to the clickHandler() function so that we know which element the event stopped at. We need to modify the <body> element's onload event handler as follows, so that it calls a second function:

```
<body onload="winload(document); stopAtDiv()">
```

The second function, stopAtDiv(), simply creates a reference to the <div> element in the document, de-registers the onclick event handler in the bubbling phase that was created by the winload() function, and, in its place, registers the cancelEvent() function to handle the event.

```
function stopAtDiv()
{
  var dbg = document.getElementById("thediv");
  dbg.removeEventListener("click", clickHandler, false);
  dbg.addEventListener("click", cancelEvent, false);
}
```

Now, if you load the document in your NN6 browser and click on the black image, the table of data will change as we can see in the screenshot below:

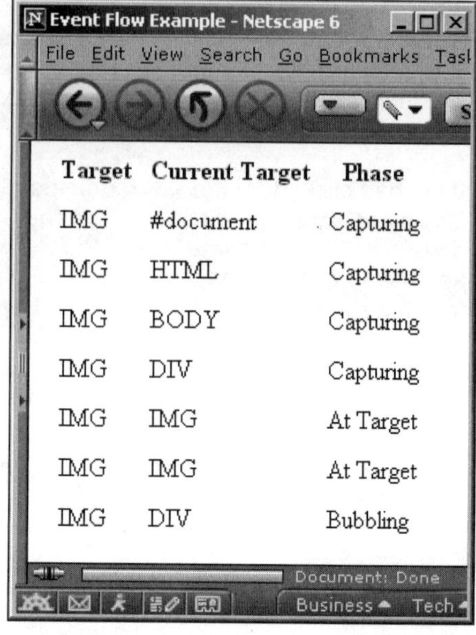

We can see here that the event handler registered to trigger the `cancelEvent()` function stops the event propagating any further past the `<div>` element. Try changing where the `cancelEvent()` function is called from – for example, change the flow phase in which it is registered, or the element on which it is triggered.

Image Viewer Application – Part 3

In Part 1 (Chapter 5), the application was presented and its purpose described – it allows different sets of image collections to be viewed. The application's display is divided into three main areas:

- Area 1 – Navigation of the different sets of images
- Area 2 – Thumbnail previews of each image within a collection
- Area 3 – Display panel for the main image

Each area was created using an `<iframe>`, and their dimensions and positions were defined by using a cascading stylesheet. For accessibility, a page was created that was a duplicate of the main page, but with the style properties of the `<iframe>` elements changed in the stylesheet so that the three areas would fit onto the screen of users with a low screen resolution. JavaScript was then deployed to detect the user's screen resolution automatically and choose, on the user's behalf, which version of the main page the application should be viewed with.

In Part 2 (Chapter 6) JavaScript was added to complete the empty functions created in Part 1. These functions were moved into an external JavaScript source file (*ImageViewerMainCode.js*), which was referenced in the main *ImageViewer.htm* file and the HTML file that creates the smaller version of the application page (*ImageViewer_smallscreen.htm*), using the `src` attribute of `<script>` elements. These functions add the ability to scroll the thumbnails in Area 2 (by clicking on the two arrow head images) and hide the animated loading image when the application first loads.

Two additional functions were defined and added to the external JavaScript source file. One of these functions, `loadNewCategoryThumbnails()`, is called after a user clicks in Area 1 on a menu option. It is passed a string URL and used to show the HTML page, in Area 2, containing the required thumbnail images. The second function, `loadNewMainImage()`, is called when a user clicks on a thumbnail image. This function uses DHTML to show the animated loading image and then sets the source location of the Area 3 `<iframe>` to the source location of an image to be viewed. When the image is displayed in Area 3, the `onload` event handler of the `<iframe>` calls the `hideImageLoadingImage()` function that, consequently, hides the animated image again.

An HTML document was created for Area 1; the document used a series of nested `<div>` elements for each of the navigable elements. In Part 2 (Chapter 6) the JavaScript functionality was added to make the navigable elements work like a TreeView navigation system. Clicking on an element will cause either a collection of thumbnails to appear in Area 2, or a sub-list of options to be displayed. By clicking on and moving the mouse over the navigable elements in Area 1, they dynamically change their style properties providing visual cues to the user.

In this final section we will finish the development of the Image Viewer application. Believe it or not, all that remains is to create the thumbnail HTML pages for display in Area 2, and the required JavaScript code to handle movement over and clicks on the thumbnail images.

Thumbnail HTML Page Template

Clicking on a navigational element in Area 1 activates the function `loadNewImageCategory()`, which is bound to the element via the `onclick` attribute in the `<div>` element. The function is passed a reference to the element clicked (using the `this` keyword) and the filename of the HTML page that contains the required set of thumbnail images.

If you look carefully at the HTML source file (`CategoryIndex.htm`) for Area 1, you will notice that for every option, and therefore every set of images, a different HTML document is required. The HTML source below shows the entire HTML that can be found in the *FlowersThumbnails.htm* file that is called by the *Flowers* option.

```
<html>
<head>
<style>
   body { margin:0px; }
   img { margin-left: 30px; border:3px solid black; }
</style>
</head>
<body background="ShortFilmStrip.gif">
  <img src="cactus_thumbnail.jpg" id="cactus1">
  <img src="rose_thumbnail.jpg" id="rose1">
</body>
</html>
```

As you can see, the HTML source is very simple – a small amount of styling, a background image to the document to provide the illusion of a filmstrip when displayed, and a set of <img> elements to import each image in the collection. Because the size of the <iframe> of Area 2 is only slightly bigger than the thumbnails, each image is immediately placed below the previous image giving the illusion of a strip of images. The left margin property of each image is 30 pixels wide and this moves the images so that they all align in the center of the background film strip image.

For each of the other thumbnail files, exactly the same HTML source is used with the exception of the <img> elements, which are changed in each file to reference the appropriate set of images.

Once the HTML source has been added to each of the thumbnail files, you will see that clicking on any option in Area 1 will update Area 2, displaying the collection of thumbnail images. What remains now is to add the JavaScript code that will allow the user to click on a thumbnail causing the full version of that image to be displayed in Area 3.

Event Binding for the Thumbnail Pages

The thumbnail pages require three events to be handled. When the mouse moves over and off an image, DHTML will be used to change the style properties of the <img> elements, toggling whether a border surrounding the image will be displayed or not. When an image is clicked, Area 3 will be updated with a new image by passing a reference (to the full image source) to the function loadNewMainImage() in the parent window.

The three events will be bound to functions after the page has finished loading. To do this, an onload event handler is added to the <body> element of each thumbnail page, as shown below:

```
<body background="ShortFilmStrip.gif" onload="initPage()">
```

When the page has loaded, the onload event handler calls the initPage() function. This function and the other functions required to handle the three mouse events will be included in an external JavaScript file. This file is imported using the src attribute of the <script> element.

```
<script language="JavaScript" src="ThumbnailPagesCode.js"></script>
```

The line above is inserted into the header section of each of the thumbnail HTML files. Using an external JavaScript source file separates the functionality from the content, modularizing the code, and making it easier to maintain and edit the JavaScript. Modularizing the code in this way allows any code changes made to be automatically imported into each HTML file.

The initPage() function is used to attach functions to the three mouse events that need to be handled, as can be seen below:

```
function initPage()
{
  document.onmouseover = document_onmouseover;
  document.onmouseout = document_onmouseout;
  document.onclick = document_onclick;
}
```

The functions are bound as objects to the document mouse event handlers and will interrogate the `event` object raised to determine over which thumbnail image the event occurred. Attaching the functions to the `document` object's event handlers is perfectly fine. The event will be raised on an element and bubbles up the document structure until the `event` object reaches the document node, and triggers the registered event handlers. When the functions are triggered, the `event` object created will possess a property that JavaScript can query to identify the source element (the thumbnail image in this case) over which the event occurred.

Let's have a look at the function `document_onmouseover()`, registered with the mouseover event. This function is used to dynamically change the border color of the image over which the mouse is passed to blue. The function definition can be seen below:

```
function document_onmouseover(eventObject)
{
  var eventSourceElement = getEventSourceElement(eventObject);
  if (eventSourceElement != null &&
      eventSourceElement.tagName.toLowerCase() == "img")
  {
    eventSourceElement.style.borderColor = "blue";
  }
}
```

Event-handling functions, as we covered earlier, are passed a reference to the `event` object as a parameter in Netscape browsers. Internet Explorer browsers, on the other hand, must obtain a reference to the `event` object from the global `event` object.

The first statement in the `document_onmouseover()` function calls another function, `getEventSourceElement()`, passing it the same parameter. This new function obtains a reference to the `event` object, either through the passed parameter or the global `event` object depending on the browser in use, and returns a reference to the source element over which the event occurred. The `if` statement then tests that the returned value is not `null` and that the source element is an `<img>` element. Note that we test using the lowercase string value of the `tagName`, thereby making sure the code works in all environments independent of the value the browser returns for the `tagName`. Knowing the event occurred over an `<img>` element, DHTML is used to change the border color of the element to blue.

The `getEventSourceElement()` function uses an `if...else` statement to test whether the parameter to the function is `null`. If the browser in use is Internet Explorer, then the parameter is `null` because this browser does not automatically pass references to `event` objects directly to the event-handling function. Alternatively, if the browser is Netscape Navigator the parameter will be an `event` object.

```
function getEventSourceElement(eventObject)
{
  var eventSourceElement;
  if (eventObject == null)
  {
    // Obtain event object source element for IE
    eventSourceElement = window.event.srcElement;
  }
  else
  {
```

```
      // Obtain event object source element for NS
      eventSourceElement = eventObject.target;
    }
    return eventSourceElement;
  }
```

Knowing now how the `document_onmouseover()` and `getEventSourceElement()` functions work, it is pretty straightforward to see how the mouseout event-handling function, `document_onmouseout()`, works. This function is defined below:

```
function document_onmouseout(eventObject)
{
  var eventSourceElement = getEventSourceElement(eventObject);
  if (eventSourceElement != null &&
      eventSourceElement.tagName.toLowerCase() == "img")
  {
    eventSourceElement.style.borderColor = "black";
  }
}
```

It should be no great surprise that the `document_onmouseout()` function is very similar to the `document_onmouseover()` function. Both perform the same action – the only difference being that in this instance the border color is changed to black (the same as the page background color), providing the illusion that the border has disappeared.

With the mouseover and mouseout event handlers complete, the user will be provided with a changing color border when they roll their mouse on and off the images. This visual cue will indicate that clicking on the image will allow a full version to be displayed in Area 3. All that remains now is to complete the `onclick` event handler function `document_onclick()`, which can be seen below:

```
function document_onclick(eventObject)
{
  var eventSourceElement = getEventSourceElement(eventObject);
  if (eventSourceElement != null &&
      eventSourceElement.tagName.toLowerCase() == "img")
  {
    var imgSrc = eventSourceElement.src;
    imgSrc = imgSrc.replace("_thumbnail","");

    parent.loadNewMainImage(imgSrc);
  }
}
```

You will notice that the function is similar to the previous two mouse event handlers, first obtaining the source element over which the event was raised. Since the source object is an `<img>` element, we know it possesses a `src` property containing the URL of the image as a string. This property is obtained and stored in the `imgSrc` variable and is used to calculate the URL of the full sized image.

Both a small thumbnail and a full-sized picture exist for each image. The file name for each thumbnail image is the same as the full-sized image with the exception that the thumbnail image contains the substring "`_thumbnail`". For example, the rose thumbnail image is called `rose_thumbnail.jpg`, and the full-sized rose image is called `rose.jpg`.

Knowing this, we can use the `replace()` method of the String object to obtain the name of the full-sized image. This method scans a string for a substring (its first parameter) and replaces the substring with an alternative (its second parameter). Using the `replace()` method on the string stored in the `imgSrc` variable, JavaScript can replace the "`_thumbnail`" substring with "" (empty quotes), thereby removing the substring and returning a string that represents the URL of the full image.

Finally the URL of the full image is passed to the `loadNewMainImage()` function in the main page, which concomitantly causes the full image to be displayed in Area 3 of the application.

That's it! All the JavaScript is complete. If you have created your own version of each of the files and JavaScript functions, you can now run the application and you will see that it functions well. You now have a base application that allows different sets of images to be presented to users; the user is able to navigate the different sets of images, select an image and view the full-sized image.

This application has been created using the information presented in this and the previous two chapters for viewing images. You now have the choice of developing the application for your own needs, for example to present a series of slides for presentation in lectures, or changing the design to fit into your own web site.

In Chapter 8 we will return to our application to give it e-commerce functionality. This will be built up, again in three parts, over Chapters 8, 9, and 10.

Summary

The DOM specification is making great strides to create platform- and vendor-neutral programming interfaces for document creation and manipulation. With the system-independent approach, it is likely that much of what you have learned here can be easily adapted to other packages that implement the DOM interfaces other than web browsers.

In relation to web browsers, the DOM APIs mean that writing cross-browser/platform code has become much easier. It is often possible to write code once for one browser and find that it works without having to write any extra code in another, especially when the DOM Core and HTML modules are used.

In this chapter we have covered how to access elements within a web page by their `id` attribute and create custom collections of elements, providing quick and easy access to elements so that JavaScript can modify the element's properties. We saw how to traverse up and down the document and manipulate its nodal structure. Finally, we looked at how XML documents can be used to import data directly into an HTML document, how to extract the data, and how to use it to build components dynamically within the page.

All these features of the DOM provide the web developer with a new and powerful means for writing richer, more complex, dynamic, and powerful web documents. Code can be written in a more timely fashion and with a greater degree of portability than previously possible.

8

- Creating your own form controls with DHTML
- Regular expressions
- E-commerce application: Part 1

Author: Paul Wilton

Advanced Form Techniques

In Chapter 4 we looked at how to access the forms, and the form elements they contain, within our HTML pages. However, we didn't cover any of the more complex form techniques. Here, we'll concentrate on these, in particular covering a technique for dynamically changing the list of options inside a select control. We'll also see that, using the DHTML techniques we saw in Chapters 6 and 7, we can create our own form controls. The advantages of this are that we can make them look more exciting than the usual rather dull gray controls, and we can create controls that don't exist by default, allowing us to obtain information from the user in a more user friendly and intuitive way.

In the previous three chapters, we have built an image viewer, one step at a time. In the second half of the chapter, we'll start converting this image viewer into an e-commerce based application that allows users to view images online, add them to a shopping basket, and order paper print versions. The e-commerce image viewer will be completed in Chapters 9 and 10.

Advanced Forms

As mentioned above, we'll first see how we can add new options to a select control that has already been loaded into the page. Then we'll see how we can create our own new DHTML form controls that allow us to go beyond boring buttons and input boxes and create more helpful user interfaces.

Adding Elements to a Select Control

It's often useful to dynamically change the options available to a user in a select control after the page has loaded. For example, a site collecting the user's personal information may have two select boxes, one allowing the user to select their country, the other their state. It would be nice to be able to dynamically change the states listed in the state box when the user changes the country. There are many browser-specific techniques for adding select control options, but here we'll cover just one way, a cross–browser technique that works with IE4+ and NN4+.

Note that, while useful in moderation, over-use of this technique may confuse the user.

When we looked at the select control in Chapter 4, we saw that it has an associated `Select` object, and that this object has the `options` array property. The `options` array contains an `Option` object for each of the `<option>` elements defined within the `<select>` element representing the select control. So, to add a new option to a select control we need to create a new `Option` object, set the text it displays and its value (that is, the `Option` object's `text` and `value` properties), and then insert it into the `options` array of the `select` object.

Removing an option from the array is even easier – we just remove the `Option` object from the `options` array by setting it to `null`.

Once `Option` objects have been added or deleted from the `options` array, the browser instantly updates the select control to show the addition or removal of the options. It also updates things like the `length` property of the `options` array to reflect the changes.

Let's create two generic functions – one to add a new option, and a second to delete an option. Create a `.js` file called `SelectElementFunctions.js` and we'll add them to it – this will make it easier to include them later in our HTML pages.

```
function addOption(optionsArray, insertAtIndex, optionText, optionValue)
{
  var indexCounter = optionsArray.length;
  optionsArray[indexCounter] = new Option();

  for (; indexCounter > insertAtIndex; indexCounter--)
  {
    optionsArray[indexCounter].text = optionsArray[indexCounter - 1].text;
    optionsArray[indexCounter].value = optionsArray[indexCounter - 1].value;
    optionsArray[indexCounter].defaultSelected =
      optionsArray[indexCounter - 1].defaultSelected;
  }

  var myNewOption = new Option(optionText,optionValue);
  optionsArray[insertAtIndex] = myNewOption;
}

function removeOption(optionsArray, removeIndex)
{
  optionsArray[removeIndex] = null;
}
```

We'll look at the `addOption()` function first. It takes four parameters; the first is the `options` array property of the `Select` object associated with the select control. The second is the array index that we want to insert the new element at in the `options` array. Remember that arrays are zero-based, so to insert an option at the top of the select control, we need an index of 0. The final two parameters are the text to be displayed for the option in the select control and the value the option should have. (Note that it's only the value of the option that gets posted to the server when the form is submitted.)

We're extending the `options` array, so the first two lines of the function create a new "blank" `Option` object and add it to the end of the array.

Now, to add our new option, we need to make room for it in the array at the index position specified by the function's parameter. We do this by moving each option below the index we require down the array. This is the task of the `for` loop. It starts at the last array element, and sets the `text`, `value`, and `defaultSelected` properties of the `Option` object in that array element to the properties of the `Option` object at the previous element, that is the array element with index `indexCounter - 1`. Setting the `defaultSelected` property means that any form resets will reset to the correct default value.

We continue looping, each time moving to the previous array element, until we have cleared a space at the array element we want to populate with our new option.

In the final two lines of the function, we create a new `Option` object based on the `optionText` and `optionValue` parameters, and insert this into the `options` array at index `insertAtIndex`, overwriting the `Option` object already there. (Although overwritten, the values of this object have already been written to the next `Option` object down the array, so the option is not lost.)

The second function, `removeOption()`, is very simple – it's barely worth a function of its own, but having one does make it easy to remember how to remove options.

The two parameters, `optionsArray` and `removeIndex`, specify the `options` array and the array index of the option to be deleted. We use this to set the `Option` object in the `options` array at position `removeIndex` to `null`, which deletes the object and removes it from the `options` array. The select control updates itself to reflect this and removes that option from display.

Now that we have these two functions, we'll create an example that puts them to use. This example consists of three form controls that may be used within a page collecting personal information.

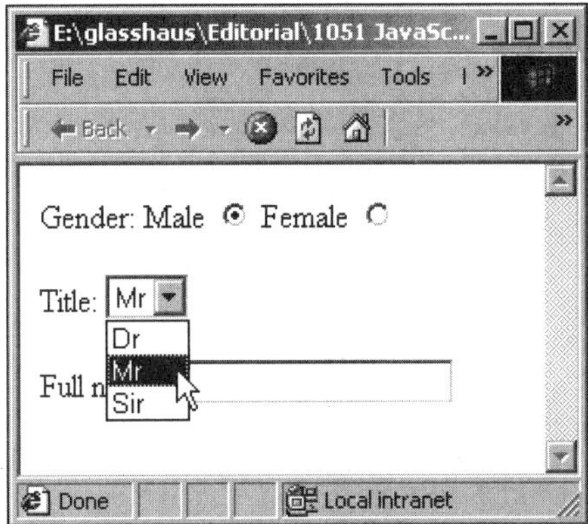

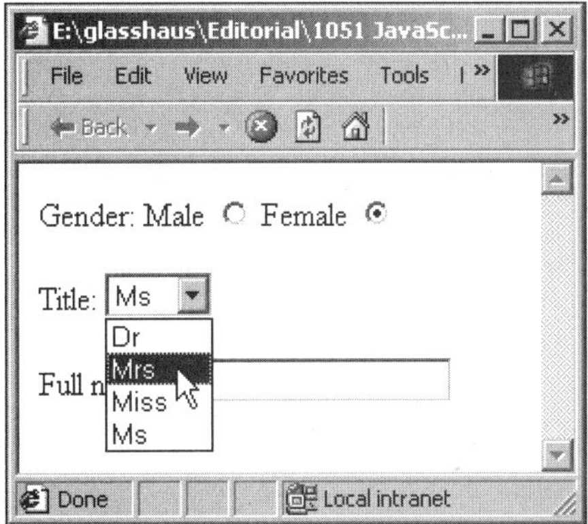

When the page first loads, the *Male* radio button is selected, and in the select control below, the title *Mr* is selected. The user can, however, change this selection to *Dr* or *Sir*. If the user selects the *Female* radio button, the select options change to *Dr*, *Mrs*, *Miss*, and *Ms* – *Ms* is the default option.

With a form of this type, we must also cater for the situation where the user fills in the controls in the "wrong order", that is chooses a title before selecting a gender. In this case, if the user chooses *Female* after selecting a *Mr* or *Sir* title, we change the selected title to *Ms* as the most generic female title. Similarly, if the user chooses a *Mrs*, *Miss* or *Ms* title before changing the radio button back to *Male*, we change the selected title to *Mr*. However, you may also want to alert the user to the mismatch they have chosen.

The example page, *AddRemoveOptionsExample.htm*, is listed below:

```
<html>
<head>
<script language="JavaScript" src="SelectElementFunctions.js"></script>
<script language="JavaScript">
  function maleOptions_onclick()
  {
    var form = document.myForm;
    var optionsArray = form.mySelectControl.options;
    var selIndex = form.mySelectControl.selectedIndex;
    var selvalue = optionsArray[selIndex].value;

    removeOption(optionsArray,1);
    removeOption(optionsArray,1);
    removeOption(optionsArray,1);
    addOption(optionsArray, 1, "Mr", "mister");
    addOption(optionsArray, 2, "Sir", "sir");

    if (selvalue=="missus" || selvalue=="miss" || selvalue=="mz")
    {
      form.mySelectControl.selectedIndex=1;
    }
    else
    {
      form.mySelectControl.selectedIndex=selIndex;
    }
  }

  function femaleOptions_onclick()
  {
    var form = document.myForm;
    var optionsArray = form.mySelectControl.options;
    var selIndex = form.mySelectControl.selectedIndex;
    var selValue = optionsArray[selIndex].value;

    removeOption(optionsArray,1);
    removeOption(optionsArray,1);
    addOption(optionsArray, 1, "Mrs", "missus");
    addOption(optionsArray, 2, "Miss", "miss");
    addOption(optionsArray, 3, "Ms", "mz");

    if (selValue=="mister" || selValue=="sir")
    {
      form.mySelectControl.selectedIndex=3;
    }
    else
    {
      form.mySelectControl.selectedIndex=selIndex;
    }
  }
</script>
</head>
<body>
```

```
<form name="myForm">
  Gender:
  Male  <input type="radio" name="gender" value="male"
               onclick="maleOptions_onclick()" checked>
  Female  <input type="radio" name="gender" value="female"
               onclick="femaleOptions_onclick()">
  <br><br>
  Title:
  <select name="mySelectControl">
    <option value="doctor">Dr</option>
    <option value="mister" selected>Mr</option>
    <option value="sir">Sir</option>
  </select>
  <br><br>
  Full name:
  <input type="text" name="fullName">
</form>
</body>
</html>
```

Let's step through the code. At the top of the page we import the `SelectElementFunctions.js` file containing our add and remove option functions:

```
<script language="JavaScript" src="SelectElementFunctions.js"></script>
```

The *Male* radio button in the body of the page is selected by default, since it has the `checked` attribute. Also, when the page is loaded, the *Title* select control is set with the options *Dr*, *Mr*, and *Sir* – *Mr* is the default since its `<option>` element contains a `selected` attribute.

The *Female* radio button has its `onclick` event handler set to call the `femaleOptions_onclick()` function from the script block in the head of the page – let's walk through that function now.

```
function femaleOptions_onclick()
{
  var form = document.myForm;
  var optionsArray = form.mySelectControl.options;
```

We first define two shortcut variables, `form` and `optionsArray`, to reference the form and the options array that we will need to use later in the function.

```
  var selIndex = form.mySelectControl.selectedIndex;
  var selValue = optionsArray[selIndex].value;
```

We then define the `selIndex` variable to hold the index of the currently selected option in the select control, and `selValue` to hold the value of that selected option.

```
  removeOption(optionsArray,1);
  removeOption(optionsArray,1);
```

Our next task is to change the options in the select control. We use the `removeOption()` function to remove the options at indexes 1 and 2 in the `options` array. If the array includes the male options list, this will be the *Mr* and *Sir* options. If it currently includes the female options, this will be the *Mrs* and *Miss* options. Notice that we pass the function index 1 in both cases – this is because once the option at index 1 is removed, the array is rearranged so that the option that was at index 2 is now at index 1.

```
addOption(optionsArray, 1, "Mrs", "missus");
addOption(optionsArray, 2, "Miss", "miss");
addOption(optionsArray, 3, "Ms", "mz");
```

We then use the `addOption()` function to add three new options to the array at index positions 1, 2, and 3. Note that, if the options list previously held female options, the *Ms* option would still be included when we start to add the three options. However, it is automatically deleted when we try to add an option with the same value, so we don't end up with two *Ms* options.

Next we have to deal with the question of which option should be selected.

```
if (selValue=="mister" || selValue=="sir")
{
  form.mySelectControl.selectedIndex=3;
}
else
{
  form.mySelectControl.selectedIndex=selIndex;
}
```

If the option that was previously selected was *Mr* or *Sir*, we set the selected option to be *Ms*. However, if it was another option (for example, *Dr*, or *Mrs*, *Miss*, or *Ms* if the previous list contained female options) we set the selected index to the previous selected index so that no change occurs.

The *Male* radio button has its `onclick` event handler set to the `maleOptions_onclick()` function, which is very similar to the `femaleOptions_onclick()` function. The only difference is in the options that are set.

Creating Your Own Controls with DHTML

The plain HTML form controls are OK, but sometimes we need something more sophisticated. Fortunately, we're not limited to plain form controls if we use DHTML inventively.

There are a few obstacles we need to overcome when creating DHTML controls. The first problem we may face is how to pass values from one of our DHTML controls to the server when the form is submitted. One way to overcome this is to use hidden textboxes. The DHTML control sets the values of these in the background, and the user never sees them, just our DHTML control. When the form is submitted to the server, the information in the hidden textboxes is posted too.

Creating DHTML controls can also be quite time consuming, so it makes sense to make their reuse as easy as possible. We can do this by using `.js` files to store the necessary script and `.css` files to store any necessary stylesheets. Ideally, we should need just a few lines of HTML in our page to make our control work – the rest should be in separate files. As well as making it easy to add the control to new pages, if any bugs are spotted we need to fix just one or two files, rather than files across every web site we've created that use the functionality. It's also vital if a control is to be reused that we have good documentation on how to use the control and how to change it to our particular needs.

There's a huge range of controls we could create, the limits being only our imagination and, perhaps, the abilities of the user's machine – anything too complex could slow things down. However, here we'll be looking at just one control in particular: a pop-up calendar control:

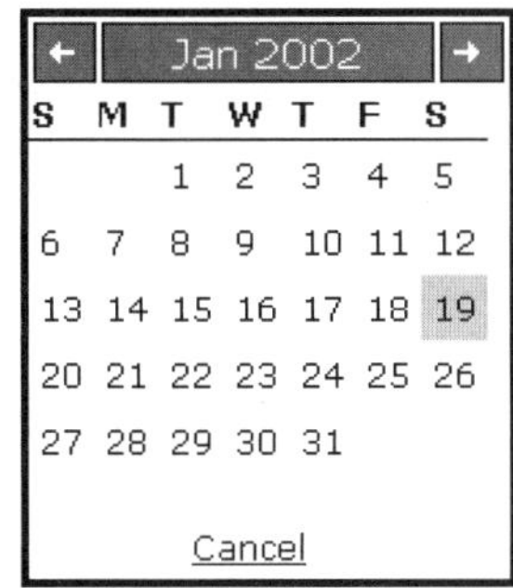

This type of control has many uses. For example, in an e-commerce site making hotel reservations, rather than simply asking the user to enter the date, they can click a button to make the pop-up calendar appear, and then easily select the date they want.

Our example consists of two pages for the control itself, and also the example HTML page that uses the control. The control consists of a code file called `CalendarScript.js` and a stylesheet file called `CalendarStyleDefinitions.css`. The example HTML page is called `PopUpCalendar.htm`. We'll look at each of these files in turn in the upcoming sections. Note that all three files must be placed in the same directory, unless you update the `src` attribute of the `<script>` element and the `href` attribute of the `<link>` element at the top of `PopUpCalendar.htm`.

Before we look at the code files in detail, it's worth taking an overview of how the control works. The calendar is actually a table, with each table cell containing a day. The table is created dynamically using JavaScript and then written into a `<div>` element. This `<div>` element is by default hidden – that is, it's positioned absolutely with off-screen coordinates. When we want to show the pop-up calendar, we create the table, write it into the `<div>` element and then move the `<div>` element onto the screen to the coordinates of the button's click event that called the calendar.

> *Note this example only works on IE4+ and NN6+; it doesn't work with NN4 because its use of layers as its technique for doing DHTML is difficult to merge with techniques for the other browsers.*

The CSS Stylesheet

The stylesheet file, `CalendarStyleDefinitions.css`, is fairly simple:

```
.calendarTable { cell-spacing: none; border-width:0px; }
.dayHeadTR {}
.dayHeadTD {font-family: verdana; font-weight:bold;font-size: 10pt;
            cell-spacing: 0px; cell-padding: 0px; border: none white 0px;
            border-bottom: solid black 1px}
.dayTD {font-family: verdana; font-weight:normal; font-size: 10pt; padding: 4px;
        cursor: pointer; cursor: hand;}
.emptyTD {font-family: verdana; font-weight:normal; font-size: 10pt; padding: 4px;
          cursor: default;}
.calendarDiv {position: absolute; left: -100px; top: -1200px; width: 180px;
              border: solid black 2px; background-color: white}
.changeMonthTD {background-color: gray; width: 20px; border: solid black 1px;
                cursor: pointer;cursor: hand}
```

```
.monthHeadingTD {font-family: verdana; font-weight:normal; font-size: 11pt;
                 background-color: gray; width: 140px; color: white;
                 border: solid black 1px; text-align: center; cursor: default;}
.monthHeadingTable { width: 100%; }
.cancelHyperlink {font-family: verdana; font-weight:normal; font-size: 9pt;
                  position: relative; left: 60px; top: -5px}
```

These ten defined styles will be used as values for the `class` attribute of various elements, to impose the specified style upon that element.

The HTML Page

The example page, *PopUpCalendar.htm*, allows us to show the calendar in use:

```
<html>
<head>
  <link rel='stylesheet' href='CalendarStyleDefinitions.css'>
  <script src="CalendarScript.js"></script>
  <script language="JavaScript">
    function onCalendarHiddenStartDate(day, month, year)
    {
      document.form1.txtStartDate.value = day + " " + month + " " + year;
    }

    function cmdShowStartDateCalendar_onclick(event)
    {
      var dateString = document.form1.txtStartDate.value;
      setSelectedDates(dateString);
      generateCalendar(mCurrentMonth,mCurrentYear, "calendarDIV");
      showCalendar(event.clientX,event.clientY, "calendarDIV",
                   onCalendarHiddenStartDate);
    }

    function onCalendarHiddenEndDate(day, month, year)
    {
      document.form1.txtEndDate.value = day + " " + month + " " + year;
    }

    function cmdShowEndDateCalendar_onclick(event)
    {
      var dateString = document.form1.txtEndDate.value;
      setSelectedDates(dateString);
      generateCalendar(mCurrentMonth,mCurrentYear, "calendarDIV");
      showCalendar(event.clientX,event.clientY, "calendarDIV",
                   onCalendarHiddenEndDate);
    }
</script>
</head>
<body>
  <form action="" method="POST" id="form1" name="form1">
    <h3>Select the start and end dates you wish to reserve the room for:</h3>
    <input type="text" name="txtStartDate">
    <input type="button" value="Select Start Date"
```

```
            name="cmdShowStartDateCalendar"
            onclick="cmdShowStartDateCalendar_onclick(event)">
    <br>
    <input type="text" name="txtEndDate">
    <input type="button" value="Select End Date"
            name="cmdShowEndDateCalendar"
            onclick="cmdShowEndDateCalendar_onclick(event)">
  </form>
  <div name="calendarDIV" id="calendarDIV" class="calendarDiv">
  </div>
</body>
</html>
```

In a browser, this page looks something like this:

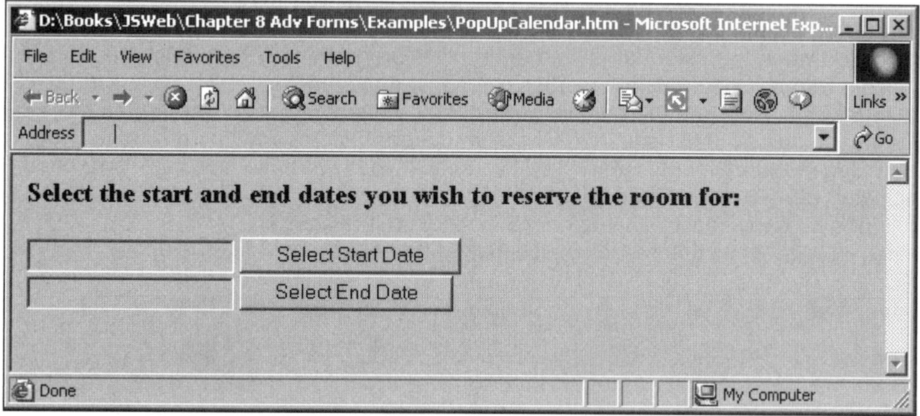

Clicking the buttons allows us to set the start and end dates of our room reservation. Once selected, the dates are shown in the textboxes. You may prefer to have a hidden textbox to hold the date information, and display the date information inside HTML text rather than textboxes – this prevents the user entering data into the textboxes in an incorrect format and forces the use of the calendar control. However, a downside to this is that if the calendar control doesn't work on the user's system, they have no way of entering the dates.

Let's look at the `cmdShowStartDateCalendar_onclick()` function from the script block in *PopUpCalendar.htm* – this is called by the *Select Start Date* button's `onclick` event handler.

The first thing to note is that we have passed the `event` object from the event handler to the function:

```
function cmdShowStartDateCalendar_onclick(event)
```

This allows us to find out where the mouse pointer was when the button was clicked, so we know where to show the calendar. As we saw in Chapter 7, IE actually uses a global `event` object, but this works here because a reference to the global `event` object has been passed. As far as NN6 goes, it has a whole new event model, but retains backwards compatibility with the simpler one we use here.

On the function's first line we set the variable `dateString` to the current value in the start date textbox:

```
var dateString = document.form1.txtStartDate.value;
```

We then use this to set the selected date for the calendar using the `setSelectedDates()` function, and then generate and show the calendar with the `generateCalendar()` and `showCalendar()` functions. These three functions are contained within *CalendarScript.js*, which we'll be having a look at shortly.

```
setSelectedDates(dateString);
generateCalendar(mCurrentMonth, mCurrentYear, "calendarDIV");
showCalendar(event.clientX, event.clientY, "calendarDIV",
             onCalendarHiddenStartDate);
```

The `showCalendar()` function is the least obvious of these. Of the function's first two parameters, `event.clientX` and `event.clientY`, the `event` is the `event` object and `clientX` and `clientY` are the positions of the mouse pointer when the event fired. The third parameter is the `id` of the `<div>` into which we'll be writing the calendar. The final parameter is the function within the HTML file to be called when the calendar is hidden. In other programming languages this sort of function is often called a **call-back function**, because it is passed to some code that calls it at some later time. It provides a way of notifying the original code of some event, in this case that the calendar has been closed. A good analogy is the situation where you phone a company and they say, "we haven't got the information at the moment, but we'll call you back when we have it. What's your phone number?" For "company" read the function originally being called, and for "phone number" read a reference to the function to be called back. The call-back function in this case is `onCalendarHiddenStartDate()`, so let's look at that next:

```
function onCalendarHiddenStartDate(day, month, year)
{
  document.form1.txtStartDate.value = day + " " + month + " " + year;
}
```

The function takes three parameters: the `day`, `month`, and `year` that the user selected. We use this data to update the *Select Start Date* textbox. Note that the month is supplied as the shortened month name rather than a number.

The two functions for the *Select End Date* button are identical to those used by the *Select Start Date* button, except it's the `txtEndDate` textbox that holds the date string.

The JavaScript Code

We'll now look through *CalendarScript.js*, where most of the action actually takes place. It is rather long, consisting of twelve functions, as well as some variable definitions, so we'll take it piece by piece.

The first thing we do is define some global variables:

```
var mSelectedDay;
var mSelectedMonth
var mSelectedYear;

var mHighlightedDay = 0;
var mCurrentMonth;
var mCurrentYear;

var mOnHideFunction;
```

The first three variables, mSelectedDay, mSelectedMonth, and mSelectedYear, will hold the date selected by the user. mHighlightedDay will hold the day that has been highlighted in the calendar, and mCurrentMonth and mCurrentYear will hold the current month and year combination that is being viewed in the calendar. mOnHideFunction will hold the call-back function we saw above, which should be called when the user chooses a date from the calendar, hiding it from view.

Recall that the HTML file called three functions from the .js file: setSelectedDates(), generateCalendar() and showCalendar(). We'll look at these in turn now; generateCalendar() actually calls several other functions, so I'll explain those at the same time.

setSelectedDates()

The purpose of this function is to take a date string and use it to set the global variables that the calendar control uses to hold the selected date. The date string supplied to the function can be any reasonable valid date, for example "31 Jan 2002", or "1/31/2002". However, if we have international visitors, for example those from the UK where date format is dd/mm/yyyy, as well as those from the US where the format is mm/dd/yyyy, we are better off using the month name to avoid confusion. In our example, the dateString parameter comes from the contents of one of the textboxes in the HTML page. These values are set either by the user (in which case you may wish to tell the user which date format to use) or by the script code (which, as you will see, uses the shortened month name format).

The setSelectedDates() function is shown below:

```
function setSelectedDates(dateString)
{
  var currentSelectedDate = new Date(dateString);

  if (isNaN(currentSelectedDate))
  {
    currentSelectedDate = new Date();
  }

  mSelectedDay = currentSelectedDate.getDate();
  mSelectedMonth = currentSelectedDate.getMonth();
  mSelectedYear = currentSelectedDate.getFullYear();

  mCurrentMonth = mSelectedMonth;
  mCurrentYear = mSelectedYear;
}
```

We create a new Date object, with the dateString parameter being passed to its constructor. If dateString does not contain a valid date, then isNaN(currentSelectedDate) will be true and the if statement will set currentSelectedDate to a new Date object without using a constructor – it will consequently be set to the current system date and time.

On the five final lines, the global variables are set to the date extracted from the Date object. Note that mCurrentMonth and mCurrentYear are set so that, when the calendar is opened, the month for the current selected date will be shown.

generateCalendar() and Associated Functions

The largest function in the *CalendarScript.js* file is that which generates the table containing the calendar, namely the `generateCalendar()` function. We'll step through it, describing the other functions it calls as we go, though we won't look into the code for these until we complete the `generateCalendar()` function so as not to disrupt the flow.

The `generateCalendar()` function takes three parameters: the month and year of the calendar to be displayed, and the `id` of the `<div>` element into which the calendar will be written. Note that the month is given as the same number that the `Date` object's `getMonth()` method would return for that month, that is month 0 is January, month 1 is February, and so on.

```
function generateCalendar(month, year, calendarDivID)
{
```

The function begins with a block of code that creates the top of the table and its heading:

```
    var headingHTML = "<table class='monthHeadingTable' border='0'>";
    headingHTML += "<tr><td class='changeMonthTD'>";
    headingHTML += "<img src='prev.gif' title='Show Previous Month' ";
    headingHTML += "onclick='goPreviousMonth(\"";
    headingHTML += calendarDivID + "\")'></td>";
    headingHTML += "<td class='monthHeadingTD'>";
    headingHTML += getMonthName(month) + " " + year + "</td>";
    headingHTML += "<td class='changeMonthTD'>";
    headingHTML += "<img src='next.gif' title='Show Next Month' ";
    headingHTML += "onclick='goNextMonth(\"";
    headingHTML += calendarDivID + "\")'></td></tr></table>";
```

This code creates the part of the calendar shown below:

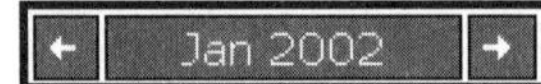

The month and year shown will be determined by the parameters `month` and `year` that were passed to the function. The look of the table is determined by styles defined in the `.css` file we created. The arrow images, when clicked, will move the calendar to the previous or next month. When we generate the HTML, we set the arrow image's `onclick` event handler to call the `goPreviousMonth()` and `goNextMonth()` functions, which are found later on in the code in `CalendarScript.js`.

The code also uses another function found later in the file, `getMonthName()` – this simply returns a three-letter shortened name for the month to display (for example, Jan for January).

So far we have just the top of our calendar heading. The next part is the display of the days of the week:

The code below creates this part of the calendar heading:

```
var tableInnerHTML = "";
tableInnerHTML = "<tr class='dayHeadTR'><TD class='dayHeadTD'>S</td>";
tableInnerHTML += "<td class='dayHeadTD'>M</td>";
tableInnerHTML += "<td class='dayHeadTD'>T</td>"
tableInnerHTML += "<td class='dayHeadTD'>W</td>";
tableInnerHTML += "<td class='dayHeadTD'>T</td>";
tableInnerHTML += "<td class='dayHeadTD'>F</td>";
tableInnerHTML += "<td class='dayHeadTD'>S</td>";
tableInnerHTML += "</tr>"
```

OK, that's the easy parts done. Now we have to create this part of the calendar:

		1	2	3	4	5
6	7	8	9	10	11	12
13	14	15	16	17	18	19
20	21	22	23	24	25	26
27	28	29	30	31		

Before we can use code to loop through the table's cells and populate them with dates, we need two pieces of information.

The first thing we need to work out is the correct column to display the number 1 in – in other words, the day of the week that the first day of the month falls on. Obviously, this will depend on the month and the year. For example, the first day of January in 2002 is a Tuesday, and so in our images the numbering of days should start under the first T for Tuesday. To find out where we need to start, we have the `getStartDayOfMonthNumber()` function, which is created later in the file. This returns a number of 0 for the first column (Sunday), 1 for the second column (Monday), etc.

The second piece of information we need is how long the month is. We find this out using the `getDaysInAMonth()` function, again created later in the file.

So, we now have our two pieces of information: the day of the week that our month starts on, and the number of days in the month. Back in the `generateCalendar()` function, we save these pieces of information to the variables `iStartDayOfMonth` and `iLastDayOfMonth`:

```
var elementIndex = 1;
var iCellCounter;
var iStartDayOfMonth = getStartDayOfMonthNumber(month,year);
var iLastDayOfMonth = getDaysInAMonth(month,year);
var tableRows = 6;
```

We can now go ahead and create the `<td>` elements that hold the days of the month in our table. Our table will have six rows: we have an outer `for` loop that iterates through these rows, the variable `weekIndex` specifying the row:

```
for (weekIndex = 1; weekIndex <= tableRows; weekIndex++)
{
  tableInnerHTML = tableInnerHTML + "<tr>";
```

Inside the outer `for` loop is an inner `for` loop that creates the `<td>` cells for that row and populates them with the dates, or blank cells. It loops through the columns using the `dayCounter` variable:

```
var dayCounter;

for (dayCounter = 1; dayCounter <= 7; dayCounter++)
{
  if (elementIndex <= iStartDayOfMonth
      ||
      elementIndex > (iLastDayOfMonth + iStartDayOfMonth) )
  {
    tableInnerHTML += "<td class='emptyTD' id='dayTD";
    tableInnerHTML += elementIndex;
    tableInnerHTML += "'> </td>";
  }
  else
  {
    tableInnerHTML += "<td class='dayTD' ";
    tableInnerHTML += " onclick='updateSelectedDate(";
    tableInnerHTML += (elementIndex - iStartDayOfMonth);
    tableInnerHTML += "," + month + ",";
    tableInnerHTML += year + "); ";
    tableInnerHTML += " hideCalendar(\"" + calendarDivID;
    tableInnerHTML += "\"); ";
    tableInnerHTML += "'id='dayTD" + elementIndex +"'>";
    tableInnerHTML += (elementIndex - iStartDayOfMonth);
    tableInnerHTML += "</td>";
  }

  elementIndex++;
}
```

This is looped through seven times, once for each day of the week. On each iteration it creates a `<td>` element, which will either be blank or will contain a number representing a date. It's the `if` statement that decides whether the cell should be blank or filled. If the `elementIndex` variable, which keeps count of each `<td>` we have created in the table, is less than or equal to the number for the first day of the week for that month or if it's greater than the number of days in the month plus the first day of the week number, then a blank `<td>` is created.

For example, January the 1st, 2002, is a Tuesday and so the first two table cells for Sunday and Monday should be left blank. Also, January has 31 days, meaning that January the 31st is on a Thursday, so the last two cells for Friday and Saturday should also be blank (as well as the next row of cells since these are not needed for this month). From the point of view of the code, the number of the first day of the week is 2 (since this quantity starts at 0) and the number of days in the month is 31, so each `<td>` with `elementIndex` <=2 or `elementIndex` > 3+31 should be blank.

Look at our example calendar below to confirm this:

The blank table cell is fairly simple – its formatting is defined by a class called `EmptyTD` in the stylesheet `CalendarStyleDefinitions.css`.

A cell with a number in is more complex. The number displayed is the current cell element index (given by the `elementIndex` variable) minus the start day of the month (given by variable `iStartDayOfMonth`), since the first day of the month won't necessarily go in the first cell in the calendar table. In addition, when the user clicks a numbered cell, we want to capture that information and update the selected date variables. Therefore, when we create the `<td>` element we add the `onclick` event handler attribute. This calls two functions: `updateSelectedDate()`, with the date, month, and year passed as parameters, and `hideCalendar()`, which removes the calendar from view and takes the `id` of the `<div>` element containing the calendar as its parameter.
Finally, the table's last row is completed.

```
    tableInnerHTML = tableInnerHTML + "</tr>";
  }
```

Note that all the HTML that is created is stored in variable `tableInnerHTML`, which we'll use in the next bit of the function to set the inner HTML of the `<div>` element:

```
  var calendarDivObject = getTagById(calendarDivID)
  calendarDivObject.innerHTML = headingHTML +
    "<table style='calendarTable' cellspacing='0'><tbody>" +
    tableInnerHTML +
    "</tbody></table>" +
    "<a href='javaScript: " +
    "cancelCalendar(\"" +
    calendarDivID + "\")' class='cancelHyperlink'>Cancel</a>";
```

First we need to get a reference to the `<div>` element's object, which we do with the `getTagById()` function created later in the file. We then set the `div` object's `innerHTML` property to the heading we created, a `<table>` tag definition, and the `tableInnerHTML` we created in the `for` loops we saw above. We also add a hyperlink onto the end of the calendar, which allows the user to cancel their action of choosing a date. The hyperlink has its `onclick` event handler set to call the `cancelCalendar()` function.

On the final lines of the `generateCalendar()` function, we shade the cell of the currently selected date if it falls within the month shown.

```
  if (mCurrentMonth == mSelectedMonth && mCurrentYear == mSelectedYear)
  {
    highlightDay(mSelectedDay, mSelectedMonth, mSelectedYear);
  }
}
```

Note the use of `highlightDay()`, another function given later in the file.

In describing `generateCalendar()`, we've touched on many functions that it calls, but have not described their code in detail. We'll do that now.

First, we have the function that retrieves elements based on their `id` attribute value:

```
function getTagById(tagId)
{
  var selectedTag;

  if (document.all)
  {
    selectedTag = document.all.item(tagId);
  }
  else
  {
    selectedTag = document.getElementById(tagId);
  }

  return selectedTag;
}
```

If we were using IE5+ and NN6+ only, then we could use just the `getElementById()` method of the `document` object, since it's supported by these DOM level 1 compliant browsers. However, by creating this function we can make our calendar control compatible with IE4 as well – given that it's only a little extra effort, it seems worth it. The function does the same as `getElementById()`, except that it also works with IE4 by using the `document.all` property supported by all IE browsers.

In the `if` statement, we check to see if `document.all` returns a value. If it does, the `selectedTag` variable is set to the object representing the element with `id` value `tagId` using the `document.all.item()` method. If `document.all` is not supported, then we use the `getElementById()` method supported by DOM level 1 compliant browsers. This does assume that this page will only be visited by IE4+ or NN6; we would need to use browser checking to ensure browsers like NN4 are directed to a page that will work for them. Finally we return the element's object to the calling function.

Next is the function that retrieves a number corresponding to the weekday of the first day of the month for any specific month and year.

```
function getStartDayOfMonthNumber(month,year)
{
  var newDate = new Date();
  newDate.setMonth(month)
  newDate.setFullYear(year);
  newDate.setDate(1);

  return newDate.getDay();
}
```

This takes the month for which we want to find the start date, and the year that the month is in, as parameters. We use these to create a new `Date` object, which we set to the first day of that month in that year. Then we simply get the day of the week this represents using the `Date` object's `getDay()` method which returns 0 for Sunday, 1 for Monday, right through to 6 for Saturday.

We also need a function that returns the number of days in a month:

```
function getDaysInAMonth(month, year)
{
  var nowDate;
  month = parseInt(month)
  year = parseInt(year)

  var monthDays = new Array(31,29,31,30,31,30,31,31,30,31,30,31)

  // If Feb then need to check for leap years
  if (month == 1)
  {
    nowDate = new Date();
    nowDate.setMonth(1);
    nowDate.setYear(year);
    nowDate.setDate(29);

    if (nowDate.getMonth() == 2)
      monthDays[1] = 28;
  }

  return monthDays[month];
}
```

The function creates an array called `monthDays`, which is initialized to the number of days in each month. We could simply return the element in this array corresponding to our month if it wasn't for February and leap years. If the month is 1, that is February, then we need to check for leap years. We do this by creating a new `Date` object, setting the month to February, the year to our specified year, and the date to 29. If February only has 28 days that year, then the value set into the `Date` object will be interpreted as 1st of March. So, if `getMonth()` returns 2 (that is, March) then we know it was a 28 day February and we update the `monthDays` array accordingly. On the final line we return the value of the `monthDays` array with the index supplied by the parameter `month`.

Next is a simple function to return a more user-friendly month name:

```
function getMonthName(month)
{
  var months = new
    Array("Jan","Feb","Mar","Apr","May","Jun",
          "Jul","Aug","Sep","Oct","Nov","Dec");
  return months[month];
}
```

It creates a new array called `months` and initializes it to the shortened names of the months. Array element 0 will be `Jan`, element 1 will be `Feb`, and so on. This array index matches the value in the parameter `month` of the `generateCalendar()` function, so we can use `month` for the index to the `months` array to return the month name.

The calendar highlights the selected date, or the current date if no date is selected, using the `highlightDay()` function:

```
function highlightDay(day, month, year)
{
  // highlight selected cell
  var idOfCellToHighlight = day + getStartDayOfMonthNumber(month,year);
  idOfCellToHighlight = "dayTD" + idOfCellToHighlight;
  getTagById(idOfCellToHighlight).style.backgroundColor = 'lightgrey';
}
```

The first task the function must do is work out which cell needs to be highlighted. It does this by adding the day of the month onto the value for the first day of the month in the calendar. In our example where Tuesday 1 Jan 2002 is the first day, the starting cell is 2. If we wanted to highlight January the 3rd, it would have a day of the month value of 3, giving a total cell number of 5. Each of the `<td>` cells has an `id` of `"dayTD"` followed by the cell number, so we can use our cell id of `dayTD5` when we call `getTagById()` on the last line to change the style of the `<td>` element to a background of light gray.

The next function is very simple. It updates the three global variables that hold the `day`, `month`, and `year` selected by the user.

```
function updateSelectedDate(day,month,year)
{
  mSelectedDay = day;
  mSelectedMonth = month;
  mSelectedYear = year;
}
```

This function is called whenever the user clicks on any of the `<td>` cells containing a date.

The next two functions we need to look at are `goPreviousMonth()` and `goNextMonth()`. These functions are called when the user clicks the left or right arrow images on the calendar. The `goPreviousMonth()` function shown below, decrements the `mCurrentMonth` variable which contains the currently displayed month. If this results in the month become less than zero, it decrements the year and sets the month to 11, that is December. Finally, we regenerate the calendar by calling the `generateCalendar()` function.

```
function goPreviousMonth(calendarDivID)
{
  mCurrentMonth--;
  if (mCurrentMonth < 0)
  {
    mCurrentMonth = 11;
    mCurrentYear--;
  }

  generateCalendar(mCurrentMonth, mCurrentYear,calendarDivID);
}
```

As can be imagined, the `goNextMonth()` function works in a similar way to the `goPreviousMonth()` one:

```
function goNextMonth(calendarDivID)
{
  mCurrentMonth++;
  if (mCurrentMonth > 11)
```

```
  {
    mCurrentMonth = 0;
    mCurrentYear++;
  }

  generateCalendar(mCurrentMonth, mCurrentYear,calendarDivID);
}
```

The obvious difference is that `mCurrentMonth` is incremented and, if this results in the month being greater than 11, the year is incremented and the month set to 0, that is January.

We then have the function that is called by the *Cancel* hyperlink (and the `hideCalendar()` function we'll see below) to move the Calendar `<div>` off screen, making it invisible to the user.

```
function cancelCalendar(calendarDivID)
{
  getTagById(calendarDivID).style.left = "-1200px";
  getTagById(calendarDivID).style.top = "-1000px";
}
```

We use the `getTagById()` function to access the `div` object containing the calendar and send it off screen by setting its `left` and `top` properties to large negative values.

Finally, we have the function that is used to hide the calendar once a date has actually been selected.

```
function hideCalendar(calendarDivID)
{
  cancelCalendar(calendarDivID);

  mOnHideFunction(mSelectedDay, getMonthName(mSelectedMonth), mSelectedYear);
}
```

This is called whenever the user clicks a cell containing a date. It first calls the `cancelCalendar()` function to move the calendar off screen. Next we make use of the `mOnHideFunction` global variable. This variable is very important and is set when the `showCalendar()` function is called (which we'll see shortly) to the call-backfunction passed as a parameter from the HTML page. We call the function `mOnHideFunction()` and pass the selected day, month, and year (the month is formatted in its short name form using the `getMonthName()` function). In our example, the `mOnHideFunction()` is either `onCalendarHiddenStartDate()` or `onCalendarHiddenEndDate()` defined in the HTML page – these insert the dates selected via the calendar into the appropriate textbox in the HTML page.

showCalendar()

We've now finished explaining `generateCalendar()` and the functions it calls in their entirety. The final function to look at from the `.js` file is the `showCalendar()` function, which needs to be called to actually show the generated control:

```
function showCalendar(xPos, yPos, calendarDivID, onHideFunction)
{
  getTagById(calendarDivID).style.left = xPos;
  getTagById(calendarDivID).style.top = yPos;
  mOnHideFunction = onHideFunction;
}
```

It takes four parameters: the x and y screen positions at which to position the control, the `id` of the `<div>` element that will hold the calendar table, and the call-backfunction that needs to be called when the control is hidden. The function uses these parameters to "show" the control, by moving it from its off-screen positions to the `left` and `top` positions specified. Then, the global variable `mOnHideFunction` is set to reference the function given in the parameter `onHideFunction`, so that it may be called by the `hideCalendar()` function, as described above.

That completes our look at the calendar control. However, there are plenty of ways to improve its look by changing the stylesheet `CalendarStyleDefinitions.css` or by adding scripting improvements, such as hiding the control after the user's mouse leaves it for more than a few seconds, should you wish to.

The E-commerce Image Viewer – Part 1

Now that we've stepped through a few advanced techniques to use with forms, we'll continue by taking a look at how the image viewer we developed in Chapters 4 to 7 can be updated to allow users to purchase prints of the images. In this chapter and the next two chapters we'll be adding the necessary code to make this work.

Interface Changes

We'll first take a look at the interface changes:

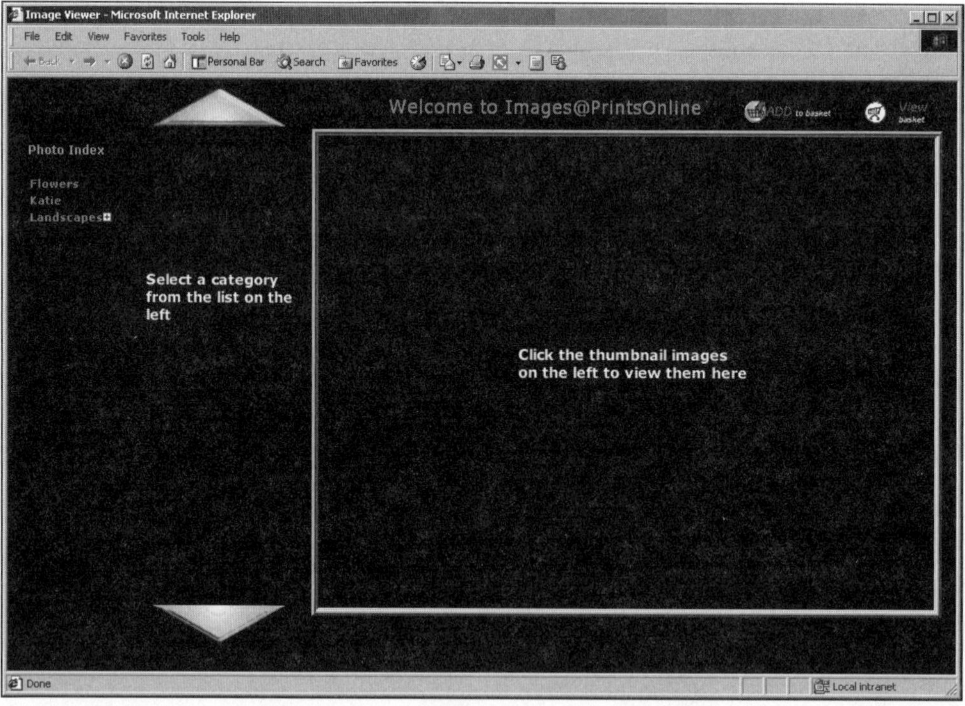

The changes here are the addition of two icons: *ADD to basket* and *View basket*. When the *ADD to basket* button is clicked, the currently selected image is added to the shopping basket. The *View basket* button, rather obviously, displays the basket's current contents in the large image window, as shown below:

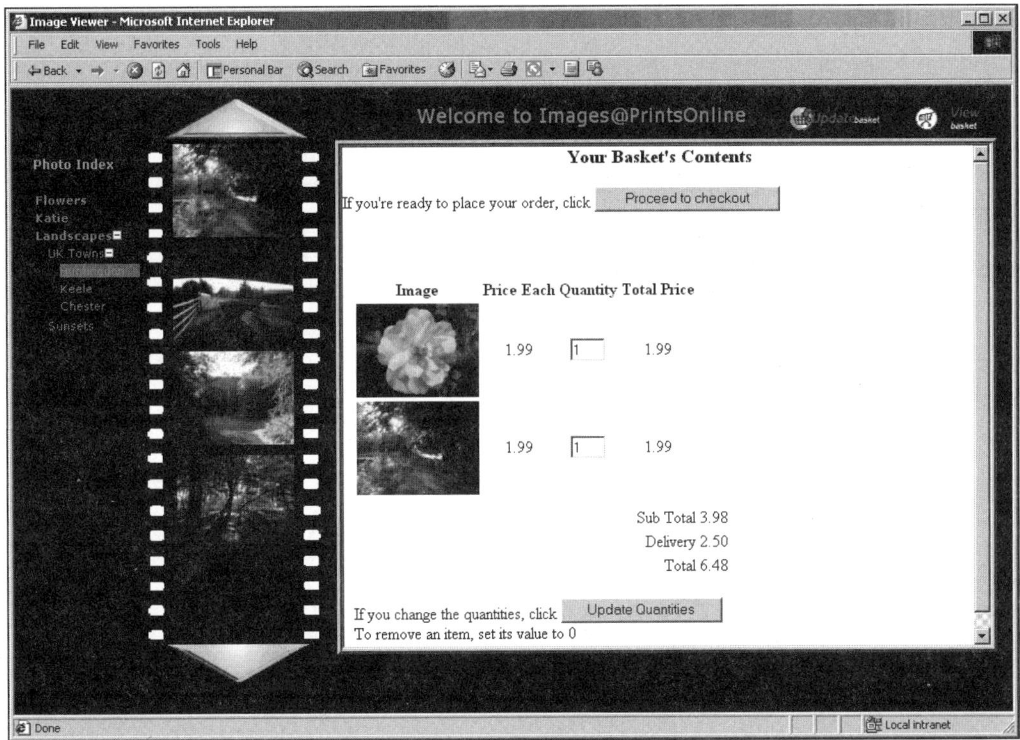

The details of the basket are shown inside the frame where the images are viewed. Another alternative would be for the details of the basket to be shown as a new complete page and then have a *Back* button to return to the image viewer. Note also that the *ADD to basket* icon has switched to *Update basket*. This, along with the *Update Quantities* button, can be clicked to update the number of quantities of each image that are wanted. If the user clicks on another thumbnail image to view it in the main image pane, then the *Update basket* icon will swap back to *ADD to basket*.

If the user leaves the web site or closes the browser, then code is used to ensure that the basket's contents are saved and can be re-accessed if they return within a 3-month period. Often users may add items to their basket, but then go away and think about it before buying. There's nothing more annoying than to come back, having decided to buy, and find that it's necessary to start over and fill your basket. By making life easier for the user, they are much more likely to buy, rather than think "I can't be bothered to start again".

At the top of the *View basket* page is the *Proceed to checkout* button. This takes the user to the first stage of the actual purchasing of the image prints:

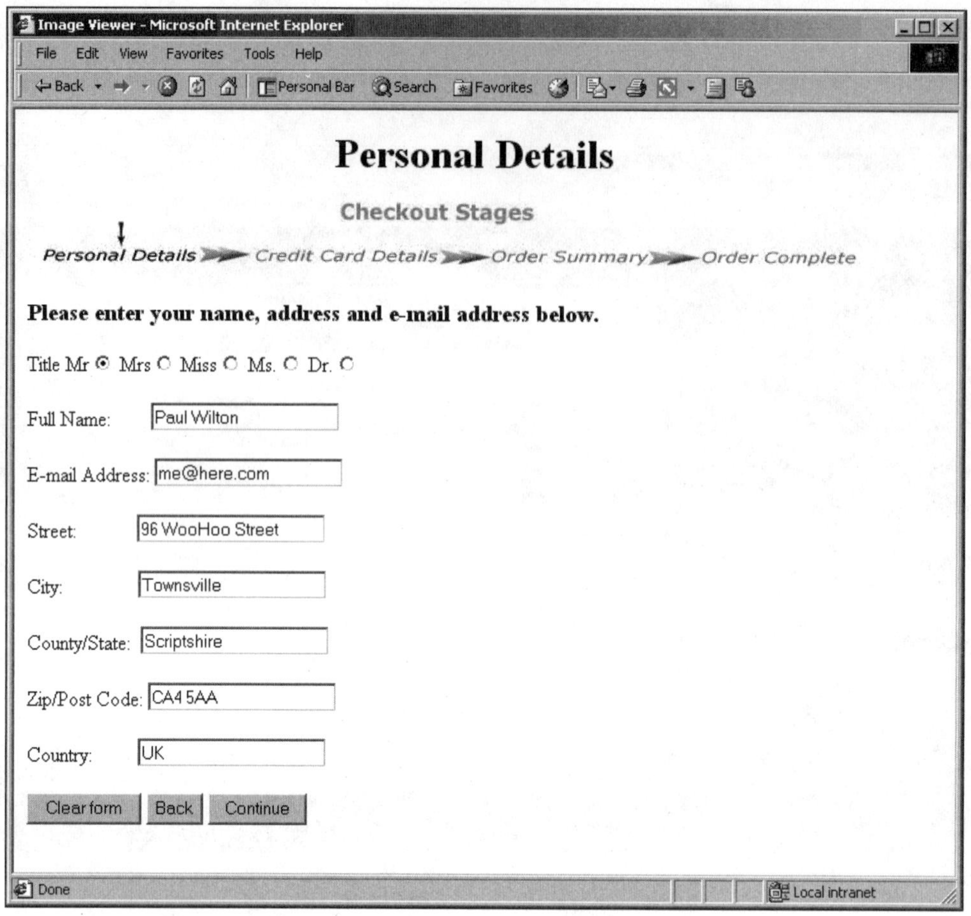

On this page, all the personal details, such as name, delivery address etc., are collected. Note that the image at the top makes it clear how many stages there are in the checkout process and what stage we are currently at. This helps reassure users and increases the likelihood of them continuing and actually purchasing items. The more feedback you can give the user about what's happening, the happier they will feel. At least now they know there are just a few pages before the process is complete.

If the *Back* button is clicked, then the user is taken back to the image viewer, but any information they have entered so far is recorded and, if they return, the form will be filled in as they left it. The record of the contents of the form is only cleared if the basket is successfully purchased, or the *Clear form* button is pressed. This again helps make life a bit easier for the user.

When the *Continue* button is clicked, the form's contents will be checked in the browser to see that they are valid. Any errors, for example invalid postal code or e-mail address formats, will be notified to the user – they won't be able to continue until they are fixed:

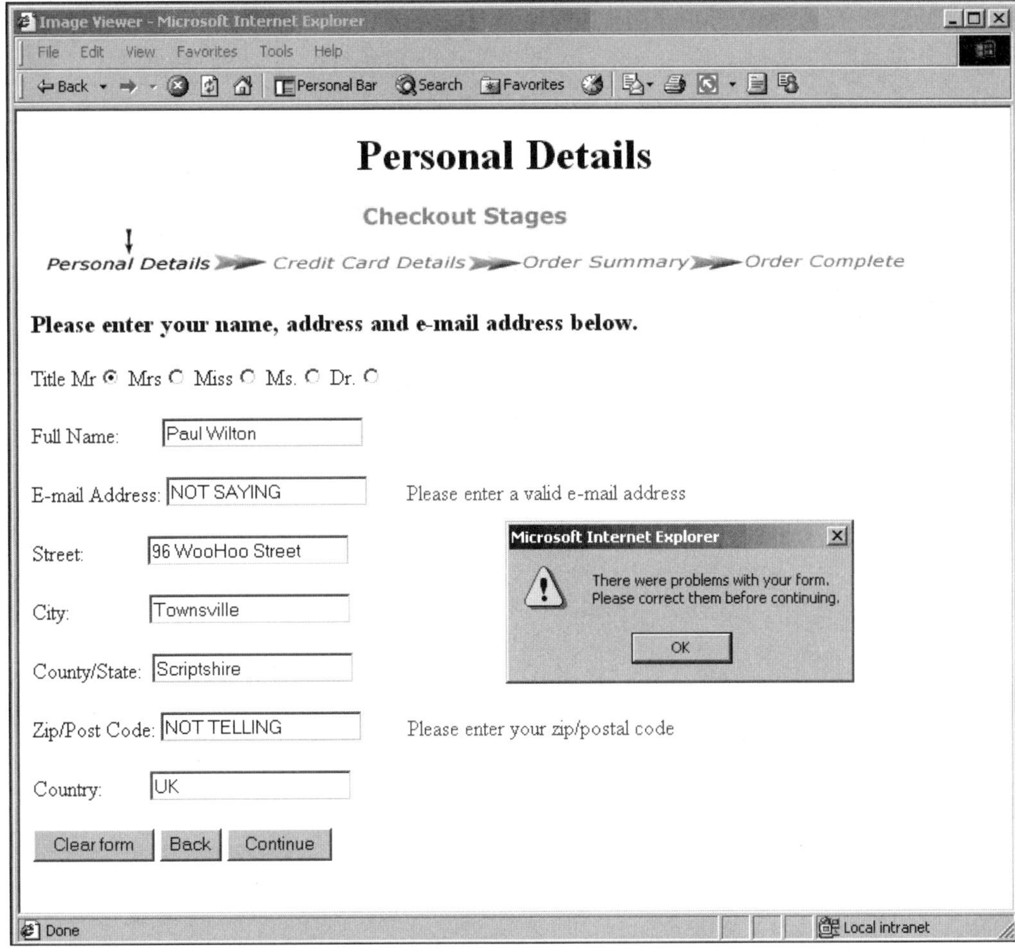

Regardless of the number of errors, only one alert box is shown. Each individual error is noted in red next to where the problem is. This is better than an alert for each error, which may get annoying.

Assuming that the form contains valid information, clicking the *Continue* button takes you to the next page:

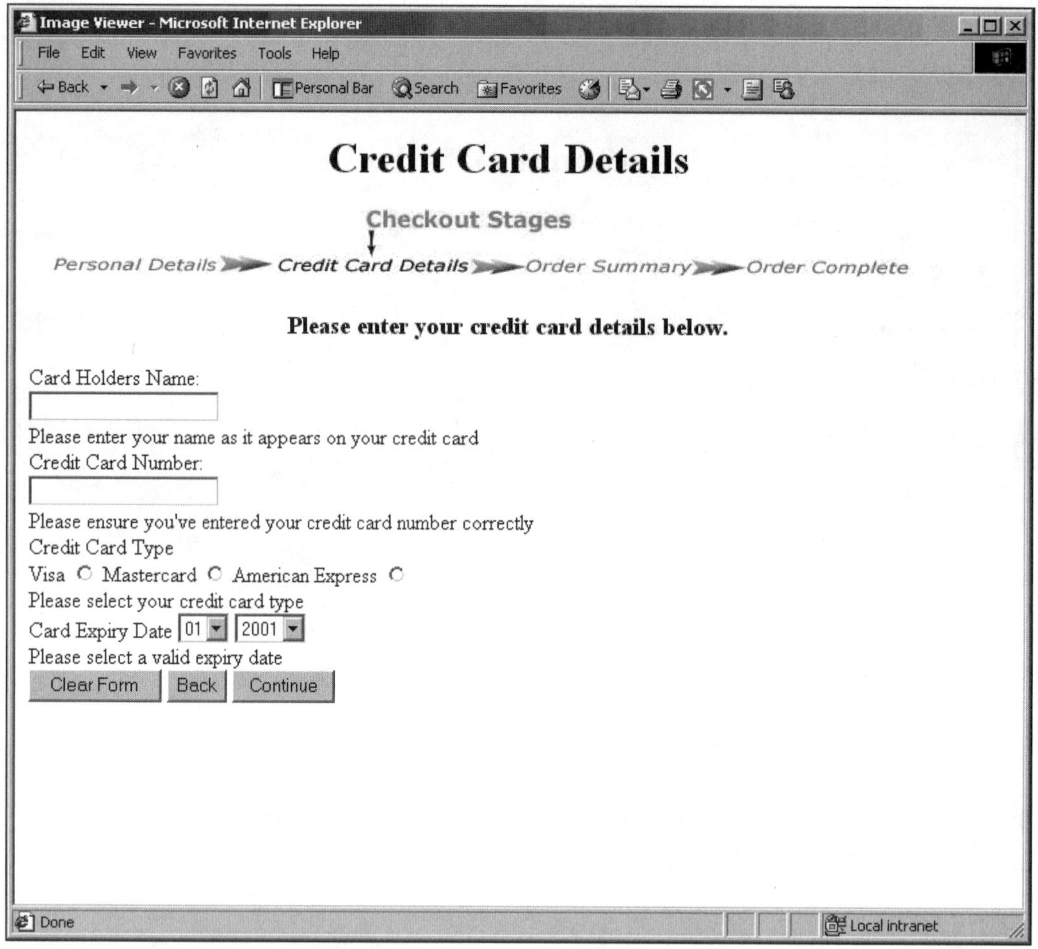

On this page we obtain the user's credit card details. Note that the heading has changed to reflect where we are in the stages of the checkout. As before, if invalid information is entered, the user will be prevented from continuing and error messages will be displayed. Note that the credit card number may or may not be entered including spaces – the code deals with this possibility. Some web sites insist you enter 1111222233334444 rather than 1111 2222 3333 4444, which is easier for humans to read. For security reasons, the details of the credit card are not stored, so leaving this page of the checkout and returning will result in them being lost.

Clicking *Continue* brings us to the final stage of the checkout before the order is actually committed:

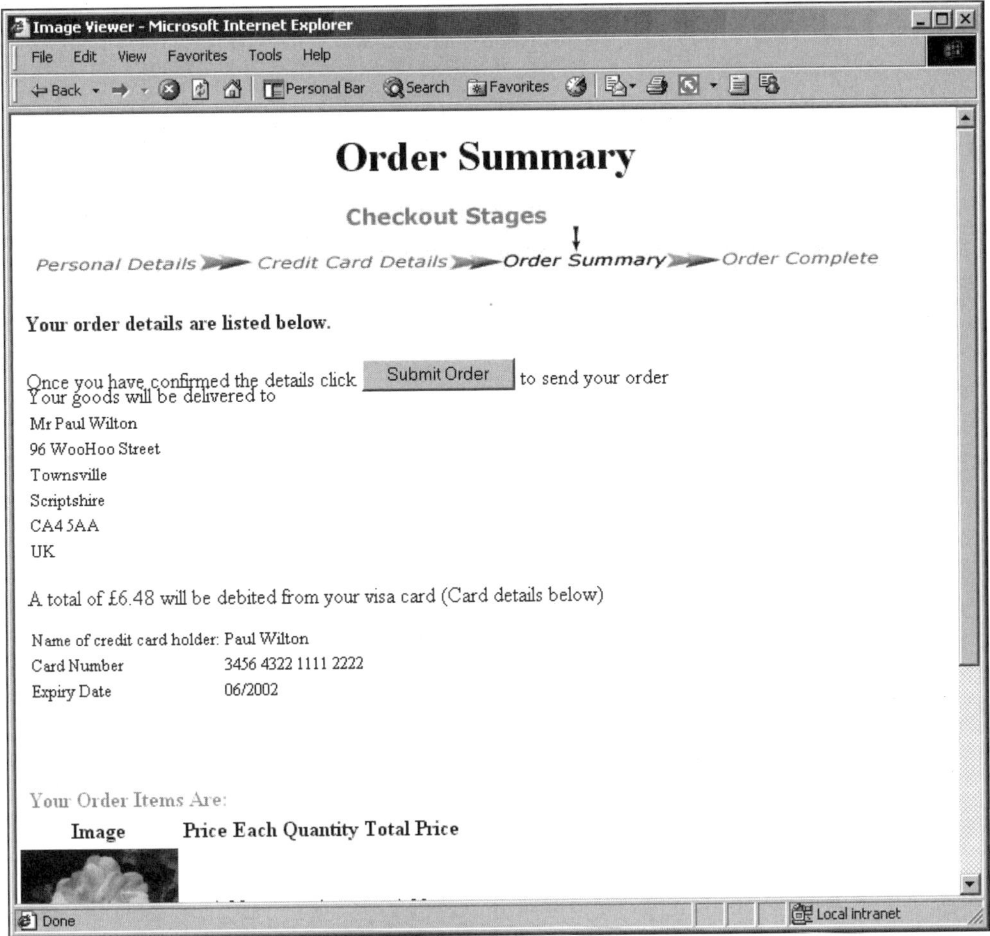

All the details of the user are displayed. Although not done here, you may prefer to show the credit card number blacked out, for example 3xxx xxxx xxxx xxx2, to prevent users in public places having someone steal their number by looking over their shoulder.

Having reviewed the order details, the user clicks *Submit Order*. It's only at this point that the information gathered from the user is actually sent to the server, where it would be processed, credit card monies taken, and someone told to dispatch the goods. In our example, it just results in this page being shown:

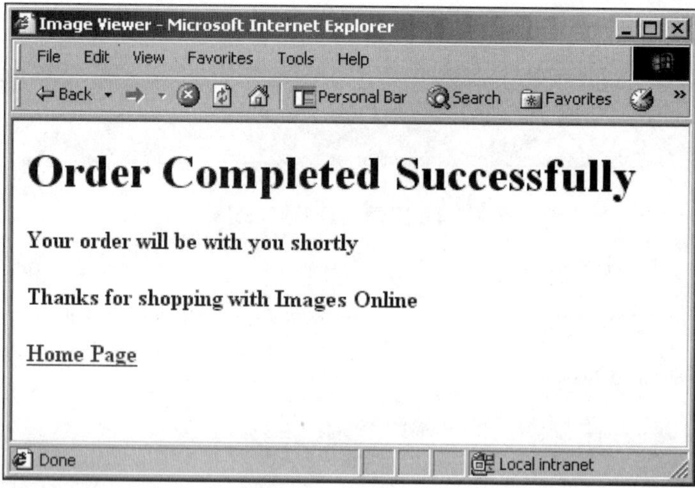

The basket and the user details that have been stored are also erased at this point.

Code Changes

That covers the interface changes, so it's now time to take an overview of the code changes.

Although the e-commerce image viewer looks virtually identical to the previous version, it is in fact now a frames-based application. The top frameset-defining page enables us to use JavaScript code that stores the shopping basket information for the duration of the customer's visit. This may seem odd, but one way of maintaining state (that is, keeping information "alive") is to store variables in a top frameset page that is never unloaded. We'll discuss this and other maintaining state techniques in Chapter 9.

The frameset page only defines one frame, namely a frame that holds the `ImageViewer.htm` page of our previous incarnation of the image viewer. In addition, the frameset page holds a lot of JavaScript code that is imported from `.js` files.

As well as the new frameset page, we also have new pages for the shopping basket and each stage of the checkout. However most of these pages contain very little or no code – almost all the code is in `.js` files, of which there are five new ones:

`CreditCard.js`	Defines a `CreditCard` class to store user's credit card details
`Customer.js`	Defines a `Customer` class to store customer details
`ecomCode.js`	General e-commerce related code
`ShoppingBasket.js`	Defines a `ShoppingBasket` and `ShoppingItem` class for creating a shopping basket
`Validate.js`	Defines a `Validate` class to validate data

We'll be creating the code for the `CreditCard.js`, `Customer.js` and `ShoppingBasket.js` files in the next chapter, and the code for `Validate.js` in Chapter 10.

For the remainder of this chapter, let's get the e-commerce application started by creating the basic HTML pages and also some of the `ecomCode.js` file. This will be built on in Chapter 9.

First we'll create the frameset page, `ImageViewerEcom.htm`:

```
<html>
<head>
  <title>Image Viewer</title>
  <script language="JavaScript" src="ShoppingBasket.js"></script>
  <script language="JavaScript" src="Validate.js"></script>
  <script language="JavaScript" src="Customer.js"></script>
  <script language="JavaScript" src="CreditCard.js"></script>
  <script language="JavaScript" src="ecomCode.js"></script>
</head>
<frameset cols="100%" border="0">
  <frame name="ImageViewerFrame" src="ImageViewer.htm">
</frameset>
</html>
```

From now on, to load our image viewer we load this page and not the original `ImageViewer.htm` page. The page is simple enough – all the code is in *.js* files yet to be created. For now, create empty files with the names: `ShoppingBasket.js`, `Validate.js`, `Customer.js`, `CreditCard.js`, and `ecomCode.js`. As we said above, we'll be adding to these in the next two chapters, though the only one of these files we'll be adding any code to later in this chapter is `ecomCode.js`.

Our next task is to create the three images for *ADD to basket*, *Update basket*, and *View basket*. These can be downloaded with the code from the book's web site.

Now we have our images, we need to add them to the `ImageViewer.htm page`. The code snippet below shows the addition of appropriate `<img>` elements within the page.

```
<img src="ImageLoadingAnimation.gif" id="imageLoadingAnimation"
     width="150" height="40" alt="Loading Image...please wait">
  <h3 id="Heading">Welcome to Images@PrintsOnline</h3>

  <img src="AddToBasket.gif" id="imageAddToBasket"
       onclick="parent.addToBasket_onclick()">
  <img src="view_basket copy.gif" id="imageViewBasket"
       onclick="parent.viewBasket_onclick()">
  <iframe name="mainImageFrame" id="mainImageFrame" src="DefaultMainImage.gif"
          scrolling="auto" frameborder="none" marginheight="0" marginwidth="0"
          onload="hideImageLoadingImage()">
  </iframe>
```

Note that the `onclick` event handlers of each image are set to call JavaScript functions – we'll need to add these functions to the `ecomCode.js` file shortly.

Another change to `ImageViewer.htm` is the addition of style definitions to the `<style>` element at the top of the page for each of the images:

```
IMG#imageLoadingAnimation
{
  left:320px; top: 10px; visibility:hidden;
}
```

```
    IMG#imageAddToBasket
    {
      position: absolute; left:770px; top: 20px;
    }

    IMG#imageViewBasket
    {
      position: absolute; left:890px; top: 20px;
    }
    H3#Heading
    {
      font: 14pt verdana; position: absolute; left:400px; top: 15px;
      color: darkorange; margin: 0px;
    }
  </style>
```

Those are all the changes that need to be made to *ImageViewer.htm*, so you can save the file and close it. However, we need to make virtually identical changes to the `ImageViewer_smallscreen.htm` page. First add the `<img>` elements:

```
<img src="ImageLoadingAnimation.gif" id="imageLoadingAnimation"
     width="150" height="40" alt="Loading Image...please wait">
<h3 id="Heading">Welcome to Images@PrintsOnline</h3>

<img src="AddToBasket.gif" id="imageAddToBasket"
     onclick="parent.addToBasket_onclick()">
<img src="view_basket copy.gif" id="imageViewBasket"
     onclick="parent.viewBasket_onclick()">
<iframe name="mainImageFrame" id="mainImageFrame" src="DefaultMainImage.gif"
        scrolling="auto" frameborder="none" marginheight="0" marginwidth="0"
        onload="hideImageLoadingImage()">
</iframe>
```

Next add the style definitions anywhere within the `<style>` element at the top of the page:

```
IMG#imageAddToBasket
{
  position: absolute; left:580px; top: 20px;
}

IMG#imageViewBasket
{
  position: absolute; left:690px; top: 20px;
}
H3#Heading
{
  font: 14pt verdana; position: absolute; left:400px; top: 15px;
  color: darkorange; margin: 0px;
}
```

That completes the changes for the `ImageViewer_smallscreen.htm` page, and it too can be saved and closed.

Now we come to the addition of code to the currently empty `ecomCode.js` file that we created above. Open it and add the following functions:

```
function addToBasket_onclick()
{

}

function viewBasket_onclick()
{
   var mainImageFrame = window.frames["ImageViewerFrame"].frames["mainImageFrame"];
   mainImageFrame.location.href = "viewbasket.htm";
   mainImageFrame.loadedImgRefId = null;
   if(document.all)
   {
      document.frames["ImageViewerFrame"].imageAddToBasket.src
="UpdateToBasket.gif";
   }
   else
   {
      window.frames["ImageViewerFrame"].document.imageAddToBasket.src =
         "UpdateToBasket.gif";
   }
}
```

These are the two functions used by the `onclick` event handlers of the `<img>` elements we have just added to `ImageViewer.htm` and `ImageViewer_smallscreen.htm`.

The first function, `addToBasket_onclick()`, is currently an empty definition – we'll be creating the classes necessary for the shopping basket in the next chapter.

The `viewBasket_onclick()` function loads the shopping basket page, *viewbasket.htm*, into the `mainImageFrame` frame. The first line of the function sets the `mainImageFrame` variable to reference the `window` object of `mainImageFrame`, where the full size images are normally loaded. The function then uses this reference to load the `viewbasket.htm` page by setting the `location` object's `href` property.

We then set variable `loadedImgRefId` to null. This variable has not yet been defined – we'll soon need to add it to the `ImageViewerMainCode.js` file we are already familiar with from the earlier incarnation of the application. Its purpose is to store a unique id for the selected image, the value of which is obtained from the id of the individual image's thumbnail `<img>` element. In a server-side based application, it's most likely that we'd have dynamically created the image thumbnails from information in a database, and that's where the unique id would have come from.

On the `viewBasket_onclick()` function's final lines we change the *ADD to basket* image for one that says *Update basket*, to reflect the changed purpose. (Notice that the way we do this depends on the browser, so we use `document.all` to check for an Internet Explorer browser.) When an image is loaded, clicking the *ADD to basket* `<img>` element causes the currently loaded main image to be added to the basket. When the shopping basket is loaded, then clicking the same `<img>` element (which is now seen as *Update basket*) causes any changes to the basket's quantities to be updated.

Let's open the `ImageViewerMainCode.js` file and add the global variable `loadedImgRefId` mentioned above:

```
var loadedImgRefId = null;
```

This can be placed at the very top of the file. We also need to change the `loadNewMainImage()` function because, as we'll see shortly, when a thumbnail image is clicked, not only do we need to load the large version of it to the main viewing frame, but we also need to note its unique id for use in the shopping basket:

```
function loadNewMainImage(imgSrc, imgRefId)
{
  var mainImgFrame = window.frames["mainImageFrame"];
  if (document.all)
  {
    document.all.imageLoadingAnimation.style.visibility = "visible";
  }

  mainImgFrame.location.href = imgSrc;
  loadedImgRefId = imgRefId;

  document.images["imageAddToBasket"].src = "AddToBasket.gif";
}
```

We've changed the function's parameters, adding `imgRefId` to the parameters passed. Near the end of the function, we have added code that sets the `loadedImgRefId` to the one passed in the `imgRefId` parameter. On the final line we make sure that, as an image is loaded in the main viewing frame rather than the shopping basket, the `<img>` element now says *ADD to basket* and not *Update basket*.

That completes the changes to `ImageViewerMainCode.js`, which can be saved and closed. We still need to update the `ThumbnailPagesCode.js`, where the `loadNewMainImage()` function is called from, since we've just changed the parameters this function takes. Alter the function `document_onclick()` as shown below:

```
function document_onclick(eventObject)
{
  var eventSourceElement = getEventSourceElement(eventObject);
  if (eventSourceElement != null && eventSourceElement.tagName == "IMG")
  {
    var imgSrc = eventSourceElement.src;
    var imgRef = eventSourceElement.id;
    imgSrc = imgSrc.replace("_thumbnail","");

    parent.loadNewMainImage(imgSrc, imgRef);
  }
}
```

This function now extracts the `id` of the thumbnail into a variable `imgRef`, and on the final line passes that as a second parameter of the `loadNewMainImage()` function.

Before we leave the e-commerce Image viewer for this chapter, let's create two final pages, `viewbasket.htm`, and `emptybasket.htm`. We'll start with `ViewBasket.htm` – this is loaded into the large image viewing pane whenever the *View basket* icon is clicked:

```
<html>
<head>
</head>
<body>
  <div align='center'>
    <h3>
      Your Basket's Contents
    </h3>
  </div>
</body>
</html>
```

So far this page is just a skeleton, but we'll be adding code to it in the next chapter.

Finally, we create `EmptyBasket.htm`, which is displayed when the basket has no contents – it is a plain HTML page with no script:

```
<html>
<head>
  <link rel='stylesheet' href='WebsiteGlobalStyle.css'></link>
  <style>
    BODY { color: white; background-color: black; }
  </style>
</head>
<body>
   <h3 style="position: absolute; top: 45%; left: 15%">
      Your basket is currently empty
   </h3>
</body>
</html>
```

That completes our look at the e-commerce updates to the image viewer for this chapter. In the next chapter we'll get the shopping basket aspect of the application working.

Regular Expressions

In the remaining two chapters of the book, we'll be looking at data – in Chapter 9 we look at storing data between pages, and in Chapter 10 we look at validating data the user has entered. One concept that is very useful when manipulating string data is that of **regular expressions**. As we'll be making extensive use of regular expressions throughout these two chapters, we'll now take a very brief look at what they are and how they work.

Regular expressions could form the topic of a whole book, so in this section we'll be aiming to give a basic insight into them without going into very much depth. However, there will be many examples of their use in the next two chapters.

What are regular expressions? Well, their name doesn't give much away about their purpose – their use is for character pattern matching. Let's use a real world example. Imagine we are searching for a person, but all we have is a faded bit of paper – the characters `Wil` are legible, but after that it's just a smudge. The name finishes with an `n` or it could be an `m`. How would regular expressions help in this situation? They let us specify that we are looking for:

- A word starting with `Wil`
- One or more characters follow the `Wil`
- Finishing with either an n or an m

These rules would match words such as:

Wilton
Williamson
Wilson
William

As we'll see in Chapter 10, regular expressions can be particularly useful in data validation. They make it easier to test whether data entered by the user matches what we expected. For example, if we asked for an e-mail address, does the string entered look like it could be valid? *me_and_you@someServer.com* could be valid, but *XXX@XXX* is not because it lacks the part after the final dot, such as *.co.uk* or *.com*.

Regular expressions have their own syntax and special characters that allow us to specify what we want to match. Let's take the example above where we have a partial name we want to match on. The regular expression for this is:

```
\bWil[a-z]+[nm]\b
```

At first sight it looks like nonsense, but if we split it up it makes sense. First we have:

```
\b
```

This is a special character in regular expression syntax that matches the boundary between characters that don't form part of a word. This ensures that words like "swilton" don't match. Next in our regular expression we have:

```
Wil
```

This is at least nice and easy – it matches the characters `Wil`. Next comes:

```
[a-z]+
```

First we specify that we want to match any of the characters inside the square brackets. This can be individual characters or, as in this case, a range of characters. Here we specify any lowercase character between a and z. Outside the square brackets we have a `+`, another special character that specifies we should match the previous item one or more times.

Next we have:

```
[nm]
```

Here we are saying we want to match any of the characters in the square brackets, in this case either an `n` or an `m`. Finally, we have another word boundary character:

```
\b
```

This is so words such as "Williams" don't match – our word must end at the `m` or `n`.

In the table below, some of the special characters that match specific classes of characters are listed. For example, `\w` matches any letter or an underscore.

Character Class	Characters it Matches	Example
\d	Any digit, includes 0-9	`\d\d` matches 72, but not aa or 7a
\D	Any character not a digit	`\D\D\D` matches abc, but not 123
\w	Any word character, such as A-Z, a-z, 0-9, and the underscore character _	`\w\w\w\w` matches Ab_2, but not £$%* or Ab_@
\W	Any non-word character	`\W` matches @, but not the letter a
\s	Any whitespace character, includes tab, newline, carriage return, formfeed, and vertical tab	
\S	Any non-whitespace character	
.	Any character except a new-line character	
[...]	Any one of the characters between the square brackets	`[abc]` will match a or b or c, but nothing else `[a-z]` will match any character in the range a to z
[^...]	Any character, except those inside the square brackets	`[^abc]` will match any character except a or b or c, but A or B or C could be matched by this pattern `[^a-z]` will match any character which is not in the range a to z, but all uppercase letters could be matched by this pattern

The next table details the repetition characters. For example, + specifies that the last item should be matched one or more times:

Special Character	Meaning	Example
`{n}`	Match `n` of the previous item	`x{2}` matches xx, but not x or xxx
`{n,}`	Match `n` or more of the previous item	`x{2,}` matches two or more x's, that is xx, xxx, xxxx, xxxxx, ...

Table continued on following page

Special Character	Meaning	Example
{n,m}	Match at least n and at most m of the preceding item	x{2,4} matches xx, xxx and xxxx, but not x or xxxxx.
?	Match the previous item zero or one times (essentially making it optional)	x? matches x or no x
+	Match the previous item one or more times	x+ matches x, or xx or xxx, or any number of x
*	Match the previous item zero or more times	x* matches no x or x or xx or any number of x
|	Match the previous or the following item	x|y matches x or y

Finally we have special characters that specify where something should be matched, for example whether the match should be at the start of a word boundary:

Position Character	Description
^	The pattern must be at the start of the string, or if it's a multi-line string, then at the beginning of a line.
$	The pattern must be at the end of the string, or if multi-line string then at the end of a line.
\b	This matches a word boundary, essentially the point between a word character and a non word character, for example the start of a word.
\B	Matches a position that is not a word boundary, for example not the start of a word.

That was a very brief introduction to regular expressions – more details can be found on the Web.

Although we have looked at the syntax of regular expressions, we've still not seen how JavaScript allows us to create them. JavaScript actually has a built-in regular expression object, which allows us to specify a regular expression. We can create it in a number of ways, but the easiest is using the method shown below:

```
var myRegularExpression = /\bWil[a-z]+[nm]\b/;
```

The / character specifies the start and end of the regular expression syntax. We can then either use the regular expression object itself or we can pass it to methods of objects such as the String object, which uses regular expressions for its `split()`, `replace()`, `search()`, and `slice()` methods. We can also specify special attributes for the regular expression object that change how it works. For example, `i` specifies that the match should be case insensitive, and `g` specifies that all matching patterns should be looked for, not just the first one.

We'll be using the regular expression object throughout the next two chapters, but let's look at two methods here: the `test()` method of the regular expression object, and the `match()` method of the String object.

The `test()` method of the regular expression object tests to see if a string, passed as a parameter, contains a matching pattern. If it does, it returns true. For example:

```
<html>
<body>
<script>
  var myRegularExpression = /\bWil[a-z]+[nm]\b/;
  if (myRegularExpression.test("Mr Bob Wilson"))
  {
    alert("A match was made");
  }
  else
  {
    alert("No match was found");
  }
</script>
</body>
</html>
```

In this case, the string `"Mr Bob Wilson"` will test true for the regular expression `\bWil[a-z]+[nm]\b`. In this case, it's `Wilson` that actually matches our regular expression.

The `match()` method of the String object will search a string and find each character pattern that matches the regular expression, returning the results in an array. For example:

```
<html>
<body>
<script>
  var names = "Bob Wilson, Guy Wilton, Susan Williams, Marie Williamson";
  var matchesMade = names.match(/\bWil[a-z]+[nm]\b/g)

  if (matchesMade)
  {
    for (var indexCounter = 0; indexCounter < matchesMade.length; indexCounter++)
    {
      document.write(matchesMade[indexCounter] + "<BR>");
    }
  }
</script>
</body>
</html>
```

The following will display in the page:

Wilson
Wilton
Williamson

These are the three items in the string `names` that match our regular expression – remember that Williams doesn't match the defined regular expression, since it doesn't end with an `n` or `m`. Notice that we set the `g` flag in the regular expression:

```
/\bWil[a-z]+[nm]\b/g
```

This will ensure that the array will contain all matches in the string. Otherwise just the first match made, Wilson in this case, will be returned and no other matches looked for.

It's useful to note that we don't create a specific regular expression object, then pass that to the `match()` method. Instead we create it inside the `match()` method's parameter. The reason it has been done this way in the example is because we have no use for the regular expression, except for use with the `match()` method. An alternative way would have been the following, if we planned to use the regular expression again:

```
var regularExpression = /\bWil[a-z]+[nm]\b/g;
var matchesMade = names.match(regularExpression);
```

This works just the same as the earlier way.

Summary

In this chapter we covered two more advanced forms techniques that we didn't look at in the earlier forms chapter, Chapter 4. We saw how to add new options to a select control, and how we can use DHTML to create new non-standard HTML controls for gathering user input.

We then started the process of converting the image viewer we created in Chapters 5, 6, and 7 into an e-commerce application. This will be completed in Chapters 9 and 10.

Finally, we took an overview of regular expressions and their syntax, since this will be used extensively throughout Chapters 9 and 10.

9

- Passing information between web pages
- Cookies
- The cookie code toolkit
- E-commerce application: Part 2

Author: Paul Wilton

Passing Information Between Web Pages and Data Storage

This chapter is all about storing and passing data on the client. We'll begin by looking at storing information that is needed by a number of pages on a web site for the duration of a user's visit. This is useful for things like storing details of a shopping basket

We can permanently store simple data on the user's computer using something called **cookies** – so we'll create functions that make cookie management easy. This allows us to store things for when the user returns to our web site, for example site preferences like language.

Finally, we'll be making more changes to the image viewer, continuing the translation of the application to an e-commerce application started in the previous chapter. By the end of this chapter, it'll have a working shopping basket and checkout.

Keeping Information Alive

One of the problems with web pages is they are essentially **stateless**, in that once you leave the page any information in variables or changes made to the page with DHTML are lost. There are many times when we want to store information for the duration of the user's visit to the site. The duration of a user's visit is called a **session**, so storing information throughout the visit is called maintaining **session state.** We'll need to maintain the details of items in our shopping cart application regardless of which pages on the web site the user browses. In this section, we'll be looking at two techniques for temporarily storing information during a session, giving the impression of **state**.

One technique for keeping information alive is to pass it from page to page through the URL. This is the first technique we'll work with, before we move on to storing information in cookies.

Passing Information with URLs

The easiest and most browser compatible client-side technique for passing information to another page is to put that information inside the URL. You've probably done this yourself when you've run a search at a site like Google. You'll see something like this:*http://www.google.co.uk/search?q=JavaScript&hl=en&btnG=Google+Search&meta=*
The first part of the URL, *www.google.co.uk/search*, specifies the server and directory. Everything following the question mark specifies the data that will be passed to the page. In this example *q* (query) is set to equal JavaScript, because this is the search term being used. The remaining parameters specify things like default language and other information needed by the server.
The good news is that not only can servers read this information; the browser on the client-side can as well. On the other hand, although you can pass quite a bit of information using URLs, they are in fact limited to around 2000 characters. And, of course, the user gets to see the information, which may or may not matter depending on the sort of information being passed.

Note that none of the examples in this section of the chapter will work with IE4 if we load the page directly from the hard drive because IE4 doesn't recognizes data passed using the file:// protocol. *We must load them from a web server for this browser. This is only a problem during testing, but is something to watch out for if you do use IE4 or earlier. It's not an issue for Netscape and IE5+.*

Data attached to a URL must be placed after a question mark after the end of the page name, like this:

http://myURL/myDirectory/somePage.htm?MyData

In this example *MyData* is the value of the data being passed. We could pass more information, like first name, second name and age like this:

http://myURL/myDirectory/somePage.htm?Paul&Wilton&33

Sending multiple pieces of data is easy – we simply use an ampersand, *&*, between each item of data to delimit it. When we receive the data, we can split it and remove the ampersands.

We read the data using the `location.search` property:

```
var receivedString = location.search;
```

In this example, the variable `receivedString` will contain `?Paul&Wilton&33`.

One of the problems associated with using this method to send data is that only certain characters are allowed in URLs. For example, standard alphabetical characters and numbers are allowed, but characters such as punctuation characters are not allowed.

We can convert the characters that aren't allowed to their character code equivalents using JavaScript. This is called **escaping**. The easiest methods for escaping and its reverse, **unescaping**, are the JavaScript `escape()` and `unescape()` functions.

The later browsers, IE5.5+ and NN6+, also support the `encodeURI()` *and* `decodeURI()` *methods, which do essentially the same thing.*

For example, if our data string is `Bob Bobkins`, then we can escape it like this:

```
var sendString = escape("Bob Bobkins");
```

Then we could decode the data we receive like this:

```
var receivedString = unescape(location.search);
```

We don't have to escape the data if it is passed as part of a hyperlink's `href` attribute because the browser does that for us.

So that's the idea behind sending data in the URL. There are three ways to get data into the URL:

- Add it to the `href` attribute of an `<a>` hyperlink element
- Using JavaScript to navigate to a new page, specifying the data with the page name
- Using a `<form>` and set its `method` attribute to `get`

This next example, `SendInfo.htm`, demonstrates each of these ways of sending data:

```
<html>
<head>
</head>
<body>

<!-- Sending data using a hyperlink -->
<a href="ReceiveInfo.htm?Bob Bobkins&32">Send Data</a>

<!-- Sending data using JavaScript to create the URL -->
<form>
  <input type="button"
         value="Button"
         name=button1
         onclick="location.href = 'ReceiveInfo.htm?' + escape('Bob Bobkins&32')">
</form>

<!-- Sending data using a form that is submitted -->
<form action="ReceiveInfo.htm" method=get name=form1>
  <input type="text" name=name>
  <input type="text" name=age>
  <input type="submit" value="Submit" id=submit1 name=submit1>
</form>
</body>
</html>
```

When loaded, the page looks like this:

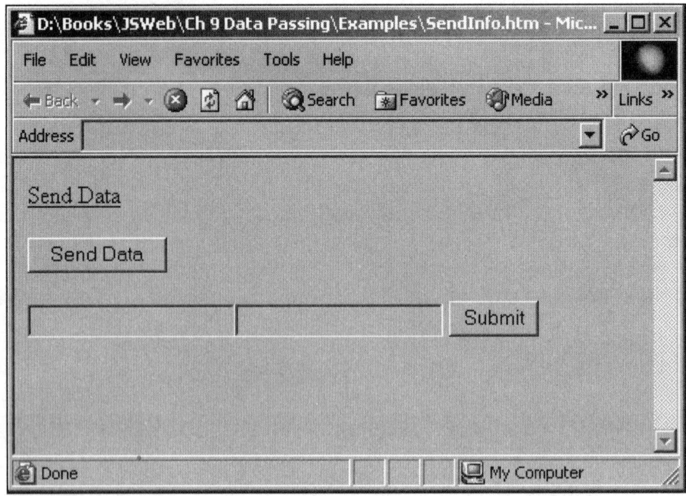

Then we just need the simple `ReceiveInfo.htm` page to receive the data:

```
<html>
<head>
</head>
<body>
  <script>
    var infoPassed = unescape(location.search);
    document.write("Info Sent is " + infoPassed);
  </script>
</body>
</html>
```

If you click the `SendInfo.htm` page's *Send Data* link or the button, then the following will be displayed by `ReceiveInfo.htm`:

Info Sent is ?Bob Bobkins&32

If, on the other hand, you write 'Bob Bobkins' into the first textboxand '32' into the second and click *Submit* then you'll get this output:

Info Sent is ?name=Bob+Bobkins&age=32&submit1=Submit

Note that when the form is sent, not only the data is sent but also *all* the controls and *all* their names – even buttons that have no real purpose in terms of providing information. The names of the controls (in this case, `name`, `age`, and `submit1`) are delimited from their values (respectively, `Bob+Bobkins`, `35`, and `Submit`) with equals signs. The form's `get` method also converts the spaces to plus signs.

So how does this work? The hyperlink is the easiest technique:

```
<a href="ReceiveInfo.htm?Bob Bobkins&32">Send Data</a>
```

Note that we don't need to escape the value of the `href` attribute in this case, because the browser does that for us.

Next we have the button and its `onclick` event handler:

```
<form>
  <input type="button"
         value="Send Data"
         name="button1"
         onclick="location.href = 'ReceiveInfo.htm?' + escape('Bob Bobkins&32')">
</form>
```

We set the `location.href` to the new page, `ReceiveInfo.htm`, add a question mark, and then the data, using `escape` so that it can be included in the URL.

The form method of sending data doesn't need any code at all:

```
<form action="ReceiveInfo.htm" method="get" name="form1">
  <input type="text" name="name">
  <input type="text" name="age">
  <input type="submit" value="Submit" id="submit1" name="submit1">
</form>
```

As long as the `method` attribute is set to `get`, then clicking the *Submit* button will send the form data in the URL. We could even use a hidden form and set the form controls using JavaScript. This method works well even with older version 3 browsers.

Finally, this code receives the data:

```
var infoPassed = unescape(location.search);
document.write("Info Sent is " + infoPassed);
```

The data is extracted from the URL and unescaped back to the original value before being stored in the `infoPassed` variable. Then the value is written into the page.

This method of receiving data is OK, but we still have the question mark and ampersands in it, so we need to extract the specific items of data. We'll create some more sophisticated code to handle data better in the `ReceiveInfo.htm` page next.

We'll use a function and an array to do this. We'll begin by creating a new function `obtainValuesPassed()`, and using `unescape()` on it as before, and then we'll remove the question mark that has been passed with the data:

```
<html>
<head>
</head>
```

```
<body>
<script>
  function obtainValuesPassed()
  {
    var infoPassed = location.search;
    infoPassed = infoPassed.replace(/\+/g," ");
    infoPassed = unescape(infoPassed);
    infoPassed = infoPassed.replace(/\?/,"");
```

We're using the `replace()` method of the `String` object to replace the addition sign with a space and to strip out the question mark.

Then we need to split the string into names and values. We'll use the `String` object's `split()` method to split the string at each point where characters matching the regular expression (passed as its only parameter) are found.

```
    var dataPairArray = infoPassed.split(/&|=/);
```

The regular expression matches either an ampersand or (the pipe symbol) an equals sign.

Then we need to use the return values of the `split()` method to populate an array with each of the matched values. So we'll create a new array and use a `for` loop to go through the `dataPairArray`, incrementing `arrayIndex` to get the value linked to each name. We'll use the data's name as the array's index at which to store the value. Then we can access the data passed using its name:

```
  var extractedData = new Array();

  for (var arrayIndex = 0; arrayIndex < dataPairArray.length; arrayIndex++)
  {
    extractedData[dataPairArray[arrayIndex]] = dataPairArray[++arrayIndex]
  }
```

The loop continues until all the data has been extracted and placed in the `extractedData` array. On the last line of the function we return this array to the calling code.

```
  var valuesPassed = obtainValuesPassed();

  document.write("Name is " + valuesPassed["name"] + "<BR>");
  document.write("Age is " + valuesPassed["age"]);
```

We set variable `valuesPassed` to the `Array` object returned by the `obtainValuesPassed()` function we just looked at.

Then all we need to do is access the values in the array using `name` and `age` as the array index. Here's the amended script:

```
<html>
<head>
</head>
<body>
```

```
<script>
  function obtainValuesPassed()
  {
    var infoPassed = location.search;
    infoPassed = infoPassed.replace(/\+/g," ");
    infoPassed = unescape(infoPassed);
    infoPassed = infoPassed.replace(/\?/,"");

    var dataPairArray = infoPassed.split(/&|=/);
    var extractedData = new Array();

    for (var arrayIndex = 0; arrayIndex < dataPairArray.length; arrayIndex++)
    {
      extractedData[dataPairArray[arrayIndex]] = dataPairArray[++arrayIndex]
    }

    return extractedData;
  }

  var valuesPassed = obtainValuesPassed();

  document.write("Name is " + valuesPassed["name"] + "<BR>");
  document.write("Age is " + valuesPassed["age"]);
</script>
</body>
</html>
```

The `obtainValuesPassed()` function only works if each data value is given a name in the sending page. If we send information using a form then this is done automatically, but it isn't if we're using the hyperlink and JavaScript methods, so we need to update the `SendInfo.htm` page. We simply add `name=` and `age=` in front of the data for the `<a>` element's `href` attribute and in the button's `onclick` attribute. This just mimics the automatic behavior of a form using the `get` method.

```
<html>
<head>
</head>
<body>
<!-- Sending data using a hyperlink -->
<a href="ReceiveInfo.htm?name=Bob Bobkins&age=32">Send Data</a>

<!-- Sending data using JavaScript to create the URL -->
<form>
  <input type="button" value="Send Data" name="button1"
         onclick="location.href = 'ReceiveInfo.htm?' +
                  escape('name=Bob Bobkins&age=32')">
</form>

<!-- Sending data using a form that is submitted -->
<form action="ReceiveInfo.htm" method="get" name="form1">
  <input type="text" name="name">
  <input type="text" name="age">
  <input type="submit" value="Submit" id="submit1" name="submit1">
</form>
</body>
</html>
```

Now, whether you click the *Send Data* hyperlink, or the button, or the form *Submit* button, you should get this written to the screen:

Name is Bob Bobkins
Age is 32

Maintaining State with Session Variables

Session variables are usually associated with server-side programming. In server-side terms a session starts when the user first visits the web site and ends once it is clear they are not going to visit more of our web pages. There aren't any automatic session variables built into browsers, but there is a simple trick that we can use to allow us to keep values in variables alive, even while the user browses to different pages on our web site.

The values of variables are usually lost when the user browses to another web page, so the simplest way to keep those values is to not change the page. No, I don't mean that you have to start building single page web sites; but instead you can use a top frame to hold the variable, and then make sure only pages inside that frame change. The frames don't have to be visible, so the user doesn't even have to know about them. As we saw in Chapter 5, it's easy to access code in other frames: all you need to do is navigate the frameset hierarchy.

Let's look at a simple example consisting of three pages – first a frameset-defining page, and then two pages that will be loaded inside the frame:

First the frameset-defining page, `SessionVariablePage.htm`, containing the session variable:

```
<html>
<head>
  <title>Welcome to my web site</title>
  <script language="JavaScript">
    var mySessionVariable = "ABC";
  </script>
</head>
<frameset cols="100%" border="0">
  <frame name="MainFrame" src="Page1.htm">
</frameset>
</html>
```

Then `page1.htm`, which is initially loaded into the frame:

```
<html>
<body>
<form name=form1>
  Session Variable
  <input type="text" name="txtSessionVar">
  <br>
  <input type="button"
         value="Write Session Var Value"
         name="cmdWriteVar"
         onclick="parent.mySessionVariable = document.form1.txtSessionVar.value">
  <input type="button"
```

```
            value="Read Session Var Value"
            name="cmdReadVar"
            onclick="document.form1.txtSessionVar.value = parent.mySessionVariable">
    </form>
    <h4><a href="page2.htm">Go to page 2</a></h4>
    </body>
    </html>
```

And then `page2.htm`, which is identical to `page1.htm` except for the following line:

```
    </form>
    <h4><a href="page1.htm">Go to page 1</a></h4>
    </body>
```

If you load up `SessionVariablePage.htm` you should see something like this:

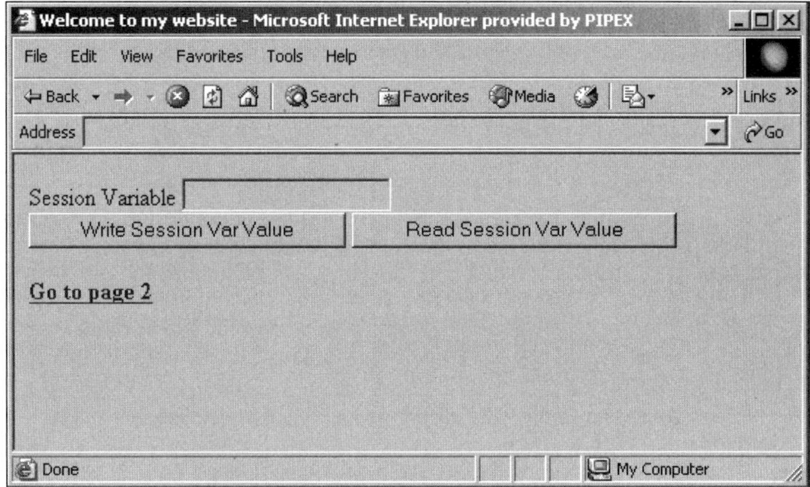

If you click the *Read Session Var Value* button, it accesses the variable stored in the top frame and writes its value (*ABC*) to the textbox. Clicking the *Write Session Var Value* button writes the current value in the textbox to the session variable in the top frame. If you set the variable to a new value in this way, click the link *Go to page 2*, and then click the *Read Session Var Value* button, you'll see that the session variable has retained its new value.

The technique and code are quite simple. We declare the variable in the frameset page:

```
    <script language='JavaScript'>
      var mySessionVariable = "ABC";
    </script>
```

Then we can access it from the page inside the frame, by using the `parent` property. For example, look at the `onclick` event handler of the *Write Session Var Value* button in both `page1.htm` and `page2.htm`:

```
onclick="parent.mySessionVariable = document.form1.txtSessionVar.value">
```

This uses the `parent` property to get a reference to the window of the frameset page and then accesses the `mySessionVariable` property inside it.

Permanently Storing Information: Cookies

We've looked at two techniques for storing data for the duration of the user's visit to our web site. There will be times, though, when you want to make a more permanent record of the data, and this is where cookies come in.

Cookies can be used for all sorts of things. We'll be using them in our e-commerce example to store the details of the customer's shopping basket even if they close the browser and return later. Cookies can also be used for storing user preferences. If we had a web site in a number of international languages, for example, then we'd want the user to select their preferred language on their first visit, and then store that preference for every subsequent visit. If their preferred language is English then we could store `Eng` in a cookie for the English language version, if it's French, `Frn`, and so on. Then, when the user returns, we simply check the value and then direct them to the correct pages.

Cookies are simply text files that store data in strings on the user's computer. Although they only hold strings, we can still use numeric or Boolean values by converting them to strings.

> Some browsers don't support cookies, and some users are uncomfortable with the idea of them and switch off cookie support entirely. We should avoid using cookies for essential functionality, and restrict their use to additional functionality for users who have them enabled. And, of course, if we absolutely can't do without them, then we need to check whether cookies will work with the user's browser, either by using code that works with or without cookies, or by notifying the user that the web site needs cookies to function correctly.

There are some default restrictions on who can read a cookie. Cookies can only be read by the page that set the cookie, or by pages in the same directory or subdirectories. You can write a cookie that specifies which pages can read it by using the `path` attribute. For example, if `path` was set to `/MyPages`, then all the pages in the directory `MyPages` and its subdirectories could read and write to the cookie.

Further, pages from a server other than the server that set the cookie can't read it, so a page on the domain *someOtherDomain.com* can't read cookie on *myDomain.com*. Again this default behavior can be changed using the `domain` attribute. We'll see how in the next section.

Cookies have a lifespan, just like variables. By default they expire as soon as the web browser is closed, so cookies used this way are called **transient cookies**. While this is fine for storing session information, if we want a more permanent record of our data we need to set the cookie's `expires` attribute.

We can have more than one cookie per web server; in fact we can have anywhere up to twenty, identifying each one using its `name` attribute. The maximum size of a single cookie is 4000 characters, including the cookie's name and value. So if we needed to store more than twenty pieces of information then we can set a single cookie to store multiple values so long as it doesn't take a cookie over its maximum size.

The fifth cookie attribute is the `secure` attribute. If it is set to true, the cookie will only be sent to the web server if it's over a secure connection, such as HTTPS. By default `secure` is false and cookies will be sent insecurely over any connection.

Now we've discussed cookies and their main attributes, we'll create some simple cookies. After we've done that we'll create a `.js` file that contains a number of useful functions that make cookie handling very easy.

Reading and Writing Cookies

Reading and writing cookies centers round the `document` object's `cookie` property. At it's most basic, a cookie has a `name` and `value`:

```
document.cookie = "MyCookieName=MyCookiesValue";
```

Reading the cookie is unfortunately not quite as simple, because `document.cookie` will return all the cookies saved on the client machine associated with the web server, so we need to extract the cookie holding the information we're looking for. If we read back the above cookie like this:

```
document.write(document.cookie);
```

then this is what would be written to the page:

MyCookieName=MyCookiesValue

If we write two cookies and read them back, as in the short example `CookieDisplay.htm` below:

```
<html>
<head>
</head>
<body>
  <script language="JavaScript">
    document.cookie = "FirstName=Cathleen";
    document.cookie = "LastName=Newman";
    document.write(document.cookie)
</script>
</body>
</html>
```

then this will be displayed:

FirstName=Cathleen; LastName=Newman

Cookies are separated using a semicolon and a space. We can use this syntax to extract the cookies using the `String` object like this (`SimpleCookieRead.htm`):

```
<html>
<head>
</head>
<body>
<script language="JavaScript">
```

```
    document.cookie = "FirstName=Cathleen";
    document.cookie = "LastName=Newman";

    function readCookie(cookieName)
    {
      cookieName += "=";
      var cookieString = document.cookie;
      var cookieStartIndex = cookieString.indexOf(cookieName) + cookieName.length;
      var cookieEndIndex = cookieString.indexOf("; ",cookieStartIndex);

      if (cookieEndIndex == -1)
      {
        var cookieValue = cookieString.substring(cookieStartIndex);
      }
      else
      {
        var cookieValue = cookieString.substring(cookieStartIndex,cookieEndIndex);
      }

      return cookieValue;
    }

    var firstName = readCookie("FirstName");
    var lastName = readCookie("LastName");
    document.write("First name is " + firstName + "<BR>");
    document.write("Last name is " + lastName)
  </script>
  </body>
  </html>
```

This displays the following in the browser:

First name is Cathleen
Last name is Newman

Look at the `readCookie()` function that does most of the work. First it takes the name of the cookie we want as a parameter. Then we add an equals sign to the end of the cookie name, because our search of the string returned by `document.cookie` will be for "cookieName=", since what follows that is the value of the cookie.

We obtain all the cookies available using `document.cookie` and store in variable `cookieString`. Our next task is to find out where the start of the cookie value we want is:

```
  var cookieStartIndex = cookieString.indexOf(cookieName) + cookieName.length;
```

We know that the value of the cookie starts right after the cookie name and an equals sign. The `indexOf()` method allows us to find the character index of the start of the cookie name. Then we add the length of the variable `cookieName` (which includes the equals sign) to that to find the character index of the start of the cookie value.

Now we need to find where the cookie's value ends and the next cookie starts, but looking for the semicolon and space that separates cookies.

```
var cookieEndIndex = cookieString.indexOf("; ",cookieStartIndex);
```

Now we know where our cookie's value starts and ends, all we need do is extract the value itself from the string using the String object's `substring()` method. We do this using an `if` loop, that looks for a `cookieEndIndex` value of `-1`. This is because we know that if the cookie being examined is the last cookie in the cookie string, or is an only cookie, then there won't be a space and a semicolon won't to be found. In that case, the end index is simply the end of the string. We therefore have an `if` statement and two ways of extracting the value depending on whether the "; " had been found:

```
if (cookieEndIndex == -1)
{
  var cookieValue = cookieString.substring(cookieStartIndex);
}
else
{
  var cookieValue = cookieString.substring(cookieStartIndex,cookieEndIndex);
}
```

On the function's final line, we return the cookie's value:

```
return cookieValue;
```

Then we use the function, extracting the `FirstName` and `LastName` values and writing them to the page.

```
var firstName = readCookie("FirstName");
var lastName = readCookie("LastName");
document.write("First name is " + firstName + "<BR>");
document.write("Last name is " + lastName)
```

Our `readCookie()` function has the benefit of being simple, and it works on early browsers like IE3 and NN3. However, as a general routine it has failings – if no cookie with the given name is found, for example, then the routine will fail. To combat these problems, in the next section we'll be creating a number of much more sophisticated and robust cookie routines.

Before we do that, though, let's see how we can set the other cookie attributes like `expires`, `path`, `domain` and `secure`. Note that we need to set the name and value of a cookie, but all the other attributes are optional – we can include as many or as few as we wish. The additional attributes are added after the `name/value` attributes of the cookie, and are separated by a semicolon and a space, like this:

```
document.cookie = "Name=Value; expires=01 Jan 2007 00:00:00 GTM; " +
                  "path=/; domain=www.mydomain.com; secure";
```

We have set the expiry date (using the `expires` attribute) to 1 Jan 2007 at midnight GMT. In order to delete an existing cookie altogether we just set its expiry date to a date in the past.

The `path` attribute in the example has been set to `/` which is the top level directory, so any page on the server can read our cookie, even if the page that sets the cookie is in a subdirectory.

The `domain` attribute has been set to `www.mydomain.com`, so the server at *mydomain.com* can view the cookie as well as the server on the domain that set the cookie.

Note that all the attributes except `secure` are set to a value. This is because `secure` is a flag. If it's present then the cookie data will only be sent over a secure connection, and if it's not then the cookie data is sent over any connection. In this case, because of the `secure` attribute flag the cookie information will only be passed if server communications are over a secure connection, for example the page has been loaded from *https://www.mydomain.com/mypage.htm.*

In the next section, amongst other things we'll create a function that makes setting the various cookie attributes easy.

Making Cookies Easy: Cookie Functions

In this section we'll create a number of functions that make working with cookies quick and easy. We'll create functions that:

- Read and write cookies
- Read and write multi-value cookies
- Delete a cookie
- Detect if cookies have been enabled

We'll finish off with an example demonstrating the functions.

Writing a Cookie

Here's the code. To make it easy to reuse the functions, simply create a file, `CookieFunctions.js` and place all the function code in it.

```
function writeCookie(cookieName,
                     cookieValue,
                     expires,
                     domain,
                     path,
                     secureFlag)
{
  if (cookieName)
  {
    var cookieDetails = cookieName + "=" + escape(cookieValue);
    cookieDetails += (expires ? "; expires=" + expires.toGMTString(): '');
    cookieDetails += (domain ? "; domain=" + domain: '');
    cookieDetails += (path ? "; path=" + path: '');
    cookieDetails += (secureFlag ? "; secure": '');
    document.cookie = cookieDetails;
  }
}
```

The function takes 6 parameters that match the attributes of a cookie (all of which are optional except the first two). The `expires` parameter must contain a `Date` object with a valid date and the `secureFlag` parameter a Boolean value, true or false. The remaining parameters are strings.

The `if` statement checks to see whether we have at least passed the cookie name – if we haven't then there's no point trying to create the cookie.

Inside the `if` statement we build up a string containing the cookie and its attributes. We start by adding the name and the cookie's value:

```
var cookieDetails = cookieName + "=" + escape(cookieValue);
```

Note that we escape the value, that is convert everything that's not letters or numbers to the character code equivalent. This is to enable us to store things like the semicolon (;) that we can't normally store in a cookie since it indicates the start of a new cookie.

All the remaining parameters are optional and we use the ternary operator (`?:`) to add them. For example:

```
cookieDetails += (expires ? "; expires=" + expires.toGMTString(): '');
```

If `expires` is undefined, that is the parameter hasn't been passed to the function, then it will be false and the code after the colon (`:`) will execute. In this case, it's an empty string so nothing will be added to our `cookieDetails` string. If `expires` does have a value, then JavaScript will evaluate it as true and the code after the question mark but before the colon will execute. In this case, the code that is added to `cookieDetails` is `"; expires=" + expires.toGMTString()`.

Using this technique allows us to make parameters optional, enabling the function to cope when one isn't passed. The principle is the same for the remaining parameters:

```
cookieDetails += (domain ? "; domain=" + domain: '');
cookieDetails += (path ? "; path=" + path: '');
cookieDetails += (secureFlag ? "; secure": '');
```

Finally, we set the `document.cookie` property to our cookie string:

```
document.cookie = cookieDetails;
```

We can call this function in a number of ways:

```
writeCookie("MyCookiesName","CookiesValue");

var expiryDate = new Date();
expiryDate.setMonth(expiryDate.getMonth() + 3);
writeCookie("MyCookiesName","CookiesValue", expiryDate);

writeCookie("MyCookiesName","CookiesValue", expiryDate,"www.mydomain.com");

writeCookie("MyCookiesName","CookiesValue", expiryDate,
            "www.mydomain.com", "/myPath");

writeCookie("MyCookiesName","CookiesValue", expiryDate,
            "www.mydomain.com", "/myPath", true);
```

Recall that the expiry date parameter needs to be a `Date` object, so we've created a new `Date` object and set its month property to the current month + 3. Then the cookie will expire in 3 months time. Or we could pass the `path` argument instead of the `domain` argument by passing `null` as the value for the `domain` argument:

```
writeCookie("MyCookiesName","CookiesValue", expiryDate,
            null, "/myPath");
```

Reading a Cookie

We're going to create two functions to read cookies. This is because the `readMultiValueCookie()` function we'll create later needs to read a cookie's escaped value. It makes sense to create a generic function here that reads a cookie to its escaped form, together with another function that unescapes this value.

```
function readUnescapedCookie(cookieName)
{
  var cookieValue = document.cookie;
  var cookieRegExp = new RegExp("\\b" + cookieName + "=([^;]*)");
  cookieValue = cookieRegExp.exec(cookieValue);

  if (cookieValue != null)
  {
    cookieValue = cookieValue[1];
  }

  return cookieValue;
}

function readCookie(cookieName)
{
  cookieValue = readUnescapedCookie(cookieName)

  if (cookieValue != null)
  {
    cookieValue = unescape(cookieValue);
  }

  return cookieValue;
}
```

Look at `readUnescapedCookie()` first. Its single parameter is a string containing the cookie's name. The next three lines deal with obtaining all the cookies, creating a regular expression to extract the cookie we want, then extracting it:

```
var cookieValue = document.cookie;
var cookieRegExp = new RegExp("\\b" + cookieName + "=([^;]*)");
cookieValue = cookieRegExp.exec(cookieValue);
```

If you remember the discussion of regular expressions at the end of Chapter 8, then you can probably translate this regular expression already. It's looking for a word boundary, followed by the cookie name, followed by an equals sign, followed by a group of zero or more characters that are not a semicolon (indicating the end of a cookie). This group of characters is the interesting part, because it is the cookie's value.

The `exec()` method of the `RegExp` object will try and match our pattern. If successful, it returns a array containing details of the match, but if it's not then it returns `null`. So the `if` statement checks that null wasn't returned, that is, it checks that the cookie and its value were found:

```
if (cookieValue != null)
{
  cookieValue = cookieValue[1];
}
```

The cookie's value is in the first regular expression group, which we access in array element 1 of `cookieValue`.

On the final line we return the cookie's value. This is the unescaped value, so we'll need to decode it before we can do anything with it.

The second function, `readCookie()`, uses the `readUnescapedCookie()` to do most of the work. The main difference is that `readCookie()` unescapes the value returned. As we can't be sure the cookie will exist, the function's `if` statement checks for a null value returned, only attempting to unescape the value if it's a valid one:

```
cookieValue = readUnescapedCookie(cookieName)

if (cookieValue != null)
{
  cookieValue = unescape(cookieValue);
}
```

Using either of the functions is very simple as show below. We simply pass the name of our cookie and store the returned value:

```
var cookieValue = readCookie("MyCookiesName");
var unescapedCookieValue = readUnescapedCookie("MyCookiesName");
```

Deleting a Cookie

You simply delete a cookie by giving it an expiry date that has already expired.

```
function deleteCookie(cookieName)
{
  var expiredDate = new Date();
  expiredDate.setMonth(-1);
  writeCookie(cookieName,"",expiredDate);
}
```

The function creates a new `Date` object, initializes it to the current date and time, and then sets the month of the date to `-1`. This sets the date to the last month of the previous year, so the previous December. Then we write the cookie using the `writeCookie()` function we already created, passing the `Date` object with the expired date to ensure that the cookie is removed.

We can call the function by passing the name of the cookie we want deleted:

```
deleteCookie("MyCookieName");
```

Writing a Multi-Value Cookie

A multi-value cookie is simply a cookie that takes more than one value. It's useful when the 20 cookie per server limit is just too restrictive for our needs. We store multiple values within the value part of the cookie, using an equals sign to associate their names and values, and delimiting them from each other using ampersands:

```
FirstMultiValue=Value1&SecondMultiValue=Value2&FinalMultiValue=FinalValue
```

The only limit on the number of multi-values we can have in a cookie is the size of data a cookie can store.

Writing a multi-value cookie is a little more complex than writing a normal cookie, because we need to take into account situations where there are already multi-values inside the cookie we're adding to, when we need to be careful not to remove the existing values. Here's the code:

```
function writeMultiValueCookie(cookieName,
                               multiValueName,
                               value,
                               expires,
                               domain,
                               path,
                               secureFlag)
{
  var cookieValue = readUnescapedCookie(cookieName);

  if (cookieValue)
  {
    var stripAttributeRegExp = new RegExp("(^|&)" + multiValueName + "=[^&]*&?");
    cookieValue = cookieValue.replace(stripAttributeRegExp,"$1");
    if (cookieValue.length != 0)
    {
      cookieValue += "&";
    }
  }
  else
  {
    cookieValue = "";
  }

  cookieValue += multiValueName + "=" + escape(value);
  var cookieDetails = cookieName + "=" + cookieValue;
  cookieDetails += (expires ? "; expires=" + expires.toGMTString(): '');
  cookieDetails += (domain ? "; domain=" + domain: '');
  cookieDetails += (path ? "; path=" + path: '');
  cookieDetails += (secureFlag ? "; secure": '');
  document.cookie = cookieDetails;
}
```

The function's parameters are identical to those of `writeCookie()` except that we need to also pass the name of the multi-value as well as the name of the cookie to write it to. The first task is to obtain the cookie with that cookie name:

```
var cookieValue = readUnescapedCookie(cookieName);
```

We then check that a matching cookie was found. If it was, then we need to ensure any multi-values within that cookie are not overwritten. If no cookie was found, then we can simply create the new cookie, and in that case we can set the cookie string to an empty string. Let's look at the code that deals with the situation where the cookie exists:

```
var stripAttributeRegExp = new RegExp("(^|&)" + multiValueName + "=[^&]*&?");
cookieValue = cookieValue.replace(stripAttributeRegExp,"$1");
if (cookieValue.length != 0)
{
cookieValue += "&";
}
```

The first line defines a regular expression that will match the multi-value name and value. It specifies that we need to match characters at the beginning of the string, or an ampersand, followed by the name of our multi-value, followed by an equals sign and a series of one or more characters that are not an ampersand. At the end we are looking for zero or one ampersands. Let's look at our example string:

```
FirstMultiValue=Value1&SecondMultiValue=Value2&FinalMultiValue=FinalValue
```

To strip out the second multi-value, the regular expression would match:

```
&SecondMultiValue=Value2&
```

On the second line we then replace the matched characters with the characters matched in the first group in the regular expression, which is either an `&` or the beginning of the string. In our example our string would become:

```
FirstMultiValue=Value1&FinalMultiValue=FinalValue
```

The second multi-value has been completely stripped out, but the ampersand between the remaining two multi-values is preserved.

We'll be adding the new multi-value onto the end of the string, so if there are existing multi-values left we need to add an ampersand to the end of the string to mark the end of the last multi-value, and this is what the `if` statement does on the final lines.

So, now we have the cookie string, which is either an empty string (if no previous cookie existed) or a string containing the multi-values other than the one we are writing to (if the cookie existed). We now need to add our new multi-value on to the end of this string:

```
cookieValue += multiValueName + "=" + escape(value);
var cookieDetails = cookieName + "=" + cookieValue;
```

This will form the name and value part of the cookie to be written. Then, as with the `writeCookie()` function, we need to add on any of the other cookie attributes that have been passed as arguments to the function:

```
cookieDetails += (expires ? "; expires=" + expires.toGMTString(): '');
cookieDetails += (domain ? "; domain=" + domain: '');
cookieDetails += (path ? "; path=" + path: '');
cookieDetails += (secureFlag ? "; secure": '');
```

On the final line the cookie is set with the contents of the multi values:

```
document.cookie = cookieDetails;
```

You can use this function the same way that you use the `writeCookie()` function with the exception that we have to specify the multi-value name:

```
writeCookie("MyCookiesName","MultiValueName", "CookiesValue");

var expiryDate = new Date();
expiryDate.setMonth(expiryDate.getMonth() + 3);
writeCookie("MyCookiesName","MultiValueName", "CookiesValue", expiryDate);

writeCookie("MyCookiesName","MultiValueName", "CookiesValue",
            expiryDate,"www.mydomain.com");

writeCookie("MyCookiesName", "MultiValueName", "CookiesValue", expiryDate,
            "www.mydomain.com", "/myPath");

writeCookie("MyCookiesName", "MultiValueName", "CookiesValue", expiryDate,
            "www.mydomain.com", "/myPath", true);
```

Reading a Multi-Value Cookie

To read a multi-value cookie, we need to first read the cookie containing the multi-values, and then extract the multi-value required.

```
function readMultiValueCookie(cookieName, multiValueName)
{
  var cookieValue = readUnescapedCookie(cookieName)

  var extractMultiValueCookieRegExp =
         new RegExp("\\b" + multiValueName + "=([^;&]*)");
  cookieValue = extractMultiValueCookieRegExp.exec(cookieValue);

  if (cookieValue != null)
  {
    cookieValue = unescape(cookieValue[1]);
  }

  return cookieValue;
}
```

The first line of the function reads the multi-value cookie using the function we created earlier. Then we create a regular expression that will match the multi-value name and value:

```
var extractMultiValueCookieRegExp = new RegExp("\\b" + multiValueName +
"=([^;&]*)");
```

The regular expression can be used to extract the cookie:

```
cookieValue = extractMultiValueCookieRegExp.exec(cookieValue);
```

The technique is nearly identical to that used to extract a cookie in the `readUnescapedCookie()` function, the only difference being that cookies are delimited by a semi-colon and our multi-values are delimited by an ampersand.

If a multi-value wasn't found then `null` will be returned. If it was found, then a special array is returned and the value of the multi-value will be in the regular expression group defined and accessible in array element 1:

```
if (cookieValue != null)
{
  cookieValue = unescape(cookieValue[1]);
}
```

Finally we return the multi-value, or `null` if none found:

```
return cookieValue;
```

Using the function is identical to `readCookie()` except that we need to pass both the cookie name and the multi-value name:

```
var multiValue = readMultiValueCookie("CookieName","MultiValueName");
```

Deleting a Multi-Value from a Cookie

If we simply want to delete all the multi-values inside a cookie then we'd use the `deleteCookie()` function and delete the whole cookie. If, on the other hand, we want to delete a specific multi-value from a cookie without deleting any other multi-values then things are a little more complicated. Here's a function that will delete specific values:

```
function deleteMultiValueCookie(cookieName,
                                multiValueName,
                                expires,
                                domain,
                                path,
                                secureFlag)
{
  var cookieValue = readUnescapedCookie(cookieName);

  if (cookieValue)
  {
    var stripAttributeRegExp = new RegExp("(^|&)" + multiValueName + "=[^&]*&?");
    cookieValue = cookieValue.replace(stripAttributeRegExp,"$1");

    if (cookieValue.length != 0)
    {
      var cookieDetails = cookieName + "=" + cookieValue;
      cookieDetails += (expires ? "; expires=" + expires.toGMTString(): '');
      cookieDetails += (domain ? "; domain=" + domain: '');
      cookieDetails += (path ? "; path=" + path: '');
      cookieDetails += (secureFlag ? "; secure": '');
      document.cookie = cookieDetails;
    }
```

```
      else
      {
        deleteCookie(cookieName);
      }
    }
  }
```

First we obtain the cookie holding the multi-value:

```
var cookieValue = readUnescapedCookie(cookieName);
```

If a value is found, then the code is similar code to that in the `writeMultiValueCookie()` function. We need to strip out the multi-value part of the cookie to be deleted without deleting the other multi-values, if any:

```
var stripAttributeRegExp = new RegExp("(^|&)" + multiValueName + "=[^&]*&?");
cookieValue = cookieValue.replace(stripAttributeRegExp,"$1");
```

If there are multi-values left when we have stripped out the ones we wanted to remove then the length of `cookieValue` will be greater than 0. In this case we need to write the remaining multi-values back into the cookie:

```
if (cookieValue.length != 0)
{
  var cookieDetails = cookieName + "=" + cookieValue;
  cookieDetails += (expires ? "; expires=" + expires.toGMTString(): '');
  cookieDetails += (domain ? "; domain=" + domain: '');
  cookieDetails += (path ? "; path=" + path: '');
  cookieDetails += (secureFlag ? "; secure": '');
  document.cookie = cookieDetails;
}
```

However, if after stripping out our multi-value the string is empty, then we may as well delete the whole cookie:

```
else
{
  deleteCookie(cookieName);
}
```

Using the function is different to the `deleteCookie()` function as we also need to supply the cookie attributes like `expires`, `domain`, `path` and so on as we do with `writeMultiValueCookie()`. We are not deleting the whole cookie, just part of it, and there is no easy way of finding out what the previously set cookie attributes were, so we have to supply them again:

```
var expiryDate = new Date();
expiryDate.setMonth(expiryDate.getMonth() + 6);
deleteMultiValueCookie("CookieName","MultiValueName",expiryDate);
```

Of course, in order to work with cookies on a user's computer, we really need to check that cookies are enabled.

Checking that Cookies are Enabled

The newer browsers, IE4+ and NN6+, support the `cookieEnabled` property of the `navigator` object, which returns `true` if cookies are enabled. The only sure way to find out if cookies are enabled on the older browsers, though, is to write a cookie and read it back. If what's read back is empty, then we know cookies don't work on this user's browser. Here's the `cookiesEnabled()` function:

```
function cookiesEnabled()
{
  var cookiesEnabled = window.navigator.cookieEnabled;

  if (!cookiesEnabled)
  {
    document.cookie = "cookiesEnabled=True";
    cookiesEnabled = new Boolean(document.cookie).valueOf();
  }

  return cookiesEnabled;
}
```

First we obtain the value of `window.navigator.cookieEnabled`, which will tell us whether cookies are enabled in IE4+ and NN6+ browsers:

```
var cookiesEnabled = window.navigator.cookieEnabled;
```

If it's false then we're either dealing with an older browser like NN4, or a newer browser that has cookies disabled. We write a simple cookie called `cookiesEnabled` and set it to the value `true`. We then read it back and convert the result to a Boolean:

```
if (!cookiesEnabled)
{
  document.cookie = "cookiesEnabled=True";
  cookiesEnabled = new Boolean(document.cookie).valueOf();
}
```

On the final line we return whether cookies were enabled:

```
return cookiesEnabled;
```

That's the last of the cookie functions that we're going to be building here. Next we'll put them to use.

Working with the Cookie Functions

In this section, we'll create a simple example to demonstrate using the `CookieFunction.js` file and the functions we've stored in it.

The script tackles one of the most irritating factors of many online forms: not saving the values that you've entered. Suppose you're running a search for a book. You enter the author's last name, the year of publication, and the publishing house, and hit the *search* button. Your initial search returns more results than you really want, so you hit the back button in order to refine it, and find that the form is completely empty. Even though you just want to add extra information, you have to fill out all the other information again too, which is a waste of time, and definitely not user-friendly.

> Although this is a great solution to the problem, you need to be careful about storing user information. Information like credit card numbers and names and addresses, for example, particularly if the user is on a public access computer rather than their home PC, really shouldn't be stored unless the user specifies that they are happy for you to do so.

In this example, we're saving the values in the form using a multi-value cookie when the page is unloaded – whether the user is browsing to another page, or web site, or just closes the browser. When the user reloads the page we simply repopulate the textboxes.

We're only saving the cookie for the duration of the session rather than long term – if the user has gone away and come back a week later, they probably don't plan to enter the same information again. This functionality would need to be changed according to the information being collected. We'd also want to incorporate a reset or clear button so that the user can wipe the details completely and start again if we were using this in an application.

Here's the code, `CookieExample.htm`:

```
<html>
<head>
<script src="CookieFunctions.js"></script>
<script>
  function window_onload()
  {
    var customerName = readMultiValueCookie("Customer", "Name")
    document.frmCookie.txtName.value = (customerName ? customerName : "");

    var customerAge = readMultiValueCookie("Customer","Age")
    document.frmCookie.txtAge.value =  (customerAge ? customerAge : "");

    var customerAddress = readMultiValueCookie("Customer", "Address")
    document.frmCookie.txtAddress.value = (customerAddress ? customerAddress :
"");
  }

  function window_onunload()
  {
    writeMultiValueCookie("Customer","Name", document.frmCookie.txtName.value)
    writeMultiValueCookie("Customer","Age", document.frmCookie.txtAge.value)

writeMultiValueCookie("Customer","Address",document.frmCookie.txtAddress.value)
  }
</script>
<title>Cookie Tester</title>
</head>
<body onload="window_onload()" onunload="window_onunload()">
  <form name="frmCookie">
    Please enter your details:
    <p>
    Name: <input type="text" name="txtName">
    <br>
```

```
      Age: <input type="text" name="txtAge">
      <br>
      Address: <input type="text" name=txtAddress>
      </p>
    </form>
  </body>
  </html>
```

Let's start by looking at the <body> element of the page:

```
<body onload="window_onload()" onunload="window_onunload()">
```

The onload event handler is set to call the window_onload() function and the onunload event handler is set to call the window_onunload() function.

In window_onload() we read back any cookie values previously saved. First, we read the Name multi-value from the Customer cookie:

```
var customerName = readMultiValueCookie("Customer", "Name")
```

This may be the first visit to the page and so the value returned may be null, something we cope with in the next line where we set the textbox's value:

```
document.frmCookie.txtName.value = (customerName ? customerName : "");
```

We're using the ternary operator. If customerName contains any value, then it will test as true and the code after the question mark will execute, simply returning customerName. If customerName is null, it will evaluate to false and the code after the colon will execute, returning an empty string.

The remaining code in the function reads in the customerAge and customerAddress multi-values and completes the age and address textboxes.

Finally, we're using the window_onunload() function to store any values entered into the textboxes as multi-values in the Customer cookie using the writeMultiValueCookie() function. We haven't passed an expiry date parameter since in this case we want the cookie to expire when the user closes their browser.

It's a simple enough script, but it improves the user experience a lot. We'll need to use a cookie in the e-commerce example, so let's start doing some more work on that next.

The E-commerce Image Viewer Application – Part 2

We'll continue the modification of the image viewer into an e-commerce application. By the end of this section we will have added the following functionality:

- Add items to the basket
- View the basket

- Save the basket if the customer leaves the web site
- Reload the basket if the customer returns to the web site from the same PC
- Create checkout pages and obtain the customer's details
- Display a final summary of the customer's details and their order

We'll be creating classes in three of the empty `.js` files we created in the last chapter. These `.js` files are included into the top frameset page `ImageViewerEcom.htm`, so that their functionality is available throughout the site.

Once we've created these classes we'll work on the `viewbasket.htm` page that shows the shopping basket's contents and is loaded into the `mainImageFrame iframe` of the `ImageViewer.htm` page. We'll also be creating new HTML pages for the checkout functionality of the site, which is used after the customer has filled their basket and is ready to buy.

Creating the Shopping Cart Classes

We'll be creating a number of classes to help us provide the functionality described above:

- `ShoppingBasket` class
- `ShoppingItem` class
- `CreditCard` class
- `Customer` class

The `ShoppingBasket` class provides all the shopping basket functionality. The `ShoppingItem` class stores information about a particular item in our basket. All the shopping items are stored as objects in the `ShoppingBasket` class. The `CreditCard` and `Customer` classes store the customer's credit card details and personal details respectively, and also provide functionality to create a summary.

The shopping basket as a whole is contained within the `ShoppingBasket` class. This class stores individual items of shopping, like a real-world shopping basket. The `ShoppingBasket` class also provides certain functionality such as allowing us to add new items of shopping to it, delete items of shopping, and so on, again just like a real-world shopping basket. We'll be storing our `ShoppingBasket` class code in the file `ShoppingBasket.js`.

Before we look further at the `ShoppingBasket` class, we need to have items to be able to store in it. This is where our `ShoppingItem` class comes in. This class's sole purpose is to store details of a particular shopping item, such as its cost, how many of that item we want, what the item is we are buying, and so on. Although a useful class, it's quite simple as we see in the next section when we create it.

The ShoppingItem Class

The class will need to store the following information about each item:

- Reference id

- Source file name and location for a thumbnail image
- Price
- Quantity required

The class is used exclusively by the `ShoppingBasket` class, so the code for the whole `ShoppingItem` class (given below) should be added to the top of the `ShoppingBasket.js` file, rather than in a file of its own.

```
function ShoppingItem(itemRefId, itemImgSrc, itemPrice, itemQty)
{
  this.itemRefId = itemRefId;
  this.itemImgSrc = itemImgSrc;
  this.itemPrice = itemPrice;
  this.itemQty = itemQty;
}

ShoppingItem.prototype.getItemRefId = function()
{
  return this.itemRefId;
}

ShoppingItem.prototype.setItemRefId = function(itemRefId)
{
  this.itemRefId = itemRefId;
}

ShoppingItem.prototype.getItemImgSrc = function()
{
  return this.itemImgSrc;
}

ShoppingItem.prototype.setItemImgSrc = function(itemImgSrc)
{
  this.itemImgSrc = itemImgSrc;
}

ShoppingItem.prototype.getItemPrice = function()
{
  return this.itemPrice;
}

ShoppingItem.prototype.setItemPrice = function(itemPrice)
{
  this.itemPrice = Number(itemPrice);
}

ShoppingItem.prototype.getItemQty = function()
{
  return this.itemQty;
}
```

```
ShoppingItem.prototype.setItemQty = function(itemQty)
{
  this.itemQty = Number(itemQty);
}
```

The class is essentially a class constructor and a series of methods that `get and set` properties. Let's start by looking at its constructor definition:

```
function ShoppingItem(itemRefId, itemImgSrc, itemPrice, itemQty)
{
  this.itemRefId = itemRefId;
  this.itemImgSrc = itemImgSrc;
  this.itemPrice = itemPrice;
  this.itemQty = itemQty;
}
```

The constructor takes four arguments, one for each of the properties of an item that we want to store. The class's properties are set using the information passed inside the method. We use the keyword `this` to specify that we mean "this" class – when an object is created based on this class, the keyword `this` refers to that object.

The remainder of the class consists of methods that allow us to get and set the four properties. We're using methods rather than the working with the variable names directly, because the technique is less prone to bugs. For example, look at the code below:

```
var myObject = new Object();
myObject.someProperty = "123";
alert(myObject.someProprty);
```

This code will fail, but without throwing any errors. This is because while I've tried to add a `someProperty` property to `"123"`, and then read the property back, I've got a typo in the property's name, which will result in an empty alert box appearing. JavaScript won't warn us of this bug – it's more than happy for us to create properties just by using them, and to read properties that have never been set. While this error isn't difficult to spot in three lines, it would be a lot harder to see if it was hidden away in the `ShoppingBasket.js` file which will contain over 350 lines.

While JavaScript lets us use non-existent properties, it won't let us use non-existent methods. This is a real bonus: it means that JavaScript's debugger will let us know if we misspell a method name, and where in the code the problem is. This is why we only access the properties of the objects based on our classes through methods, and not by using the property names directly.

Each of the properties has its own `get` and `set` method, created in the same way for each property. Since the differences between these pairs of methods are just the property and function names, we'll look at just the `itemRefId` methods:

```
ShoppingItem.prototype.getItemRefId = function()
{
  return this.itemRefId;
}

ShoppingItem.prototype.setItemRefId = function(itemRefId)
```

```
{
  this.itemRefId = itemRefId;
}
```

The first method returns the value of the `itemRefId` property, again using the keyword `this` to ensure it returns the value of the current object instance of the class.

The second method takes the new `itemRefId` as an argument and uses this to set the `itemRefId` property to a new value.

The ShoppingBasket Class

The `ShoppingBasket` class contains the following thirteen methods:

`addItem()`	Adds a new shopping item to the basket
`deleteItem()`	Deletes an existing shopping item
`fixDecimalPlaces()`	Fixes a number to a specific number of decimal places
`getBasketHTML()`	Gets the HTML required to display the shopping basket
`isEmpty()`	Checks if there are any items in the shopping basket
`setQty()`	Sets the quantity of a particular item in the basket
`updateBasketWithForm()`	Updates the quantities in a basket using information in a form
`saveBasket()`	Saves the basket if the user leaves the web site
`getCookieValue()`	Obtains the value of a specific cookie
`loadBasket()`	Loads the basket when the user returns to the web site
`getTotalIncDelivery()`	Obtains the total cost of the basket plus delivery costs
`getHiddenInputHTML()`	Gets the HTML required to create hidden form textboxes so that the basket contents can be posted in a form to the server
`clearBasket()`	Clears all the basket's contents

All the code for these methods needs to be added to the `ShoppingBasket.js` file, underneath the code for the `ShoppingItem` class that we just added to it. One essential method that we haven't listed is the class constructor – we'll start with that, before describing the others.

Constructor Method

This constructor is used to initialize the class object. It goes in the `ShoppingBasket.js` file:

```
function ShoppingBasket()
{
  this.items = new Object();
  this.numItems = 0;
  this.deliveryCost = "2.50";
}
```

First, we set the `items` property to a new `Object`. This is a plain object that we'll be using as an **associate array**, which is an array whose elements we can access using a string rather than an index number. We'll be storing the `ShoppingItem` class objects inside it, each object representing an item of shopping in our basket, and using the `itemRefId` property of the `ShoppingItem` object as its index in the array.

Next we set the `numItems` property to `0` and the `deliveryCost` property to `"2.50"`. Having a global variable like this for the delivery cost means that if we decide to change the cost we only need to change the code in one place.

Note that we won't access any of the properties from outside the class itself – all access to the class is strictly via its methods only. This makes it easier to keep track of where the class variables are being changed and prevents typo errors going unnoticed.

addItem() Method

As the name suggests, the `addItem()` method adds a new shopping item to the shopping basket.

```
ShoppingBasket.prototype.addItem = function(itemRefId,
                                            itemImgSrc,
                                            itemPrice,
                                            itemQty)
{
  if (typeof(this.items[itemRefId]) == "undefined")
  {
    this.items[itemRefId] = new
      ShoppingItem(itemRefId,itemImgSrc,itemPrice,itemQty);
    this.numItems++;
  }
  else
  {
    this.items[itemRefId].setItemQty(itemQty);
  }
}
```

The method's parameters are required to create a new `ShoppingItem` class object: a unique reference id for the item, the source for the image's thumbnail, its price, and the quantity to be ordered.

On the first line we check to see if an item of this reference id is already in the shopping basket:

```
  if (typeof(this.items[itemRefId]) == "undefined")
```

If `this.items[itemRefId]` returns a type of `undefined`, then no match has been found so we need to create a new `ShoppingItem` class object and add it to the basket. It is added as an element of the `items` array, `items` being a property of the `ShoppingBasket` class:

```
    this.items[itemRefId] = new
      ShoppingItem(itemRefId,itemImgSrc,itemPrice,itemQty);
    this.numItems++;
```

The `numItems` property is also updated to keep track of the number of items in our basket.

If the basket already had an item with that particular reference id, then the code in the `else` clause executes. Instead of creating a new `ShoppingItem` object, it simply updates the quantity required of the existing item:

```
else
{
  this.items[itemRefId].setItemQty(itemQty);
}
```

deleteItem() Method

This method completely removes an item from the shopping basket:

```
ShoppingBasket.prototype.deleteItem = function(itemRefId)
{
  if (typeof(this.items[itemRefId]) != "undefined")
  {
    delete this.items[itemRefId];
    this.numItems--;
  }
}
```

The `if` statement checks first to see if the item to be removed is actually in the basket, using the same technique as we saw with the `addItem()` method above. We remove the item using the JavaScript operator `delete`, which removes an item from the `items` array with the reference id as specified in `itemRefId`. On the final line, we update our `numItems` property to make sure we keep track of the basket size.

fixDecimalPlaces() Method

We've already seen this function in Chapter 3, so won't do more than list its code here. Its purpose is to fix a number to a specific number of decimal places. We need it in our application so that we can display our prices in full: $1.10 rather than $1.1, for example.

```
ShoppingBasket.prototype.fixDecimalPlaces = function
  (fixNumber, decimalPlaces)
{
  var lDiv = Math.pow(10,decimalPlaces);
  fixNumber = new String((Math.round(fixNumber * (lDiv)))/lDiv)

  var zerosRequired;
  var decimalPointLocation = fixNumber.lastIndexOf(".");
  if (decimalPointLocation == -1)
  {
    fixNumber = fixNumber + ".";
    zerosRequired = decimalPlaces;
  }
  else
  {
    zerosRequired = decimalPlaces - (fixNumber.length -
      decimalPointLocation - 1);
  }
```

```
    for (; zerosRequired > 0; zerosRequired--)
      fixNumber = fixNumber + "0";

    return fixNumber;
  }
```

getBasketHTML() Method

The next method is rather long, but is not actually that complicated. Its purpose is to go through the basket's contents and create the HTML required to display the items to the user. The display will look something like this:

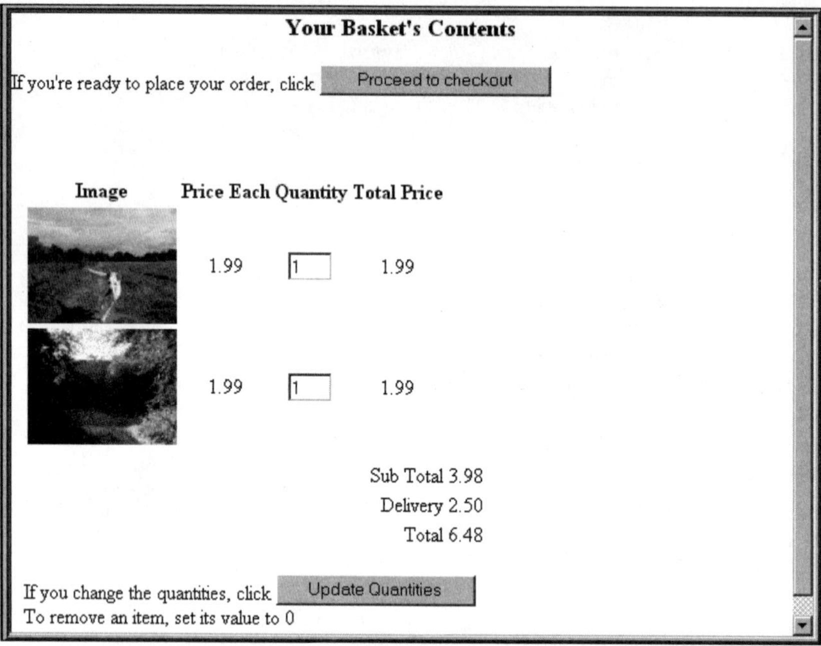

The HTML displays a thumbnail of the image, its price, the quantity ordered and the total price (the quantity ordered multiplied by the individual item's price). A summary of the subtotal cost of all the items, the shipping costs, and the final total is also displayed. The *Update Quantities* button allows customers to update their order.

Although this code is long, you'll see, as we go though it a section at the time, that it's mostly simple concatenation of strings to build up the HTML. Add it to `ShoppingBasket.js` as we go through.

The first thing to note is that the method takes one parameter, a Boolean value, which indicates whether the displayed basket should be updateable. If it's updateable, the quantities ordered of each item are written into textboxes, as in the previous screenshot, so that the user can change them. Also an *Update Basket* button is added at the end of the page to allow the user to make the updates permanent. We use a version of the basket that's not updateable for the final summary display of the checkout, in which quantities are given as hard-coded HTML, rather than inside textboxes, and there is no *Update Basket* button.

```
ShoppingBasket.prototype.getBasketHTML = function(isBasketUpdateable)
{
```

At the top of the function, we declare the variable `basketHTML`, which holds the HTML that will display the baskets contents. Then, if `isBasketUpdateable` is true, we write out a `<form>` element, since we'll have textboxes in the `basketHTML` and some browsers, like NN4, won't display form elements (such as `<input>`) unless they are in a `<form>`.

```
  var basketHTML = "";

  if (isBasketUpdateable)
  {
    basketHTML = "<FORM name=basketForm>";
  }
```

Then we start the `<table>` element and write the table cells containing the basket's heading:

```
  basketHTML += "<table class=BasketTable><tr class=HeadTR>";
  basketHTML += "<th class=BasketHeading>Image</th>";
  basketHTML += "<th class=BasketHeading>Price Each</th>";
  basketHTML += "<th class=BasketHeading>Quantity</th>";
  basketHTML += "<th class=BasketHeading>Total Price</th></tr>";
```

We declare some variables that will be used in generating the list of items in the basket. For example, `basketTotalCost` keeps a running total of the cost of items in the basket. Following this is the start of the large `for` loop that will loop through each item in our `items` array:

```
  var basketItem;
  var basketTotalCost = 0;
  var itemTotalCost = 0;
  var thumbnailSrc = "";

  for (basketItem in this.items)
  {
```

The first thing we come to inside the `for` loop is the code that generates the thumbnail images for that particular basket item:

```
    // Description
    basketHTML += "<tr><td align=center class=ImgThumbnail>";
    basketHTML += "<img src='"

    thumbnailSrc = this.items[basketItem].getItemImgSrc();
    thumbnailSrc = thumbnailSrc.replace(".jpg","");
    thumbnailSrc = thumbnailSrc + "_thumbnail.jpg";

    basketHTML += thumbnailSrc;
    basketHTML += "'></td>";
```

We create the <tr> element for that basket item, then the <td> element to contain the thumbnail <img> element. The src property for the <img> element comes from the ShoppingItem object's getItemImgSrc() method. However, this actually gives the source of the full image and not the thumbnail. To get the thumbnail image we just add _thumbnail.jpg onto the end, having first removed the .jpg. Obviously, this will only work if the image thumbnails are all given the same name as the larger image but with the suffix _thumbnail.

Next we add the price table element. The code is fairly self-explanatory:

```
// Price
basketHTML += "<td align=center class=Price>";
basketHTML += this.items[basketItem].getItemPrice();
basketHTML += "</td>";
```

Adding the quantity table element is slightly trickier, because the HTML required depends on whether it's an updateable basket requiring textboxes or a non-updateable basket that just needs read-only HTML:

```
// Qty
basketHTML += "<td align=center class=Price>";

if (isBasketUpdateable)
{
  basketHTML += "<input type=text size=2 maxlength=2 name='" +
  this.items[basketItem].getItemRefId() + "' ";
  basketHTML += "value=" + this.items[basketItem].getItemQty();
  basketHTML += ">";
}
else
{
  basketHTML += this.items[basketItem].getItemQty();
}

basketHTML += "</td>";
```

If the basket is to be updateable, then we write an <input> element into the <td> element and put the quantity value in its value attribute. Note that the name given to the <input> element is the reference id of the item; we'll need this later when we come to update the basket and need to know what item we are updating.

In the else statement we simply write the quantity into the <td> element.

Next, we calculate the total cost of that item, that is the item quantity multiplied by the individual item cost. We add this figure to the basketTotalCost variable which is keeping a running total of the cost of items in the basket:

```
itemTotalCost = this.items[basketItem].getItemQty() *
  this.items[basketItem].getItemPrice();

basketTotalCost += itemTotalCost;
```

Finally we are at the end of the for loop. We write a <td> element containing the total cost of that line, which we just calculated above, then write the <tr> element's closing tag:

```
    // Total Item Price
    basketHTML += "<td align=center class=Price>";
    basketHTML += this.fixDecimalPlaces(itemTotalCost, 2);
    basketHTML += "</td>";
    basketHTML += "</tr>";
  }
```

The `for` loop iterates until all the basket items have had their details written into the HTML table. After that, we need to create the final basket summary where we list the total cost of the basket, the delivery cost, and the total cost including delivery. There's a lot of code, but again it's simple concatenation. First we add the basket subtotal HTML:

```
// Cost Summary
basketHTML += "<tr><td colspan=4 align=right class=BasketSummary "
basketHTML += "style='padding-top: 10px'>";
basketHTML += "Sub Total</td>";
basketHTML += "<td align='center' class= "
           + "'BasketSummary' style='padding-top: 10px'>";
basketHTML += this.fixDecimalPlaces(basketTotalCost,2);
basketHTML += "</td></tr>";
```

Note we use the `fixDecimalPlaces()` method we created earlier to make sure that the subtotal is show with two decimal places.

Next we display the delivery cost:

```
// Delivery Cost
basketHTML += "<tr><td colspan=4 align=right "
           +"class='BasketSummary'>Delivery</td>";
basketHTML += "<td  align=center class=BasketSummary>"
           + this.deliveryCost + "</td></tr>";
```

Finally, we add the total for the whole basket including delivery:

```
// Total
basketHTML += "<tr><td colspan=4 align=right "
           + "class='BasketSummary'>Total</TD>";
basketHTML += "<td align=center class=BasketSummary>";
basketHTML += this.fixDecimalPlaces(basketTotalCost
           + Number(this.deliveryCost), 2);
basketHTML += "</td></tr></table>";
```

We also make sure the `<table>` element's closing tag is added, since that completes the basket display.

The final addition to the page is the *Update Basket* button, but only if the basket is updateable:

```
if (isBasketUpdateable)
{
  basketHTML += "<p>If you change the quantities, click ";
  basketHTML += "<input name='Submit' type='submit' "
             +"value='Update Quantities' ";
```

```
        basketHTML += "onClick='updateBasket()'>";
        basketHTML += "<br>To remove an item, set its value to 0"
                   +"</p></form>";
    }
```

The `onclick` event handler of the button is set to call the function `updateBasket()`, (we'll create this function later), which must be inside the same page as the shopping basket HTML, otherwise the call to find the method will fail.

Finally we return the HTML:

```
    return basketHTML;
}
```

isEmpty() Method

This method simply returns a Boolean indicating whether the basket contains items or is empty:

```
ShoppingBasket.prototype.isEmpty = function()
{
  if (this.numItems < 1)
  {
    return true;
  }
  else
  {
    return false;
  }
}
```

If the value of `numItems` is less than one, then the basket is empty and we return `true`; otherwise the basket clearly contains items and `false` is returned.

setQty() Method

This method takes two parameters. The first is the `itemRefId` of the item, and second parameter is the new quantity.

```
ShoppingBasket.prototype.setQty = function(itemRefId, itemQty)
{
  if (itemQty < 1)
  {
    this.deleteItem(itemRefId);
  }
  else
  {
    this.items[itemRefId].setItemQty(itemQty);
  }
}
```

Note that if `itemQty` is less than one, then we delete the item from the basket. This means the customer can remove an item from the shopping basket by entering 0 into the appropriate textbox in our basket display form.

updateBasketWithForm() Method

When we generate the HTML for viewing the basket using the `getBasketHTML()` method we saw earlier, we add textboxes to display the quantities of each item if the basket is updateable. The customer can enter new quantities into these textboxes. The purpose of the `updateBasketWithForm()` method is to loop through the quantity textboxes in the form, and use the quantities to update the basket.

```
ShoppingBasket.prototype.updateBasketWithForm = function(basketForm)
{
  var itemRefId;
  var numFormElements = basketForm.length;
  var basketFormElements = basketForm.elements;

  for (var elementIndex = 0; elementIndex < numFormElements; elementIndex++)
  {
    if (basketFormElements[elementIndex].type == "text")
    {
      itemRefId = basketFormElements[elementIndex].name;
      itemQty = parseInt(basketFormElements[elementIndex].value);
      if (!isNaN(itemQty))
      {
        this.setQty(itemRefId,itemQty);
      }
    }
  }
}
```

The method's parameter is a `form` object, namely the form containing the textboxes that will be used to update the basket.

At the top of the method we declare our variables. Variable `itemRefId` will hold the `itemRefId` of each item we update, `numFormElements` is set to the length of the form, so we know how many times to loop, and finally `basketFormElements` is set to reference the `elements` array property of the `form` object.

Next comes the start of the `for` loop that will loop through each element in the form:

```
  for (var elementIndex = 0; elementIndex < numFormElements; elementIndex++)
  {
```

Inside the `for` loop is an `if` statement. This checks to see that the element is a textbox, because we have other elements in the form, like the *Update Basket* button:

```
    if (basketFormElements[elementIndex].type == "text")
    {
      itemRefId = basketFormElements[elementIndex].name;
      itemQty = parseInt(basketFormElements[elementIndex].value);
      if (!isNaN(itemQty))
      {
        this.setQty(itemRefId,itemQty);
      }
```

When we created the <input> element in the `getBasketHTML()` method, we set its name to the reference id of the image. We use this on the first line of the `if` statement to obtain the reference id of the item to be updated. Then, we obtain the quantity from the form element's `value` property and use the JavaScript `parseInt()` function to convert it to a number.

We check that the quantity the user entered really is a number; if so, we set the quantity using the `setQty()` method.

The `for` loop keeps iterating until all the <input> elements have been used to update the basket.

saveBasket() Method

If the customer leaves the web site without buying the items in their shopping basket, then we want to save the items for their return. They may have gone away for a number of reasons, and if they haven't deliberately emptied the fields then there's a good chance they want to come back and start again where they left off. It'll make life easier for them if they don't have to refill their basket. (I recommend that you go one step further in a real e-commerce application and add a link or button that allows the user to clear their basket in one step.)

```
ShoppingBasket.prototype.saveBasket = function()
{
  if (!this.isEmpty())
  {
    var basketDetails = "";
    var cookieExpires;

    for (basketItem in this.items)
    {
      basketDetails += this.items[basketItem].getItemRefId() + "`";
      basketDetails += this.items[basketItem].getItemImgSrc() + "`";
      basketDetails += this.items[basketItem].getItemPrice() + "`";
      basketDetails += this.items[basketItem].getItemQty() + "¬";
    }

    basketDetails = basketDetails.substring(0,basketDetails.length - 1);
    basketDetails = escape(basketDetails);

    var nowDate = new Date();
    nowDate.setMonth(nowDate.getMonth() + 3);
    cookieExpires = nowDate.toGMTString();

    document.cookie = "ImageShopBasket=" + basketDetails
      + ";expires=" + cookieExpires + ";";
  }
  else
  {
    document.cookie = "ImageShopBasket= "
      +";expires=1 Jan 2000 00:00:00";
  }
}
```

The first thing the method does is check to see if there is actually anything in the basket:

```
if (!this.isEmpty())
{
```

If it's not empty, we store the basket. If it is empty, then the `else` statement expires the cookie to delete it.

Let's look at the code that stores the basket. It begins by going through all the items in the basket and retrieving the information about each one so we can save it:

```
var basketDetails = "";
var cookieExpires;

for (basketItem in this.items)
{
  basketDetails += this.items[basketItem].getItemRefId() + "`";
  basketDetails += this.items[basketItem].getItemImgSrc() + "`";
  basketDetails += this.items[basketItem].getItemPrice() + "`";
  basketDetails += this.items[basketItem].getItemQty() + "";
}
```

We are generating a string value that will be stored inside a cookie. So that we know where each bit of information starts and ends in the string, we use the grave accent (`) to delimit them. On the customer's return we'll reload the basket, splitting each item's data at the grave accent so that we can get to the specific information, (the reference id, img source, price, and quantity) for that item. On the last line we add the quantity, using the not sign (¬) to mark the end of one item's data and the start of the next.

For example, here's a basket with two items in it represented by a string. The first item has the id `cactus1`, the image source `cactus.jpg`, the price 1.99, and quantity of 1, and the second item has the id `rose1`, image source `rose.jpg`, price of 1.99, and again quantity of 1:

```
"cactus1`cactus.jpg`1.99`1¬rose1`rose.jpg`1.99`1
```

If the item the script is working on is the last item then we need to chop off the last delimiter:

```
basketDetails =
  basketDetails.substring(0,basketDetails.length - 1);
```

Next we escape the details of the basket items and create a new expiry date, which will be 3 months ahead. We can probably assume that if the customer hasn't returned within three months, they are not planning on buying the items:

```
basketDetails = escape(basketDetails);
var nowDate = new Date();
nowDate.setMonth(nowDate.getMonth() + 3);
cookieExpires = nowDate.toGMTString();
```

Finally we set the new cookie with the details of the basket's contents:

```
document.cookie = "ImageShopBasket=" + basketDetails
  + ";expires=" + cookieExpires + ";";
```

getCookieValue() Method

This method, which is used by the `loadBasket()` method, extracts a specific cookie from the `document.cookie` property. It should look familiar – it's based on the cookie methods we built earlier in the chapter:

```
ShoppingBasket.prototype.getCookieValue = function(cookieName)
{
  var cookieValue = document.cookie;
  var cookieRegExp = new RegExp("\\b" + cookieName + "=([^;]+)");
  cookieValue = cookieRegExp.exec(cookieValue);

  if (cookieValue != null)
  {
    cookieValue = cookieValue[1];
    cookieValue = unescape(cookieValue);
  }

  return cookieValue;
}
```

First we obtain the `document.cookie` value. Then we create a regular expression that matches the cookie. The regular expression will look for a word boundary, followed by the cookie name, followed by an equals sign, and then followed by a group of one or more characters that are not a semicolon (remember a semicolon indicates the end of a cookie). As in the earlier example, the group of characters contains the cookie value.

The `exec()` method of the `RegExp` object will try and match our pattern. If successful, it returns an array containing details of the match. If the match is not found then it returns `null`.

We check to see if the cookie was found, that is `null` was not returned. If it wasn't `null`, then we extract the value of the group inside the regular expression, then unescape its value.

Finally, either the cookie's value or `null` (if it wasn't found) is returned.

loadBasket() Method

As the name suggests, this loads the basket if the user returns to the web site after an absence:

```
ShoppingBasket.prototype.loadBasket = function()
{
  var basketItems;
  var basketItemNum;
  var itemDetail;
  var itemRefId = "";
  var itemImgSrc = "";
  var itemPrice = "";
  var itemQty = "";

  var basketDetails = this.getCookieValue("ImageShopBasket");
  if (basketDetails != null)
  {
    basketItems = basketDetails.split('¬');
```

```
      for (basketItemNum in basketItems)
      {
        basketItem = basketItems[basketItemNum];
        basketItem = basketItem.split('`');

        itemRefId = basketItem[0];
        itemImgSrc =basketItem[1];
        itemPrice = basketItem[2];
        itemQty = basketItem[3];
        this.addItem(itemRefId, itemImgSrc,itemPrice, itemQty);
      }
    }
  }
```

At the start of the method, we declare the variables we'll be using. Then we obtain the saved basket details using the `getCookieValue()` method we just looked at.

Assuming a cookie was found, (so `basketDetails` does not equal `null`) then we need to extract all the item details and repopulate the basket. First, we need to split the cookie string where the not sign (¬) character is found. (Remember that this was the character we used to mark the end of an item's details when we saved the cookie in the `saveBasket()` method.)

The result of the split is an array stored in `basketItems`. Each array element contains the details for one item. We need to loop through that array with a `for` loop, and add each item to the basket.

When we saved the basket, we delimited the individual bits of data for an item (that is quantity, item reference, etc.) using the grave accent (`). So, we split each element of the `basketItems` array at the grave accent and store the resulting array in `basketItem`. Once we've done that we can access each bit of information for an item in turn by accessing the elements of the `basketItem` array. Having obtained all the information we need, on the last line of the `for` loop we use the `addItem()` method to add the item to the basket.

The `for` loop iterates until all the items have been added, and the basket has been recreated as the customer left it.

getTotalIncDelivery() Method

This method gets the total cost of the basket plus the cost of delivery. It's used in the final checkout summary page when we tell the user how much will be deducted from their card.

```
ShoppingBasket.prototype.getTotalIncDelivery = function()
{
  var basketTotalCost = 0;
  var basketItem;
  var itemTotalCost = 0;

  for (basketItem in this.items)
  {
    itemTotalCost = this.items[basketItem].getItemQty() *
      this.items[basketItem].getItemPrice();
    basketTotalCost += itemTotalCost;
```

```
    }

    basketTotalCost += Number(this.deliveryCost);
    basketTotalCost = this.fixDecimalPlaces(basketTotalCost,2);
    return basketTotalCost;
  }
```

We use a `for` loop to iterate through the basket, calculating the cost of a particular item multiplied by the quantity required, and add this to the running total stored in `basketTotalCost`.

After the `for` loop, we add the cost of delivery. The delivery cost, held in the `deliveryCost` property of the `ShoppingBasket` class object, is a string. We need to convert it to a number before adding it to the total cost, otherwise JavaScript will concatenate and not add the values.

We then convert the number so that it is fixed to two decimal places, and return the result.

getHiddenInputHTML() Method

We display a summary of the order in the final checkout summary screen. When the user clicks to buy the items, a form `post` would send the information to the server. However, currently the information is held purely as client-side information in JavaScript. We need to create a hidden form that contains details of the items the customer wants to purchase, and post the form. The `getHiddenInputHTML()` method creates a hidden form containing details of the basket items inside hidden textboxes:

```
ShoppingBasket.prototype.getHiddenInputHTML = function()
{
  var hiddenInputHTML = "";
  var basketItem;

  for (basketItem in this.items)
  {
    // Ref
    hiddenInputHTML += "<input type='hidden' name='";
    hiddenInputHTML += this.items[basketItem].getItemRefId() + "_RefId'";
    hiddenInputHTML += " value=" + this.items[basketItem].getItemRefId();
    hiddenInputHTML += ">";

    // Qty
    hiddenInputHTML += "<input type='hidden' name='";
    hiddenInputHTML += this.items[basketItem].getItemRefId() + "_Qty'";
    hiddenInputHTML += " value=" + this.items[basketItem].getItemQty();
    hiddenInputHTML += ">";
  }

  return hiddenInputHTML;
}
```

The code loops through the `ShoppingItem` objects in the `items` array representing our basket, and uses the details to generate the HTML necessary to create a form. However, note that we only create two hidden textboxes – one to hold the unique reference id and the other to hold the quantity required. We are assuming that the server can use a database to look up the remaining information, except customer and card detail information we will obtained shortly, so long as the unique reference id is passed.

clearBasket() Method

The final method for this class clears the shopping basket of all items, and is used after the customer has successfully completed an order:

```
ShoppingBasket.prototype.clearBasket = function()
{
  this.items = new Object();
  this.numItems = 0;
  document.cookie = "ImageShopBasket= ;expires=1 Jan 2000 00:00:00";
}
```

We set the `items` array property of the `shoppingBasket` to a new `Object`, set `numItems` in the basket to `0`, and make sure the cookie holding the basket details is cleared by expiring it.

That is the end of the `ShoppingBasket` class. Before we change the web site, we have two more classes to create: the `CreditCard` class and the `Customer` class, so we'll look at these next.

The CreditCard Class

Although it contains quite a bit of code, this class is very simple and is mainly a convenient way of storing information about the customer's credit card. It has eight methods that simply allow us to get or set the following values:

`cardType`	Type of card, (visa, American Express etc.)
`cardHolderName`	Name of card holder
`cardnumber`	Credit card number
`cardExpires`	Expiry date of credit card

We saw the technique of getting and setting object properties like this when we looked at the `ShoppingItem` class.

The class also has another method, `getCreditCardDetailsSummary()`, which creates HTML to summarize the credit card details entered by the customer. It's used in the final checkout page where the whole order is summarized for confirmation prior to the customer making their purchase. As no information is passed server-side with this class until the very final post on the summary page, there are no security issues on the server-side or between the client and server. The main risk is the user leaving their browser open having filled in their credit card details.

The class and its methods are stored in the file `CreditCard.js`:

```
function CreditCard() {}

CreditCard.prototype.setCardType = function(cardType)
{
  this.cardType = cardType;
}

CreditCard.prototype.getCardType = function()
{
```

```
  return this.cardType;
}

CreditCard.prototype.setCardHolderName = function(cardHolderName)
{
  this.cardHolderName = cardHolderName;
}

CreditCard.prototype.getCardHolderName = function()
{
  return this.cardHolderName;
}

CreditCard.prototype.setCardNumber = function(cardNumber)
{
  this.cardNumber = cardNumber;
}

CreditCard.prototype.getCardNumber = function()
{
  return this.cardNumber;
}

CreditCard.prototype.setCardExpires = function(cardExpires)
{
  this.cardExpires = cardExpires;
}

CreditCard.prototype.getCardExpires = function()
{
  return this.cardExpires;
}

CreditCard.prototype.getCreditCardDetailsSummary = function()
{
  var summaryHTML = "<table class='Summary'>";
  summaryHTML += "<tr><td>Name of credit card holder: </td>";
  summaryHTML += "<td>" + this.getCardHolderName() + "</td></tr>";
  summaryHTML += "<tr><td>Card Number</td>";
  summaryHTML += "<td>" + this.getCardNumber() + "</td></tr>";
  summaryHTML += "<tr><td>Expiry Date</td>";
  summaryHTML += "<td>" + this.getCardExpires() + "</td></tr>";
  summaryHTML += "</table>";

  return summaryHTML;
}
```

The Customer Class

This class is very similar to the `CreditCard` class. It has various properties for storing information, methods to set and get these properties, and a method to summarize the information. This is the information stored by the `Customer` class:

`title`	Customer title. For example, Miss, Mrs, Mr
`fullName`	Customer's full name
`email`	Customer's e-mail address
`street`	Customer's house number/name and street name
`city`	Customer's city
`locality`	Customer's state or county
`postalCode`	Customer's zip or post code
`country`	Customer's country

Although the properties that are get and set and the summary information is different, all the techniques are identical to the ones we saw with the `CreditCard` class, so we won't discuss the code. We'll just list it – all contained within the file `Customer.js`:

```
function Customer() {}

Customer.prototype.getCustomerDetailsSummary = function ()
{
  var summaryHTML = "Your goods will be delivered to "
    + "<table class='Summary'>";
  summaryHTML += "<tr><td>" + this.getTitle() + " " + this.getFullName()
    + "</td></tr>";
  summaryHTML += "<tr><td>" + this.getStreet() + "</td></tr>";
  summaryHTML += "<tr><td>" + this.getCity() + "</td></tr>";
  summaryHTML += "<tr><td>" + this.getLocality() + "</td></tr>";
  summaryHTML += "<tr><td>" + this.getPostalCode() + "</td></tr>";
  summaryHTML += "<tr><td>" + this.getCountry() + "</td></tr>";
  summaryHTML += "</table>"

  return summaryHTML;
}

Customer.prototype.setTitle = function(title)
{
  this.title = title;
}

Customer.prototype.getTitle = function()
{
  return this.title;
}

Customer.prototype.setFullName = function(fullName)
{
  this.fullName = fullName;
}

Customer.prototype.getFullName = function()
{
```

```
    return this.fullName;
  }

  Customer.prototype.setEmail = function(email)
  {
    this.email = email;
  }

  Customer.prototype.getEmail = function()
  {
    return this.email;
  }

  Customer.prototype.setStreet = function(street)
  {
    this.street = street;
  }

  Customer.prototype.getStreet = function()
  {
    return this.street;
  }

  Customer.prototype.setCity = function(city)
  {
    this.city = city;
  }

  Customer.prototype.getCity = function()
  {
    return this.city;
  }

  Customer.prototype.setLocality = function(locality)
  {
    this.locality = locality;
  }

  Customer.prototype.getLocality = function()
  {
    return this.locality;
  }

  Customer.prototype.setPostalCode = function(postalCode)
  {
    this.postalCode = postalCode;
  }

  Customer.prototype.getPostalCode = function()
  {
    return this.postalCode;
  }

  Customer.prototype.setCountry = function(country)
```

```
{
  this.country = country;
}

Customer.prototype.getCountry = function()
{
  return this.country;
}
```

Using the Classes

Now that we have created our `ShoppingBasket`, `CreditCard`, and `Customer` classes, we can use them to make our shopping basket functionality work, and to create the checkout.

Adding Items to the basket

In Chapter 8, we added an *ADD To Basket* image to `ImageViewer.htm` with an event handler pointing to the `addToBasket()` function. We created this function in `ecomCode.js`, but it was an empty function. We'll return to that function now and add some code.

The first thing we need to do is add the following to the top of the `ecomCode.js` file (outside the functions):

```
var myBasket = new ShoppingBasket();
var thisCustomer = new Customer();
var customerCreditCard = new CreditCard();
```

The `ecomCode.js` page is loaded as part of the top frameset-defining page, `ImageViewerEcom.htm`. When it loads, the code above will create global variables called `myBasket`, `thisCustomer`, and `customerCreditCard`, and set them to a new object instance of the `ShoppingBasket` class, `CreditCard` class and `Customer` class.

At the end of Chapter 8, the `addToBasket()` function was defined but empty – we need to add the following code to it:

```
function addToBasket_onclick()
{
  var imageViewerPage = window.frames["ImageViewerFrame"];
  var mainImageFrame = imageViewerPage.frames["mainImageFrame"];

  if (mainImageFrame.updateBasket )
  {
    mainImageFrame.updateBasket();
  }
  else if (imageViewerPage.loadedImgRefId == null)
  {
    alert("Please click on the image\nyou want to add to the basket then"
      +"\nclick the add button to add it");
  }
  else
  {
    myBasket.addItem(window.frames["ImageViewerFrame"].loadedImgRefId,
                     mainImageFrame.location.href, 1.99, 1)
    viewBasket_onclick();
  }
}
```

At the top of the function we declare two variables to hold references to the `window` object of the page that contains the image viewer page – the top frameset page `ImageViewerEcom.htm` and the `window` object of the `iframe` that displays either the larger image of a thumbnail or the shopping basket.

Next we need to check what sort of page is loaded in the image viewer main frame. If it's an image then we need to add the selected image to the basket, and if it's the shopping basket then we need to update the basket. This page contains the `updateBasket()` function, which lets us know if the shopping basket page is loaded. We test whether `mainImageFrame.updateBasket()` returns a value in the `if` statement. If it does, it will evaluate to `true` and the code in the `if` statement will execute, updating the basket using the `updateBasket()` function (we'll come to this soon).

If it wasn't the shopping basket page that was loaded, then it could be the case that the customer has not selected an image. We can test for this since the `loadedImgRefId` variable in the main image viewer page will be `null`. If so, we can't add anything to the basket and just need to notify the customer that they need to select an image first, before they can add it to the basket.

If it's not the shopping basket page, and an image is loaded, then in the final `else` statement we add the image to the basket. We use the `addItem()` method of the `ShoppingBasket` class to do the hard work. Recall that the `addItem()` method takes four parameters:

- The reference id that comes from the selected `<image>` element's `id` attribute.
- The `location.href` of the frame viewing the image provides the image source.
- The price. In a more sophisticated e-commerce system, we'd obviously want to be setting prices as well. We'd also want to obtain this value from a database rather than hardcode it; it's easier to update prices if we can just change a database and not have to edit HTML pages.
- The quantity is assumed to be 1. If the customer wants more, they can update the basket from the shopping basket view.

On the final line of the function, we call the `viewBasket_onclick()` function added to `ecomCode.js` in the previous chapter, which causes the now changed basket to be displayed. It helps confirm to the customer that something did just happen and the basket has changed.

That completes the *Add to Basket* functionality and for now we can save and close the `ecomCode.js`. Now we need to add some code to view the basket.

Viewing the Basket

In the previous chapter, we added a *View Basket* button to the `ImageViewer.htm` page. Its `onclick` event handler was connected to the `viewBasket_onclick()` function, which we created in `ecomCode.js`. This function caused the `viewbasket.htm` page to be displayed.

What we need to do now is update the `viewbasket.htm` page and add the HTML and code to display the basket:

```
<html>
<head>
  <link rel='stylesheet' href='Web siteGlobalStyle.css'>
  <script language='JavaScript'>
    var imageViewerPage = window.parent.parent;
```

```
      if (imageViewerPage.myBasket.isEmpty())
      {
        window.location.href = "emptybasket.htm";
      }
    </script>
  </head>
  <body>
    <div align='center'>
      <h3>
        Your Basket's Contents
      </h3>
    </div>
    <form name='frmItems'>
      <p align='left'>
        If you're ready to place your order, click
        <input type='Button' name='cmdCheckout'
          value='Proceed to checkout'
          onClick='window.parent.location.href="PersonalDetails.htm"'>
      </p>
    </form>
    <div id='basketDisplayDiv' style='position: absolute; left: 10px; top: 125px;'>
      <script language='JavaScript'>
        document.write(imageViewerPage.myBasket.getBasketHTML(true));
      </script>
    </div>
  </body>
  </html>
```

The first change is the addition of a form, `frmItems`, which contains a button. When clicked, this takes the customer to the `PersonalDetails.htm` page. (We'll create this later in the chapter. It's the first page in the checkout.)

Below that is the `<div>` element into which the HTML displaying the basket is written. We use the `document` object's `write()` method to write the HTML, obtained using the Shopping Basket's `getBasketHTML()` method. Note that we pass `true` to the method. This tells it to produce a basket with updateable quantities – the textboxes displaying the quantities.

Finally there is some new script code at the top of the page. First we set the `imageViewerPage` variable to the location of the current page's `parent.parent`, that is the very top frameset-defining page, the page which contains the `myBasket ShoppingBasket` object. We use this to check in the `if` statement whether the basket is empty. If it is, we redirect the page to the `emptybasket.htm` page we created in the previous chapter. Keep the `viewbasket.htm` page loaded in your HTML editor, as we'll be amending it further in the *Updating*, *Saving*, and *Loading Basket* sections below.

Updating the basket

In the `viewbasket.htm` page, add the following to the top script block:

```
if (imageViewerPage.myBasket.isEmpty())
{
  window.location.href = "emptybasket.htm";
}
```

```
    function updateBasket()
    {
      var basketForm = document.basketForm;
      var imageViewerPage = window.parent.parent;
      imageViewerPage.myBasket.updateBasketWithForm(basketForm);
      location.reload();
    }
</script>
```

The new function is `updateBasket()`. This updates the basket when either the *Update Basket* button is pressed in the basket view page or the *Update* image is clicked in the main frame (in this case, the function `addToBasket_onclick()` is called, which then calls the `updateBasket()` function if the basket is loaded in the image viewer frame).

The first thing the function does is obtain a reference to the `basketForm`. This is the form containing details of the items in the basket and the quantities required. The customer may have changed the quantities required by entering the numbers in the textboxes.

We then set variable `imageViewerPage` to the top frameset page, `ImageViewerEcom.htm`, where most of the e-commerce code is contained. Then we call the `updateBasketWithForm()` method of the `ShoppingBasket` object. We pass it the form object containing the basket details and it uses this to update the basket items stored in the `ShoppingBasket` object stored in variable `myBasket` in the top frameset page.

Finally the page is reloaded, so that the changes to the basket are displayed.

Saving and Loading the Basket when the Customer Leaves/Returns

The first change we need to make for this functionality is to `viewbasket.htm`. Whenever it's loaded, we'll save the basket to the customer's computer:

```
<div id='basketDisplayDiv' style='position: absolute; left: 10px; top: 125px;'>
  <script language='JavaScript'>
    document.write(imageViewerPage.myBasket.getBasketHTML(true));
    imageViewerPage.myBasket.saveBasket ();
  </script>
</div>
```

Now, as well as writing the basket to the page, it also saves it, using the `saveBasket()` method we created for the `ShoppingBasket` class.

We've finished the changes to the `viewbasket.htm` page, so that can be saved and closed.

We now need to load and change the `ecomCode.js` page, adding the following code to the top of the file:

```
var myBasket = new ShoppingBasket();
myBasket.loadBasket();
```

We use the `loadBasket()` method of the `ShoppingBasket` object to load the shopping basket's contents back in when the customer returns to the web site. We can save and close this page for now, though there are still more changes to it in the next section.

Creating the Checkout

In this section we create the four pages that constitute the checkout part of the e-commerce application. The first page obtains the customer's name and address details, the second their credit card details, the third displays a summary of the order, and the fourth is simply a "thanks for placing your order" page.

Obtaining Customer Name/Address Details

The `PersonalDetails.htm` page is listed below. Although the page is big, for the most part it's basic HTML and form controls. We'll take it piece by piece. First the top section, which simply provides a few new styles:

```
<html>
<head>
  <link rel='stylesheet' href='Web siteGlobalStyle.css'>
  <style>
    DIV.FormElementError
    {
      position: relative;
      left: 280px;
      top: -20px;
      color: red;
      visibility: hidden;
    }

    SPAN.FormElementError
    {
      position: relative;
      left: 280px;
      top: -20px;
      color: red;
      visibility: hidden;
    }

    input.TextBox
    {
      width: 150px;
    }
  </style>
```

We next have a script block containing three functions.

The `loadForm()` function is called by the `window` object's `onload` event handler, and its purpose is to reload any values the user typed into the form. Let's say the user types in some information, then goes to the credit card page, then the order summary page, and at that point spots a mistake in their postal code. They click the *Back* button and go back to this page to correct the mistake. If we don't save the values in the form, then the user is going to have to start all over again filling in the form. We save them the trouble by saving any form values when the page is unloaded – we'll see the save function in a minute – and reload them using this `loadForm()` function.

```
  <script language='JavaScript'>
    function loadForm()
    {
```

At the top of the function, we set variables to reference the `customer` object in the top frame and also our form in this page:

```
var customer = parent.thisCustomer;
var form = document.frmCustomer;
```

We only want to load the form values if there have been values saved, so we check for this in the `if` statement:

```
if (typeof(customer.getFullName()) != "undefined")
{
```

If there are values, then we load the form's `<input>` elements with these values:

```
  form.txtFullName_compulsory_alphabetic.value = customer.getFullName();
  form.txtEmail_compulsory_email.value = customer.getEmail();
  form.txtStreet_compulsory_alphanumeric.value = customer.getStreet();
  form.txtCity_compulsory_alphanumeric.value = customer.getCity();
  form.txtLocality_compulsory_alphanumeric.value =
    customer.getLocality();
  form.txtPostalCode_compulsory_postcode.value =
    customer.getPostalCode();
  form.txtCountry_compulsory_alphabetic.value = customer.getCountry();
```

Resetting the radio controls with the title requires slightly more work – we use a `switch` statement to check the value stored in the title and set the radio controls accordingly:

```
  switch (customer.getTitle())
  {
    case "Mr":
      form.radTitle_Compulsory[0].checked = true;
      break;
    case "Mrs":
      form.radTitle_Compulsory[1].checked = true;
      break;
    case "Miss":
      form.radTitle_Compulsory[2].checked = true;
      break;
    case "Ms.":
      form.radTitle_Compulsory[3].checked = true;
      break;
    case "Dr.":
      form.radTitle_Compulsory[4].checked = true;
      break;
  }

  form.radTitle_Compulsory.value = "Mrs";
}
}
```

Next is the `saveForm()` function, which saves the contents of the form when the page is unloaded.

We need to do this to keep a record of the customer details for use when the form is posted to the server on the final checkout page, as well as to save details for cases where a user backtracks to change their data.

```
    function saveForm()
    {
```

Again, first we reference the `customer` object and the form:

```
      var customer = parent.thisCustomer;
      var form = document.frmCustomer;
```

Then we set the `customer` object's properties using its set methods. It's pretty simple, with the exception of the radio button. For this, we use the `getSelectedRadioValue()` method, which we'll need to add to the `ecomCode.js` page shortly:

```
      // get value of title radio button
      var titleValue;
      titleValue = parent.getSelectedRadioValue(form.radTitle_Compulsory);
      customer.setTitle(titleValue);
      customer.setFullName(form.txtFullName_compulsory_alphabetic.value);
      customer.setEmail(form.txtEmail_compulsory_email.value);
      customer.setStreet(form.txtStreet_compulsory_alphanumeric.value);
      customer.setCity(form.txtCity_compulsory_alphanumeric.value);
      customer.setLocality(form.txtLocality_compulsory_alphanumeric.value);
      customer.setPostalCode(form.txtPostalCode_compulsory_postcode.value);
      customer.setCountry(form.txtCountry_compulsory_alphabetic.value)
    }
```

The third and final function is the `cmdSubmit_onclick()` function, where just one line of code takes the page to the next stage in the checkout – the obtaining credit card details stage.

```
    function cmdSubmit_onclick()
    {
      window.location.href = "CheckoutCredit.htm";
    }
  </script>
</head>
```

In the main body of the page, we add the input elements to gather information about the customer. You may notice `<div>` elements after each form element, which seem unnecessary. The purpose of these is to show or hide form validation error messages – we'll be adding the form validation code in Chapter 10.

```
<body onload="loadForm()" onunload="saveForm()">
  <h1 align=center>Personal Details</h1>
  <center>
    <img src="CheckoutStage1.jpg">
  </center>
```

```
<h3>
  Please enter your name, address and e-mail address below.<BR>
</h3>

<form name='frmCustomer'>
  <!-- Title -->
  <div>
    Title
    Mr<input name='radTitle_Compulsory' type='radio' value='Mr'></input>
    Mrs<input name='radTitle_Compulsory' type='radio' value='Mrs'></input>
    Miss<input name='radTitle_Compulsory' type='radio' value='Miss'></input>
    Ms.<input name='radTitle_Compulsory' type='radio' value='Ms.'></input>
    Dr.<input name='radTitle_Compulsory' type='radio' value='Dr.'></input>
    <div id='TitleError' name='TitleError' class='FormElementError'>
      Please select your title
    </div>
  </div>
  <!-- Full Name -->
  <div>
    Full Name:       
    <input name='txtFullName_compulsory_alphabetic' maxlength='150'
      class='TextBox' ></input>
    <div id='FullNameError' name='FullNameError' class='FormElementError'>
      Please enter your full name
    </div>
  </div>
  <!-- Email -->
  <div>
    E-mail Address:
    <input name='txtEmail_compulsory_email' class='TextBox'
      maxlength='75'></input>
    <div id='EmailError' name='EmailError' class='FormElementError'>
      Please enter a valid e-mail address
    </div>
  </div>
  <!-- Street -->
  <div>
    Street:           
    <input name='txtStreet_compulsory_alphanumeric' class='TextBox'
      maxlength='75'></input>
    <div id='StreetError' name='StreetError' class='FormElementError'>
      Please enter your house number and street name
    </div>
  </div>
  <!-- City -->
  <div>
    City:            
    <input name='txtCity_compulsory_alphanumeric' class='TextBox'
      maxlength='50'></input>
    <div id='CityError' name='CityError' class='FormElementError'>
      Please enter a valid city name
    </div>
  </div>
  <!-- County/State -->
```

```
    <div>
      County/State: 
      <input name='txtLocality_compulsory_alphanumeric'
        class='TextBox' maxlength='50'></input>
      <div id='LocalityError' name='LocalityError' class='FormElementError'>
        Please enter the state
      </div>
    </div>
    <!-- Post/Zip Code -->
    <div>
      Zip/Post Code:
      <input name='txtPostalCode_compulsory_postcode' class='TextBox'
        maxlength='15'></input>
      <div id='PostalCodeError' name='PostalCodeError' class='FormElementError'>
        Please enter your zip/postal code
      </div>
    </div>
    <!-- Country -->
    <div>
      Country:        
      <input name='txtCountry_compulsory_alphabetic' class='TextBox'
        maxlength='50'></input>
      <div id='CountryError' name='CountryError' class='FormElementError'>
        Please enter your country name
      </div>
    </div>

    <input type='reset' name='cmdReset' value='Clear form'>
    <input type='button' name='cmdPrevious' value='Back'
      onClick='history.back()'></input>
    <input type='button' name='cmdSubmit' value='Continue'
      onClick='cmdSubmit_onclick()'></input>
  </form>
</body>
</html>
```

We've finished for now with `PersonalDetails.htm`. We now need to add the `getSelectedRadioValue()` function to the `ecomCode.js` page:

```
function getSelectedRadioValue(radioGroup)
{
  var selectedRadioValue = "";
  var radIndex;

  for (radIndex = 0; radIndex < radioGroup.length; radIndex++)
  {
    if (radioGroup[radIndex].checked)
    {
      selectedRadioValue = radioGroup[radIndex].value;
      break;
    }
  }
  return selectedRadioValue;
}
```

If this function looks suspiciously familiar, it's because we created it in Chapter 4 when we looked at interacting with the browser and accessing forms.

Obtaining Credit Card Details

This page needs to be saved as `CheckoutCredit.htm`:

```
<html>
<head>
  <link rel='stylesheet' href='Web siteGlobalStyle.css'>

 <style>
 DIV.FormElementError
 {
 position: relative;
 left: 280px;
 top: -20px;
 color: red;
 visibility: hidden;
 }
 </style>

  <script language='JavaScript'>
    function cmdContinue_onclick(theForm)
    {
      var selectedMonth =
        theForm.cboExpMonth.options[theForm.cboExpMonth.selectedIndex].value;
      var selectedYear =
        theForm.cboExpYear.options[theForm.cboExpYear.selectedIndex].value;
      var cardType =
        parent.getSelectedRadioValue(theForm.radCardType_Compulsory);
      var cardNumber =
        theForm.txtCardNumber_Compulsory_Alphanumeric.value;
      parent.customerCreditCard.setCardType(cardType);
      parent.customerCreditCard.setCardHolderName
        (theForm.txtCardHolderName_Compulsory_Alphabetic.value);
      parent.customerCreditCard.setCardNumber(cardNumber);
      parent.customerCreditCard.setCardExpires(selectedMonth + "/" +
selectedYear);
      window.location.href = "CheckoutConfirm.htm";
    }
  </script>
</head>
<body>
  <h1 align=center>Credit Card Details</h1>
  <center>
    <img src='CheckoutStage2.jpg'>
  </center>
  <h3>
    <p align='center'>Please enter your credit card details below. </p>
  </h3>
  <form name='frmCCDetails'>
    <div>
      Card Holders Name:
      <br>
```

```
    <input type='TEXT' name='txtCardHolderName_Compulsory_Alphabetic'
      maxlength='50'></input>
    <div id='CardHolderNameError' name='CardHolderNameError'
      class='FormElementError'>
      Please enter your name as it appears on your credit card
    </div>
  </div>
  <div>
    Credit Card Number:
    <br>
    <input type='TEXT' name='txtCardNumber_Compulsory_Alphanumeric'
      maxlength='20'></input>
    <div id='CardNumberError' name='CardNumberError'
      class='FormElementError'>
      Please ensure you've entered your credit card number correctly
    </div>
  </div>
  <div>
    Credit Card Type
    <br>
    Visa <input name='radCardType_Compulsory' type='radio' value='visa'></input>
    Mastercard <input name='radCardType_Compulsory' type='radio'
      value='mastercard'></input>
    American Express <input name='radCardType_Compulsory' type='radio'
      value='amex'></input>
    <div id='CardTypeError' name='CardTypeError'
      class='FormElementError' style='left:320px'>
      Please select your credit card type
    </div>
  </div>
  <div>
    Card Expiry Date
    <select name='cboExpMonth' size='1'>
      <option value='01'>01</option>
      <option value='02'>02</option>
      <option value='03'>03</option>
      <option value='04'>04</option>
      <option value='05'>05</option>
      <option value='06'>06</option>
      <option value='07'>07</option>
      <option value='08'>08</option>
      <option value='09'>09</option>
      <option value='10'>10</option>
      <option value='11'>11</option>
      <option value='12'>12</option>
    </select>
    <select name='cboExpYear' size='1'>
      <option value='2001'>2001</option>
      <option value='2002'>2002</option>
      <option value='2003'>2003</option>
      <option value='2004'>2004</option>
      <option value='2005'>2005</option>
      <option value='2006'>2006</option>
    </select>
```

```
        <div id='CardExpiryError' name='CardExpiryError' class='FormElementError'>
          Please select a valid expiry date
        </div>
      </div>

      <input name='reset' type='reset' value='Clear Form'></input>
      <input name='cmdPrevious' type='button' value='Back'
        onClick='history.back()'>
      <input name='cmdContinue' type='button' value='Continue'
        onClick='cmdContinue_onclick(document.frmCCDetails)'>
    </form>
  </body>
  </html>
```

We don't save and reload the form details for this page for security reasons. However we do need to make a note of the data entered, and we store this information in the `CreditCard` object we declared in the `ecomCode.js` file.

The storing of the form details occurs when the *Continue* button is clicked, whose `onclick` event handler calls the `cmdContinue_onclick()` function. The first thing this function does is to get the values of the selected credit card expiry month and year:

```
          var selectedMonth =
              theForm.cboExpMonth.options[theForm.cboExpMonth.selectedIndex]
              .value;

           var selectedYear =
             theForm.cboExpYear.options[theForm.cboExpYear.selectedIndex]
             .value;
```

Then we obtain the selected card type from the radio buttons using the `getSelectedRadioValue()` function we recently created in the `ecomCode.js` file. Next, we obtain the card number.

```
  var cardType = parent.getSelectedRadioValue(theForm.radCardType_Compulsory);

  var cardNumber = theForm.txtCardNumber_Compulsory_Alphanumeric.value;
```

Finally, we fill the `creditcard` object referenced in the `customerCreditCard` global variable defined in the `ecomCode.js` file with the values we have extracted from the form:

```
              parent.customerCreditCard.setCardType(cardType);
              parent.customerCreditCard.setCardHolderName
                 (theForm.txtCardHolderName_Compulsory_Alphabetic.value);
              parent.customerCreditCard.setCardNumber(cardNumber);
              parent.customerCreditCard.setCardExpires(selectedMonth + "/"
                 + selectedYear);

              window.location.href = "CheckoutConfirm.htm";
```

On the last line of the function we navigate to the final checkout page, where we confirm the customers order.

Displaying the Final Summary

This page needs to be saved as `CheckoutConfirm.htm`. Its function is to display all the details the customer has entered, including all the items they want to purchase. It helps reassure the customer that they have entered their order correctly, and gives them a chance to go back and change things if they spot a mistake.
Starting at the top of the page, after the necessary heading tags, we have the first script block.

```
<html>
<head>
  <script>
    if (parent.myBasket.isEmpty())
    {
      window.location.href = "emptybasket.htm";
    }
  </script>
```

If the basket is empty, then there is no order to submit, so we take the user to the `emptybasket.htm` page. This is to prevent the situation where the user manages to navigate to this page using a different method than the checkout stages – if, for example, they found one of these pages using a search engine.

We include some extra styles to be used:

```
  <title>Confirm Details</title>
  <link rel=stylesheet href="Web siteGlobalStyle.css">
  <style>
    table.Summary
      {
        font-size: 10pt;
      }
    div.AddressSummary, div.CreditCardSummary,
      div.AmountSummary, div.BasketSummary, div.OrderItemsAre
    {
      position: absolute;
      left: 10px;
    }
    div.AddressSummary
    {
      top: 200px;
    }
    div.CreditCardSummary
    {
      top:350px;
    }
    div.AmountSummary
    {
      top: 380px;
      color: darkorange;
      font-weight: bolder;
    }
    div.BasketSummary
    {
```

```
      left: 0px;
      top: 520px;
    }
    div.OrderItemsAre
    {
      top: 500px;
      color: darkorange;
      font-weight: bolder;
    }
  </style>
</head>
```

Then we need to get the details for the customer and their shopping basket to the server – currently they are only held client-side. The easiest way is using a form `post`. To do this, we create hidden input controls, one for each item of data that needs to be sent:

```
<body>
  <form action='OrderComplete.htm' method='post' name='frmOrder'>
    <!-- Name/Address Details -->
    <input type='HIDDEN' name='txtTitle' value=''></input>
    <input type='HIDDEN' name='txtFullName' value=''></input>
    <input type='HIDDEN' name='txtEmail' value=''></input>
    <input type='HIDDEN' name='txtStreet' value=''></input>
    <input type='HIDDEN' name='txtCity' value=''></input>
    <input type='HIDDEN' name='txtLocality' value=''></input>
    <input type='HIDDEN' name='txtPostalCode' value=''></input>
    <input type='HIDDEN' name='txtCountry' value=''></input>

    <!-- Credit Card Details -->
    <input type='HIDDEN' name='txtCardHolderName' value=''></input>
    <input type='HIDDEN' name='txtCardNumber' value=''></input>
    <input type='HIDDEN' NAME='txtCardType' value=''></input>
    <input type='HIDDEN' name='txtCardExpires' value=''></input>
```

In the script that follows this, we fill the hidden input controls with data from the `Customer` and `CreditCard` objects that are stored in the `thisCustomer` and `customerCreditCard` global variables in `ecomCode.js`:

```
    <script language='JavaScript'>
      var form = document.frmOrder;
      form.txtTitle.value = parent.thisCustomer.getTitle();
      form.txtFullName.value = parent.thisCustomer.getFullName();
      form.txtEmail.value = parent.thisCustomer.getEmail();
      form.txtStreet.value = parent.thisCustomer.getStreet();
      form.txtCity.value = parent.thisCustomer.getCity();
      form.txtLocality.value = parent.thisCustomer.getLocality();
      form.txtPostalCode.value = parent.thisCustomer.getPostalCode();
      form.txtCountry.value = parent.thisCustomer.getCountry();
      form.txtCardHolderName.value =
parent.customerCreditCard.getCardHolderName();
      form.txtCardNumber.value = parent.customerCreditCard.getCardNumber();
      form.txtCardType.value = parent.customerCreditCard.getCardType();
      form.txtCardExpires.value = parent.customerCreditCard.getCardExpires();
      document.write(parent.myBasket.getHiddenInputHTML());
    </script>
```

Note that on the last line we write into the page the results returned by the `ShoppingBasket` class's `getHiddenInputHTML()` method. This method generates hidden input controls for each item in the shopping basket, so that the item reference id and quantity required will also be posted to the server.

The next task is to display the summary of the order details. First we generate the customer's details, name, and address:

```
    <h1 align=center>Order Summary</h1>
    <center>
      <img src="CheckoutStage3.jpg">
    </center>

    <!-- Summarize Order details -->
    <h4>Your order details are listed below.</h4>
    <p>Once you have confirmed the details click
    <input type='button' name='cmdSubmit'
      onClick='window.location.href = "OrderComplete.htm"'
      value='Submit Order'>
    </input>
    to send your order
    </p>
  </form>

  <!-- Summary of name and address for delivery -->
  <div id='divAddressSummary' class='AddressSummary'>
    <script language='JavaScript'>
      var customerSummaryHTML = parent.thisCustomer.getCustomerDetailsSummary();
      document.write(customerSummaryHTML);
    </script>
  </div>
```

We use the `getCustomerDetailsSummary()` method of the `Customer` class to do the hard work of generating the summary. Next we generate the credit card details summary:

```
  <!-- Summary of amount to be charged to credit card -->
  <div id='divAmountSummary' class='AmountSummary'>
    <script language='JavaScript'>
      var cardSummaryHTML =
        parent.customerCreditCard.getCreditCardDetailsSummary();
      document.write(cardSummaryHTML);
    </script>
  </div>
```

This time it's the `CreditCard` class that provides the summary HTML. To reassure the customer with the exact amount that will be debited from their card, we create a summary of this too:

```
  <!-- Show summary of card details -->
  <div id='divCreditCardSummary' class='CreditCardSummary'>
    <script language='JavaScript'>
      var cardDebitSummaryHTML = "A total of &pound;";
      cardDebitSummaryHTML += parent.myBasket.getTotalIncDelivery();
      cardDebitSummaryHTML += " will be debited from your ";
```

```
        cardDebitSummaryHTML += parent.customerCreditCard.getCardType();
        cardDebitSummaryHTML += " card (Card details below)";
        document.write(cardDebitSummaryHTML);
      </script>
    </div>
```

We use the `getTotalIncDelivery()` of the `ShoppingBasket` class to find out the amount, and the `CreditCard` class to get the card name.

The final task of this page is to display a summary of the items the customer is purchasing. This summary is nearly identical to the summary when viewing the basket – the only difference is that this summary is not updateable, which is why `false` is passed as the argument to the `getBasketHTML()` method:

```
    <div id='divOrderItemsAre' class='OrderItemsAre'>
      Your Order Items Are:
    </div>

    <!-- Summary of items in order -->
    <div id='divBasketSummary' class='BasketSummary'>
      <script language='JavaScript'>
        var orderItemsSummaryHTML = parent.myBasket.getBasketHTML(false);
        document.write(orderItemsSummaryHTML);
      </script>
    </div>
  </body>
  </html>
```

The customer clicks the *Submit Order* button and is taken to our final page for this chapter, the `OrderComplete.htm` page.

Completing The Order

Usually, we would expect that when an order is sent to the server, a whole load of behind-the-scenes processing would take place. For example, we'd update the stock database, notify someone of the items to be sent out, and deduct the money from the customer's credit card. However, as we only cover client-side technologies in this book, in this example we simply display a "thank you" page, `OrderComplete.htm`:

```
  <html>
  <head>
    <link rel='stylesheet' href='Web siteGlobalStyle.css'>
    <title>Order Complete</title>
  </head>
  <body onLoad='window.parent.resetShoppingApp()'>
    <h1>Order Completed Successfully</h1>
    <h4>Your order will be with you shortly</h4>
    <h4>Thanks for shopping with Images Online</h4>
    <h4><a href='ImageViewerEcom.htm'>Home Page</a></h4>
  </body>
  </html>
```

The `onload` event handler calls a function in the top frame, `resetShoppingApp()`. This clears the shopping basket and resets the variables holding customer and credit card objects to new objects. We need to add this function to the file `ecomCode.js`:

```
function resetShoppingApp()
{
      myBasket.clearBasket();
      thisCustomer = new Customer();
         customerCreditCard = new CreditCard();
}
```

This completes all of the code changes to the e-commerce image viewer for this chapter. In the next chapter we'll take the final step of looking at form validation and applying that to our application.

Summary

In this chapter, we've looked at how we can store data temporarily and pass it from page to page client-side. We saw two techniques for this: first placing the data in the URL, and second using JavaScript global variables in a top frame page that doesn't get unloaded.

We then looked at how we could permanently store data on the user's computer. JavaScript doesn't allow unlimited access to the user's hard drive, but it does allow us to store character data using cookies. We saw how to use cookies, and then looked at various cookie functions that made using them easy.

Finally, we made major changes to the image viewer application. We created the shopping basket and also the checkout aspects of the application using JavaScript classes, instances of which represent real-world items. In particular, a `ShoppingBasket` class models the shopping basket of the real world, a `Customer` class represents a customer, and a `CreditCard` class represents the customer's credit card.

In the next and final chapter, we'll be looking at advanced form validation techniques and applying those to the checkout of the image viewer application.

10

- Form information validation
- Form validation code library
- E-commerce application: Part 3

Author: Paul Wilton

Data Validation Techniques

There are many ways for a user to provide information to a web application. It is most commonly achieved via forms, but also through prompt boxes and via DHTML techniques. Sometimes users will deliberately enter incorrect information, but most of the time, if the data is wrong in some way, it's an honest mistake on their part. Perhaps they do not understand what data needs to be entered or what format to enter it in. While we can go to some lengths to make this clear within our HTML pages, we still need some technique for checking the validity of the data they enter. It's much more user friendly if we let them know what's wrong at the time the problem occurs, rather than on another page, or (even worse) not at all. In this chapter, we'll be looking at how we can validate information entered by the user and let them know right away if something is amiss.

Throughout the chapter, we'll create a special validation class, adding methods that check various types of data as we go. We'll be able to check the validity of simple numbers and strings, right through to more complex data, such as credit card details and postal or zip codes. We'll then extend the class for use with the e-commerce image viewer. In particular, we'll see how we can automate form checking, so that a large form can be checked with just a few lines of code via method calls.

Validation of Different Types of Information

In this section, we'll be building up our JavaScript `Validate` class, adding methods to check various different types of data. We'll start with basic data checking, for example checking that a string only contains letters of the alphabet, and not numbers and punctuation. We'll then move on to more complex examples, such as e-mail addresses and credit card details.

Note, however, that there is only so much we can check client-side. For example, we can check that the format of an e-mail address is valid, but we can't check that someone has actually set up and is using the address. We could perhaps perform more stringent checks with server-side processing, but our client-side checks do help reduce the need for server-side processing since many of the errors are spotted and dealt with client-side. It's also more user-friendly if we can warn the user of errors right away, rather than making them wait for server processing and page loads.

Before we start looking at the individual data-checking methods, we need to create our class constructor, and add it to the currently empty `Validate.js` file we created in Chapter 8 for our e-commerce application:

```
function Validate() {}
```

Although it doesn't do much, we need it for our class to work.

We'll go on in the following sections to look at many methods that we'll add to the class using the `prototype` property we have used in earlier classes – if the class doesn't contain the validation method you want, it will be very easy to create and add it to the `Validate.js` file yourself.

Most of our checking will involve regular expressions – these make checking for patterns of characters very easy. All of the methods take at least one parameter, which is the data to be validated. They also all return a Boolean value, which is either `true` if the data was valid or `false` if invalid.

Validating Characters

Our first set of methods looks at the validation of sequences of letters, numbers, and spaces.

Letters of the Alphabet, Numbers, and Spaces Only

As with all the methods we give here, add this to the `Validate.js` file:

```
Validate.prototype.isOnlyAlphaNumeric = function(string)
{
  var invalidCharactersRegExp = /[^a-z\d ]/i;
  var isValid = !(invalidCharactersRegExp.test(string));

  return isValid;
}
```

On the first line, we create a new regular expression object containing the regular expression:

```
/[^a-z\d ]/i
```

This regular expression specifies the characters that are invalid in our string. The ^ character says, "not one of the characters in the square brackets", that is not a letter of the alphabet (`a-z`) or a digit (`\d`) or a space (note the space just before the closing square bracket). We have set the case insensitive flag, `i`, at the end, so that neither uppercase nor lowercase letters of the alphabet are matched by the expression.

We then test to see if any invalid characters are found in our string:

```
var isValid = !(invalidCharactersRegExp.test(string));
```

If the `string` parameter's value contains one of the invalid characters specified by the regular expression, then `invalidCharactersRegExp.test(string)` returns `true` (since one of the invalid characters has been found). However, we want the `isValid` variable to contain `true` if the string was valid, that is if no invalid characters were found, so we reverse the result of `invalidCharactersRegExp.test(string)` using the `!` character. Now, if invalid characters are found, `invalidCharactersRegExp.test(string)` returns `true`, which `!` reverses, so that `isValid` contains `false`.

On the final line, we return the Boolean value contained in `isValid`.

Note that this method simply checks that characters other than letters, numbers, and spaces don't appear in the string. In particular, an empty string doesn't contain these characters, so will pass this test. Also, a string that contains just spaces, such as "   ", doesn't contain any of these characters, so it will also pass this test. It may be that a more stringent test than this is needed for your data.

Letters of the Alphabet and Numbers Only

As you'll see, this method is nearly identical to that described above:

```
Validate.prototype.isOnlyAlphaNumericNoSpace = function(string)
{
  var invalidCharactersRegExp = /[^a-z\d]/i;
  var isValid = !(invalidCharactersRegExp.test(string));

  return isValid;
}
```

The only difference is the regular expression used:

```
/[^a-z\d]/i
```

Note that no space is specified, so now only letters and numbers are valid, not spaces. Again, this method does not specify that there must be characters in the tested string, so an empty string will pass this test.

Letters of the Alphabet and Spaces Only

Again, this method is very similar to those already seen.

```
Validate.prototype.isOnlyAlphabetic = function(string)
{
  invalidCharactersRegExp = /[^a-z ]/i;
  var isValid = !(invalidCharactersRegExp.test(string));

  return isValid;
}
```

The regular expression used is now:

```
/[^a-z ]/i
```

Since no `\d` is specified, only letters and spaces are valid, not numbers. An empty string and strings containing only spaces will pass this test.

Validating Password Characters

This method is a little different to those already looked at, although it starts in a similar way:

```
Validate.prototype.isValidPasswordCharacters = function(password)
{
  var invalidCharactersRegExp = /[^a-z\d]/i;
```

```
    var isValid = !(invalidCharactersRegExp.test(password));
    if (isValid)
    {
      isValid = (password.length >= 8 && password.length <= 16);
    }

    return isValid;
  }
```

This time, we specify the regular expression as:

```
/[^a-z\d]/i
```

Anything that is not a letter of the alphabet character or a number is invalid, meaning that a password should only be made up of these characters. If you need to check for passwords that can contain other characters, you would need to alter this regular expression.

As in earlier methods, we test for invalid characters:

```
var isValid = !(invalidCharactersRegExp.test(password));
```

However, we now go further and also check the length of the string in the parameter `password`:

```
if (isValid)
{
  isValid = (password.length >= 8 && password.length <= 16);
}
```

Even if a password contains valid characters, it will only be valid if it has a specified length. Here, we say it must be at least eight but no more than sixteen characters in length. It's quite common to specify that passwords should be more than just a few characters if they are to be secure, and we may not want to have to store passwords over a certain length. If the length parameters don't suit us, then it's easy enough to modify the method.

Validating Numbers

In this section, we look at various methods for validating different types of numbers. These techniques are a little different to the methods we have seen so far – rather than just checking that a string doesn't contain specific characters, we check whether or not it has a specific format.

Positive Numbers Only

We start with a method to check that the passed string contains only positive numbers, such as 4, 7654, and 74.743.

```
Validate.prototype.isOnlyNumeric = function(string)
{
  var validFormatRegExp = /^\d*(\.\d+)?$/;
  var isValid = validFormatRegExp.test(string);

  return isValid;
}
```

First we define our regular expression that specifies the correct format for the string:

```
/^\d*(\.\d+)?$/
```

The surrounding `^` and `$` characters mean that the expression must appear at the beginning and the end of the string. In real terms, this means that the expression must match the whole string – the string cannot contain any other characters.

Then, `\d*` means that the pattern must start with zero or more digits. `(\.\d+)?` means that this may optionally be followed by a pattern containing a dot and one or more digits. Note that the dot is preceded by a `\` since it is a special character in regular expression syntax, so we need to tell JavaScript that we mean a real dot.

Note that patterns such as 04.500 match this regular expression, though we may not wish to allow numbers of that format.

We then test our string against this regular expression. If our string contains a pattern that matches the regular expression, the `isValid` variable will be set to `true`; otherwise it will be set to `false`. `isValid` is then returned by the method.

As with all methods so far, an empty string will match this pattern – we can use this method to test for non-compulsory data.

Integer Numbers Only

Our next method checks for integers, that is a number with no floating point part.

```
Validate.prototype.isValidInteger = function(string)
{
  var validFormatRegExp = /^((\+|-)\d)?\d*$/;
  var isValid = validFormatRegExp.test(string);

  return isValid;
}
```

This is similar to the method above, except that the decimal point is now invalid and we do allow a positive or negative sign:

```
/^((\+|-)\d)?\d*$/
```

This regular expression specifies that the string may optionally start with a + or - sign, but if it does, this must be followed by at least one digit. This is followed by zero or more digits. The `^` and `$` characters again make sure that no other characters are allowed before or after the pattern.

Examples of valid strings are +123, 234, 0, and -2445234. Invalid strings include ++123, ABC, 1.23, and 1234ABC.

Note that strings such as -0, and 0054 match this regular expression, though we may not want strings in this format.

As in the *Positive Numbers Only* method, we test our string against the regular expression, and return the variable `isValid`, which contains the result of this test.

Note that we could have written the regular expression as `/^(\+|-)?\d+$/`. However, this would not match an empty string – this is something we want to match, so that this method can be used to check for non-compulsory data.

Floating Point Numbers Only

Next we check for positive or negative floating point numbers, that is numbers that may contain a decimal point.

```
Validate.prototype.isValidFloatingPoint = function(string)
{
  var validFormatRegExp = /^((\+|-)\d)?\d*(\.\d+)?$/;
  var isValid = validFormatRegExp.test(string);

  return isValid;
}
```

This time the regular expression specifies that digits, minus signs and decimal points are allowed:

```
/^((\+|-)\d)?\d*(\.\d+)?$/
```

The ^ and $ characters again specify that our pattern must match the whole string we test it against.

The pattern `((\+|-)\d)?` specifies that the pattern can start with a + or a -, and that if it does, it must be followed by a digit – this is to prevent + alone being valid. It does however mean that +.5 is not valid, thought +0.5 will be.

Next we specify that zero or more digits can follow using the `\d*`. Finally we have `(\.\d+)?`, which optionally matches a decimal point and any numbers following it.

Note that, as with all the methods we have seen so far, an empty string is valid. The methods don't make the entering of data compulsory, but rather confirm that data if entered is of a valid type.

Validating the Age of a Person

Our next method checks that the specified value is logical for the type of data supplied, in this case the age of a person.

```
Validate.prototype.isValidAge = function(age)
{
  var isValid = false;
  if (this.isInteger(age))
  {
    isValid = (parseInt(age) >= 0 && parseInt(age) < 140)
  }

  return isValid;
}
```

This is similar to our password-validating function in that we not only check that the characters are valid, but also that the data is within a certain range.

First we use the `isInteger()` method to check that we have integer data:

```
if (this.isInteger(age))
```

If it does, then inside the `if` statement we check that the age is within the range 0 to 140. If some medical miracle changes human life expectancy, then we would need to update our code, but otherwise it seems a reasonable range.

Finally we return `isValid`, which returns `true` if the passed `age` parameter is a valid age.

Validating a Telephone Number

So far the data being checked has been fairly simple. However, telephone numbers are much more of a challenge to validate. The problems are:

- Phone numbers differ from country to country
- There are different ways of entering a valid number, for example adding the international code or not

One way to make it clear what we expect in terms of the format of the telephone number is to split the telephone number input into separate boxes, for example one box labeled for the international dialing code, one for the area code, one for the number itself and finally one for the extension number, if applicable.

Another alternative, which we look at here, is to use regular expressions to match variations of international phone numbers. For example, any of the following are valid:

- +1 (123) 123 4567
- 02312 345 5467 56
- +44 (123) 123 4567
- +44 (123) 123 4567 ext 123
- +44 (20) 789 4567

You can find out more information on world telephone numbering systems at *http://phonebooth.interocitor.net/wtng/*.

The variations our regular expression needs to deal with (optionally separated by spaces) are:

- The international number – a + followed by 1 to 3 digits (optional)
- The local area code – 2 to 5 digits, sometimes in parentheses (compulsory)
- The actual subscriber number – 3 to 10 digits, sometimes with a space after the first 3 (compulsory)

* An extension number – 2 to 5 digits, preceded by x, ext, xtn, extn, or extension (optional)

Obviously there will be countries where this won't work – this is something we'd need to deal with based on where we hoped the web site would be used from.

OK, let's create the method with these needs:

```
Validate.prototype.isValidTelephoneNum = function(telephoneNum)
{
  var validFormatRegExp = /^(\+\d{1,3} ?)?(\(\d{1,5}\)|\d{1,5}) ?\d{3} ?\d{0,7}
                          ( ?(x|xtn|ext|extn|extension)?\.? ?\d{1,5})?$/i
  var isValid = validFormatRegExp.test(telephoneNum);

  return isValid;
}
```

So far the regular expressions for checking validity have been fairly simple, so the one in this method comes as a bit of a shock:

```
/^(\+\d{1,3} ?)?(\(\d{1,5}\)|\d{1,5}) ?\d{3} ?\d{0,7}
( ?(x|xtn|ext|extn|extension)?\.? ?\d{1,5})?$/i
```

Although it looks nightmarishly long and complex, if we break it down it's not so bad at all. (In fact, it's so long that the width of this book results in it being split – make sure you type it in on one line.)

We'll start with the pattern that matches an international dialing code:

```
(\+\d{1,3} ?)?
```

So far we're matching a plus sign (`\+`) followed by 1 to 3 digits (`\d{1,3}`) and an optional space (` ?`). Note that, since the + character is a special character with a special meaning in regular expression syntax, we add a \ character in front of it to specify that we mean an actual + character. The characters are wrapped inside parentheses to specify a group of characters. We match this group of characters zero or one times – as indicated by the `?` character after the closing parenthesis of the group.

Next we have a pattern that will match the area code:

```
(\(\d{1,5}\)|\d{1,5})
```

This pattern is contained in parentheses, which designate it as a group of characters, and matches either 1 to 5 digits in parentheses (`\(\d{1,5}\)`) or just 1 to 5 digits (`\d{1,5}`). Again, since the parentheses characters are special characters in regular expression syntax and we want to match actual parentheses, we need the \ character in front of them. Also note the use of the pipe symbol (|) which means "OR" or "match either of these two patterns".

Next we match the subscriber number.

```
 ?\d{3} ?\d{0,7}
```

Note that there is a space before the first `?` – this space and question mark mean "match zero or one space". This is followed by three digits (`\d{3}`), another "zero or one space", and finally between zero and seven digits (`\d{0,7}`).

Finally we add the part to cope with an optional extension number:

```
( ?(x|xtn|ext|extn|extension)?\.? ?\d{1,5})?
```

This group is optional, since its parentheses are followed by a question mark. The group itself checks for an optional space, optionally followed by one of `x`, `ext`, `xtn`, `extn`, and `extension`, followed by zero or one dots (note the `\` character, since `.` is a special character in regular expression syntax), followed by zero or one space, followed by between one and five digits.

Putting these four patterns together, we have the whole regular expression, apart from the surrounding syntax: recall that the regular expression starts with `/^` and ends with `$/i`. The i flag indicates that the regular expression is case insensitive. The `/` characters indicate that the contained code is a regular expression. So, that just leaves the `^` and `$` characters. As we've seen previously, these mean that the string we test the regular expression against can contain no other characters before or after the pattern.

OK, that's the scary regular expression out of the way. The method that uses it should be fairly familiar by now. First, we create the regular expression object:

```
var validFormatRegExp = /^(\+\d{1,3} ?)?(\(\d{1,5}\)|\d{1,5}) ?\d{3} ?\d{0,7}
                        ( ?(x|xtn|ext|extn|extension)?\.? ?\d{1,5})?$/i
```

Then, we test our string using the regular expression:

```
var isValid = validFormatRegExp.test(telephoneNum);
```

Finally, the method returns the `isValid` variable.

Validating a Postal Code

We just about managed to check worldwide telephone numbers, but to do the same for postal codes would be something of a major challenge. Instead, we'll create a method that only checks for US Zip codes and UK post codes. If we needed to check for other countries, then the code would need modifying.

International users will obviously find being asked to provide a postal code, and subsequently being told that their code is invalid, very annoying. Only use this validation code if you are sure it will not cause problems to the user.

Again, it's important to note that this method only checks that the postal code format is valid – there's no easy way client-side to check that the postal code does exist and is actually in use.

```
Validate.prototype.isValidPostalCode = function(postalCode)
{
  var validFormat = /^(\d{5}(-\d{4})?|[a-z][a-z]?\d\d? ?\d[a-z][a-z])$/i
  var isValid = validFormat.test(postalCode);
  return isValid;
}
```

The method is much the same as those we have already seen, so we'll start by looking at the regular expression:

```
/^(\d{5}(-\d{4})?|[a-z][a-z]?\d\d? ?\d[a-z][a-z])$/i
```

This is actually in two parts: the first part checks for zip codes and the second part checks UK post codes. We'll start by looking at the zip code part.

Zip codes can be in one of two formats – either five digits (12345), or five digits followed by a dash and four digits (12345-1234)

The zip code regular expression to match these is this:

```
\d{5}(-\d{4})?
```

This matches five digits, followed by an optional group that matches a dash followed by four digits.

For a regular expression that covers UK post codes, let's consider their various formats. UK post code formats are one or two letters, followed by either one or two digits, followed by an optional space, followed by a digit, and then two letters. Valid examples include: CH3 9DR, PR29 1XX, and C27 3AH.

Based on this, our pattern is:

```
[a-z][a-z]?\d\d? ?\d[a-z][a-z]
```

The two patterns that match zip codes and post codes are combined using the | character to mean "match one or the other" and grouped using parentheses:

```
(\d{5}(-\d{4})?|[a-z][a-z]?\d\d? ?\d[a-z][a-z])
```

We then add the ^ character at the start and $ character at the end of the pattern to be sure that the only information in the string is the postal code, and surround the string by the regular expression delimiter character /. Although postal codes should be uppercase, it is still valid for them to be lowercase, so we have also set the case-insensitive flag i:

```
/^(\d{5}(-\d{4})?|[a-z][a-z]?\d\d? ?\d[a-z][a-z])$/i
```

The remainder of the method uses this regular expression to test that the format of the characters in the data matches the valid format of a postal code:

```
var isValid = validFormat.test(postalCode);
```

Validating an E-mail Address

Before we start working on a regular expression to match e-mail addresses, we need to look at the types of valid e-mail addresses we can possibly have:

- someone@mailserver.com

- someone@mailserver.info
- someone@mailserver.ca
- someone@mailserver.co.uk
- someone@mailserver.org.uk
- someone@mailserver.win.net
- someone.something@mailserver.com
- someone@subdomain.mailserver.com
- someone.something@subdomain.mailserver.com

That's quite a list and a lot of variations we need to cope with. The method to do that is shown below:

```
Validate.prototype.isValidEmail = function(email)
{
  var validFormatRegExp =
    /^\w(\.?\w)*@\w(\.?[-\w])*\.[a-z]{2,4}$/i;
  var isValid = validFormatRegExp.test(email);

  return isValid;
}
```

We can see that it's yet another complicated regular expression:

```
/^\w(\.?\w)*@\w(\.?[-\w])*\.[a-z]{2,4}$/i
```

Again, this wasn't built in one go but in stages, so let's break it down and discuss it in more manageable bites.

First, let's deal with the part of the address up to and including the `@` symbol. All e-mail addresses start with one or more of the `\w` class of characters – these are all letters, all digits, and the underscore character (_). So we start our pattern with this:

```
\w
```

Following this, we can have any sequence of \w characters, dashes, and dots. However, we can't have two dots in a row – each dot must always be followed by either a \w or a dash character. The pattern \.?[\w-] matches any \w or dash character, or a dot followed by any \w or dash character (recall that the dot is a special symbol in regular expression syntax and so needs to be preceded by a \, and that a question mark means that the preceding symbol is optional). We add zero or more of this pattern onto our regular expression (indicated by the * character), followed by the compulsory @ symbol:

```
\w(\.?[\w-])*@
```

Dealing with the part after the `@` is a little easier, because we already have some of the code written. After the `@` part of the address, we want to match "mailserver" or "subdomain.mailserver", which is the same as "someone" and "someone.something" that we have matched previously. So we can make our regular expression:

\w(\.?[\w-])*@\w(\.?[\w-])*

Now we need to add support for the end of the e-mail address. This combination of dots and letters varies enormously, from a dot followed by between two and four letters, to a dot, two to four letters, another dot, and another two to four letters. Of course, this changes all the time as new suffixes are ratified. Here, we will just check for a dot followed by between two and four letters – any other dots and letters will be covered by the previous `\w(\.?[\w-])*` pattern.

```
\.[a-z]{2,4}
```

So, our full pattern is:

```
\w(\.?[\w-])*@\w(\.?[\w-])*\.[a-z]{2,4}
```

We still need to make sure that there is only an e-mail address in the string and nothing else. Currently, something like "!!!!someone.something@domain.com!!!!!!" would be valid.

We need to add the `^` character to specify that the pattern should be at the beginning of the string and the `$` character to specify that the pattern should be at the end of the string, as well as the `/` characters to delimit the regular expression:

```
/^\w(\.?[\w-])*@\w(\.?[\w-])*\.[a-z]{2,4}$/i
```

As case does not affect the validity, we've added an `i` flag to make it case insensitive too.

After creating the regular expression, the remainder of our method is fairly easy. We test to see whether the format is valid, and then return the result. Although the regular expression matches virtually all of the combinations currently available, as new domain top level names and variations are created, we may need to update our regular expression to match them.

Validating Dates

In this section, we look at validating dates. We first look at simple dates, and then dates specific to a particular type of data such as date of birth or credit card expiry dates.

Validating a Date

The method to validate a date takes three parameters: day of the month, the month name, and a four-digit year. The month name can be the shortened 3-letter version or the full name.

We could have created a method that accepted the month number (`0-11`), but this can be problematic because of differences in how countries specify the date. For example in the US, we usually say "month day year", whereas in the UK "day month year" is more common. Using a number for the month may lead to unexpected dates being set, where the month is treated as the day.

```
Validate.prototype.isValidDate = function(day, month, year)
{
  var isValid = true;
```

```
    var enteredDate = new Date(day + " " + month + " " + year);
    if (enteredDate.getDate() != day)
    {
      isValid = false;
    }

    return isValid;
  }
```

This method checks that the supplied day, month, and year are a valid combination. For example, it checks that the date is not the 32nd of January or the 29th of February in a year that is not a leap year. The method does this by creating a new `Date` object based on the parameters supplied:

```
    var enteredDate = new Date(day + " " + month + " " + year);
```

If the date was not valid, then the `day` parameter passed and the value returned by the `Date` object's `getDate()` method will be different:

```
    if (enteredDate.getDate() != day)
    {
      isValid = false;
    }
```

In this case, `isValid` is set to the value `false` (note, it was initialized to `true` at the start of the method). `isValid` is then returned by the method.

Validating a Date of Birth

When validating a date of birth, we must first validate the date as above, and then check that the birth year is possible for someone still alive today. As before, the parameters are a date in the month, a shortened or full name of a month, and a four-digit year.

```
  Validate.prototype.isValidDateOfBirth = function(day, month, year)
  {
    var isValid = true;
    var nowDate = new Date();
    year = parseInt(year);
    var dateOfBirth = new Date(day + " " + month + " " + year);

    if (!this.isValidDate(day,month,year))
    {
      isValid = false;
    }
    else if (dateOfBirth > nowDate || (year + 140) < nowDate.getFullYear())
    {
      isValid = false;
    }

    return isValid;
  }
```

This method first creates a `Date` object with no parameters – this will be set to the current system's date. Then, as we saw in the previous method, we check that the date passed via the parameters is a valid date:

```
var nowDate = new Date();
year = parseInt(year);
var dateOfBirth =  new Date(day + " " + month + " " + year);

if (!this.isValidDate(day,month,year))
{
  isValid = false;
}
```

Next we need to check that the date of birth is one that could be valid for someone alive today. Someone claiming to have been born in 1750 has either found the secret to eternal life or has entered their date of birth incorrectly. They must also be mistaken if they claim to have been born in the future. The `else` statement checks that the date entered is not a future date (in which case the date will be greater than the current date we stored in `nowDate`) and that it's not further into the past than 140 years, on the assumption that few people live longer than 140 years:

```
else if (dateOfBirth > nowDate || (year + 140) < nowDate.getFullYear())
{
  isValid = false;
}
```

Validating a Credit Card Expiry Date

A valid credit card expiry date is a month and year combination that is not already in the past.

```
Validate.prototype.isValidCreditCardExpiry = function(expiresMonth, expiresYear)
{
  var isValid = true;
  var nowDate = new Date();
  if (expiresMonth < (nowDate.getMonth() + 1) &&
      expiresYear == nowDate.getFullYear())
  {
    isValid = false;
  }
  else if (expiresYear < nowDate.getFullYear())
  {
    isValid = false;
  }

  return isValid;
}
```

This method takes two parameters, the card's two-digit expiry month (01 for January, up to 12 for December) and a four-digit expiry year. We need to check that one of the following two conditions hold:

- The expiry year is the current year, and the expiry month is later in the year than the current month
- The expiry year is greater than the current year.

If today's date is June 2003, then 05/2003 is invalid, but 06/2003, 10/2003 and 01/2004 are valid.

The first `if` statement checks whether the expiry month is before the current month in the current year:

```
if (expiresMonth < (nowDate.getMonth() + 1) &&
    expiresYear == nowDate.getFullYear())
{
  isValid = false;
}
```

Then the `else if` statement checks whether the expiry year is prior to the current year:

```
else if (expiresYear < nowDate.getFullYear())
{
  isValid = false;
}
```

If either of the `if` statements' conditions are `true`, then `isValid` is set to `false`.

Validating a Credit Card Number

Our final validation method checks whether a credit card number could be a valid card number. Note that I say "could be" rather than "is" – just because the number is valid, doesn't mean that the card has been allocated or that it has not been canceled, if it was allocated. Only server-side processing can possibly validate a card number. However, what we can do here is check that the user hasn't made an accidental mistake so that we can get them to rectify any mistakes before we attempt server-side checks.

As we'll see shortly, validating a credit card is much more complex than any of the validation methods we have created so far. There are three checks we can perform client-side:

- Check that only numbers or spaces are given in the credit card number – not letters or other characters.
- Check that, for the given card type, the number of digits given is valid and the prefix to the number is valid.
- Use the Luhn formula to check the validity of the entered credit card number. This is a special algorithm that can be applied to most credit card numbers to check that the number would be valid.

We'll be using all three of these checks in our method.

```
Validate.prototype.isValidCreditCardNumber = function(cardNumber, cardType)
{
  var isValid = false;
  var ccCheckRegExp = /[^\d ]/;
  isValid = !ccCheckRegExp.test(cardNumber);

  if (isValid)
  {
```

```
      var cardNumbersOnly = cardNumber.replace(/ /g,"");
      var cardNumberLength = cardNumbersOnly.length;
      var lengthIsValid = false;
      var prefixIsValid = false;
      var prefixRegExp;

      switch(cardType)
      {
        case "mastercard":
          lengthIsValid = (cardNumberLength == 16);
          prefixRegExp = /^5[1-5]/;
          break;

        case "visa":
          lengthIsValid = (cardNumberLength == 16 || cardNumberLength == 13);
          prefixRegExp = /^4/;
          break;

        case "amex":
          lengthIsValid = (cardNumberLength == 15);
          prefixRegExp = /^3(4|7)/;
          break;

        default:
          prefixRegExp = /^$/;
          alert("Card type not found");
      }

      prefixIsValid = prefixRegExp.test(cardNumbersOnly);
      isValid = prefixIsValid && lengthIsValid;
    }

    if (isValid)
    {
      var numberProduct;
      var numberProductDigitIndex;
      var checkSumTotal = 0;

      for (digitCounter = cardNumberLength - 1;
        digitCounter > 0;
        digitCounter--)
      {
        checkSumTotal += parseInt (cardNumbersOnly.charAt(digitCounter));
        digitCounter--;
        numberProduct = String((cardNumbersOnly.charAt(digitCounter) * 2));
        for (var productDigitCounter = 0;
          productDigitCounter < numberProduct.length;
          productDigitCounter++)
        {
          checkSumTotal +=
            parseInt(numberProduct.charAt(productDigitCounter));
        }
      }

      isValid = (checkSumTotal % 10 == 0);
    }

    return isValid;
  }
```

We'll take this method step by step. Note first of all, that the method takes two parameters – the card number and the card type (`mastercard`, `amex`, and `visa` are valid card types that we will cater for here, though the method could be extended for other card types).

The first part of the method checks that only numbers or spaces have been entered:

```
var isValid = false;
var ccCheckRegExp = /[^\d ]/;
isValid = !ccCheckRegExp.test(cardNumber);
```

The regular expression `/[^\d ]/` will match invalid characters (any character that is not a digit or a space). When we test the card number against the regular expression on the third line, as in previous methods, we use the `!` character to reverse the logic, so that `isValid` is set to `false` if invalid characters are found in the card number.

The next part of the method checks that the card has a valid prefix, that is it starts with the correct numbers for that card type, and contains the correct number of digits, again specific to a card type. The prefixes and lengths for some commonly available cards are shown below:

Card Type	Prefix	Number of Digits
Visa	4	13,16
Mastercard	51-55	16
American Express	34,37	15

You can find more information on card details at *http://www.beachnet.com/~hstiles/cardtype.html.*

First we strip out any spaces the user may have put in their credit card number when they entered it:

```
if (isValid)
{
  var cardNumbersOnly = cardNumber.replace(/ /g,"");
  var cardNumberLength = cardNumbersOnly.length;
  var lengthIsValid = false;
  var prefixIsValid = false;
  var prefixRegExp;
```

The `if` statement checks whether the previous validation (that the card number only contained numbers or spaces) found the number to be valid, and only proceeds with the next check if it did. Then, using a regular expression (a space between the `/` regular expression delimiters, together with the global flag `g`) and the String object's `replace()` method, we strip out the spaces.

Variable `cardNumberLength` is set to the length of the string (the number of digits in the string). The variables `lengthIsValid` and `prefixIsValid` will store Boolean values indicating the validity of the length and prefix checks that we do next.

We now need to check the `cardType` parameter of the method and, from that, decide what the prefix to the card number should be and how long the number should be.

The `switch` statement checks the card type to see which, if any, of the known card types is found:

```
switch(cardType)
{
  case "mastercard":
    lengthIsValid = (cardNumberLength == 16);
    prefixRegExp = /^5[1-5]/;
    break;

  case "visa":
    lengthIsValid = (cardNumberLength == 16 || cardNumberLength == 13);
    prefixRegExp = /^4/;
    break;

  case "amex":
    lengthIsValid = (cardNumberLength == 15);
    prefixRegExp = /^3(4|7)/;
    break;

  default:
    prefixRegExp = /^$/;
    alert("Card type not found");
}
```

In each `case` statement, we set `lengthIsValid` to the Boolean returned by the logical expression that checks for the correct card length. Then we create a regular expression that will check for the correct prefix for that card. In the `default` case, we create a regular expression that matches nothing, and warn the customer that their card type hasn't been found. If we want to allow different cards, for example diners club, then our `switch` statement simply needs an extra `case` adding to match the new type of card's parameters, that is size and start digits.

We next check the prefix using the regular expression set in the relevant `case` statement, and then set `isValid` to the results of the logical addition `prefixIsValid` AND `lengthIsValid`, which will be `true` only if both these values are `true`:

```
prefixIsValid = prefixRegExp.test(cardNumbersOnly);
isValid = prefixIsValid && lengthIsValid;
```

OK, that's the two easy checks done. Now we have the part of the method that checks the card number using the **Luhn formula**, which works with almost all card types. This special formula, also known as **Modula 10** or **Mod 10**, tells us whether the number it is applied to could be a valid number. Obviously, it doesn't guarantee that the number is actually in use, only that it could be used.

We'll walk through the basic formula, using the credit card number 4221 3456 1243 1237 as an example:

1. Start with the second digit from last in the card number. Moving backwards towards the first digit in the number, double each alternate digit.

   In our example, we would double the bold numbers in **4**2**2**1 **3**4**5**6 **1**2**4**3 **1**2**3**7 to give us:

   (4x2), (2x2), (3x2), (5x2), (1x2), (4x2), (1x2), (3x2)

   which is:

   8, 4, 6, 10, 2, 8, 2, 6

2. Take the results of the doubling, add each of the individual digits in each doubled number together, and then add to the running total.

   In our example we have:

   8 + 4 + 6 + (1 + 0) + 2 + 8 + 2 + 6 = 37

3. Add all the non-doubled digits from the credit card number together

   In our example we have:

   2 + 1 + 4 + 6 + 2 + 3 + 2 + 7 = 27

4. Add the values calculated in step 2 and step 3 together.

   In our example:

   37 + 27 = 64

5. Take the value calculated in step 4 and calculate the remainder when it is divided by 10. If the remainder is zero, then it's a valid number, otherwise it's invalid.

   In our example:

   64 / 10 = 6 with remainder 4.

   So, our example number is not a valid card number, as the remainder is not 0.

Now we understand how it works, let's look at the code in our method that uses it.

First we check if `isValid` is `true` (that is, if all other checks so far proved satisfactory). Then, after our variable declarations, we have the main `for` loop that will go through the credit card number a digit at a time starting with the last digit and moving to the first.

```
if (isValid)
{
  var numberProduct;
  var numberProductDigitIndex;
  var checkSumTotal = 0;

  for (digitCounter = cardNumberLength - 1;
    digitCounter > 0;
    digitCounter--)
  {
```

In this `for` loop we do a number of things. Firstly we add a digit's value to the running total, `checkSumTotal`.

```
    checkSumTotal += parseInt (cardNumbersOnly.charAt(digitCounter));
```

Then we move to the digit that is one nearer the start of the card number string. We multiply this next digit by 2.

```
digitCounter--;
numberProduct = String((cardNumbersOnly.charAt(digitCounter) * 2));
```

We take the digits forming the results of the product calculation and in the inner `for` loop we add these digits to the running total.

```
for (var productDigitCounter = 0;
  productDigitCounter < numberProduct.length;
  productDigitCounter++)
{
  checkSumTotal +=
    parseInt(numberProduct.charAt(productDigitCounter));
}
```

Our outer `for` loop continues by moving to the next digit to the left, and iterates until we reach the first digit in the credit card number string.

If we think back to the explanation of the Luhn formula, our approach is out of step in that we are not doing step 1, then step 2, and so on, but instead are merging steps 1 – 4 and processing the number on a digit by digit basis, keeping a running total. It amounts to exactly the same thing, but reduces the number of loops required.

Let's summarize the steps in our outer and inner `for` loops:

- Extract the character whose position is specified by `digitCounter`, from the string in `cardNumbersOnly`.
- Add this number to our running total, which is kept in variable `checkSumTotal`.
- Decrement the character counter, `digitCounter`. This now refers to the next digit to the left in our string `cardNumbersOnly`.
- Extract the next digit, convert it to a number, and then double it. This is all done on one line and this product is stored in variable `numberProduct`.
- Convert the product calculated in step 4 to a string.
- Loop through each digit in the product string, convert it to an integer, and add to the running total. This is our inner `for` loop. For example, if the character extracted in step 4 was 8, its product would be 16, and so we'd add 1 and then 6 to our running total.
- Decrement the `digitCounter` and move to step 1.

In the table below, we show what digits are extracted and what values added to the running total for the example card number 4221 3456 1243 1287.

Character Extracted	What happens to it	What happens to running total	Running total Value
7	Added to running total	Running total (0) + character extracted (7)	7
8	Doubled (16), then each digit in the product added to running total	Running total (7) + first digit in product (1) + second digit in product (6)	14
2	Added to running total	Running total (14) + character extracted (2)	16
1	Doubled (2), then each digit in the product added to running total	Running total (16) + first digit in product (2)	18
3	Added to running total	Running total (18) + character extracted (3)	21
4	Doubled (8), then each digit in the product added to running total	Running total (21) + first digit in product (8)	29
2	Added to running total	Running total (29) + character extracted (2)	31
1	Doubled (2), then each digit in the product added to running total	Running total (31) + first digit in product (2)	33
6	Added to running total	Running total (33) + character extracted (6)	39
5	Doubled (10), then each digit in the product added to running total	Running total (39) + first digit in product (1) + second digit in product(0)	40
4	Added to running total	Running total (40) + character extracted (4)	44
3	Doubled (6), then each digit in the product added to running total	Running total (44) + first digit in product (6)	50
1	Added to running total	Running total (50) + character extracted (1)	51
2	Doubled (4), then each digit in the product added to running total	Running total (51) + first digit in product (4)	55
2	Added to running total	Running total (55) + character extracted (2)	57
4	Doubled (8), then each digit in the product added to running total	Running total (57) + first digit in product (8)	65

Once we have our result, in the table above that's 65, we then find its modulus 10 value, that is the remainder left over when the running total is divided by ten. If it's zero, we have ourselves a valid credit card number, otherwise it's a fake. We set `isValid` to the result of the Boolean expression comparing the remainder to zero – if `true` it's valid, if `false` it's invalid. In our example, we have 65, the modulus 10 value of which is 5, so the example number is invalid – you didn't really think I'd give my credit card number out now did you?

Image Viewer E-commerce Application – Part 3

It's time to complete the image viewer's conversion to an e-commerce application. So far we have everything working, except the validation of the form fields when the user enters data in the checkout part of the application. If we enter "Donald Duck" as our credit card number, the application happily accepts it. In this final section, we rectify that and make use of our `Validate` class to validate our forms.

However, we'll be doing more than just using the `Validate` class – in the next section we extend its capabilities to make it easier to use.

Adding Automatic Form Validation

Writing code to check each input box or radio button in a form can be quite tedious. It would be great if we could just somehow say, "this input box must contain a valid e-mail address and must be filled in, this input box can contain any text, and one of these radio buttons must be selected", so that our code automatically knew what validation technique to use for each form element. For some of the image viewer application's textbox and radio controls, we are going to extend the `Validate` class and add a way of doing this.

First, we need to decide on a way of letting our code know what sort of data a form element should contain. For example, in the case of a radio button, we simply want to specify that one of the radio buttons in the group must be selected. To achieve this in a cross-browser compatible way, we'll be using the `name` attribute of the form element to specify:

- Whether the form element is compulsory, that is the user must have entered or selected a value.
- What sort of data a form element should contain. This applies to textboxes only, since radio buttons already have values set.

Let's look at an example `<input>` element:

```
<input name="txtFullName_Compulsory_alphabetic" maxlength="150" class="TextBox" >
```

Look at the `name` given to the element, and note that as well as the usual form element name there is also:

```
_Compulsory_alphabetic
```

This has specified that the element is compulsory (some value must be entered) and that the value must contain only alphabetic characters. We'll see what other data types we can use shortly.

If we want a form element to be compulsory *and* specify the data type, then we just add them one after the other, as in the above example: `_Compulsory_alphabetic`. We need to make sure we get the order correct, that is first specify if the element is compulsory and then specify the type of data: `_alphabetic_Compulsory` is not valid.

If we don't need a form element to be compulsory, but any data entered must be of a valid alphabetic type, we would write `_NotCompulsory_alphabetic`. Note this won't work with data types where the format is important as well as the characters entered, so it will work with an alphabetic check, but not a post code check. This is because the non-format checking validation methods allow empty strings to be valid. The format specific methods don't allow an empty string to be valid, and so are always compulsory.

If we don't want a form element to be part of the automatic validation process, then we simply leave off both the compulsory and data type parts of the name string so that it will be ignored.

We can also add `_Compulsory` to radio button groups where we want to ensure that the user has selected one of the buttons. However, as we set their value ourselves, we don't check radio button groups for data type validity.

The variations possible are summarized below:

Action	**Postfix For Name Value**	**Example**
Don't validate at all	nothing	`name="MyElementsName"`
Check the element has been filled in, but don't check the data type	`_Compulsory`	`name="MyElementsName_Compulsory"`
Check the type of the data, if any, but the data is not compulsory	`_NotCompulsory_datatype`	`name="MyElementsName_NotCompulsory_alphabetic"`
Check that the element has been filled in and check the type of the data	`_Compulsory_datatype`	`name="MyElementsName_Compulsory_alphabetic"`

The range of data types that can be checked is determined by the data validation methods in our `Validate` class. The full list of possible data types is shown in the table below:

Identifier	**Method of Validate class Used**	**Can use with _NotCompulsory?**
`_alphanumeric`	`isOnlyAlphaNumeric()`	yes
`_alphanumericnospace`	`isOnlyAlphaNumericNoSpace()`	yes

Table continued on following page

Identifier	Method of Validate class Used	Can use with _NotCompulsory?
_alphabetic	isOnlyAlphabetic()	yes
_numeric	isOnlyNumeric()	yes
_integer	isValidInteger()	yes
_floatingpoint	isValidFloatingPoint()	yes
_age	isValidAge()	no
_password	isValidPassword()	no
_telephone	isValidTelephoneNum()	no
_postcode	isValidPostalCode()	no
_email	isValidEmail()	no

Looking at the table, we can see certain types of data are not listed. For example, there is no identifier for validating dates, credit card expiry dates, or credit card numbers. This is because those data types usually rely on more than one form element. For example, with a credit card number, the validity of the number depends on the card type entered as well as the card number entered. To avoid making things too complex, we have not attempted to check data that is dependent on more than one form element.

OK, so we have a way of checking if the data entered is valid, but how do we notify the user? Well, the easy option would be a series of alerts for each form element the user has not filled in correctly. However, as we mentioned in Chapter 8, this can be annoying to the user, so we adopt a different technique. Next to each form element is a hidden `<div>` element, which we fill with an appropriate error message in red. For example:

E-mail Address: [ ] Please enter a valid e-mail address

Here, no e-mail address was entered, so when the user clicked *Continue*, the form checking spotted the mistake and displayed the error message `<div>`. However, how will our code know the name of the appropriate `<div>`? The easiest cross-browser way of doing this is to have a naming convention.

In our naming convention, the name of the form element itself must start with a three-letter identifier, such as `txt` for a textbox, `pwd` for a password element or `cbo` for a drop-down combo box. You can use whatever identifiers you like as long as they are three characters long and at the start of the name. Recall that the name may also end with the compulsory and datatype identifiers described above.

To be able to find the appropriate `<div>` for each form element, we say that the `id` of the error `<div>` must contain the name of the associated form element, but without the three-letter identifier, the compulsory and datatype identifier, and with the word `Error` added at the end. Based on the form element example above, where our element has the name `txtFullName_Compulsory_alphabetic`, the error `<div>` would have an `id` value of `FullNameError`.

An example of an <input> element and its associated error <div> taken from the *PersonalDetails.htm* page of our application is shown below:

```
<div>
  Full Name :
  <br>
  <input name="txtFullName_Compulsory_alphabetic" maxlength="150" class="TextBox">
  <div id="FullNameError" name="FullNameError" class="FormElementError">
    Please enter your full name
  </div>
</DIV>
```

We may not want to position elements on the page absolutely, so the form element and the error displaying <div> are both wrapped inside an outer <div> that acts as a container. We can then specify the position of the error <div> relative to the outer container <div>, but don't need to make the outer <div> absolutely or relatively positioned.

Now we have an idea of how it works, let's create the code we need.

Automatic Checking of Text Boxes and Radio Button Groups

The code to do the automatic checking is split into six methods:

Method	Purpose
`checkFormValid()`	This is the main method we use to start the checking
`isTextElementValid()`	Used by `checkFormValid()` to check text elements
`isElementDataValid()`	Used by `isTextElementValid()` to check data type is valid
`isOneRadioButtonInGroupSelected()`	Used by `checkFormValid()` to check one radio button in a group is selected
`showErrorDiv()`	Displays an error <div>
`hideErrorDiv()`	Hides an error <div>

Let's look at each of these methods in turn, adding them to the *Validate.js* file we started earlier in this chapter.

checkFormValid() Method

This is the key method as far as automatically validating a form goes. This method will go through the form, which is passed as its first parameter, and look at each form element in turn. If the form element is either a textbox or a radio button, then the method checks to see if a value should have been entered. Additionally, in the case of a textbox, it checks what type of data that value should be. If an error is found, then the error <div> is displayed for that element.

```
Validate.prototype.checkFormValid = function(theForm, theDocument)
{
  var isWholeFormValid = true;
  var isValid = true;
  var theElement;
  var isToBeValidatedElementRegExp = /(_Compulsory)|(_NotCompulsory)/i;
  var isCompulsoryRegExp = /(_Compulsory)/i;
  var validDataTypeRegExp = /_[a-zA-Z]+$/i;
  var invalidDataType;
  var elementName;
  var errorDivId;
  var isCompulsoryElement;
  var isToBeCheckedElement;
  var isTextBoxElement;

  // Check textboxes completed and/or correct data type
  for (var formElementCounter = 0; formElementCounter < theForm.length;
       formElementCounter++)
  {
    theElement = theForm.elements[formElementCounter];
    elementName = theElement.name;

    isCompulsoryElement = isCompulsoryRegExp.test(elementName);
    isToBeValidatedElement = isToBeValidatedElementRegExp.test(elementName);

    if (isToBeValidatedElement)
    {
      errorDivId = theElement.name;
      errorDivId = errorDivId.slice(3,errorDivId.indexOf("_")) + "Error";
      this.hideErrorDiv(errorDivId, theDocument);

      isTextBoxElement =  theElement.type == "text" ||
                          theElement.type == "password" ||
                          theElement.type == "file";

      if ( isTextBoxElement )
      {
        isValid = this.isTextElementValid(theElement,
                                          validDataTypeRegExp,
                                          isCompulsoryElement);

        if ( !isValid )
        {
          this.showErrorDiv(errorDivId,theDocument);
          isWholeFormValid = false;
        }
      }

      //Check compulsory radio buttons completed
      else if (theElement.type == "radio")
      {
        if (isCompulsoryElement)
        {
          elementName = theElement.name;
```

```
          theElement = theForm.elements[theElement.name];
          isValid = this.isOneRadioButtonInGroupSelected(theElement);

          if (isValid == false)
          {
            this.showErrorDiv(errorDivId,theDocument);
            isWholeFormValid = false;
          }

          do
          {
            formElementCounter++;
            theElement = theForm.elements[formElementCounter];
          }
          while (theElement.name == elementName &&
            formElementCounter < theForm.length)
          formElementCounter--;
        }
      }
    }
  }

  return isWholeFormValid;
}
```

This is the key method that a web page needs to call to validate a form automatically. It has two parameters, the form to be checked and also the `document` object of the page containing the form. We'll use the `document` object to access the error `<div>` elements. At the top of the method we have our variable declarations – notice the three regular expressions which will be used later to check the names of elements to see if they need checking and what data they should contain:

```
var isWholeFormValid = true;
var isValid = true;
var theElement;
var isToBeValidatedElementRegExp = /(_Compulsory)|(_NotCompulsory)/i;
var isCompulsoryRegExp = /(_Compulsory)/i;
var validDataTypeRegExp = /_[a-zA-Z]+$/i;
var invalidDataType;
var elementName;
var errorDivId;
var isCompulsoryElement;
var isToBeCheckedElement;
var isTextBoxElement;
```

Then comes the main `for` loop that will loop through each element in the form. We start at the top of the loop by using the regular expressions we mentioned above to check whether the element is compulsory, and also whether the element needs checking at all. Remember, a compulsory element is any element with `_Compulsory` in the name and an element to be checked for any reason is one with `_Compulsory` or `_NotCompulsory` in the name.

```
for (var formElementCounter = 0; formElementCounter < theForm.length;
     formElementCounter++)
{
  theElement = theForm.elements[formElementCounter];
  elementName = theElement.name;
```

```
isCompulsoryElement = isCompulsoryRegExp.test(elementName);
isToBeValidatedElement = isToBeValidatedElementRegExp.test(elementName);
```

If we find that it is an element to be validated (`isToBeValidatedElement` is `true`), then in the `if` statement we first set `errorDivId` to the name of the associated `<div>` element with the error message inside. Remember, the error `<div>` element's `id` is the same as the name of the form element, but without the first three characters, excluding anything after the _, and with `Error` added at the end. The error `<div>` will be used to display an error message, if it turns out that the field is compulsory and has not been filled in or a data type has been specified and the field contains invalid data. We don't know yet whether the data is valid, so in the final line below we hide the error `<div>`. Why do this? Well, when the page first loads, all the error `<div>` elements will be hidden, since the stylesheet specifies this. If the user clicks *Continue* to submit the form, it's then checked and the error `<div>` elements for any invalid elements are shown. Hopefully, the user corrects the errors and tries again – in this case, we want to make sure that all previous errors are hidden. We can then recheck the form and show just those that are still in error, if any.

```
if (isToBeValidatedElement)
{
  errorDivId = theElement.name;
  errorDivId = errorDivId.slice(3,errorDivId.indexOf("_")) + "Error";
  this.hideErrorDiv(errorDivId,theDocument);
```

Next we need to decide whether the element is a text type element – this includes the textbox, password box, and file element. If it's a text element of some sort, then we first check its data validity by calling the `isTextElementValid()` method of the `Validate` class (this class). We'll see how this method works shortly. If `isValid` has not been set to `true`, then we display the error `<div>` by calling the `showErrorDiv()` method of this class (hence the `this` keyword). We also set the variable `isWholeFormValid` to `false` – this will be the value returned by the `isFormValid()` method, indicating that one or more elements had invalid data or were not completed when they should have been.

```
isTextBoxElement = theElement.type == "text" ||
                   theElement.type == "password" ||
                   theElement.type == "file";

if ( isTextBoxElement )
{
  isValid = this.isTextElementValid(theElement,
                                    validDataTypeRegExp,
                                    isCompulsoryElement);

  if ( !isValid )
  {
    this.showErrorDiv(errorDivId,theDocument);
    isWholeFormValid = false;
  }
}
```

In the `else` statement, we then check to see if this is a radio button element. If it is a radio button, then we check to see if this is a compulsory element. (This should always be the case – if a radio button is non-compulsory, it should not have `_Compulsory` or `_NonCompulsory` added to its name, and so should not fall into this loop at all. However, this check does a double check on this.) If it is compulsory, then we need to get a reference to the radio button group as a whole and not an individual element in it. We do this by getting the `name` of the element and then using that with the form's `elements` array. We pass this reference to the `isOneRadioButtonInGroupSelected()` method of this class (the `Validate` class), which will loop through the radio button group and check that one element has been selected, returning `true` if it has and `false` otherwise. In one of our previous examples in Chapter 4, we saw that getting the index of the selected radio buttons needed an iteration over an array of radio buttons, and this is exactly what this method does.

```
    else if (theElement.type == "radio")
    {
      if (isCompulsoryElement)
      {
        elementName = theElement.name;
        theElement = theForm.elements[theElement.name];
        isValid = this.isOneRadioButtonInGroupSelected(theElement);
```

If `isValid` is `false`, (no radio button was selected), then we show the applicable error `<div>` by calling the `showErrorDiv()` method of this class, passing it the `errorDivId` and the `document` of the page containing the form. As with the textbox code, we set `isWholeFormValid` to `false` – this is the variable that will be returned by `isFormValid()`.

```
        if (isValid == false)
        {
          this.showErrorDiv(errorDivId,theDocument);
          isWholeFormValid = false;
        }
```

We then come to a `do...while` loop whose purpose is to simply move the `formElementCounter` on to the next element past those in the radio button group we've already checked. Radio buttons in a group have the same name, so we just need to keep looping until the name changes or we've reached the end of the form. This is required because the `length` property of the form `elements` array only returns the total number of elements, without regard to their name, so this would even apply to a combo box. At the end of the loop we decrement the `formElementCounter` by one – this is to allow for the fact that when the main `for` loop re-iterates, it will increment the `formElementCounter` by one and, because we are already pointing to the next element due to our `while` loop, it would mean we'd skip an element that may need validating.

```
        do
        {
          formElementCounter++;
          theElement = theForm.elements[formElementCounter];
        }
        while (theElement.name == elementName &&
               formElementCounter < theForm.length)
          formElementCounter--;
```

That ends our `if` and `else` statements for radio button checking, and our `for` loop that iterates over the form elements. Finally, at the end of the method, we return our findings as to whether the form was completely valid or not:

```
    return isWholeFormValid;
```

isTextElementValid() Method

This method does the actual checking of any individual text element whose name contains `_Compulsory` or `_NonCompulsory`. The method, shown below, takes three parameters: the element's object, a `RegExp` object that we'll use to obtain the data type information from the name, and the Boolean value stored in `isCompulsoryElement`.

```
Validate.prototype.isTextElementValid = function(theElement,
                                             validDataTypeRegExp,
                                             isCompulsoryElement)
{
  var isValid = true;
  var validDataType;

  if (isCompulsoryElement && theElement.value == "")
  {
    isValid = false;
  }
  else
  {
    validDataType = validDataTypeRegExp.exec(theElement.name)[0];
    validDataType = validDataType.toLowerCase();
    if (validDataType != "_compulsory")
    {
      isValid = this.isElementDataValid(theElement.value,validDataType)
    }
  }

  return isValid;
}
```

Inside the method, we first check whether the element is compulsory and contains no value. If this is the case, `isValid` is set to `false`.

Otherwise, we go about checking whether the information entered by the user is valid for the datatype format specified. The naming conventions we have used should now be clear. We execute the regular expression on the element name, This returns an array containing all the matches for an underscore character followed by a sequence of letters, that also ends at the end of the string – this means the array will only contain one element. We place this element into the variable `validDataType`, and set this to lowercase to avoid problems with, for example, `_IsValidEmail` and `_isvalidEmail` being treated differently. Getting the case wrong for the data type definitions in the name when creating our forms would be very easy and a hassle to spot.

In the `if` statement we need to check that the control did actually have a specified data type and was not just compulsory, otherwise our data type regular expression will lead us to checking for a non-existent data type called `_compulsory`.

Finally, we set `isValid` to the value returned by the `isElementDataValid()` method of this class, which does the actual data validity checking. Then `isValid` is returned to the calling function to indicate the validity of the element checked.

isElementDataValid() Method

This method is basically one big `switch` statement in which we call the relevant data validation method of our `Validate` class based on the `validDataType` parameter that we extracted in the `isTextElementValid()` method above. This parameter contains the data type defined in the form element's name. The methods called are those we created earlier in the chapter to validate various types of data. If we wanted to extend our automatic checking, then we need only create the validation method that will check the additional data type and then add a relevant data type name to this method.

```
Validate.prototype.isElementDataValid = function(elementValue, validDataType)
{
  var isValid = false;

  switch (validDataType)
  {
    case "_alphanumeric":
      isValid = this.isOnlyAlphaNumeric(elementValue);
      break;

    case "_alphanumericnospace":
      isValid = this.isOnlyAlphaNumericNoSpace (elementValue);
      break;

    case "_alphabetic":
      isValid = this.isOnlyAlphabetic(elementValue);
      break;

    case "_numeric":
      isValid = this.isOnlyNumeric(elementValue);
      break;

    case "_integer":
      isValid = this.isValidInteger(elementValue);
      break;

    case "_floatingpoint":
      isValid = this.isValidFloatingPoint(elementValue);
      break;

    case "_age":
      isValid = isValidAge(elementValue);
      break;

    case "_password":
      isValid = isValidPassword(elementValue);
      break;

    case "_telephone":
      isValid = isValidTelephoneNum(elementValue);
      break;

    case "_postcode":
      isValid = this.isValidPostalCode(elementValue);
```

```
      break;

    case "_email":
      isValid = this.isValidEmail(elementValue);
      break;

    default:
      alert("Error unidentified element data type");
  }

  return isValid;
}
```

isOneRadioButtonInGroupSelected() Method

This method loops through the radio button group passed as a parameter and checks to see if any radio button in the group has been checked. We set `isValid` to the `checked` property of each radio button as we loop through. If at any point `isValid` is `true`, that is the radio button is checked, we break out of the loop. If it is never `true`, then `isValid` remains at its initialization value of `false`. The value of `isValid` is returned at the end of the method.

```
Validate.prototype.isOneRadioButtonInGroupSelected = function(theElement)
{
  var radioCounter;
  var isValid = false;

  for (radioCounter = theElement.length - 1; radioCounter >= 0; radioCounter--)
  {
    isValid = theElement[radioCounter].checked;
    if (isValid)
    {
      break;
    }
  }

  return isValid;
}
```

showErrorDiv() Method

We can access any `<div>` element using its `id` value, and change its properties dynamically. To show the error, we use the `<div>` element's `visibility` property. The syntax for different browsers is different because they support DOM in a different fashion, but the basic idea remains the same – runtime modification to the contents and/or attributes of any element.

This method takes two parameters, the `id` of the error `<div>` and the `document` object of the page containing the form. Because IE4+, NN4, and NN6 access elements in a page differently, we have a series of `if` statements each containing a different means of changing the `<div>` element's visibility based on what each browser supports.

```
Validate.prototype.showErrorDiv = function (errorDescripDivId,
                                            theDocument)
{
```

```
    if (document.layers)
    {
      theDocument.layers[errorDescripDivId].visibility = "visible";
    }
    else if (document.all)
    {
      theDocument.all[errorDescripDivId].style.visibility = "visible";
    }
    else
    {
      theDocument.getElementById(errorDescripDivId).style.visibility = "visible";
    }
  }
```

NN4 uses layers, so if `document.layers` is not `null`, then the first `if` statement's condition will evaluate to `true`, and the code it contains will be evaluated.

IE4+ supports `document.all` (and NN6 does not) so we use that in the second `if` statement to make sure only IE attempts to execute the contained code.

Finally, we have worked on the assumption that if nothing else has worked, the browser must be NN6 and its DOM-based `getElementById()` method will work. You may wish to alter this to cover the less common browsers, such as Opera. This method will also work on IE5+, but for simplicity we stick with the `document.all` method for all IE browsers. If you expect visitors to have browsers supporting none of these techniques, then you would have to add the specific code or spot them in advance and not use the automatic form validation.

hideErrorDiv() Method

This is identical to the `showErrorDiv()` method in every respect except it hides the `<div>` by setting its `visibility` style property to `hidden`. The method is used by the `checkFormValid()` method to hide error `<div>` elements that were previously shown in the page due to incorrect data being entered in them by the user, but which are now valid.

```
  Validate.prototype.hideErrorDiv = function (errorDescripDivId, theDocument)
  {
    if (theDocument.layers)
    {
      theDocument.layers[errorDescripDivId].visibility = "hidden";
    }
    else if (document.all)
    {
      theDocument.all[errorDescripDivId].style.visibility = "hidden"
    }
    else
    {
      theDocument.getElementById(errorDescripDivId).style.visibility = "hidden"
    }
  }
```

Updating the Personal Details Page

All the hard work has now been done – we can sit back, relax, and make use of the code in the `Validate` class within our application.

Before we load up the `PersonalDetails.htm` page and change it, we first need to change the `ecomCode.js` file and add the following somewhere near the top:

```
var validator = new Validate();
```

This creates a new object based on our `Validate` class. Note that have already added the `<script>` element that imports the `Validate.js` file in to the `ImageViewerEcom.htm` page.

Now we can edit our `PersonalDetails.htm` page and alter the `cmdSubmit_onclick()` function as shown below:

```
function cmdSubmit_onclick()
{
   if (parent.validator.checkFormValid(document.frmCustomer,
      window.document))
   {
      window.location.href = "CheckoutCredit.htm";
   }
   else
   {
      alert("There were problems with your form.\n"
         + "Please correct them before continuing.");
   }
}
```

Previously, clicking the *Continue* button simply took the customer to the next page. Now it performs validation by calling the `Validate` class's `checkFormValid()` method. We pass it the `form` object of the form containing the customer details, and also the current page's `document` object. The `Validate` object is actually imported into the top frame, hence our `parent` prefix. If `true` is returned, then the page is valid and we take the user to the next stage in the checkout, the `CheckoutCredit.htm` page.

If the form is not valid then we alert the user. Remember that, as well as this alert box, the `checkFormValid()` method of the `Validate` object will show the error `<div>` elements, so that the customer knows which form elements were incorrectly completed.

Updating the Credit Card Details Page

The final page we need to change is `CheckoutCredit.htm`. In particular, we need to change the function `cmdContinue_onclick()`.

The first change is that we declare a variable `isValid` and initialize it to `true`.

```
function cmdContinue_onclick(theForm)
{
   var isValid = true;
```

Our next task is to obtain the credit card expiry date, and check if this is valid:

```
var selectedMonth =
   theForm.cboExpMonth.options[theForm.cboExpMonth.selectedIndex]
   .value;

var selectedYear =
  theForm.cboExpYear.options[theForm.cboExpYear.selectedIndex]
  .value;

if (parent.validator.isValidCreditCardExpiry
    (selectedMonth,selectedYear) == false)
 {
    isValid = false;
    parent.validator.showErrorDiv("CardExpiryError",
       window.document);
 }
 else
 {
    parent.validator.hideErrorDiv("CardExpiryError",
       window.document);
 }
```

Checking the card expiry date requires two fields and it's not one of the data types that we can automatically check with our `Validate` class. Instead, we extract the date from the select elements, then use the `Validate` class's `isValidCreditCardExpiry()` method to check the validity. If invalid, then we display the error `<div>` using the `showErrorDiv()` method of the `Validate` class. Otherwise we hide it in the `else` statement. Why do we need to hide it? Well, when the page first loads all the error `<div>` elements are hidden. But, let's say the customer enters the card number and the expiry date incorrectly, then clicks to continue. At this point, the page does not change – instead we spot the error and show the error `<div>` elements. The customer then corrects the expiry date error, but is still getting the credit card details wrong. In this case we want to make sure the card expiry error `<div>` is hidden and only the error `<div>` next to the card number is shown.

Next we use the automatic form checking function `checkFormValid()` to check the name input box and that a card type radio button has been selected:

```
 if (parent.validator.checkFormValid(document.frmCCDetails,
    window.document) == false)
 {
    isValid = false;
 }
 else
 {
    var cardType =
       parent.getSelectedRadioValue(theForm.radCardType_Compulsory);

    var cardNumber =
       theForm.txtCardNumber_Compulsory_Alphanumeric.value;
```

We get the card number and type, and then move on to the final task of validating the card number:

```
            if (parent.validator.isValidCreditCardNumber(cardNumber,
               cardType) == false)
            {
               parent.validator.showErrorDiv("CardNumberError",
                  window.document);
                  isValid = false;
            }
         }
```

Using the `Validate` class's `isValidCreditCardNumber()`, we check the card number's validity. If it's not valid, the appropriate error `<div>` element is shown using `showErrorDiv()`.

If everything is valid, then we store the card details, and then load the final checkout page.

```
         if (isValid)
         {
            parent.customerCreditCard.setCardType(cardType);
            parent.customerCreditCard.setCardHolderName
               (theForm.txtCardHolderName_Compulsory_Alphabetic.value);
            parent.customerCreditCard.setCardNumber(cardNumber);
            parent.customerCreditCard.setCardExpires(selectedMonth + "/"
               + selectedYear)

            window.location.href = "CheckoutConfirm.htm";
         }
```

Otherwise we alert the customer to the error and give them the chance to fix it.

```
         else
         {
            alert("There were problems with your form.\n" +
               "Please correct them before continuing.");
         }
      }
```

Summary

In this chapter we created the `Validate` class. This class wraps up various data validation methods and can be easily used again and again in our web pages. It may not contain all the data validation methods you'll need, but that's not a problem as you can easily extend the class and add new ones.

We then extended the class for our e-commerce image viewer application to allow it to automatically check some form elements. By using a naming convention, we could specify whether an input element should have been filled or a radio button from a group should have been selected, and also specify what type of data an input element should contain to be valid. We wrote a function that, when called, goes through all the elements in a form – any invalid ones have the error `<div>` element next to them displayed. That completes the e-commerce image viewer application.

Index

A Guide to the Index

The index is arranged hierarchically, in alphabetical order. Most second-level entries and many third-level entries also occur as first-level entries. This is to ensure that users will find the information they require however they choose to search for it.

D

E

F

G

H

I

J

K

L

M

N

O

P

R

S

W